M000113782

More Praise for

Mergers & Acquisitions: An Insider's Guide to the Purchase and Sale of Middle Market Business Interests

"Mr. Roberts has written a timeless contribution to the art of getting business transactions completed. His years of experience allow him to provide invaluable insights into the nuances of successful deal completion. It gets better: The wisdom is communicated in a highly readable format spiced with on-point illustrations, examples, stories and informed opinions. This book must be on the short list of every investment banker and business owner seeking to gain that all important advantage in today's competitive markets."

> —Scott D. Miller, CPA/ABV, CVA, author of The Adviser's Guide
> to Mergers, Acquisitions, and Sales of Closely Held Businesses:
> Advanced Case Analysis and Buying and Selling Businesses:
> The CPA's role.

"Dennis does a tremendous job of looking beyond all of the technical jargon that clutters the world of investment banking, and focusing on the key elements of how deals actually get done. This is a refreshing book, with engaging real-world teachings and clever insights from one of the masters of mid-market M&A."

> —Howard Johnson, President,
> Veracap Corporate Finance Limited,
> Toronto, Canada

"Dennis understands the psyche of the middle market and translates his years of experience into a practical, entertaining yet technical text. Bankers and business operators, on either side of a transaction, will benefit from studying at the foot of the master."

> —Martin O'Neill, Author,
> Building Business Value and Coauthor,
> Act Like an *Owner*

Mergers & Acquisitions

Mergers & Acquisitions

An Insider's Guide to the Purchase and Sale of Middle Market Business Interests

The Middle Market is Different/ Tales of a Deal Junkie
and
The Business of Middle Market Investment Banking

DENNIS J. ROBERTS

WILEY
John Wiley & Sons, Inc.

This book is printed on acid-free paper. ⊗

Copyright © 2009 by John Wiley & Sons, Inc. All rights reserved.

Published by John Wiley & Sons, Inc., Hoboken, New Jersey.
Published simultaneously in Canada.

No part of this publication may be reproduced, stored in a retrieval system, or
transmitted in any form or by any means, electronic, mechanical, photocopying,
recording, scanning, or otherwise, except as permitted under Section 107 or 108 of the
1976 United States Copyright Act, without either the prior written permission of the
Publisher, or authorization through payment of the appropriate per-copy fee to the
Copyright Clearance Center, Inc., 222 Rosewood Drive, Danvers, MA 01923,
978-750-8400, fax 978-646-8600, or on the Web at www.copyright.com. Requests to the
Publisher for permission should be addressed to the Permissions Department, John
Wiley & Sons, Inc., 111 River Street, Hoboken, NJ 07030, 201-748-6011,
fax 201-748-6008, or online at http://www.wiley.com/go/permissions.

Limit of Liability/Disclaimer of Warranty: While the publisher and author have used their
best efforts in preparing this book, they make no representations or warranties with
respect to the accuracy or completeness of the contents of this book and specifically
disclaim any implied warranties of merchantability or fitness for a particular purpose. No
warranty may be created or extended by sales representatives or written sales materials.
The advice and strategies contained herein may not be suitable for your situation. You
should consult with a professional where appropriate. Neither the publisher nor author
shall be liable for any loss of profit or any other commercial damages, including but not
limited to special, incidental, consequential, or other damages.

For general information on our other products and services, or technical support, please
contact our Customer Care Department within the United States at 800-762-2974, outside
the United States at 317-572-3993 or fax 317-572-4002.

Wiley also publishes its books in a variety of electronic formats. Some content that
appears in print may not be available in electronic books.

For more information about Wiley products, visit our Web site at www.wiley.com.

Library of Congress Cataloging-in-Publication Data:
Roberts, Dennis J.
  Mergers & acquisitions: an insider's guide to the purchase and sale of
middle market business interests / Dennis J. Roberts.
      p. cm.
    Includes index.
    ISBN 978-0-470-26210-8 (cloth)
  1. Consolidation and merger of corporations—United States. I. Title.
  HG4028.M4R626 2009
  658.1'62—dc22
                                                        2008035469

Printed in the United States of America

10 9 8 7 6 5 4 3 2 1

"Some men know the price of everything and the value of nothing."
Oscar Wilde

Contents

About the Author

D ennis J. Roberts, CVA,CPA*/ABV (*no longer practicing), is the chairman of a very active M&A investment bank (The McLean Group) with offices in approximately 30 cities in the United States and Canada. Having acted as the investment banker advisor on numerous transactions over many years, he is also a formal business valuator, having done such prominent business valuations as the Nixon Watergate tapes. He was also the founder and chairman of a multistate regional commercial national banking company. He was a member of the initial committee that established the first eight part AICPA training modules on business valuation for CPAs. He has lectured, taught, and authored courses on M&A subjects for numerous audiences and professional groups, such as the National Association of Certified Valuation Analysts, The Alliance of Merger and Acquisition Advisors, university graduate programs, and many others, including having been engaged as a lecturer by other privately owned M&A investment banks. He lives in Fairfax, Virginia, with his wife Robin Quattlebaum.

Acknowledgments

Acknowledgments seem almost routine, a mere formality . . . but they are not to authors. This is a very small and totally inadequate way of saying "Thank God you were there, or my screw-ups would have been even greater than they are." Not that any of the following contributed in any way to those screw-ups that still remain.

Thanks to Steve Meltzer and Enrique Brito for very detailed word-by-word reviews; Joe Loughran for very helpful edits of my early drafts; Andrew Smith, Andrew Sherman, Chuck Andrews, and Scott Miller for useful insights and comments that I incorporated in one way or the other; Howard Johnson, my co-teacher, who helped me develop many of the thoughts and the overall body of knowledge here years ago (albeit with a Canadian accent); William Offutt, who reviewed and made excellent suggestions on the tax chapter of the book; and all of them for their intelligent comments, observations, and "in the nick of time" course corrections.

Parnell Black, the founder and CEO of The National Association of Certified Valuations Analysts (NACVA), and Mike Nall, the founder and CEO of the Alliance of M&A Advisors (AMAA) deserve special mention, as they were both instrumental in my own learning by allowing me to teach and create courses for them over many years.

Again, as in most books, I would like to make a dedication—but in no way as a mere matter of routine, for without the love and patience of family, I would not be able to do what I do. So;

To my children
Debbie, Cathy, and David
And my wife
Robin Quattlebaum

Dennis J. Roberts, 2008

Foreword

A difference of opinion is what makes horse races and missionaries.

Will Rogers

Blessed are they who can laugh at themselves, for they shall never cease to be amused.

Anonymous

This book is intended as a textbook and perhaps a reference book for training those who seek a Middle Market investment banking career. It is intentionally not meant to be a "technical" book. Enough of those have been written, and I do not believe we need yet another. Enough of my students over the years have either had technical training (accountants, valuation experts, MBAs, finance majors, and so forth), or maybe do not really care to go into those subjects too deeply (business owners, managers, and entrepreneurs).

In fact, the problem in my view with most Middle Market M&A texts is that they are too technical at the expense of "feel," and feel is what my students tell me they want. Were I to organize a course from scratch (and I have), I would first teach the elusive feel and only later add the technical subjects that flesh out feel and are frankly secondary to it.

In the 1930s, Percy Boomer wrote one of the best books on golf ever written, *On Learning Golf.* Percy rightly believed golf was mainly about feel. In this regard, Middle Market M&A quite arguably is a lot like golf. A thorough knowledge of technique alone always proves a poor substitute for a honed feel of the swing in each transaction. Even though I took it up rather late in life, I love golf. Initially I read everything I could put my hands on in terms of the golf swing but it was often (in fact usually) years later only when I successfully actually did something that I had read about that the light came on: "Oh. That is what they meant. I can actually feel it." While there is a limit to what a book can do, what I have attempted here is to short cut some of that time between acquiring technique and experiencing "feel."

Another virtue of this book is that it uniquely addresses not only the art and science of Middle Market M&A but, at the same time, the buy and sell sides, while admittedly placing more emphasis on the latter.

Finally, other M&A professionals and investment bankers might glean something from peeking into the tent of a fellow M&A professional's experiences, if for no reason other than to satisfy their curiosity. And if this book should happen occasionally to fall into the hands of a Middle Market business seller, or buyer, or capital seeker, then so be it. That would not displease me at all, as there is information here that will be of much assistance to them, too, in conducting their own transactions. It might also prove of use to them in the choice of the best banker available for the task at hand.

I want to warn my readers up front that they are likely to encounter a lot of apparent redundancy in this book. This is for two very conscious reasons: First I have always taught that way, starting with the general and then restating it but in increasingly granular levels. The second is that by its very nature, M&A and this book as result cannot be either proceed nor be taught in an entirely linear fashion. For example, the concepts of preliminary valuations, Letters of Intent (LOI's) and balance sheet conventions among others by necessity need to appear in various chapters but in slightly different contexts. Also because this book was written to be a reference book as opposed to a "read straight thru" book for those who preferred it that way, I will occasionally repeat some earlier material for the convenience of my readers.

Preface: A Profession

A Career in Middle Market Investment Banking

Since my early days, I have never looked back. Never made so much money either (or gone for such long stretches wondering where the next payday was coming from), but after a while money doesn't mean that much. I think the excitement of dealmaking is a sufficient reward in itself for those of us attracted to this kind of work.

And you meet some pretty cool people too, even in the Middle Market. Heads of state of very large nations, admirals, generals, senior White House officials, senators, congressman, cabinet officers, CEOs of many large companies and many more smaller ones, private equity group and angel investors, all equally interesting people. Not everybody may want to be a dealmaker (actually, in my heart, I think they do), but everyone seems at least intrigued by what we do.

And it leads to the damnedest places. One of my jobs as an investment banker and valuation analyst was to value the Nixon Watergate tapes—who would have thought? I wouldn't trade this career for anything, with the possible exception of time with my family and my periodic sojourns to my home in Mexico for tequila and sun breaks.

The Origins of a Deal Junkie

Washington, DC—March 1967 *and* Manhattan, New York City— June 1970

As a newly minted—and very wet behind the ears—CPA, I sat at my desk in a client's office in suburban Washington, DC, ticking off audit steps and found myself quite frankly bored to death. I could not imagine doing anything remotely similar to this kind of work for the rest of my life. The notion of how stultifying this work was became even clearer to me as I overheard apparently intense negotiations transpiring in the office next door. Just a few feet away from me, on the other side of a very thin wall, the owners of our client firm, a decent-sized construction company, their investment banker, and a team representing the prospective buyers were hammering out a proposed merger agreement. I couldn't tell exactly what was going on, but I had enough of a clue to know that I was interested.

Three years later, having made some progress up through the accounting ranks, I found myself in the richly furnished and very large board room of a Wall Street investment bank, listening attentively to a similar and no less heated discussion regarding the merger of a large Middle Market company, to be followed by an initial public offering (IPO). I was there as an audit support staff member for a CPA firm (and pretty much tolerated as a trained fly on the wall) as some of the critical issues that bore on whether this multistage deal was to get done were of an accounting nature. The alternate pounding on the table going on between the chairman of the major investment bank and his associates on one hand and the senior audit partner of a "big eight" accounting firm and his fellow auditors on the other was exciting and intimidating to me at the same time. Frankly, it was like watching tag-team wrestling in suits.

Those two particular experiences, in Washington, DC, and New York City, had given me a peek inside the tents where, in my opinion, the real gods of business, at least the ones that grabbed my attention (dealmakers), held court, consummated mergers, and did acquisition transactions. They most definitely were not dazzling, white-bearded men in white robes inaccessible to mere mortals like me. But in the moment they might as well have been, because even though I knew I wanted to walk among them, I didn't know how to get there. And I had to get there, because simply hearing and seeing them do their deals got my juices flowing. Let others start and run businesses, account for them, keep them out of legal trouble, and/or market their goods and services. Those jobs were not for me. I wanted "to do deals," even if I wasn't yet clear as to what all that entailed.

The Deal Junkie Arrives (Almost)

Savannah, GA—May 1989

My brand new partners and I were ensconced in offices located in a pleasant and recently revitalized part of town, close to the river. There was an attractiveness there that derived from a particularly successful blending of the qualities of Old and New South. I was really happy to be there. Looking around the boardroom table at my new colleagues, I thought, I have found it. After 20 years of enjoying the wheeling and dealing of financial services transactions close to but not really directly in the M&A arena, I believe I have finally found a place where

I can capitalize on everything I have learned along the way by just, well . . . doing deals. *In the industrial south, this relatively small boutique firm had a great reputation for executing the kinds of transaction in industries that were traditional for the south at that time: textiles, furniture, food manufacturing and services, and so on. The information technology boom was still a few years away. On that May 1989 afternoon in Savannah, I wanted to believe the sunlight streaming into our boardroom was a harbinger of good things to come. But even then, I had much more work and much more learning to do.*

By 1984, my experiences as a senior partner in public accounting, focusing a good deal of my career on transaction advisory services, had led to my becoming founder, chairman, and CEO of a publicly owned, multistate banking company. A few other entrepreneurial undertakings, launched in my spare time, also had proved instructive, as I developed at least a few (fewer than I realized) of the necessary skills for successful M&A investment banking. But I was totally prepared to live by my wits and experience, and I was sure that with just a little additional refinement of my skills, I would be ready to go. Or, at least, so I thought. Certainly, the complementary skills of my new partners gathered around our boardroom table were all I needed now. But this was not quite true . . . as I was to find out.

Why Another M&A Book?

What I would come to understand soon enough was that there was no better place to learn what I needed to learn than on the job, dealing with real-world M&A deals mainly. My partners would prove helpful, of course, but only intermittently so. In part, this reflected a simple fact of life: Middle Market M&A investment banking was a notoriously unstable business and, as a result, its practitioners faced very high career "mortality" rates. Relatively few Middle Market M&A intermediaries weathered the financial valleys (deep and sometimes protracted) in this very lumpy and cyclical business long enough to enjoy the rewards of teaching the next generation. Furthermore, a lot of the professionals in this business, being retired industry executives, were doing M&A consulting as a sort of retirement avocation and were somewhat lone wolves, only in it for few years.

A recent Internet Amazon search for M&A-related books identified over 26,000 references in seconds. Doubtless, there are more out there. So why write another? In point of fact, very few books separately address the unique issues and circumstances of Middle Market M&A. Colleagues, students, clients, and other Middle Market M&A practitioners tell me the same thing. The books that do address the Middle Market often fail to acknowledge the very different circumstances, perspectives, and practices of the sales-side on the one hand and the buy-side on the other, addressing the two as if they were all but interchangeable. They are not. As a result, inexperienced practitioners, prospective clients, and readers may well walk away with serious misconceptions of the differences in practice between the two sides. I frequently have seen novice sales-siders, overconfident due to having read one text or another on Middle Market M&A, rushing into meetings to support their clients' positions with all manner of financial models and calculations that would be more appropriate on the buy side.

Middle Market M&A literature today also tends to address the art of the deal or the science of it, but seldom both. The art and the science are equally important and ever-present in the real world. Developing a facility for one at the expense of the other routinely proves less than ideal.

And then there are those who do and those who teach. Much of our Middle Market literature appears to me to have been written by authors who do not really do deals (business valuators, accountants, etc.), and while these books can make a valuable contribution, they do not give a sense of the feel of M&A, as it is practiced outside of a textbook or a classroom.

> *In quarterly board meetings with my partners in Savannah over the next few years, I came to realize that most of them were "winging it" to some degree as they did their M&A deals. I learned that many M&A transactions are facilitated successfully almost in spite of the alleged professional firepower hired by clients. But deals got done. It was as though the "Will to Transact" itself was sufficiently powerful to overcome many obstacles, including the more-than-occasional lack of experience or necessary capabilities on the part of some of the Middle Market investment bankers ostensibly managing the transaction process.*

My Intended Audience

Over the course of the past 15 years, I have traveled extensively to teach Middle Market M&A fundamentals to business owners and executives, attorneys, accountants, and business valuation experts serving a Middle Market clientele, as well as some seasoned and some newly minted investment bankers. Some of the bankers are at the beginning of their careers, and some of whom enjoy swapping war stories and experiences with another veteran of the M&A wars. What I gained over time by teaching innumerable seminars and workshops to these three groups was a growing insight into those different perspectives.

I admit to having slanted this book more to the sales-side perspective—consciously and for several reasons without having ignored the buy side altogether however. First, most buyers are larger companies with professional, in-house M&A and corporate development staff. Many, if not most, sellers will complete only one or two M&A transactions in the course of a career. Yet that deal (or those deals) most likely will be the largest and most significant financial transactions of their lifetimes. By definition, the inexperience of these essentially novice sellers can prove financially catastrophic as they negotiate transactions with a buyers' full-time, professional M&A staffs. This book is partly written to help them prepare for such transactions and to provide some suggestions as to what to look for in the sales-side M&A investment bankers and other professionals they will hire to protect their interests throughout the process.

But I also hope this book will prove of some value to in-house, professional buy-side M&A practitioners, as it addresses the techniques employed by professional, sell-side investment bankers in negotiating and transacting deals. Having trained buy-side in-house staff, I often have found them in want of an appreciation of the sales side and its techniques, which too often can put the buy side at a disadvantage it does not need to suffer.

Happy Families

As Tolstoy said, "Happy families are all alike; every unhappy family is unhappy in its own way." The ways to ineptly sell, or buy for that matter, a Middle Market business in the six to twelve months typically required to close a transaction are legion. This book will address the many challenges, pitfalls and difficulties inherent in transactions involving Middle Market businesses. Admittedly, every M&A transaction is, by definition, unique but they also share many commonalities, even across industries.

After all the deals, all the clients, all the books, and all the colleagues met along the way (good and bad), I believe I've learned a great deal about the work I love. But I have never found all I've learned about the art and the science of the Middle Market M&A work I've pursued for half a lifetime brought together in one place. That is why I wrote this book, and I hope my fascination with and love of this profession comes through clearly and will be shared by my readers in a sufficient number of cases to have made this worth the writing.

Dennis J. Roberts
McLean, Virginia (Washington, DC)
November 2008

Disclaimers, Apologies, and Modest Lies

I have a higher and greater standard of principle. Washington could not lie. I can but I won't.

Mark Twain

A little inaccuracy sometimes saves a ton of explanation.

Saki (H.H. Munro)

Every war story or anecdote recounted in this book to illustrate one principle or another is true. Even so, fictitious names, dates, locations, and transaction amounts are employed in the retelling to preserve the privacy of all parties to these transactions and events. My use of some obfuscation reflects a continuing commitment to preserve my clients' confidentiality, even years later. Like most investment banks, my firm publishes "tombstones" reporting summary transaction information with the prior approval of our clients. As a result, if a sleuth in our Google world succeeded in matching an anecdote to a tombstone, I and my investment bank might well face an outraged former client whose trust we would have violated.

This book has been written over a number of years. Much in it has been inevitably addressed elsewhere in the huge plethora of M&A literature (maybe 75% of the material, with the balance being some notable exceptions, such as M&A conventions, the Rules of Five and Ten, pricing a company, etc.) but my point was to bring it all together in one place for the first time. If I have failed to appropriately credit any of my sources (cryptoamnesia), it is only because after 15 or more years of sporadic writing and teaching, it is impossible to remember where I learned all of this myself. I do know that some of it certainly came from my own reading but only if corroborated by subsequent experience, much more of it from original on the job experience, and a good deal of it from my colleagues.

Finally, I have written this book so that it can be read straight through or can be skipped around as one desires and finds useful.

CHAPTER 1

The Middle Market Is Different!

Business Process Innovation, Growth Spurts, Regulatory Imperatives, and Capital

Historically, at least for the last 120 years or so, the United States' mergers and acquisitions (M&A) activity has paralleled business growth spurts, regulatory imperatives, or both. In turn, business growth spurts have been driven by business process innovation, particularly in transportation and communications infrastructures and most recently in technology. A third ingredient for this stew, along with businesses growth spurts and regulatory imperatives, is the need for ample excess capital to properly flavor the pot.

In the late 1800s and very early 1900s, the real and effective establishment of a national railroad system was a primary driver of a rapidly expanding U.S. economy, and of course high stock prices and new capital were an accompaniment. Typically, during periods of innovation, monopolies or seeming monopolies tend to develop (witness Microsoft in our own era), people complain, regulators react, and thus did this first wave finally slow down with a 1904 U.S. Supreme Court decision which frowned upon the monopoly situations and the ever-larger companies that were developing. In fact, the first regulation to emerge regarding M&A in the United States was the Sherman Act in 1890.

By the 1920s, the continued substantial improvement of transportation (automobiles and trucks) and communications systems (widespread use of radio and telephone) were driving a thriving U.S. economy. A booming stock market meant abundant capital, and mergers and acquisitions predictably resulted. Since horizontal merger activity had been discouraged by the Supreme Court earlier, the tendency during this period was to merge forward or backward through the supply chain. History has well memorialized that this wave in turn ended with (but that is not to suggest that it caused) the 1929 crash of the stock market; the impediment to the capital markets was to last at least 30 years.

Despite the World Wars, 30 fairly quiet business years followed, with steadily increasing improvements in infrastructure. These improvements occurred partly out of concern for national transportation policy prompted by the wartime activity of the Second World War, and of course communications took center stage again (television) as a marketing device. By the 1960s, 14 years after World War II, business seemed ready to truly grow again. Fourteen years of veterans' housing programs and job and educational opportunities began to show real results in the economy. Another factor, the "military industrial complex," accompanied growth in national government spending. By this time, though, regulators and politicians were opposed to either type of merger, sideways or up and down, that might impede free competition. The result was a tendency toward mergers and acquisitions to form conglomerates, driven by the desire to employ capital and grow large without running afoul of regulators, politicians, and courts. But conglomerates were not succeeding particularly well because focus and as a result, good operating practices were dampened. In addition, the passage of antitrust laws started to make even conglomerate mergers of disparate parts more difficult.

M&A resumed again in the 1980s, fueled by junk-bond financing, leveraged buyouts, and strong stock prices. It was also driven in part by financial engineering—mostly from arbitrage, in which the real money was made from the deal by the promoters themselves as opposed to improved operations. The 1980s' financially engineered deals were somewhat different from the type we were to see in the 1990s (many now in the Middle Market) from roll-up groups.

By the 1990s, we were beginning to see a great influx of capital driven in one way or another by the productivity and consumerism of those ubiquitous baby boomers (the sons and daughters of World War II veterans), the youngest of whom were then entering their 50s, as well as from the abrupt turn toward deregulation of industries such as banks, utilities, communications, and airlines, among others. Consolidation was another factor and to some degree a result, especially when it was conducted by the financially engineered roll-up groups, which, just like their counterparts in the 1980s, made their money when the deal was done by rolling up and repackaging Middle Market businesses as public companies, not as a rule by conducting sound financial operations. Of course, the mid-1990s was also the dawn of the information age, and that too was accelerating the pace of business and the pace of change in business enormously. The end of this last wave paralleled the telecom and dot.com crash of 2000. Much of M&A was Wall Street activity, but a more than gradual and steady incursion was coming from the Middle Market and Main Street in the 90's.

Since 2003, we have been observing another wave that by now heavily involves the Middle Market. The Middle Market, as of early 2008, accounts for approximately 300 to 350 deals per quarter in the United States and Europe respectively, when the deals are defined as those with transaction values in excess of $30 million. Larger business are seen as necessary to successfully compete in the competitive global economy as well as in cross-border transactions, which are of course a product of that global economy. Technology, often developed by Middle Market companies, is being acquired by larger companies through acquisitions. In addition, massive changes in the health care, communications, and financial services industries (usually associated with technology advances) are also drivers, especially Middle Market drivers. Increased government spending associated with war and terrorism, as well as huge influxes of capital from private equity groups and hedge funds, are also real factors.

Not "Mom-and-Pop" Businesses

I did not write this book to address the roughly 80% of U.S. businesses (Mom-and-Pop businesses) that typically are served by business brokers. But I do want to discuss them briefly.

Mom-and-Pop businesses typically are valued using rules of thumb that are not grounded in finance theory, particularly return on investment calculations. Furthermore, Mom-and-Pops typically generate very little interest among the predominant strategic and financial buyers of Middle Market businesses. If I define "Mom and Pop" as businesses with at least one employee and with less than one million dollars in annual sales there are some 4.5 million of them in the United States and these resoundingly affirm the genius of Adam Smith: capitalism really does work and flourish. Mom-and-Pop businesses are also frequently called "lifestyle businesses," because quite often their proprietors launched them to suit lifestyle preferences: to escape the "rat race," to control their own destinies, or just to get a foothold in American capitalism. Such lifestyle businesses often result in longer hours and far greater challenges for their founders/proprietors than the former nine-to-five jobs ever required. Still, the financial and psychological rewards can be significant.

Mom-and-Pop businesses provide an underpinning for our economy. They constitute the starting line in the entrepreneurial marathons for millions of citizens, who in turn employ millions more. While most Mom-and-Pop businesses will remain Mom-and-Pops throughout their business lifecycles, many thousands of them eventually will become Middle Market businesses. In addition, first- and second-generation entrepreneurial families running corner stores across America frequently produce third- and fourth-generation MBAs and CEOs in the Middle and Upper Markets.

For the most part, though, Mom-and-Pop businesses cannot be valued with the primary techniques used in the Middle Market, in which business valuation is based on return on investment (ROI). The impracticality of applying Middle Market valuation tools to Mom-and-Pop firms quickly becomes obvious. Why would someone pay, say, $300,000 (probably on terms) to buy a corner business that nets its owner $60,000 a year in return for the owner's 80-hour work weeks? So Mom-and-Pop businesses tend to be valued according to rules of thumb that take into consideration their type and other factors, but typically do not give that much explicit weight to return on investment.

The Upper Market

Nor is this book intended to address the Upper Market, which usually is considered to comprise companies with $1 billion or more in annual sales.[1] Such companies in turn command valuations of at least $500 million and up—often considerably more in the case of publicly held companies. Upper Market businesses account for less than 1% of U.S. firms and are mostly, but by no means always, public companies. Middle Market firms, unlike their Upper Market counterparts, typically are owned by ten or fewer individuals. Often, they boast only one owner. Upper Market firms generally are publicly owned by thousands of stockholders.

In the Middle Market, the term *merger* is for the most part a misnomer. A merger fundamentally implies that both companies will continue to exist with more or less the same original owners (stockholders), albeit in a combined sort of way in the form of a new and larger company. This scenario is much more a "Wall Street" or Upper Market phenomenon than it is a Middle Market concept. In the Middle Market, the vast majority of deals involve *acquisitions*, in which one company and its shareholders acquire another company, and the shareholder-owners of the acquired company are no longer involved in its ownership.

Furthermore, the idea of hostile takeovers is also pretty much a Wall Street or Upper Market phenomenon, as the majority of Middle Market companies are not publicly owned and thus not subject to hostile takeovers.

Additionally, whether the deal is *accretive* or *dilutive* is not usually a real issue (as it is in Upper Market deals) when it comes to the effect on earnings in Middle Market deals. There is usually no public stock market to judge, more or less immediately, the deal and the immediate increase or decrease in the blended trading prices of the two companies' shares.

Finally, the time it takes to market and sell a Middle Market company is usually far longer (6 to 24 months) than the time it takes to do a deal in the Upper Markets, especially as Upper Market companies are more frequently one-on-one deals, whether hostile or friendly. The Middle Market is fundamentally inefficient when it comes to M&A transactions. As a result of Middle Market owners' natural concerns with confidentiality, a central computer-based market (i.e., a stock market, where these businesses could be traded) is basically impossible and impractical. Difficulties in finding all possible capable buyers contribute to this inefficiency. For these and other reasons startup investment banks who deal in the middle market typically have very short life spans, estimated at 24 to 36 months, and usually employ only one or two people. While success payoffs can be large, this is not a field for the faint of heart or for those with a paucity of cash reserves. I intend to make the reasons for this apparent later in this book.

What Exactly Is the Middle Market?

The Middle Market is extraordinary for its diversity and breadth of opportunities. But what exactly is the Middle Market? A typical characterization among M&A professionals views the Middle Market as businesses with values of from $1.5 million to $250 million. Others suggest that Middle Market businesses range from $5 million to $500 million in value. The point is, there is no standard definition.

For example, Bank of America Business Capital defines Middle Market firms as those businesses generating revenues of between $25 million and $1 billion. (This would suggest that their sizes in terms of value are $12.5 million to $500 million). As defined by the Bank of America, some 50,000 Middle Market businesses account for approximately 25% of the U.S. gross national product (GNP). On the other hand, the U.S. Department of Commerce reports that there are approximately 300,000 Middle Market companies that, according to its own definition, generate $5 million to $250 million in annual revenues.

To put the M&A business opportunity for Middle Market investment bankers into perspective, consider this: The U.S. Census Bureau, in 2002, estimated there were a total of 5,697,759 businesses in the United States,[2] with aggregate sales totaling in excess of $22 trillion. Assuming a very conservative two-to-one revenue to value ratio,[3] that equates a market value of $11 trillion. While the census data indicates that many of the totals are small businesses (under $1 million in sales), just over 21%, or 1.2 million, are Middle Market firms with sales of $1 million to $1 billion annually. Collectively, these 1.2 million firms had sales totaling $9.8 trillion and carry a conservative market value of $4.9 trillion.

Middle Market business also constitute a driving force in the U.S. economy, accounting for fully 68% of our GNP, according to the Department of Commerce. Clearly, no matter how you slice it, the Middle Market is huge as an engine of the U.S. economy. It also presents incredible opportunities to investment banking specialists representing its business owners.

If we assume the widest range of revenues ($5 million to $1 billion), this translates into business with average values of about half that, or $2.5 million to $500 million. This definition is probably a pretty good one that most would accept. Furthermore, in practice, most M&A professionals agree that the lower Middle Market (which is the most robust segment of the Middle Market in terms of numbers of deals) is in the $2.5 million to perhaps $150 million value sector which could also be stated as $5 million to $300 million in sales.

Does Size (Alone) Matter?

Even size can be a gray area in defining the Middle Market, though. Many ostensibly Middle Market businesses generate sales of between $4 million and $8 million without ever being of any interest to strategic buyers. These are very difficult firms to find buyers for, as they are of no interest to strategic buyers and too large for individual buyers. Many of these firms will take two or more years to be sold or perhaps will never be sold, at least other than to management, which is something that should always be given serious consideration in these cases. If they are fortunate, they might be sold to another buyer in the same industry, but not one that has formally mounted a strategic acquisition program (thereby truly meeting the definition of a "strategic buyer") in other words a passive buyer and therefore not willing to pay top dollar. These same-industry buyers are what I will call later *opportunistic industry buyers*. I would suggest that such ostensibly Middle Market firms as I describe here are in fact are really larger and more sophisticated Mom-and-Pop hybrids.

But just as there are firms that would qualify as Middle Market on the basis of revenues but for all intents and purposes remain Mom-and-Pop companies, so too are there firms that would appear to be Mom-and-Pops on a revenue basis that in fact should be considered Middle Market firms, based on their business prospects and scalability. For example, I have participated in the sale of several businesses generating less than $1 million in annual revenues that sold for more than $20 million. Such firms are recognized easily, based on "killer app" goods and/or services and on their scalability and future prospects. They often are either growing very rapidly or have the potential to do so. Frequently, they are technology businesses that have something very special to offer both their current clients and the strategic buyers that compete aggressively to acquire them.

Brokers and Investment Bankers Servicing the Three Markets

Middle Market investment bankers quite understandably are more interested in a business's likely market value than its revenues when determining whether or not to represent a prospective client. Their fees ultimately will be reflect the selling price of the business. At a bare minimum, most serious Middle Market investment banks would have a substantial retainer and a minimum fee of $200,000, and would expect a prospective client to be worth at the very least $3 to $4 million in the marketplace and be attractive to serious strategic buyers before agreeing to represent it, leaving businesses of lesser value to business brokers, consultants, and, not infrequently, freelancing accountants.

More akin to residential real estate agents, business brokers usually operate as relatively nontechnical "matchmakers," marketing their clients through newspaper classified advertisements, online advertisements, and tabloid-type catalogues of "businesses for sale." They typically charge fees of around 10% of the transaction values (which are usually under $1 million) and mostly operate with no retainer. Business brokers do provide Mom-and-Pop firms with valuable, if somewhat nontechnical, support. Unlike investment bankers, who usually focus more on sellers than on buyers (strategic and financial buyers can be easily identified, once a sales side client has been engaged an investment banker), business brokers tend to develop stables of (usually individual or similar smaller business) buyers to whom they present their new sales "listings."

Finally Wall Street and/or major regional investment banks serve the Upper Market by providing services in support of mergers and acquisitions of large companies, divestitures, and leveraged buyouts, among other transactions including initial public offerings (IPOs) of stock.

Chapter Highlights

- The Middle Market has been described in various ways by different authors and organizations, but a good definition would be businesses having from $2 million to $500 million in revenues.
- At its broadest definitional limits, Middle Market firms generate from $4 million to $1 billion in annual revenues, so for all practical estimation purposes, Middle Market firms so defined generate from $2 million and $500 million in business value.
- The Middle Market represents approximately 21% of U.S. businesses, while Mom-and-Pop firms (often lifestyle businesses for which formal financial theory valuations seldom are relevant or applicable) account for 79% of businesses. Upper Market firms account for the remaining less than 1%.

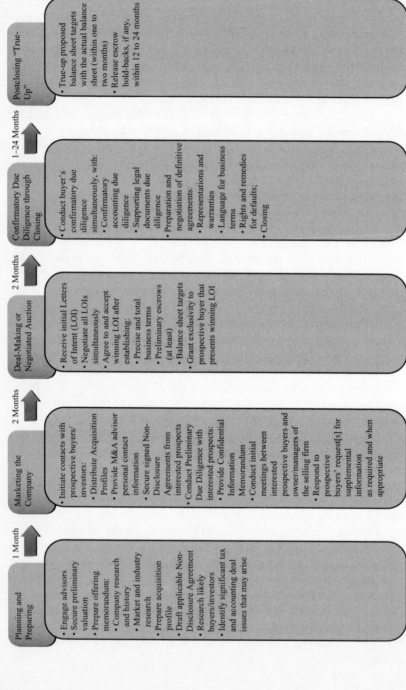

Planning and Preparing	Marketing the Company	Deal-Making or Negotiated Auction	Confirmatory Due Diligence through Closing	Postclosing "True-Up"
1 Month	2 Months	2 Months	1–24 Months	

Planning and Preparing
- Engage advisors
- Secure preliminary valuation
- Prepare offering memorandum:
- Company research and history
- Market and industry research
- Prepare acquisition profile
- Draft applicable Non-Disclosure Agreement
- Research likely buyers/investors
- Identify significant tax and accounting deal issues that may arise

Marketing the Company
- Initiate contacts with prospective buyers/investors:
- Distribute Acquisition Profiles
- Provide M&A advisor personal contact information
- Secure signed Non-Disclosure Agreements from interested prospects
- Conduct Preliminary Due Diligence with interested prospects:
- Provide Confidential Information Memorandum
- Conduct initial meetings between interested prospective buyers and owner/managers of the selling firm
- Respond to prospective buyers' request[s] for supplemental information as required and when appropriate

Deal-Making or Negotiated Auction
- Receive initial Letters of Intent (LOI)
- Negotiate all LOIs simultaneously
- Agree to and accept winning LOI after establishing:
- Precise and total business terms
- Preliminary escrows (at least)
- Balance sheet targets
- Grant exclusivity to prospective buyer that presents winning LOI

Confirmatory Due Diligence through Closing
- Conduct buyer's confirmatory due diligence simultaneously, with:
- Confirmatory accounting due diligence
- Supporting legal documents due diligence
- Preparation and negotiation of definitive agreements:
- Representations and warranties
- Language for business terms
- Rights and remedies for defaults;
- Closing

Postclosing "True-Up"
- True-up proposed balance sheet targets with the actual balance sheet (within one to two months)
- Release escrow hold-backs, if any, within 12 to 24 months

EXHIBIT 1.1 The M&A Process from Start to Finish

- Mom-and-Pops are sold with the assistance of business brokers who develop stables of buyers for these smaller firms.
- Sales of Middle Market and Upper Market firms are transacted by boutique or large investment banks.
- Middle Market businesses are usually represented by investment bankers who are more concerned with sellers, inasmuch as buyers for these attractive business are usually not that difficult to locate.

Exhibit 1.1 gives an overview of the M&A process.

Notes

1. In point of fact, there is really no consensus agreement on where the Middle Market ends and the Upper Market begins. I do not think anyone would argue though with an upper limit on the former of $1 billion in sales (which in turn suggests about $500 million in value). As a practical matter between $500 million in value and $1 billion is a rarified area and most Middle Market transactions in the M&A world are substantially under even $500 million in value.
2. This excludes some 17,600,000 "businesses" that have no employees.
3. For a basis for this assumption, see Chapter 23, the Rules of Five and Ten.

CHAPTER 2

Drivers of Middle Market Activity and the Sellers

Liquidity and Umbrella Drinks

In the first decade of the 21st century, Middle Market mergers and acquisitions (M&A) activity is driven by several unique factors, some old but many of them new. The first is liquidity. Many attractive Middle Market businesses have ten or fewer owners. Precisely because Middle Market firms have so few principal shareholders, they often find themselves up for sale when liquidity issues arise. For example, one or more owners may wish to leave the business to happily retire (I like to call them "umbrella-drink sellers"), or may need to exit due to other lifestyle issues. Health issues, divorce, and death among the principal owners' group may lead to a sale if the owner's heirs or partners cannot accommodate each others' needs. Selling a partial interest in a Middle Market business is not as easy as selling a partial interest in a public company, where ordinarily, a simple call to your stock broker will do the trick. If the interest is big enough, it may result in having to put the whole company, not just the partial interest, on the market. Of course, in a case where the liquidity problem (or just the desire for liquidity) is with one of the majority owners, it will almost certainly result in a sale if there are no other options—and frequently there are not.

Baby Boomers

There are also the ubiquitous baby boomers, no less a driving force in Middle Market M&A than in all other aspects of life in the late 20th and early 21st centuries. The eldest members of the 78-million-strong baby boom generation turned 60 in 2006. The youngest boomers will turn 66 (our government's estimate for the most common retirement age) in 2030, about 22 years from now. Many baby boomer entrepreneurs will sell the Middle

Market businesses they founded, and this factor will remain a major driving force in M&A for at least two more decades. To put this transaction data into perspective, consider this: Based on data supplied by the U.S. Census Bureau in 2002 there are just about 1.2 million Middle Market firms with sales of $1 million to $1 billion annually. Collectively, these 1.2 million firms had sales totaling $9.8 trillion and carry a conservative market value of $4.9. And the boomers own about 800 thousand of these businesses. Between 2011 and 2029 (19 years) an average of 43 thousand of these a year will be disposed of, about 2/3 of these by sale. These are huge numbers and unprecedented.

Technology and the Information Age

This is not your mother's Middle Market. Technological advances have dramatically transformed the Middle Market of 2008 from that of 1966. Consider that the first widespread use of the Internet was in 1995. Consider that the amount of technical information in the world doubles every 24 months. Well known as "Moore's Law."

Today, many Middle Market firms will have dramatically shortened business life cycles as new technologies are developed and adapted throughout the global economy. New technologies and approaches launched by Middle Market firms routinely disrupt and eclipse other Middle Market—even Upper Market—firms, and sometimes entire industries. Light-speed advancement in disruptive technologies is the rule, forcing survivors to become increasingly more proactive and infinitely more responsive vis-à-vis their clients and prospects . . . or die. Middle Market firms that rest on their laurels, growing complacent with past achievements, will, not *may*, wake up one day soon to find themselves in the "buggy whip business," figuratively speaking.

Creative destruction always has been a force to be reckoned with in capitalist systems. It existed in the United States in 1908 and 1808. But in 2006, the ever-increasing speed of technological advances has accelerated the process to an astonishing degree. As a result, business life cycles (or at least "business as normal" life cycles) have been truncated no less dramatically among businesses that rely on technology than among those that develop technologies. Ten years ago, the Internet was effectively in its infancy for the vast majority of the world. Since then, the Internet has radically transformed our world, our economy, and virtually every business in the United States and elsewhere. A good illustration of this is that the average existence of a company in the Standard & Poor's (S&P) 500 index, which shows that annual turnover 50 years ago was 25 to 35 years, versus today's 12 to 14 years.

The Middle Market business life cycle—the time elapsed from founding to exiting, or at least to growing by acquisitions of other Middle Market business—has gone from 25 years or more, historically, to 2 to 5 years in and even less in some technology or technology-dependent businesses, with most of that acceleration being realized in the last ten years. The radical shortening of business life cycles, in turn, has had an enormous impact not only on Middle Market business operations but also on the timing, frequency and execution of the sale of Middle Market firms as well.

It's Not Your Father's M&A World, Either

McLean, VA—April 2006,
I looked around the large meeting room, rehearsing in my mind some brief remarks to introduce the panel of experts that would discuss business and M&A transactions with India. I was not sure whether it would be taken as offensive or humorous, but my temptation was to make a comment somewhat along the lines that when I was 12 years old (53 years ago admittedly), the breadth of my knowledge of India was more or less covered by Rudyard Kipling's famous British Empire novels, and that it would be in fact another 40 (circa 2000) years before my awareness of India had much improved, at least in terms of doing business with it. My god I can barely believe how small the world has become in terms of commerce in the last ten years.

According to a major M&A reporting service, as far back as the early 1990s about 25% to 33% of announced M&A transactions were cross-border deals, admittedly mostly between U.S. companies and companies in the Western Europe and the UK. However, in very recent years, with the fall of the Soviet Union, an increasing number of deals are being done with Eastern European businesses. According to one study, about 75% of all Middle Market acquisitions of European targets by non-European acquirers were by U.S. acquirers.

And then there is China. I can only imagine what this world will look like 25 years from now, when China is likely the dominant financial player in the world. It is predicted that in ten years, China will be the largest English-speaking country in the world.

And we must consider the rest of the developing and developed world: the Pacific Rim basin; Mexico and Canada (post-NAFTA[1]); Israel and the Middle East; and so on. I would love to devote a whole chapter to this subject, but it is outside the scope of this book. Suffice it to say that this is not your father's M&A world. The one-world phenomenon is everywhere around us, especially including Middle Market M&A transactions. Most

Middle Market M&A firms worth their salt either have offices, have correspondent offices, or are members of global affiliations of international M&A firms and depend heavily on these to service their U.S. clients. On a final note, it is interesting to contemplate, for me at least, the degree to which Middle Market M&A activity will contribute to smoothing out the geopolitical differences between historically insular nations, whose internal focus has led for eons to so much war and strife. People historically tend to be less antagonistic when they have fair trade with each other.

The Glass Ceiling that Sometimes Drives Transactions

In the Middle Market, as in many other upward-growth paths, there exists a "glass ceiling," a point where a Middle Market company's resources no longer keep up with its growth or its growth opportunities. The resources that are lacking may involve leadership, experience, financial resources, or insufficient access to distribution or supply channels, among other factors. In short, successful Middle Market firms often outgrow their owner/founders or capital resource limitations. The glass ceiling tends to emerge when Middle Market companies reach $10 million to $20 million in annual revenues. Many Middle Market business owners often find that the best way to break through the ceiling is to find the necessary resources by merging with, or selling out to, a larger company—even if it means relinquishing much, if not all, of the ownership of the business.

Big Fish and Little Fish

Business is sort of an ecosystem for sure, and in all ecosystems, the big fish eat the little fish in order to survive. This is not a new phenomenon in M&A, but it is a more frequent phenomenon as the pace of business life changes. Survival of the fittest is not just a Darwinian construct for living creatures. It is equally applicable to business, especially the Middle Market sea, which is, after all, the spawning ground for the Upper Markets.

Chapter Highlights

Principal drivers in the sale of Middle Market firms include:

- Liquidity and or retirement
- Baby boomers coming into retirement age

- Shortened business life cycles due to technology and the information age
- Global expansion into a one-world economy
- Glass ceilings for Middle Market businesses
- The corporate food chain

Note

1. NAFTA, enacted 14 years ago, now eliminates tariffs on more than 70% of the products and services that the United States, Mexico, and Canada sell each other.

CHAPTER 3

Finding—and Understanding—Buyers in the Middle Market

Washington, DC—1962

My wife and I left the settlement attorney's office both exhilarated and exhausted. The settlement attorney was probably beyond exhausted and more than a little exasperated. As 20-year-olds, we were making our first house purchase, and we were as nervous and as diligent as if we were summiting Mt. Everest at its slipperiest point while storm warnings were being sounded. After all, $14,000 was a hell of a lot of money. The package of closing documents consisted of a settlement sheet, a deed of trust, and two or three other pieces of paperwork, and we reviewed and questioned them relentlessly for two hours.

Scared Money

Times have changed. Anyone who has settled on the purchase or refinance of a home in the past 15 years knows that the transaction involves enough documentation to fill a bushel basket. The closing of my last residential settlement, circa 2005, involved more money than I ever could have imagined a home purchase would involve. In 2005, the purchase price of a roof over my head seemed more in line with the after-tax proceeds of a midsized lottery jackpot. In 2005, I signed all those documents more or less without reading them, no more than glanced at the bottom line on the settlement sheet, and departed the settlement attorney's office within 25 minutes of my arrival. That is what some would call confidant, experienced money.

While "scared" money occasionally plays a role in an individual *smaller* Middle Market mergers and acquisitions (M&A) transactions, it does not do so in the overall transaction arena. But the scared money buyer is a type I want to make you aware of, because all M&A practitioners and many very small Middle Market sellers (deal values usually under $5 to $7 million) will encounter them. Scared money is almost always far too sensitive to risk ever "pulling the trigger" on a Middle Market M&A transaction, even when ample justification exists to close the deal. Recognize and avoid scared money in Middle Market M&A transactions or, at the very least, do not expect scared money to consummate the deal. I will discuss this class of Middle Market buyer as we proceed.

Understanding Buyer and Investor Types

This chapter will focus on how to identify buyers that on the one hand primarily are associated directly or indirectly with the seller's industry or on the other hand operate in other industries but may find the seller attractive as a strategic acquisition. Sellers are likely to encounter both as well as other types of buyers in any given M&A transaction and these respective buyer types routinely make offers that incorporate very different values and transaction terms.

Active Middle Market buyers may be sorted into several fairly distinct categories, and it is worthwhile to do so to gain a greater understanding of who they are and how they act. As Sun Tzu, the 6th-century BC military strategist, more or less said, half the battle is knowing your opponent. Well . . . he said something like that anyway.

Consolidators or Roll-Up Promoters

Consolidators or roll-up promoters were especially active during the late 1990s, and they were a Middle Market business owner's dream (and his or her investment banker's dream as well!). They still pop up from time to time and will continue to do so. Count on it! As buyers, consolidators or roll-up promoters were a seller's dream, because in industries they were "rolling up," they often were willing to pay prices for sellers' businesses that typically reflected very significant premiums over what the sellers otherwise might be offered.

The premiums offered by consolidators or roll-up promoters reflected the fact that roll-ups often were done in haste in anticipation of a planned initial public offering (IPO). The buyers expected that the arbitrage—the mark-up between what they expected to realize when selling their roll-up into the public market and the price they paid for the collection of private Middle Market firms they rolled up—would be substantial, and quite often, the pay-off to these promoters was in fact astronomical. Then again, the Middle Market sellers themselves made out quite well.

So if the private Middle Market sellers made out quite well and the roll-up promoters often did extraordinarily well . . . this was terrific news all around, right? Well, almost but not quite, because virtually every last one of these roll-ups became one of the worst nightmares public shareholders ever could have imagined.

Here's how the game was played. Promoters happened upon a highly fragmented industry, bought up scores of companies within it and combined them into one company that they then sold into the public market in an IPO. By taking their roll-ups public, the promoters routinely realized substantial mark-ups (arbitrage) over the cost of acquiring all of the component private companies. The ostensible justifications for such mark-ups included "economies of scale" and other synergies that would be achieved by lumping together those scores of smaller businesses. Even so, the IPOs invariably were launched before those economies of scale and synergies were realized or even proved to be remotely achievable. Yet roll-up promoters descended like locusts upon Middle Market and Mom-and-Pop industries alike, across such disparate industries as funeral parlors, trash haulers, ambulance services, heating- and air-conditioning service companies (HVAC), and office supply stores. You name a fragmented industry and someone was likely rolling it up in the late 90's.

The fundamentals of roll-ups proved problematic for several reasons. First, for the most part they were driven by promoters—MBAs and financial engineers who had minimal operational experience running businesses. Those promoters realized early on that their upside profit potential was huge and, once they cashed out or generated exceptional returns through a public offering, they did not need to hang around to deliver the promised economies or synergies. This is not to suggest that in all cases there was an intentional disregard for their investors, as there was certainly more than a little naïveté on the part of many of these promoters, too.

Second, the idea that significant economies of scale could or would be realized by these ad hoc agglomerations of small Middle Market (or Mom-and-Pop) companies proved fallacious. A miscellaneous collection of small businesses does not a big business make. This is especially true among Middle Market firms where, once the ink has dried on the closing documents, the acquirer must "manage" scores of entrepreneurs who remain highly independent-minded and quite difficult to lead. The fact that the rolled-up Middle Market operations routinely were strewn across a continent, with little more to connect them to one another but a new, seemingly alien home office and senior management made things all the more difficult. Talk about herding cats! Inevitably, the cats could usually not be herded, and, as I have said, public shareholder/investors in the rolled-up enterprises paid the downside price more often than not. Roll-ups came, conquered unsuspecting public shareholders, collapsed (or severely contracted), and then disappeared from the scene more or less in the very late 1990s as a major buy side modus operandi, as the investing public caught on.

Will roll-ups ever return? You can bet on it. For that matter, they have not entirely disappeared. Memories will fade, and a new generation of MBAs and financial engineers and other such whiz kids will return, most likely offering some variation of the roll-up. There will always be another gold rush somewhere (recently renewable energy, particularly biofuels—ethanol, biodiesel). When roll-ups return, in whatever form, prospective public shareholders would do well to remember the 1990s and the saying so often attributed (without substantiation, in fact) to P.T. Barnum: "There is a sucker born every minute." At the same time, if and when roll-ups do return and as they occasionally even now arise, those Middle Market business owners lucky enough to find themselves in an industry being rolled-up should consider quite seriously this huge opportunity to maximize the value of their enterprises while they can. The one caveat: they must insist on receiving the bulk of the selling price in cash, not stock.

Strategic Industry Buyers

Strategic industry buyers may resemble roll-up promoters at first glance, but that is where the similarities end. The most significant difference between strategic industry buyers and roll-up promoters is that the former tend to be Upper Market businesses and larger public companies, which conduct consolidations under the direction and management of operations executives. While strategic industry buyers are motivated by economies of scale, entry into new markets, and other synergies to be realized through their acquisitions, they do not start off with the notion that cobbling together scores of Middle Market businesses will guarantee success.

Unlike roll-up promoters, strategic industry buyers already have attained critical mass in the Middle or Upper Market enterprise that serves as their acquisition platform. And they only pursue (or at least try to pursue) acquisitions that complement the established enterprise. In short, strategic industry buyers tend to be highly-motivated, very good buyers, among the very best buyers that Middle Market sellers could want.

Financial Buyers and Private Equity Groups

In the 1990s and earlier, the term *financial buyer* was often considered to be a pejorative. These were the types of buyers who, as a real estate investor acquaintance once bragged to me, made their money when they bought the property. In other words, they always tried to buy on the cheap. While they are technically financial buyers, today's private equity groups (PEGs) are very significant M&A participants, accounting for approximately 25% to 33% of the Middle Market deals done. Private equity actively invests at all stages, from early stage companies (venture capital) to later stage transactions.

From a source of cash point of view, the term private equity group is somewhat of a misnomer, since most investments in private equity funds are made through college endowments, large pension plans, insurance company portfolios, and so forth, although recently some PEGs have raised money through the public sale of stock. Among such investors in these funds, private equity holdings often are considered part of their alternative asset investment programs, quite separate and distinct from the more conservative stocks and bonds that typically account for up to 95% of most endowments, pension funds, and similar investor types. These investors tend to be motivated to set aside 5% (and recently, through greed, maybe a lot more) of their assets in alternative investment vehicles in hopes of "catching a ride" on the occasional home run or at least a stream of doubles.

There are approximately 8,000 PEGs operating. Typically, they are structured to allow their own investors certain first-out, guaranteed-return-on-investment rights, after which point all gains are divided along the lines of 80% (to the investors) and 20% (to the organizers), the latter being known as a "carried interest." The management of PEGs usually is paid fees amounting to 1.5% to 2.5% of fund assets to cover salaries, professional fees, and other expenses. What PEG management is motivated by is the 20% carried interest it will receive on investment gains after the fund has achieved a baseline financial return to its investors.

PEG investments usually are organized under limited partnerships or LLCs, with specific and limited lifespans of eight to ten years. There needs to be an end to the fund so the final tallies of profits and losses can be made and distributed. As a result, for all practical purposes, the investment time horizon—the time between purchasing a stake in an enterprise and cashing out of it—averages four to seven years. This time span reflects the fact that it takes some time to invest the PEG's funds fully and, at the back end, it takes time to unwind its investment positions.[1]

Private equity groups typically launch with $150 to $250 million in assets at the very minimum. Smaller funds usually cannot operate efficiently, given that their staff must be specialized and labor-intensive. A 2% annual management fee on funds of this size should suffice to pay management expenses.

VENTURE CAPITALISTS   For purposes of distinguishing between the different types and preferred investments of PEGs, I will denominate early-stage investors as venture capitalists (VCs), although in the 1990s most PEGs were known as VCs. Early-stage VCs were among the most prominent investors in companies that led the dot.com boom of 1997 through the spring of 2000. They invested early and often, in thousands of start-up enterprises. Historically (as with roll-ups, but much more dramatically), the dot.com era led to a bubble and a collapse. As of 2008, much of the wreckage left behind by the surge of ill-conceived (and often even more poorly executed) "new paradigm" enterprises launched before the bubble burst has been cleared away. Many VCs (but by no means all) had been run, or at least very heavily populated, by 30-something MBAs without a lick of operating experience who embraced all the usual clichés of "new paradigm" hype that are always so credulously repeated right up until the latest boom goes bust. Of course, the 30-something MBAs who have zero operating chops or real-world experience with past bubbles and collapses were investing tens of billions of dollars of other people's money in "killer-app" businesses launched by 20-somethings, whose business concepts and plans often barely exceeded, at least in quality, a few scribbles on the back of an envelope. The dot.com bubble was déjà vu all over again—the latest in a parade of disruptions and faux disruptions dating back to tulip manias and beyond, probably throughout the history of human commerce.

VCs are still here, though, and a lot wiser, too. Many of them, in fact, moved away from early-stage business investments into later- or more mature-stage investments after the crash of 2000. These come broadly in two flavors: Funds that like to buy entire businesses and funds that prefer to buy majority or minority interests but keep the original owners along for the ride. For ease in discussion, I will denominate these as portfolio funds and recapitalization funds, respectively.

Unlike their later-stage PEG counterparts, true early-stage VCs invest funds that usually can only be used to grow the enterprise. VC investments usually do not allow founders or other early investors to take cash "off the table."

LATER-STAGE PRIVATE EQUITY GROUPS (PORTFOLIO FUNDS AND RECAPITALIZATION FUNDS)   Later-stage private equity groups have grown enormously active in recent years, investing in post–start-up, relatively more mature businesses, and are now a dominant buyer type in the Middle Market M&A world. Investments by later-stage PEGs hit record levels in the second half of 2006, after raising some $360 billion in capital that year (much of which and more remains uninvested as of mid-2008.) About two-thirds of these funds are North America–based.

Despite investing in businesses that are much more mature than start-ups, per se, later-stage PEGs still must have significant growth prospects if they are to attract investment capital. Typically, a PEG tries to realize something like a 35% compound growth rate in value (value needs to double about every two years) to be deemed a real success. As I have already said, later-stage PEGs include portfolio funds and recapitalization funds. Again, the primary difference between these two groups is stylistic.

Portfolio funds routinely buy the whole company, while recapitalization funds prefer to leave the sellers in place with significant minority interests of 20% to 40%. Occasionally, however, recapitalization investor PEGs do allow the sellers to retain a majority stake in the company in which they invest. The essence of a recap PEG is to allow sellers to take money off the table while offering opportunities for a second "dip" when the PEG cashes out through an IPO or other sale (M&A) by going along for the ride. The key in a recapitalization transaction, then, is to deal with a PEG that has ample funds for expansion and growth and, ideally, the industry connections (smart money) to accomplish that.

Recapitalization investor and portfolio PEGs usually place as much value on upper level management as on the investment opportunity itself. "Add-ons," "tuck-ins," or "bolt-ons" to the original platform company can and frequently are undertaken when operating and management structures or platforms already exist to absorb the new acquisitions. In many respects, PEG investors of both types are similar to—and now, for the most part, highly competitive with—strategic industry buyers in the M&A auction market.

HEDGE FUNDS Once the domain primarily of the superrich for all sorts of esoteric investments, hedge funds are a relatively new arrival in the M&A marketplace. In financial terms, to *hedge* is to manage and/or diversify investment risk by creating derivative or counter-positions in securities, currencies, or other vehicles. The original hedge funds, established 30 or 40 years ago, sought to post superior investment returns while carefully managing and minimizing downside risk. Hedge funds have transformed over the course of the past decade. Recently, they have entered the Middle Market and have begun behaving much like PEGs. Unlike PEGs, however, hedge funds often appear to be crazy patchwork quilts of very different investments, but they now include Middle Market companies in their appetites, sometimes voraciously. As of late 2006, some 13,000 hedge funds were operating.

THE IMPORTANCE OF DEAL STRUCTURE AND RESEARCH WHEN WORKING WITH PRIVATE EQUITY GROUPS PEGs mostly leverage their deals with debt in addition to using their own equity (leveraged buy-outs, or LBOs), so sellers who retain a significant position in their companies need to consider this factor. The business, post acquisition, very likely will be highly leveraged by third-party debt following the closing of the deal. Such leveraged transactions are less common to nonexistent among early stage (venture capital) deals, to the extent at least that they would appear on the investees' balance sheet, and of course they have no consequences to the seller on total buyouts.

But otherwise, they most certainly do matter, big time, in a partial interest deals in which sellers retain some equity.

Why does this matter? Because the seller's equity will be subordinated to virtually all other securities if a deal sours. Lenders—whether senior, mezzanine (subordinate), cash flow, or asset-based—will all be able to get out first if trouble arises. Private equity group investors may well find themselves to at least some degree in the same boat as the sellers—with equity positions at risk—but private equity group investors typically have equity positions giving the PEGs preferences over the original sellers.

Additionally, PEG investments in any individual seller's company will represent only a portion of their overall holdings (which, for the most part, constitute "other people's money" anyway), whereas for sellers themselves, the stakes they retain in their former companies are likely to represent significant personal wealth.

These PEG investor preferences usually take the form of preferred stock with preferred dividends, first-out rights, and preferred redemption and liquidation rights. In addition, even in a situation where the PEG has a minority interest, it will, through corporate governance or shareholder agreements, be more or less in control of events. Negotiating deal terms when transacting with PEGs is one area where the advice of experienced investment bankers and transaction attorneys becomes critical, as there are no hard and fast rules and terms often vary from PEG to PEG, from deal to deal, and even from coast to coast.

Lastly, the same due diligence should be performed on a prospective PEG recapitalization investor as on any financial decision that will have great impact on the seller's financial life. Is this a smart money investor (see above)? How large is the fund? When was it organized? When will it likely be liquidated? Who would the client be working with post-deal? What do other earlier investees think of this fund and its management?

Individual Buyers and Scared Money

Individual buyers are highly unusual in the Middle Market, both from the perspective of deal frequency and deal size. In most cases of very small deals (under $5 to $7 million in transaction value), closing a Middle Market acquisition requires prospective buyers to part with approximately one-half of the seller's business's value in available cash. And very few people, relatively speaking, find themselves in a position or with an appetite to pay out—and put at risk—$2.5 million to $3.5 million in cash to purchase a Middle Market business. Even those who possess as much as $2.5 million would find themselves psychologically averse to investing virtually their entire net worth in the purchase of a business. Occasionally, individuals do appear both willing and able to transact deals by having sufficient individual or pooled financial resources (and access to supplementary financing as required) to compete with other participants in a negotiated auction. Even so, such individuals (sometimes smaller Middle Market companies), despite having the resources to compete, rarely have the strategic motivation to do so. Strategic motivation implies an edge that reflects an ongoing buyer's business significantly enough to warrant the pursuit of add-ons or complementary acquisitions, so even more capital is likely to be needed down the road.

Nonstrategic Industry Buyers: Bottom Feeders

Nonstrategic industry buyers present problems and challenges that at first glance appear counterintuitive. Do not assume that because a buyer is already in a business like the seller's, he or she will pay a reasonable price. Unless an industry player has mounted a conscious (formal) plan to acquire other competitors, he or she will not likely be a good buyer. This is what I refer as a nonstrategic industry buyer.

Posit the sale of a fairly large Middle Market printing company based in San Francisco, CA, that has annual revenues of $50 million. The business is worth approximately $15 million. An inexperienced Middle Market investment banker might recommend selling the company by finding a larger competitor in a city within a 200-mile radius or so. Sacramento, San Mateo, and the Silicon Valley come to mind. However, there may be no active, strategically motivated buyers within that 200-mile radius. Such nonstrategic industry buyers as do exist regionally will typically prove both coy and cynical: they are willing to consider an acquisition, but only at a rock-bottom price. These bottom feeders capitalize on their own indifference to the prospective acquisition to extract substantial price concessions from prospective sellers who are unwilling or unable to look further afield for potential strategic buyers. These types of bottom feeders are not good buyers and should be avoided at all costs. Unfortunately, it is all too often the case that these nonmotivated buyers constitute the only real possibilities when the sale of the business is motivated by some disaster and was not planned for well in advance.

Management Buyouts (The Good, the Bad, and the Ugly)

Management buyouts sometimes offer a problematic source of Middle Market buyers and sometimes offer an opportunity. Two major problems can arise. First, financing may be difficult to obtain unless the sellers (Middle Market owners) are willing to extend a substantial portion of the purchase price in promissory debt (seller take-back) notes to the management buyers. Management usually must be capable of investing funds equal to a minimum of about 20% to 33% of the business's investment value before debt sponsors would be willing to come up with the balance of funds necessary to close the transaction and that assumes good collateral is available.

Another approach available to management (and the sellers) is the recapitalization type of PEG, referred to earlier in this chapter. In this case, management will go along for the ride, with the PEG being the real owner and management having perhaps 10% ownership initially, with maybe another 10% available from incentive stock options if all goes well. Of course, those PEG sponsors will first want to assure themselves that the prospective management team has the requisite capabilities to lead effectively while the business's own potential remains bright.

It takes a good business to attract the interest of outside sponsors, a point that sometimes conflicts directly with a second problem that arises where Middle Market management buyouts are concerned. That second problem, from the seller's perspective, is that management buyouts (where management, as opposed to a PEG, will be the true owners) require that a purchase price for the business be negotiated as it always is, but pricing a business in the absence of a fully orchestrated negotiated auction is unlikely to establish a business value that accurately reflects actual market value especially in a negotiated auction with several suitors. The value of the seller's business can be appraised, but virtually all such appraisals are by necessity hypothetical in nature and rarely reflect actual investment values that might be derived from an auction with a number of competing bidders.

So, assuming that financing can be found, how do management buyouts ever get transacted? Some sellers may feel sufficiently benevolent towards the longstanding managements that, in fact, helped them build their businesses that they are willing to reward them by selling the business at some price that may fall short of the business's likely true value. Occasionally, a seller's estate may be similarly disposed toward long-time management, especially when a quick sale is desirable and when it is in the best interest of all to hold the company together.

But management buyouts can be a real boon for certain types of business sellers in cases where the business may have no real appeal to private equity groups or strategic buyers, and sellers may deem management to be its best, and most likely, and sometimes only prospective buyers.

MANAGEMENT BUYOUTS AND PUBLIC COMPANY DIVESTITURES Management buyouts are also frequently entertained when a public company decides to spin off a division or other unwanted assets quickly. Rather than belabor the process by initiating an auction, the public company chooses to sell the assets to management. Alternatively, it is not unusual that after management has taken a company public, and the company falters in turn, management may pursue a buyback.

Management buyouts of divisions or of entire companies can be tinged with cronyism, though, when a select group of insiders receives an extraordinary opportunity to become owners of an enterprise. On the other hand, in a hard-nosed corporate environment, management may be given no greater consideration than any other potential buyer and will have to compete in an auction and . . . Because of large firm politics, sometimes even less consideration is given to them than to an outside buyer. Management in these cases is also stuck between a fiduciary responsibility to get the best price for the corporate parent that owns the division or subsidiary and its own desire to negotiate a good deal for itself. These are not easy transactions by any stretch of the imagination. I recently observed a management team for whom my firm had raised the capital fail to get the deal, even when it offered the best terms and price. The alleged reason was that the parent felt that the customers would be better served in the hands of the larger outside buyer. Corporate politics . . . who knows? Of course, if the management team is really strong, it may have some negotiating leverage along the lines of "if this business is sold to someone else, we will find it necessary to seek other employment." This is a dangerous card that has to be subtly, carefully, and usually very politely played.

ABSENTEE OWNERS AND MANAGEMENT BUYOUTS IN PRIVATELY HELD COMPANIES

While I will address this again in a later chapter, one classical management buy-out scenario, in the case of privately held Middle Market companies, is likely to be expressly or implicitly antagonistic: the buyout of passive and/or absentee owners by an ambitious and aggressive management team that does not believe it has been sufficiently rewarded in the past for achievements leading to the business's success.

Tensions arising between aggressive management teams and passive (absentee) owners often force a management buyout, because under certain circumstances, management can have a significant impact on the seller's ability to close a transaction with an outside party. Such management influence may range from subtle hints of a general lack of cooperation with passive/absentee owners, to what in some cases would appear to be outright blackmail, especially in the case of absentee owners. Sellers may undertake preventive measures if they are able to anticipate such problems well in advance, which I will discuss later in Chapter 5.

ESOPs Employee stock ownership plans (ESOPs) were created during the somewhat egalitarian euphoria of the 1960s, when social scientists theorized that employees who owned shares in the businesses for which they worked would, in fact, work harder. I will tell you, based on 40-plus years of advising Middle Market business, that on the front lines of business operations and management, virtually no one believes this, nor has anyone seen this theory proved true. I call this theory ESOPs' fable. The 80/20 Rule is a more commonly held and documented belief; it holds that 20% of a firm's employees account for 80% of its success.

That said, ESOPs may be quite useful as a financing mechanism in employee buyouts, although extreme caution is advised. ESOPs essentially provide sellers of Middle Market businesses a means of selling out to their employees by taking advantage of the tax deductibility built into qualified retirement and pension plans by law, which allows a trust to be formed that, in turn, is wholly or partly funded by the business's profits (a form of tax qualified pension plan). Then, the sellers have the trust invest its money by acquiring the business. The owner effectively is allowing his employees to acquire his business with the business's profit, which in effect is the owner's own money. However, this solution can still work well and make sense in the right circumstances.

Two factors make this alternative workable. First, the owners (of the business being acquired) receive tax deductions for monies they give their employees (through the trust) to acquire the business. At marginal tax brackets approaching 40% or more, this can make a huge difference in financing the deal. Second, leverage often makes the deal work. Banks and specialty lenders that lend to ESOPs in turn make payouts to the seller, who does not have to wait for his money. The tax-deductible qualified retirement plan contributions made by the business are then used to pay back the loan.

ESOPs do pose some problems. As with any management or employee buyout, determining the value of the business being sold can be very difficult. Valuations must be determined by a professional valuator. ESOPs are heavily regulated by the IRS and the Department of Labor. With professional valuators estimating valuations strictly based on stand-alone financial performance (as opposed to the investment value, which may be derived by several prospective buyers bidding in a negotiated auction) on the one hand, and the IRS and Department of Labor heavily scrutinizing such transactions on the other, the sellers are highly unlikely to maximize the investment value of their businesses when selling to ESOPs. Another problem: Advantages provided by leverage (having the ESOP trust borrow some part of the business's purchase price) are often limited to about one-third of the business's value initially. Meanwhile, in case of default, the seller should never forget that it is still his own business, more or less, that is collateralizing the loan until he is totally paid out.

In the final analysis, ESOPs have their place and their purpose, but for the vast majority of Middle Market business sellers, ESOPs make the most sense when there is no other way out. In that particular case, they are an excellent tool in the box of professional M&A advisors.

Offshore Buyers

Sellers and their Middle Market investment bankers should never limit their search for prospective buyers to the United States, because international buyers—mostly from Western Europe, but increasingly from other nations, especially India—account for increasingly larger roles in the acquisitions of U.S. Middle Market businesses. As I am completing this book in the spring of 2008, the decline in U.S. currency values. relative especially to the United Kingdom and Western Europe, make the acquisition of U.S. business by acquirers in those countries particularly attractive. It is easy to see how a relatively inexperienced consultant undertaking the occasional M&A engagement for a client ("Anybody can do this stuff...right?") or a seller attempting to close a sale on his own very likely would overlook a big portion of his potential buyer market.

Identifying Potential Buyers

These days, every good-sized Middle Market investment bank avails itself of extraordinary—and very expensive—research tools, which help them identify and locate suitable prospective buyers and/or investors for their sales-side clients' businesses. Investment banks' research staffs usually conduct the necessary database and related research long before initial approaches to prospective buyers are made.

The research databases and related tools allow them not only to explore fully all the potential investor classes and types on behalf of their sellers, but also to think "outside the box" as much as their personal creative talents or limitations allow. It is critically important to sellers that their investment bankers do not simply add additional names to lists of prospective buyers already known to the seller. Middle Market investment bankers can and should have both the tools and the motivation to look further afield for prospective buyers that might not be obvious candidates at first glance. One useful approach, when looking further afield, is to consider Silo Mates, Tunnels, Ladders, Maps, and Clients.

Silo Mates

Silo Mates are often larger or public companies operating in the seller's business type or industry that might have an interest in acquiring the seller. Identifying Silo Mate enterprises takes very little effort and no imagination. Not surprisingly, the Silo Mate approach frequently fails to identify the best prospective buyers. Even so, Silo companies account for about 25%

of prospective buyers in many cases (the others being PEGs, international companies, and outside-the-box buyers. Even among the Silos, great care should be taken to identify especially prospective buyers that might benefit from potential synergies. A Silo Mate company will not realize synergies automatically simply because it represents a larger version of the Seller; if that were possible, Middle Market sellers would be well-advised simply to undertake massive contacts among prospective buyers operating in their respective industries and simply hope for the best. Silo Mate companies should not be discounted, however, and when up-front research suggests strong potential synergies, the seller and/or his investment banker would do well to approach the prospective Silo Mate buyer, well-armed with research. An understanding of those potential synergies should be hip-pocketed when the initial contact is made, because if the Silo company is interested in the seller, the subsequent communications of those potential synergies might greatly increase the buyer's interest.

Tunnels

Tunnels speak to prospective buyers who do not operate in the client's business or supply chain directly but nevertheless would benefit from entering the seller's business. Businesses occupying adjacent Silos might well be willing to "tunnel over" and take a look at the prospective seller. Firms selling computer printers might well benefit from selling computer paper, for example. Tunneling to an adjacent or nearby Silo often proves as successful as any other approach, and should be included in any sales-side representation that is conscientiously carried out for a client. Wholesaler and retailer catalogues (along with the research databases, of course) are potentially great places for analysts to seek out such connections.

In one case, one of my firms' investment banking clients in a motorcycle-related industry was seeking potential buyers that were less obvious than those that might be surfaced by using a "bigger company, same business" approach. The solution: We researched wholesaler's catalogues for related industries, a tack that generated dozens of potential leads for likely Tunnel buyers, and achieved a very successful outcome for the client. To carry this just a step further, the rather obvious but simple example of printers and printer paper quite easily could be researched by obtaining catalogues from a few big-box stationers. Other potential buyers, in the case of printers, might include manufacturers of printer stands, printer cartridges, cables, etc.

In one transaction with a former client, a paper company purchased a large direct mail company, a move that made tremendous sense in retrospect given the huge quantity of paper consumed by the direct mail company. Such approaches may sound simple, but can work really well for Middle Market sellers. As usual, the simplest ideas quite often are the best ones.

Ladders and Supply Chains

The supply chain Ladder offers another fairly basic way to consider potential buyers. A Middle Market investment banker representing a prospective seller who manufactures widgets should "look both ways" vis-à-vis the supply chain by identifying 1) the businesses that mine or manufacture the basic materials from which widgets are made, and 2) the firms that sell widgets at retail.

Mapping Buyers

Last but not least, Mapping prospective buyers entails the obvious tactic of identifying businesses that are likely to gain a particular advantage by acquiring the seller for the purpose of entering new geographical markets. This approach overlaps all of the others previously discussed, to some degree. Prospective sellers and their investment bankers should especially not forget to Map prospective offshore buyers, which, as we have already said, account for a substantial number of U.S. Middle Market transactions.

Clients

It has been estimated that Middle Market sellers identify the ultimate buyer of their businesses—at the very least as one of a number of prospective buyer candidates they share with their investment bankers at the onset of an engagement—fully one-third of the time. Inexperienced Middle Market investment bankers too often are reticent when it comes to asking the seller which buyers he thinks would constitute good acquirers. But when you come right down to it, this should be among the very first questions a Middle Market investment banker asks his sales-side client. Too many investment bankers labor under the matchmaker myth, believing themselves solely responsible for identifying prospective buyers. Some may fear that simply asking the question might cause the seller to doubt their abilities and/or ask for a reduction when it comes to the payment of fees. Those inexperienced investment bankers who are reluctant to ask a seller to provide a list of potential buyers miss the point of the relationship: it is a collaboration between the seller and his investment banker that is intended to maximize the seller's investment value. The seller brings his typically highly-specialized knowledge of his own industry to the table, while the investment banker contributes an invaluable understanding of negotiating auctions and related technical skills, including of course possessing large databases of buyers himself.

Jersey City, NJ—June 2003

Wow! *Colby and I walked into the large conference room to meet the M&A Red Team for a Fortune 500 company to discuss targets for their acquisition program. In the room, there were at least 50 chairs arranged classroom style, and 45 of those are occupied. (Turned out that five people are running late.) Mr. Big, the COO, had decided to go into the government contracting business, and the order was handed down the line: "Go and buy something." Having been just hired as buy-side consultants, we were there on our first meeting to discuss possibilities and parameters. In all fairness, "something" had already been defined as falling into any of maybe 12 categories. Already stunned by the size of the meeting, we were even more taken aback when we were told that there would be another 20 people tied in on a conference line. The meeting started to go downhill from there, as everybody wanted a say. Even from our vantage point, some of the internal politics also became quite obvious quite quickly.*

I barely suppressed (actually took some comfort in, I admit) a quote I heard attributed to the late Fred Allen that went something like: "A conference is a gathering of important people who singly can do nothing, but together can decide that nothing can be done." And another from the humorist Dave Barry: "Meetings are an addictive, highly self-indulgent activity that corporations and other large organizations habitually engage in only because they cannot actually masturbate." Actually, I loved these clients. The problem was not the people, but organizational behavior run amuck.

Which Door to Open to the Buyers?

Having identified a potential buyer, how does one make the proper first approach? Many buyers of Middle Market businesses are larger public companies that all-too-often are highly bureaucratic and/or decentralized. While larger public companies have in-house M&A or corporate development staffs, no such group, representing any randomly-chosen public company, will operate quite the same as any other. Some in-house M&A or corporate development staffs operate as pure bean counters. They establish a valuation for a potential acquisition and they want to stick to it (and maybe even try to stick it to the seller!). Other such staffs may include extraordinarily creative corporate development officers who are capable of discerning investment value potential. Most staffs will include a mix of bean counters and creative corporate development officers. But Middle Market business owner/entrepreneurs who are interested in selling their businesses to public companies tend to approach the companies' M&A or corporate development teams directly. This quite often turns out to be a mistake.

In my experience the best way to approach a public company almost always is by directly contacting a division or operational executive with sufficient authority and clout to consider the opportunity and subsequently lobby for it within the company. Obviously, the ideal candidate will be the executive whose division stands to benefit most by acquiring the seller. Because many, if not all, public company in-house M&A and corporate development groups are relegated to number crunching and are very much removed from operational aspects of their firms, they are more likely than not to take no action on a potential transaction unless directed to "crunch numbers on it" by senior executives. Additionally, number crunchers employed by many large public buyers frequently kill deals when acting on their own initiative (or without strong encouragement to green light a deal from above), because they implicitly are rewarded for not making mistakes. Often, the best way to guarantee not to make a mistake is not to do the deal.

A related buy-side challenge arises when the buyer company makes the mistake of leaving the divisional executive–cum–deal champion in charge of deal negotiations, instead of its in-house M&A staff: the divisional executive's eagerness to consummate such a deal very well could result in the company's paying a higher price than necessary to close it. On the other hand, his inexperience in negotiating M&A transactions could just as likely kill the deal. Ideally, buy-side larger companies have these two groups share the task of preliminary evaluation, valuation, and negotiation, but in large bureaucracies this can be a tough thing to pull off without at the same time involving too many people.

McLean, VA and San Francisco, CA—June 2008

This email was sent today (almost) verbatim from one of our experienced bankers to a colleague member of our firm on the West Coast:

"My suggestion to you as a next step would be to call them later this coming week and highlight our related expertise, real-world management experience in the industry, tombstones, and ongoing contacts/participation at industry trade shows and conventions. As you may know, most investment bankers market their deals to the corporate development departments of prospective buyers. Because of the particular expertise we have, we take advantage, where possible, of our access to the people who are responsible for revenue. They are the ones who ultimately appreciate the value and potential of the acquisition and who hopefully will drive the corporate development people to want to do the deal. Corporate development people are generally gatekeepers who find reasons (at times) not to do deals unless they are told to do them. I draw the analogy to looking

for a job. Would you look for a job by contacting the HR department of a company or by going to the decision maker (when known)? HR people usually filter candidates without appreciating the bigger picture. We believe that our approach enhances deal-closing potential, as well as the opportunity to create interest and potentially higher valuations."

Chapter Highlights

- Classic buyer types, each with separate and distinct motivations and deal structures, include:
  - Consolidators or roll-up promoters
  - Strategic industry buyers
  - Private equity groups
  - Venture capitalists
  - Nonstrategic industry buyers
  - Individual buyers
  - Management buyouts
  - Hedge funds
  - ESOPs
  - Offshore buyers
- Buyers can be found:
  - In Silos (same-industry buyers)
  - In Tunnels (related-industry buyers)
  - On Ladders (supply-chain analysis)
  - On Maps (geographical buyers)
  - Clients
- The best way to identify a strategic buyer is by finding a division or product leader/executive.
- On the buy side, the best way to conduct an acquisition search, evaluation, valuation, and negotiations is a team approach between bean counters (M&A people) and deal champions (division executives), but with preferably a very few people involved—perhaps two or three at the most.

Note

1. Commonly, to the extent that a PEG fund has not unwound its investments at the end of the partnership life, the remaining portfolio may be transferred forward to a new fund with the consent of the original investors.

CHAPTER 4

Preparing a Middle Market Business for Sale and Running the Business while Selling It

Memphis, TN—June 2001

This was my second trip to Memphis to meet with the board and CEO of a technology Middle Market client which had asked us to provide a preliminary valuation, in this case with a full value-driver analysis, in anticipation of selling this decent-sized operation. We had sent a copy of the preliminary valuation and value driver analysis to them several days ago in preparation for this meeting and were here to discuss it and move forward with the sale of the business for them.

Charlie, a CEO whom I had just recently met through a referral, was one of those thoughtful guys that you instantly liked and respected, and that respect was well-justified. This company was his third home run in about 30 years. I guess I also liked him because he was about my age, and for once I did not have to feel like somebody's grandfather.

Charlie took a pull on his pipe. Very charming, *I thought,* and rare to see one of those these days. *"Dennis."* he started out, *"there is good news and there is bad news."*

I thought to myself, how many times have I heard that one in my career? *The bad news, in my experience, usually trumped the good news, so I braced for the worst.*

"The bad news is that we have decided to hold off the sale of the company." (Yep, there it was.) "After a lot of conversation, we believe your value-driver analyses pointed out some tactics and strategies that we can adopt for the next several years and then really come out of this with

a home run and not just a triple." (Charlie was a pretty modest guy; I thought he had a home run already.)

Charlie went on, "We began reformulating our strategic plan around improving some of the negative value drivers and enhancing some of the positive ones your firm's report discussed. Your report was really an eye opener."

I was not really sure how I felt about this . . . mixed feelings, for sure. The good news was that we were developing a trusting client relationship, and we would probably work with them on the sale of their company . . . just not now.

Charlie was not through. Another characteristic of his was kindly blunt-ness. "Now before you get too big a head, there was nothing in your report that was of the nature of, well, let's call it 'miraculous informa-tion.' But it did cause us to slow down and reflect on what we could still accomplish with just a few moves."

I was not too deflated by Charlie's bluntness. Well . . . maybe a little. But after all, I have been a consultant long enough and hired enough of them myself to have no problem with the fact that much of consulting is just regurgitating back to the client what they "sort of" knew already, maybe with a different ribbon around it and perhaps thought out and articulated slightly differently. The benefit to me was when I needed an outside opinion myself; I usually had not had the time or the clarity to develop my own thoughts fully.

As Middle Market business owners create companies to build value, the actual realization of that value via an eventual exit strategy should always be in the back of their minds, and it should be monitored on a regular basis to produce a frame of reference or an easy-to-measure status report. This advantage can be most readily accomplished by obtaining a thorough and periodic preliminary valuation analysis, even where the business is not for sale and not likely to be for years.

I will address the concept of a preliminary valuation elsewhere in this book, in the context of a client and his investment banker getting a prelim-inary handle on what value range a business is likely to bring just before entering the sales process, and I will also distinguish that type of valuation from the more formal types used for courtroom, accounting, and tax plan-ning purposes. However, I want to discuss here another use of what is still a preliminary valuation, but with a serious analysis of the value drivers of the subject company.

It is not my intent to list all of the value drivers (positive and negative) that can affect the value of a particular company in this book (although

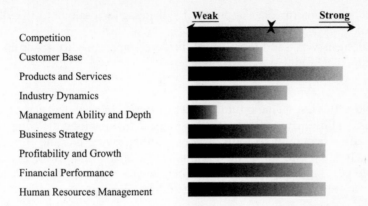

EXHIBIT 4.1 Preliminary Valuation as a Re-engineering or Strategic Planning Document

Exhibit 4.1 captures many of them). Suffice it to say that these drivers can usually be stated in number of categories (a sort of a strengths-and-weaknesses analysis performed by a professional in the context of valuation), including growth rates, customer concentrations, threat of competition, management structure, and so forth. My firm has long applied these more detailed analyses not just as an estimate of preliminary value, but also as a tool many of our clients use for reengineering their businesses, even when they are not immediately for sale.

A number of years ago, these preliminary valuations, in a less detailed fashion, were used simply to estimate value before going into the marketplace to sell a business, and that was their original intent. Gradually, we and our clients began to realize that these valuations were also a valuable tactical tool in running their businesses, too. Many of our clients actually update these more-detailed analyses every several years now. The fact of the matter is that what makes a business valuable upon its sale also makes it valuable while it is being run. This is, in fact, the ideal starting point for business owners who are willing to take the long view, as discussed below, and I heartily recommend this approach.

Three Periods to Prepare to Sell a Middle Market Business

In my experience, Middle Market business owners tend to prepare for the sales of their companies in one of three ways:

- Taking the long view, by preparing the business for sale over the course of three to four years out

- Taking an intermediate approach, by planning for a sale 12 to 18 months out
- Taking a very-short-term, even "fire-drill" approach to a sale in the immediate future

Often, this last scenario is triggered by external or unanticipated circumstances: an unsolicited offer for the business, a death among the company's principal owners, and so forth. It goes without saying that the "fire sale" approach is, far and away, the least attractive of the options for planning the sale of a business, but it still can be effective if the client is willing to devote at least a little time to planning and/or "cleanup."

Long-Term: Preparing the Business for Sale Three to Four Years Out or More

Every Middle Market entrepreneur spends a substantial amount of time strategizing how to grow his business, and should spend no less time considering how to build investment value—and how to realize it—in his company as it evolves. Whenever possible, Middle Market business owner(s) should make the time to perform a comprehensive inspection/tour (figuratively, anyway) of their business to identify issues that should be addressed, cleaned-up, and/or enhanced to make the business more successful and eventually more attractive to prospective buyers. One way to do this, which I have discussed, is by securing a preliminary valuation from a professional who can provide this assessment, and then by following the strategic and tactical plan that will suggest itself out of this preliminary valuation.

How might a Middle Market business owner/principal best prepare, long-term, for the sale of his company three to four years hence? One might start by reverse-engineering the process from the end game of an envisioned, highly successful sale of the business. First (or last) of all, the owner/principals of the business would have developed it to the point that it performed optimally against a series of metrics, or value drivers, which maximized its investment value to a group of several prospective buyers in a negotiated auction. The metrics, or value drivers, of A+ Middle Market companies would include highly experienced management teams that are not overly reliant on a single owner and/or manager; steady (or better) growth rates in revenues and profitability; product and/or service excellence that affords the company leadership in its business sector, with luck; barriers to entry that discourage competitors; and a broad client base that minimizes risks of an over-reliance on any one or more of the company's top customers, etc.

With such end-game value drivers clearly in mind, owners can then ask themselves: "Where are we now vis-à-vis these performance standards? Three to four years' lead time gives owner/principals plenty of time to earn an A+ for their companies, but only if they are willing to step back and critically evaluate where they stand now. This process automatically establishes a strategic plan, on which basis a tactical plan may be developed to transform the company into a more highly saleable business in the future.

Intermediate-Term: Just Before the Business Goes on the Market, One to One-and-One-Half Years Out

Middle Market owner/entrepreneurs planning to sell their businesses in the short-term—in the coming year or slightly more, for example—can undertake a number of presale initiatives that should enhance their businesses' investment values substantially. Such initiatives include:

- Cleaning up the business' accounting and tax records ... and hiring a CPA, if one is not already onboard to do so (and to make other bookkeeping recommendations, as appropriate). I repeat this elsewhere in this book, but one of the most frequent causes of deal failure or at least major adjustments to transaction value is the fallout from incomplete or inappropriate application of accounting principles when they are discovered after the Letter of Intent.
- Establishing an effective management team whose members work well together, and improving that team if possible. Prospective buyers who are confident that the business's managers can handle the company's postacquisition transition successfully (especially when the owner/entrepreneur is expected to depart) are usually more likely to pay a premium than those expecting wholesale replacements of, or departures by, management team members. The exception, of course, is the case where the new ownership intends to replace management with its own, but this should not be assumed.
- Locking in that management team now (See Chapter 5).
- Cleaning up or clarifying major contractual relationships with customers, suppliers, landlords, and so forth
- Registering and protecting trademarks, patents, and copyrights, where appropriate
- Seeking out favorable media coverage for your business, products, services, and personnel, if possible. No buyer is immune to being somewhat influenced by this. The media, especially business media, hunger for content to fill their weekly or monthly needs. Often, media coverage

is not all that hard to obtain, but if the business is sufficiently large and it is warranted, a good PR firm can be a big help.

- Reviewing Occupational Safety and Health (OSHA) compliance issues and conforming to them, if you are in the appropriate industry. This will be a serious buyer issue.
- Reviewing any hazardous waste issues (environmental waste issues), getting into compliance with regulations (or at least assessing their impact), and, if necessary, getting independent studies, which are usually conducted as Phase One or Phase Two environmental studies, where appropriate.
- Ensuring that all licenses and permits and tax registration are in order; the buyer may eventfully need a legal opinion that they are.
- Firming up or clearing up important customer and supplier contracts.
- Cleaning up any corporate minutes and ensuring they are up-to-date.
- Cleaning and organizing the shop, office, and plant. Yes, a little beautification can do a great deal of good, as it suggests a level of professionalism and attention to detail that inspires greater confidence among prospective acquirers.[1] Eye-appeal is seldom among a business's key value drivers, but it definitely can enhance a business's investment value by subtlety impressing potential buyers.

Short-Term: While the Business Actually Is Being Sold, Within 12 Months of Closing the Deal

Washington, DC—July 2001

"You did what?" asked Greg, one of our senior investment bankers. It was a steam-room hot summer day in DC. (Why does this damned humidity seem to be so much higher than 100% on these 100-degree summer days? And how could it be that the office's air-conditioning system decided to fail today, making our offices even less hospitable than even the hazy murk outside our windows suggested it should be?) Tempers were flaring as temperatures rose.

"You did what?" Greg repeated. A born-and-bred New Yorker, Greg tended to speak in a voice that could have boomed out across two blocks of his native Manhattan, clearly audible by all within that not-that-short radius. From his office next to mine, his screaming into the phone at an upstate New York client gave my southern ears an earful, to be sure. Fortunately, they were friends.

"You say you just bought a new $5 million printing press? Let me get this straight. We are going to settlement on the sale of your business in two weeks and you just went out and bought a new $5 million printing press?"

Good Lord—they were on speakerphone, I realized soon enough, as Greg's client, a great guy, responded, "Yeah, but it was too good a deal to resist. It was a great price on a great press. When business volume picks up in another year or two, the buyer will really need this press, so I could not resist."

Greg was not simply New Yorker–blunt. Greg was blunt enough to abash most New Yorkers. One thin office wall away, I just shook my head, thankful that Reed, a fellow New Yorker, probably could hold his own in this conversation. But buying a $5 million printing press two weeks before closing? I all but willed myself to remain seated at my own desk so as not to rise up, walk over into Greg's office and chew Reed a new one myself. Then again, my own Texas-cum-New England upbringing had instilled in me a usual commitment to genteel conversation that, if abandoned, too-often raised mere confrontations to matters of honor that not all that long ago resulted in duels at 40 paces. I bit my tongue, held my seat, and braced my ears against the inescapable.

"Listen, you idiot," Greg continued, but not in those words, exactly (I thanked heaven that Reed was a long-time friend and confidante of Greg's). "The purchase contract for the company is $10 million. Why in the hell do you think the buyer is coming up with another $5 million for that printing press, and why would he even want to anyway?"

"Well, maybe I will lease it to him or something," Reed answered, in a tone that suggested he was beginning to understand Greg's grave concern.

"Yeah," countered Greg, "and how much might he pay for that lease?"

"Well, let's say maybe $75,000 a month will cover the printing press and then they will have it when the market turns around and ah … he is, ah … ready to … ah … use it." As longer pauses punctuated each word, Reed seemed to be getting the point, however tardily.

"Okay, $75,000 a month comes to about a $900,000-a-year hit to cash flow. And since we sold the company to the buyer for five times earnings, I'm guessing that you will be willing to reduce the $10 million purchase price of your company by, say, $4.5 million? Is that what you're thinking? Because that's what the buyer's going to be thinking."

Reed, somewhere out there, had fallen silent. After a minute or so, Greg tried another tack: "Can you just sell the damned press on the market?"

Reed was speaking in a near-whisper now, "Well, used printing presses do not command a high price once they have been installed somewhere. And I would have to pay another $150,000 to have it dismantled and removed." Oh well!

However preposterous the above story may sound, it really happened.

I would like to make a few points concerning short-term business operations once Middle Market owners have decided to sell and during the period that they are selling the company. The sale of a Middle Market businesses is time-consuming, requiring six to twelve months on average (and sometimes much longer) to consummate and close a deal. But even when all of that up-front time is invested, the outcome of a deal, or even a closing, is by no means certain.

In other words, it might not actually get done, and in general the best interim philosophy is to approach the sale as if it will not happen. As time passes, any number of issues can hinder the progress of a deal or even blow it up. These include changes in the macro economy, force-majeure events like 9/11, changes in the outlook of the industry in which the company operates, the sale of similar companies at unexpectedly low purchase prices, sudden negative changes in the business's own financial and/or operational performance that may take some time to correct ... the list goes on. Experienced investment bankers have weathered all of these challenges and more, while deals blew up, resulted in "fire sale" valuations, were tabled, or ... sometimes ... proceeded to successful conclusions because the Middle Market owner responded quickly to the issues at hand and minimized their impact on the sale. Timing, luck, and responsiveness all come into play in Middle Market investment banking and sales of Middle Market companies. A balance must be struck, though it can admittedly be a tenuous one, between running the business as though it were a going concern (not one up for sale) while recognizing that it is, in fact, up for sale.

Buyers do not generally like big changes once they have done their initial preliminary due diligence and decided to move forward, but on the other hand, as I have said, there is no certainty that a deal will ever get done until the fat lady sings. Yes, this is a bit of a conundrum, but things tend to work out best when the scale favors the going-concern scenario (assuming the business will not be sold and making most decisions on that assumption, especially during the early part of the sales process). Never forget that running the business as a going concern in most cases suits prospective buyers perfectly, because they are the ones who will continue to run it as one should they win the negotiated auction.

Managerial decisions made by sellers solely in the interest of the immediate expedience of selling the company often tend to prove counterproductive in the long term, as their consequences may yield materially damaging results if the business is not sold. When in doubt—or even when not in doubt—Middle Market owners should consult their investment bankers regarding this type of decision. They pay their investment bankers quite well to advise on precisely those decisions.

A business is always changing and will always change throughout the course of its existence. The bottom line: Stay flexible and keep options open. Should a Middle Market owner (while the business is for sale) sign a new, long-term lease for office or manufacturing facilities when short-term renewals are available? Probably not. Should he undertake a major but not critically necessary plant renewal project while the business is for sale? Again, probably not. But should he continue to expand his marketing budget? Maybe so. Many longer-term decisions that do not immediately produce cash flows (or may even decrease them) can be normalized or rationalized out from current operations by the investment banker when he restates his client's financial statements so as to affect transaction value only minimally, if at all.

Litigation

That we live in a particularly litigious age has escaped no one's attention. Middle Market business owners may find it all but impossible to prevent parties from suing them in an era in which weird tort law and astonishingly aggressive attorneys too often enable minimally inconvenienced third parties to dream of lottery jackpot–sized returns for insignificant complaints. That said, Middle Market business owners while the business is for sale should do whatever they can to avoid initiating and/or instigating litigation, especially where relatively unimportant matters are concerned. Litigation intended to prove a point, exact revenge, win minor damages, etc., should be avoided at almost all costs where the owner(s) would be a plaintiff. When litigation results in countersuits and other escalations, it does nothing to advance, and everything to threaten, a successful deal closing.

Complications posed by ongoing litigation are nearly limitless. If a Middle Market business owner/entrepreneur involved in litigation draw nears a closing on the sale of his firm, a savvy counterparty to the litigation very likely will make every effort to leverage those circumstances to maximize his own outcome. Should a sale close before such litigation has been concluded, the buyer inevitably will require the Middle Market business owner/entrepreneur to agree to concessions and conditions—most certainly including escrowed amounts to cover any reasonably anticipated outcomes and then some—that put the seller at a clear disadvantage. When likely outcomes of litigation cannot be estimated with a high level of confidence, prospective buyers very likely will disappear altogether, requiring the would-be seller to take his business off the market indefinitely.

Summing Up

While it is all but impossible to catalog all of the issues and decision points that may arise in the course of selling or preparing for the sale of a Middle Market business, this chapter attempts to address the most important points. Prepare for the sale as far in advance as the client can and be careful about making decisions during the sales process itself. The best recommendation one can give prospective sellers: Consider each such issue potentially pivotal to the prospective sale, while consulting an investment banker and other trusted advisors to ensure that the decisions made balance the dual polarities of the company's long term future and avoid too-big changes during the sales process.

Chapter Highlights

- Middle Market business owners should consider, whether contemplating a sale of a business or not, obtaining a preliminary valuation with detailed analyses of business value drivers to provide a strategic and tactical plan for current operations.
- Prospective sellers of Middle Market businesses tend to operate within the construct of any one of three primary scenarios:
  - *Long-term planning, three to four years out:* Identifying the positive and negative business value drivers that will affect the ultimate investment value of their firm and proceeding to re-engineer the business to optimize that value. This is the phase in which obtaining a value driver analysis is the most beneficial.
  - *Near-term planning, one year out:* Cleaning-up accounting systems and contracts, locking in management teams, and generally rationalizing and smoothing ongoing operations where and to the extent appropriate.
  - *Imminent, the sales period itself (of from six 12 months or more):* When the seller should run the business as a going concern—as prospective buyers themselves in fact see the business—while avoiding wherever possible any new long-term commitments, major changes in business operations, or actions that might result in litigation.
- There is a subtle balance between focusing on selling the business and making necessary decisions to run the business day-to-day. The objective is not to hurt the business's long-term prospects by postponing operating decisions that are good for its future while at the same time avoiding large changes in the businesses fundamentals. These are tricky decisions, and the best advice here is to seek out the advice of a very experienced mergers and acquisitions (M&A) banker.

Note

1. I am reminded of a statement by a slight business acquaintance of mine who founded a new passenger airline in the 1980's. It was along the lines of: "If the drop down tables in the passenger compartment have coffee stains, a passenger may assume less than adequate engine maintenance."

CHAPTER 5

Rewarding and Retaining Key Staff in Connection with a Business Sale: Blackmail or Justice?

Sudden Severe Storm Warnings

Overview

Many Middle Market business owners will be in for a significant shock when the day to sell comes and they find that key employees and management are suddenly not on their side. I have referred to this in the past as "strange, if predictable, behaviors around large sums of money." There are various ways to go wrong with key employees when selling a Middle Market business, and the intent of this chapter is to forewarn against them and provide some advice on how to avoid or mitigate them. This chapter may seem both overkill and overwrought, except to experienced mergers and acquisitions (M&A) dealmakers. The problems enumerated are not at all uncommon; in my experience, they occur with alarming frequency in Middle Market deals. Middle Market M&A practitioners are well-advised to raise the all-important question very early on in discussions with prospective sellers: What has been promised to whom and on what basis? Have any such promises been documented? Investment bankers and sellers who fail to address this issue risk working for months on a transaction that may falter or fail at the very last moment. Promises of compensation or a share in the proceeds from the sale of a business, made by a Middle Market owner to minority shareholders and/or key employees, constitute a sleeper issue that, if inadequately addressed, can prove disastrous. Offhand remarks made or not made by owners can prove no less disastrous if minority shareholders and/or key employees misinterpreted or imagined promises of greater compensation or greater shares in the proceeds pending the sale of the firm.

Washington, DC—March 2000
Promises, promises

It was a Friday morning. I should have been feeling pretty good: The week was almost over, I had a Saturday tee time, and we were enjoying the first decent, if early, golfing weather of the year. I was determined to play as much as I could that season, to knock a few more strokes off my embarrassingly high handicap.

But my stomach was sinking as my partner told me that it looks like months of very hard work on a $50-million business might have proved to be a dry well, at least for the time being. It is particularly painful when these dry wells happen for all the wrong reasons, and this was the second time this year that we had run into the same problem and for the same wrong reasons. The owner had made some promises, at least allegedly, to a senior executive and minority partner, perhaps more or less vaguely, that she would share in some way and "be taken care of" when it came time to sell the business, with an amount higher than her actual legal ownership would give her the right to claim.

My thoughts ran very quickly into a stream of questions. When did this happen? Where did it happen? Was it at some office Christmas party, after too much holiday cheer and eggnog? Who knows?

Two imploding deals in one year—one on the East Coast, one on the West, for almost identical reasons, one with a senior executive, the other with a minority partner—made it even worse.

Admittedly, in each case the complainant actually was running the business, or a big part of it. Each had been relatively indispensable in creating the enterprise that was to be sold. The East Coast deal's senior executive, a woman who clearly had been instrumental in building the business, was no less certain to play a major role in transitioning the business to the new buyer. Yet she was balking just short of the finish line for the deal. She was claiming she had been promised, albeit not in writing, a bigger stake in the sale proceeds than she now appeared poised to receive. The West Coast deal had been on the verge of foundering because an influential executive, who also was a minority partner himself, was claiming to have been promised an additional share of sale proceeds, once again without anything committed to paper.

I asked my partner Mike, what he thought. "How the hell would I know?" he answered, unhelpfully. I understood his frustration all too well, having found myself no less confounded, and no less irascible, when on both coasts the disputants seemed to be claiming something they were not (at least apparently legally) entitled to. And it was impossible to know what the facts were, and where, how, and by whom those facts had been misinterpreted or maybe even distorted. Assumptions get made, even over the sketchiest of remarks, and then they become set in the concrete of selective recollections. Months or years later, these recollections resurface as a deal is about to be done, when the business is about to be sold. Seasoned investment bankers will tell you this happens time and time again.

Not-insubstantial settlements were necessary to get these deals done . . . but they did get done. This time anyway.

Key Employee Rewards in General

Entire books have been written about the intricacies of rewarding key employees. Potential rewards run the gamut from stock options and other ownership plans, bonus arrangements, stay bonuses, phantom stock option plans, and numerous variants thereof. This chapter will not address the many permutations by which key employees may be compensated. Rather, it will focus on five basic issues that must be addressed from the point of view of a sale of a business:

- The need to arrange to retain key personnel to a point sometime after the sale
- The need to arrange for nonintervention and/or noncompete agreements with key personnel
- The need to arrange stay bonuses, timing them properly, and avoiding overpaying them
- The need to arrange to document promises that might have been made earlier, and to avoid making vague promises
- The special problems of absentee owner, key employees, and key employee rewards

The Need to Reward Certain Key Employees

Rewarding key personnel is an important element of many Middle Market M&A transactions. While buyers may offer moderate signing bonuses to newly-acquired key employees in an M&A transaction, and/or include them in buyer stock option plans, the burden for both rewarding and retaining key the seller when selling a Middle Market company. Sharing sales proceeds with key employees often reflects altruism and a sense of fairness. Sellers often acknowledge the instrumental roles such employees have played in helping build the company. Beyond altruism, however, sellers recognize that their businesses will depend in large part on the continuing commitment of those key employees if they are to achieve a successful transition to new ownership. Thus, it is very much in the seller's interests to establish incentives that encourage key employees to remain with the company through a transition period of from one to three years post-sale. A buyer's biggest fear—and this point will bear occasional repeating throughout this book—is that it will settle on the purchase of a business on Friday, only to find itself the owner of an entirely different enterprise when it opens the doors for business on Monday. Among the biggest risks in this regard is that a critical mass of key employees will disappear between that Friday closing and the start of business Monday, at least figuratively.

Counterproductive Rewards

Whether rewarding key employees is altruistic, fair, or simply prudent business practice may remain a matter of debate, but sellers should consider very carefully the nature and size of such rewards, lest the rewards themselves prove to be counterproductive. Imagine a scenario under which a seller awards a key employee 10% of the proceeds from the sale of his $20 million business. The receipt of a $2 million windfall could tempt many employees into immediate retirement—particularly those in mid- to late-career who already have been investing for retirement for many years. A younger key employee, though he or she might be years or decades from retirement, could look upon a $2 million windfall as an invitation to pursue an entirely different career or to take an extended sabbatical from the workforce. Even if the seller is certain that financial incentives paid to key employees will not tempt those employees to leave the company, the buyer very likely will have serious misgivings. Occasionally, those concerns could make the buyer reluctant to acquire the business, especially when the seller intends an immediate exit from the business following the closing.

Timing Reward Payments

The *timing* of reward payments to key employees is therefore of critical importance. Ideally, the proceeds should vest in accordance with a schedule that encourages them to remain with the company for two to three years. In my experience, otherwise well-intentioned sellers overlook vesting consideration alternatives at least 50% of the time. Three principal elements should be incorporated within any agreement to reward key employees upon the sale of a company. In return for their incentive payments, those employees must:

- Agree to remain with the company for a specified transition period following the sale
- Agree not to compete with the company for a specified period following the sale and/or not to interfere (nonintervention agreements) with clients/customers and employees of the company in a manner detrimental to its interests
- Not be paid their key employee incentive rewards or bonuses until they have satisfied these and related requirements in full

Timing Tax Issues in Rewarding Key Employees

The timing and execution of legally binding key employee incentive agreements also may be of crucial importance due to capital gains holding period requirements. Inappropriate or ill-advised timing, or having the employees paid by the wrong party (whether that is the buyer or the seller) often may wipe out 25% or more of the benefit to the sellers, would-be recipients, or both, depending on the specific tax strategy. In the absence of written documentation, oral promises to pay such incentives are unlikely to stand up for tax purposes when it comes to establishing a date that can be used to determine whether such payments to key employees will be accorded long-term capital gains treatment or whether they qualify as capital gains at all. Sellers and their key employees should consult tax counsel to ensure that such plans reflect their mutual interests and tax considerations.

The Importance of Clarity and Documentation—Avoiding Vague Promises

When sellers make unspecified, undocumented, general promises to "share the rewards with" key employees, the "how much?" question inevitably arises and almost invariably creates real problems when the company is about to be sold. This problem is especially acute if noncompete and nonintervention agreements have not already been executed—or even if they have been, in cases where the employee's presence in the continuing business is important. In any case, sellers and key employees often find themselves entertaining substantial differences of opinion when it comes to defining and interpreting how much will be shared when the business is sold. A lack of documentation compounds these issues, especially when a seller is likely to close a transaction in return for substantial financial proceeds. Key employees may feel cheated, while sellers feel blackmailed. Litigation may be and often is threatened or initiated. When buyers become aware of these problems, they are reluctant to proceed with the transaction. Would-be buyers understand all too well that potentially alienated key employees are less likely to prove effective in achieving a successful transition and continued operation of the business. In short, sellers should document all incentives for key employees in detail and in advance, so that these arrangements can have a sound legal basis and be clearly understood by both parties. Sellers also should construct and communicate the terms of such arrangements to prospective recipients well in advance of a sale of their business, to ensure that the key employees remain onboard and motivated throughout the transition period. Finally, allowing or encouraging a kind of unstated understanding of greater rewards to develop on the part of the key employee is serious mistake—and not an uncommon one, unfortunately.

When to Negotiate Noncompete and Nonintervention Agreements with Key Employees

Sellers should procure noncompete and/or nonintervention agreements from their key employees long before it becomes apparent that the business is for sale. Ideal points are when they are hired or when they receive a serious promotion or increase in compensation or responsibilities. In the absence of long term, in-advance-of-sale arrangements, nonintervention agreements may be more readily negotiable with key employees when combined with other devices or inducements, especially properly thought-out incentive and retention payments to be made in connection with the sale of the company.

Blackmail or Reasonable Compensation?

One man's inducement may well be another man's blackmail. If clarity and documentation of stay bonuses or shares of sales proceeds are not established well in advance, sellers may believe they are being forced, unfairly, to pay substantial sums of money to long-time employees (to whom they once entrusted the company and whom they are likely to feel they rewarded sufficiently for years) in the face of an implied threat by those same employees to launch a competing enterprise that will plunder the company's own client lists and employment rosters or, more subtly, just fail to cooperate in the transfer of important relationships to the new owner/buyers.

Key employees, on the other hand, are likely to consider such arrangements to be justifiable and equitable. After all, in their minds, the seller is likely to reap substantial profits from the eventual sale of a company the key employees helped build. Furthermore, key employees may be quite right in arguing that the sellers' wishing to restrict their own post-closing employment options must, and should, pay for the privilege. Meanwhile, seller and buyer alike will seek contractual assurances that key employees either remain with the company and/or decline to compete or interfere with it for a year or more following the closing of a sale.

Noncompete Agreements *and* Sellers

Some employees, of course, may also be sellers and significant owners, and while it may be somewhat of a non sequitur in this chapter, since we are discussing noncompete agreements, this is a good place to clarify the issue of noncompete agreements when it comes to owner/employees who are also sellers. For buyers, there is no getting around the critical importance of securing noncompete agreements from majority owner/sellers. The greater the financial consideration realized by sellers in the sales transaction, the more legally enforceable these noncompetes with them tend to be. Courts in general have ruled that a buyer is entitled to get what he or she paid for. In the case of key employees who are not owners, onerous noncompete agreements tend to be difficult to enforce as unreasonable violations of right-to-work principles.

Nonintervention Agreements

Nonintervention agreements are intended to protect sellers and buyers alike. Nonintervention agreements specifically prohibit sellers, minority owners, and/or key employees who execute them from interfering with the company's existing customers, contracts, and/or employees. As I have already said, nonintervention agreements tend to be more enforceable and more effective against nonowner key employees than noncompetes, as they do not prevent future employment, just the pilfering of valuable relationships.

Being Alert to Potential Problems When Promises Made Are Not Consistent with the Duties and/or Influence of Key Employees

Even when a prospective seller carefully documents the benefits key employees will realize, complications may still arise on the eve of the settlement of the sale. When key employees believe the rewards they will realize are inadequate, given the sales proceeds, trouble may still result. Essentially, by definition, sellers will want to offer key employees financial rewards and inducements they believe to be completely appropriate and objectively fair. But if sellers and key employees cannot bridge any gaps separating their respective expectations, very little recourse short of litigation is available to them. In fact, the discontent of key employees at a critical point in the closing of a deal can implode that deal altogether, as buyers shy away from bad feelings, potential bad faith, and postclosing implications for their prospective acquisition. Key employees might become very vocal in their disagreement precisely because of the leverage they can wield in their own interests preclosing. That said, key employees should avoid acting in a manner so clearly intent upon queering the deal that they run the risk of being sued by the seller for tortious interference. Nevertheless, most sellers want to avoid litigation on the eve of the sale, and this does leave key employees a great deal of practical if not legal leeway. In some cases, key employees may impact the deal more subtly, but still materially, simply by resigning or at least threatening to resign.

A Way to Avoid Key Employee Problems in the First Place

Sellers' intent upon minimizing the preclosing and posttransaction risks posed by key employees may pursue an entirely different course of action over time: develop a management team that is sufficiently broad and deep in experience and expertise that no individual employees are critical to the company's continuing success. This may seem a tall order at first, but it is achievable. Sellers who can create a management team of sufficient strength to obviate the need for single key employees very likely will choose to incentivize that team following a sale of the company without having to pay out the sums that single key employees might demand.

The Special Problems of Absentee Owners

Experienced Middle Market M&A intermediaries and their sales-side clients should pay particular attention to key employee issues when the sellers have been absentee owners for some time. Sooner or later, many owners of successful Middle Market enterprises realize that they have established companies that can operate reasonably well without their full-time (or even part-time) attention. Some owners may step away from day-to-day operations long before an exit opportunity materializes or is desired. The success of such companies may reflect the ability of key employees to take over relationships with major clients or other important company staff while building new client relationships, altogether independent of the absentee owner. As the absentee owner loosens his grip on the reins, his connections to clients, vendors, managers, and employees gradually but steadily erode. Key employees' psychic "ownership" in the company steadily increases.

Such transformations from owner to key employee dependence may be even more rapid and stark in companies where rapid technological changes force companies to accelerate product and service innovations or die. Absentee owners who become concerned and attempt to re-establish their dominance by asserting a tighter grip on the reins are more likely than not to exacerbate tensions with key employees, who will begin to take umbrage at efforts to interfere. "What does [the absentee owner] know anymore, anyway? The industry has changed and the business has changed with it. [The absentee owner] should just leave us alone to make him his money. He only shows up at dividend time these days, anyway."

Under these circumstances, absentee owners' efforts to sell their companies could be complicated by an all-out scramble to ensure that those on whom the company depends can be encouraged to remain with the firm through its sale and transition under new ownership. Even more so, their key employees—recognizing the extraordinary leverage they can exercise in advancing or imploding a deal—may try to exact significant concessions from the absentee owner/seller in return for allowing the deal to go forward and for promising to remain with the firm. Should the absentee owner/seller balk at financial incentives that key employees believe are commensurate with their contributions, entire executive staffs may rebel, one way or another, in full view of a prospective buyer or buyers. On such occasions, absentee owners might wish to consider selling the entire company—or at least a part of it—to the key employees themselves. A leveraged buyout or various gradual management buyout structures might be considered.

Absentee Owners . . . Maybe the Best Advice to Consider . . .

Alternatively, Middle Market business owners who realize that they are at eventual risk of becoming absentee owners should consider pursuing an exit strategy while they are on board and in charge of their enterprises. In fact, this is my usual advice to older clients who, having established successful businesses, are considering becoming absentee owners.

Wrap-Up

Key employees do not get to be key employees without making substantial contributions to the creation, development, and long-term success of the company of which they are a part. Sellers who are intent upon achieving a successful sale and a smooth transition will act cautiously and with great prudence to ensure that key employees receive adequate rewards that are documented fully and unambiguously, presented in a timely fashion, and which vest in alignment with noncompete, nonintervention agreements and desired transition stay periods.

Chapter Highlights

- Prospective sellers of Middle Market businesses should ensure that all exit strategy-related incentive and reward plans communicated with minority owners and key employees—whether informally or via formal agreements—are clarified, formally documented, revisited, and reaffirmed with those minority owners and key employees before launching the sale of the company, so as to avoid serious problems once a negotiated auction with buyers has begun.
- Bonuses and incentives payable to key employees in return for their remaining with the company through a postsale transition should vest gradually over the course of the entire transition period; immediate—or accelerated—vesting of such incentives may encourage key employees to jump ship on buyers prematurely, especially when the bonus is substantial.
- Sellers should secure noncompete and nonintervention agreements with key employees *well in advance* of the announcement of the imminent sale of their companies to encourage key employees to remain with the company through its sale and transition and to discourage them from departing the company to compete with the buyer.
- Noncompete agreements with sellers of Middle Market businesses are usually very enforceable, but may be less so with employees, where the agreements are too broad in scope.
- Absentee owners are particularly likely to face serious problems should key employees balk at their plans to sell the business and/or the financial inducements they propose to keep key employees onboard through a postsale transition under new ownership. The best ways to avoid such difficulties are: 1) Do not become absentee owners in the first place; 2) Seriously consider selling the firm before becoming an absentee owner; or 3) Seriously consider selling the company to an investor group led by key employees.

CHAPTER 6

Crystal Balls and Timing the Sale of a Middle Market Business

History repeats itself. That is one of the things that is wrong with history.
Clarence Darrow

Fairfax, VA—June 1995
I was on a conference call with Nelson, discussing whether or not it was time to sell the $40 million technology staffing business he had founded. Delightful guy, with more graduate degrees than you could hang on one wall, thoughtful, bright and pleasant.

But we were disagreeing.

And Nelson clearly was winning the debate. It was not that I found myself in the "usual suspect role" of mergers and acquisitions (M&A) investment banker (who was simply by trying to convince someone to sell.). Nelson trusted my objectivity; he just did not share my opinion. Nelson and I really did like one another, and have ever since; in fact, over the course of another 13 years, we long since became good friends.

At the time, we were in the dawn of the technology boom. There were not enough qualified technologists available, and everyone was trying to stay on top of the rapid changes in technology. We were all running just to stay in place. Meanwhile, everyone from Vice President Al Gore on down was singing the praises of outsourcing jobs around the globe.

So businessmen like Nelson, who provided technology staffing services to other businesses, found their businesses growing at compounded annual rates of 40% or so, while generating extraordinary profits. And when they sold, they were generating EBIT multiples of as high as 12 times. I was trying to suggest to Nelson that now might the ideal time to grab the money and run.

But Nelson was taking a different position. "Why not hang in there and enjoy this, rack up a few more years of 40% growth?" The sky itself was not even a limit in 1995. "Sure," he argued, "sooner or later, after several years, the technology staffing industry is going to take a breather, but like all markets, it will come back. A bull market in stocks returns once everyone has turned bearish. Right?"

Nelson's confidence, in fact, made me all the more uncertain. I now wish, looking back, that I had been a little more experienced with M&A cycles, as I might have been able to show Nelson what was about to happen to him if he hung on. Sadly, those multiples within couple of years dropped from 12 times EBITDA to 4.5 times, as all of the growth in the industry disappeared for various reasons—as it always does in every industry.

Bubbles, Cycles, and Business Values

Determining more or less the right time to sell a business at its maximum value is not always a luxury available to Middle Market owners, who sometimes find their hands forced by distress sales arising from family health issues or death, from partnership disputes, or from business difficulties. Fortunately, some issues that might motivate the sales of Middle Market businesses come naturally and can be anticipated: retirement age, the desire to change lifestyles, etc.

Timing a market to a certain degree is not entirely out of the question. Circumstances and conditions regularly arise that encourage sellers to make an educated choice. This is particularly true in regard to the "bubble" phenomena that arise irregularly in many Middle Market business sectors. Prospective sellers, recognizing that they and their companies are positioned in the right place at the right time, will try to sell into the bubble. During the mid- to late 1990s, for example, a number of industries experienced bubbles driven in large part by the dot.com and technology booms. For example, at the time, the outsourcing of professional IT services proved so popular, so "hot," that it was for all practical purposes a gold rush. Firms everywhere recognized the need to jump on the technology bandwagon by transforming their in-house IT capabilities. Consumers of these services confronted a very limited supply of adequately-trained "techies" (who themselves understandably commanded high compensation packages) on one hand, and on the other hand they acknowledged their own reluctance to take on the expense of a permanent IT staff to address requirements they considered to be a temporary need. As a result, the investment values of IT staffing and IT project management firms skyrocketed. The IT staffing and IT project management industries—and the individual firms within them—began posting

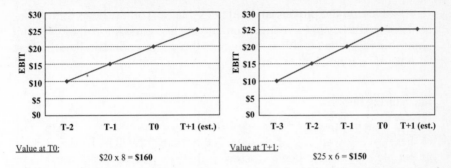

EXHIBIT 6.1 Timing the Deal or Waiting for Next Year's Growth: A Potentially Costly Trap

compound annual growth rates of 40% or better overnight. In turn, buyers of these businesses very soon began offering EBIT multiples of 10, 11, and higher to willing sellers (see Exhibit 6.1).

Current Bubbles

But bubbles collapse, and when they do, they cause significant market devaluation of the business that originally benefited. From 2003 through 2008, the government contracting industry has been experiencing a bubble driven by dramatic increases in the industry's M&A activity. In the aftermath of 9/11, federal government spending on defense and homeland security (among other areas) exploded, while government contractors, like IT staffing companies before them, realized double-digit growth rates that in turn generated investment valuations in the range of ten to twelve times EBIT—*and in some cases much, much higher.* As recently as the year 2000, it was quite difficult to sell a government contractor for anything more than four to five times EBIT.[1] This particular bubble is an unusually long one, as it was event-driven (by 9/11, the Iraq War, etc); however, beginning in 2007 and continuing into 2008, it is showing significant signs of weakening. Health care services and health care technology, as other examples, are also currently experiencing a big boom in growth, and consequently the multiples being paid. Timing is everything in these bubbles, and it should be considered carefully if a business finds itself in the midst of one. Bubbles are driven by sudden and rapid growth in an industry, and it is unrealistic to think that any industry can maintain a high rate of growth forever or even for long. This is especially true in the technology age where virtually all businesses and industries are seeing light speed changes in operating methods and whole market places and the ways they are serviced change almost overnight.

Bubbles are the proverbial flood tides that float all the boats in that particular sea. The key to surviving, even thriving in them is knowing something about bubbles—being able to recognize them and understanding the best time to sell during them.

Recognizing Bubbles

How does a business owner recognize that his industry is experiencing one of these cycles? Well, first of all, there is the "buzz." It will be loud and clear, as people everywhere begin discussing the exceptional transaction values that companies in industry X are generating. Another clue comes from the Rules of Five (See Chapter 23), which argue that when Middle Market businesses sell for more than five times cash flow (EBIT, etc.), financial engineering roll-ups excepted, the higher multiple must be justified by some kind of near-term earnings growth that justifies it. This mindset may govern the sale of a single Middle Market business or any number of businesses in a "bubble" industry in which the overall growth rate is floating everybody's boat. So the first key to a possible bubble phenomenon is the situation in which many companies (not just a few, as a single company may command a high multiple just due to its own high growth rate) within a single industry are receiving purchase multiples well in excess of five. Usually these will be found in the range of, say eight to twelve or higher as multiples of EBIT or EBITDA.

When EBITDA multiples do reach the eight to twelve range, Middle Market business owner/entrepreneurs should realize that the very peak of the cycle is approaching and the collapse of the bubble may well be drawing near.[2] EBITDA multiples of eight to twelve tend to be realized *three-quarters of the way into the cycle*, at which point buyers are likely to pay the highest investment values to be realized over the bubble's lifecycle, because there seems to still be growth ahead, and buyers always buy the future. At the peak (end) of the bubble, most of the growth has been achieved; of course, buyers become aware of that, so multiples begin to recede rapidly back to five or so. Forewarned is forearmed: when buyers are willing to pay seven to twelve times EBITDA (there are, of course, exceptions in some bubbles, where even higher multiples can be paid, but seven to twelve is a good time to become keenly alert to the possible end of a bubble), they very likely are paying the highest purchase price they will on anticipated future growth of the seller's business.

Bubbles and Their Duration

Bubbles tend to last for three to four years before collapsing.[3] This was true of the staffing and IT staffing explosions, the dot.com boom (later "bomb"), the telecom industry bubble, and the roll-up era. Bubbles eventually collapse, because they inevitably lead to consolidation, and consolidators (the buyers) inevitably become satiated, especially as rising transaction valuations tend to wring the upside growth and profit potential out of successively more expensive acquisitions. The other factor, of course, is the consumption of the goods or services being offered by the bubble industry. Eventually, an equilibrium between supply and demand is reached. Bubbles, in short, are market hiccups.

As I have said already, Middle Market business owners who are fortunate enough to find themselves operating in an industry experiencing a bubble should give serious consideration to taking fullest advantage of the rapidly inflating business valuations before they inevitably collapse. Twenty/twenty hindsight can be extraordinarily expensive, and once the bubble has collapsed, it is unlikely to revisit the industry affected for a long, long time. To the extent it does, it will almost certainly be in a *very different form*, involving new business processes and technologies.

Bubbles, a Summary So Far . . . Catching the Wave

So what can we do with this information and how can we use it? Well, we can at least know the following things and then act accordingly:

- Bubbles are probably occurring when there is buzz and when many companies within an industry are selling for multiples that far exceed the norm in the Middle Market of about five times EBTIDA.
- Bubbles typically last about three to four years.
- The highest multiples are paid when the bubble is about three-quarters over. This is when there is still foreseeable growth left in the bubble curve and buyers are willing to pay for it.
- At the top of the bubble, multiples will usually recede back to somewhere around five times.

Bubbles and Recurrences

The extreme improbability of a bubble's recurrence in precisely the same way in the same industry is due especially to the effects of the so-called "Information and Technology Age." The Information Age effect may lead seasoned investment bankers to revisit the advice they might once have offered before the early 1990s as to who should and who should not have to seriously consider taking advantage of these high-valuation business cycles. Once upon a time, one might have considered the age of the seller to be a major factor in the sell/do not sell decision while a bubble was inflating. The argument, of course, would have gone like this: The 55-year-old owner contemplating retirement should seize the opportunity to exit at the top of the valuation cycle or as close to that as he can. But maybe the 25-year-old owner should stick around, waiting for the next cycle. After all, he has plenty of time to catch another wave. Does he not?

But age may no longer be a good—or wise—criterion, precisely because bubbles that have occurred after the early 1990s are so unlikely to recur in the same way in the same industry. Those Middle Market business owners fortunate enough to find themselves operating in an industry that is enjoying a bubble, seriously should consider selling, whatever their age. In client representation, of course, the art is being able to covey this to your client without being perceived as simply trying to sign up a new client.

Ambitious younger owners also may decide that they can lead their businesses through long years of growth and dramatic transformation that might well generate a significantly higher valuation down the road. But this is a very big bet, and *clear-headedness* is absolutely critical to the owner's realistic assessment of his or her capabilities, the business's potential, the industry's mid- and long-term prospects, and his or her own staying power. One way to look at this is to consider that if an owner passes an opportunity to sell at the top of a bubble, at, say, a valuation of $25 million, then he is in effect making a $25 million bet that something better will come down the pike . . . if he hangs in there long enough (see Exhibit 6.2). The age of a business owner is clearly no longer a clear indication of whether to take advantage of a bubble.

From the other side, the buyers' side, owners of mature buy-side businesses may want to stay in the game to benefit from the growth and values they believe they can achieve by acquiring market share during a bubble, even if they seem to pay dearly for it at the time. Such decisions should be approached with extreme caution because, as I have said, valuation multiples tend to peak in the third quarter of the overall cycle, and buyers who buy in the bubble will need to depend on generating their own values from sheer size, market domination, and economies of scale that result from bubble period acquisitions.

Other Timing Opportunities—Roll-Ups

In addition to industry bubbles, when the roll-up phenomenon returns (see Chapter 3)—as it inevitably will, in some form or other—Middle Market owners whose businesses operate in an industry that is being rolled up should also seriously consider the opportunity to sell out at substantial premiums that are unlikely to be realized elsewhere. Where roll-ups are involved, sellers benefit by sharing, at least as beneficiaries in part, the substantial arbitrage roll-up sponsors expect to realize between the private

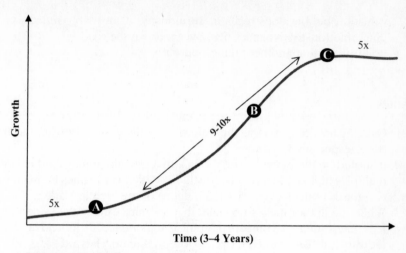

A: Beginning of the bubble
B: Bubble at 75%—highest multiples
C: Bubble's peak—already decreasing multiples
Explanation of EBITDA multiples:
   • No bubble/flat growth = 5× EBITDA
   • Bubble/accelerated growth = 9–10× EBITDA

EXHIBIT 6.2 Growth Curve and Optimum Selling Time

valuations paid for Middle Market companies and the value they can bring
when sold into the public market via initial public offerings (IPOs). Roll-up
promoters, in effect, are willing to share some of their anticipated profits
with Middle Market businesses owners to ensure they can assemble an
enterprise to bring to the public IPO markets. *Carpe diem* is usually the
order of the day for sellers in these conditions.

Chapter Highlights

Middle Market businesses hoping to sell their companies during a market
bubble should be alert to the following:

- Bubbles are of finite duration, and usually last no more than three to
  four years. The highest investment values are likely to be paid somewhere in the vicinity of the third quarter of the bubble's lifecycle.
- Bubbles are unlikely to recur, once they collapse—at least, never in
  the same way in the same industry. On the rare occasions when a

valuation bubble does recur in an industry, it invariably reflects very different industry dynamics many years down the road.

■ Roll-ups present another timing opportunity.

Notes

1. Once again I refer you to the Rule of Five discussed elsewhere in this book, especially in Chapter 23.
2. It should be mentioned here, though, that size alone may tend to drive multiples higher, as to very large Middle Market companies in the upper two thirds (values over say $150 million) of the Middle Market.
3. While the author makes no claim that they are exactly the same thing, it is interesting to compare empirical experience in individual M&A industry bubbles to Kitchin Cycles (Joseph Kitchin, Harvard Press, 1923), which identified economic cycles as lasting from about 39 to about 41 months. These are often interpreted as inventory cycles too.

CHAPTER 7

The Confidential Information Memorandum

New York, NY—1994

John, our Director of Engagement Support Services, was furious. He had written the fifth draft of a client's Confidential Information Memorandum (CIM), and the client for whom it was written remained unhappy. I was puzzled myself. No question about it: the business was highly technical, involving myriad potential applications of the technology ... but John was a Harvard Business School graduate, a Stanford journalism major, and a very talented writer. And the client was about to fire us.

I looked out the train window as we headed back to Washington, DC. "John, what do you think is going here? You have spent hours with this guy, and I know you have done all the standard research, been to New York City twice to visit with the client. What is going on?"

Fortunately, we had both had a glass of wine as we traveled south through New Jersey, and I could see that John was calming down, a bit anyway.

"Dennis. I am telling you that this guy has no clear concept of his own business. You ask him for an elevator speech and he gives you the Great American Novel—and it is a bad novel at that. And he really will not take the time to work with us to get his own story right. That is why this turkey of a CIM is all over the place, and why I just have not gotten a handle on it myself. If he can not explain his own business, how can I?"

I nodded and sipped some more wine. It had been a long day. Trains sure beat cars. At least you can commiserate with a colleague over wine in a train when all goes wrong; that is a very bad idea in a car, and planes to New York are no pleasure.

Postscript: *It turned out that we lost the client. He took his business off the market. There was probably more going on than met the eye, anyway.*

65

This guy was basically treating his business as a mini-conglomerate with no clear direction (including in his own mind), and he would not take direction from us either. That is the way the business goes sometimes.

The Acquisition Profile

Among the first documents in the mergers and acquisitions (M&A) sales process, in terms of prospective buyer communications, is the Acquisition Profile (see Exhibit 7.1). But it is often prepared after the Confidential Information Memorandum, as it really is a summary of that document, obscured to a degree to preserve client anonymity until a non-disclosure agreement (see Chapter 8) is signed by the buyer.

Confidential Information Memoranda—Overview

The Confidential Information Memorandum sports various noms de plume: the CIM, the Offering Memorandum, the Information Memorandum, the Book, and probably a few others. No matter what you call it, the CIM serves a variety of purposes in profiling a company and positioning it for sale. It serves as a preliminary due diligence document, since actual due diligence will be performed after all the major deal points are agreed upon. It helps control the agenda, allowing the seller to direct prospective buyers' attention to particular aspects of the seller's company, and provides an opportunity to confront weaknesses or challenges on the seller's own terms. From another point of view, it may be a securities document, which must be prepared with all the due care that this implies.

Each of these aspects of the CIM is critical to the successful sale of a Middle Market company, and each requires careful consideration by seller and investment banker alike. The CIM usually takes from a month to a month and a half to assemble. This is not to say that 30 to 45 full calendar days are required to complete the CIM, but rather that gathering of substantial information and input from the client, performing any needed additional research, writing and editing the document, and obtaining sign-off approval by the seller will tend to unfold over the course of a month to a month and one half.

Clients and Confidential Information Memoranda: An Intense Collaboration

From the investment banker's perspective, the most important aspect of collaborating with the client in the writing of the CIM is the invaluable

Telecommunications and Information Technology Services
Federal Contractor Company Profile

Charles Smith
Csmith@mcleanllc.com
703-827-0200 ext. 101

Mike Moore Mmoore@mcleanllc.com
Mmoore@mcleanllc.com
703-720-7980

Leading provider of satellite and terrestrial telecommunication networks, integrated information technology solutions, and professional services to the U.S. government and corporate sectors

- FY03 revenue: $300 million
- FY04E revenue: $325 million
- 500% revenue growth since 2000
- $295 million backlog
- Marquee federal client base, including Department of Defense, Department of Homeland Security, intelligence agencies, and multiple civilian agencies

Business Description: The Company is a proven Telecommunication and Information Technology Services company that provides total solutions for the secure coordination, synchronization, access, and delivery of mission-critical information. The Company's areas of expertise revolve around innovative satellite communications systems, terrestrial fiber-based connectivity, server-based communication networks, and information technology services.

Founded in 1991, the Company is ISO-9001 certified and has compiled a record of outstanding financial performance. The Company has been profitable since inception, and over the last three years has seen revenue grow 500%, reaching $64 million during 2003. This track record of dynamic growth is expected to continue into the future, and on the basis of current backlog, the Company conservatively expects to surpass $112 million in 2004 revenues. The Company's experienced management team has reaped numerous awards while successfully directing this growth and ensuring financial stability, building infrastructure, and maintaining the corporate culture of client focus and commitment to quality.

Services: Headquartered in the greater Washington, DC area, the Company is a leading provider of satellite and terrestrial telecommunication networks, integrated information technology solutions, and professional services to the U.S. government and corporate sectors. The Company's staff of nearly 400 experienced professionals offers a full range of services from each of its core capabilities—Telecommunications Services, Information Technology Solutions, and Professional Services. The Company is a trusted partner for enterprises seeking quality solutions, using the latest telecommunications and information technologies to provide superior, cost-effective, and responsive end-to-end innovative services designed to meet the Company's customers' complex requirements.

Market: Federal IT contractors have continued to command high valuations within the public and private marketplaces as the environment of multiyear contracts in which they operate allows the markets solid visibility into revenue, cash flow, and earnings, unlike many of their commercial counterparts. The government's commitment to technology transformation and consolidation continues to drive sizeable IT spending. The FY04 federal budget request in appropriations for technology was an increase of almost 13% over the prior year, and IT outsourcing is expected to continue to grow at double-digit rates. An additional $30 to $40 billion is estimated to be spent annually on classified intelligence-related initiatives. Satellite communications, one of the Company's areas of expertise, has seen a continual expansion of services and applications over the past several years, and has created a market opportunity for which the Company is well-positioned. For example, the Pentagon plans to spend $1.5 billion on commercial satellite services over the next five years.

Opportunity: The Company is actively seeking a merger or acquisition with a firm that can strategically benefit from the Company's significant capabilities in telecommunications and IT, the value of its cleared personnel, the Company's in-place infrastructure, and the importance of its long-term contracts. The Company's established reputation for excellence within the government market represents an outstanding acquisition opportunity for a firm seeking to enter the federal marketplace, or for a firm with already established government contractor credentials that is seeking to expand its customer base or create new areas of corporate capabilities.

	2000	2001	2002	2003	2004E
Revenue	$15,000,000	$25,000,000	$70,000,000	$300,000,000	$325,000,000

This profile is intended for qualified or accredited strategic buyers only and was prepared by the McLean Group, LLC from information provided primarily by the Company which has not been verified. The McLean Group does not make any representation, express or implied, as to the accuracy or completeness of the information. It is the responsibility of the buyer to perform its own due diligence to verify the information. This confidential profile may not be reproduced or quoted without written permission of The McLean Group, LLC. This profile is not an offering for the sale of securities.

EXHIBIT 7.1 Sample Company Acquisition Profile

opportunity to really get to know a client and his company quite well in a relatively short period of time. No matter how well an investment banker may know an industry, every company is different. Any number of experienced investment bankers will note with some astonishment that when they ask new clients to describe for them, for the first time, the business they really are in and what they believe to be their companies' strengths and weaknesses to be, these clients quite often are at least a little stumped—at least in terms at expressing this well.

This is not so surprising, really. Middle Market business owners tend to throw themselves headlong into their businesses. Their hours can be extraordinarily punishing, their efforts bordering on the Herculean. The business owners who succeed in building companies suitable for sale tend to excel at being many things to many customers and clients. Once they have made the decision to sell and have been confronted with the question, "What is your core business and where are your key strengths?" they routinely find themselves too-long-immersed in their companies to come up with a *succinct response* without some collaborative work with their advisors. This is where the investment banker and his research staff come in: his job is to help the seller create the "elevator speech" that captures the essence of the company and its key success factors as well as the challenges it faces, its shortcomings, and what it is doing or what opportunities this presents to rise to the former and overcome the latter.

Capturing that essence of the company—both in its own right and as a competitor in the industry or industries in which it finds itself—requires close and careful collaboration. The client should take the role of telling his story, providing supporting documentation, and, at the very least; assisting the banker in editing the document (several times usually) to ensure that it tells his company's story effectively. It is the seller's business, and no one can know that business better than the seller himself—even if he has not yet learned to express that well in the context of a likely sale.

Sometimes, sellers appear to believe that investment bankers are solely responsible for preparing the CIM. Such misapprehensions may arise when investment bankers "oversell" themselves, giving prospective and actual clients alike the impression that the investment banker prepares and writes the CIM in return for the retainer paid him by the seller. The retainer is to retain the investment bank and would be more accurately characterized as a commitment fee. It is not for the preparation of the CIM, although that is certainly part of the overall engagement. Obviously, the investment banker is obligated to incorporate into the CIM the requisite market research that yields insights as to the company's performance vis-à-vis its competitors.

The investment banker is responsible for organizing the CIM in a manner consistent with its investment banking purpose. Having gathered insights from the seller into the seller's company, assembled a selection of the seller's collateral materials (e.g., marketing and Web site materials, capabilities statements, and the like), and completed additional research on the company and its industry, the investment banker will take the first cut at drafting the CIM. But as I have said, the best and most effective CIMs require several iterative edits going back and forth between the client, the investment banker, and the investment banking analyst supporting the assignment.

Typical Confidential Information Memorandum Content

A CIM typically includes the following, more or less in order:

- A lead page, which is an executive summary of the CIM itself and incorporates such brief financial highlights as the past few years' revenues, growth, and profitability. The executive summary often constitutes the basis—or entirety—of the Acquisition Profile which is used to solict the interest of buyers without disclosing the name of the client/seller.
- An overview of the seller's business: what it does, what it is about, and more.
- A description of the seller's industry and the industry's own prospects (usually based on market research undertaken by the investment banker and his or her staff), which provides insights into how the seller's business fits within its industry, etc.; this often includes a list of the business's primary competitors, as well.
- When and as relevant, a history of the seller's business: when it was established, its principal owner(s), its corporate structure, and its tax elections, among other things.
- A description of the seller's special processes, approaches, and technology, to the extent appropriate.
- Seller strengths and opportunities and even—if not especially— "weaknesses," which are best dealt with in the CIM up front, rather than later.
- A synopsis, at least, of the seller's most important leases and similar financial/contractual commitments (always a question of materiality) of which the buyer should be made aware. Information relevant to this synopsis routinely is footnoted in accountant-prepared financial statements (which often prove useful in the crafting of the CIM beyond the presentation of the financials themselves).
- A description of the seller's work force, including an organizational chart listing key executives and managers; a summary of the educational backgrounds of key staff members, where relevant; and employee headcounts by department or business area. Note that names should not as a rule be provided at this point, as doing so risks the poaching of key personnel; therefore, all information relating to key personnel should usually be provided by job title rather than by name.
- Descriptions of major contracts and or customers—but, again, usually without names at this stage.

- Normalized and recast financial statements presenting the businesses financial statements, especially operating statements in an investment banking format as opposed to a tax or standard financial statement format.
- Appendices that include the seller's financial statements, preferably prepared by independent certified public accountants, that establish credibility on the one hand while providing a point of reference for the normalized, recast financial statements presented in the CIM on the other. The inclusion of recent tax returns sometimes proves helpful as well; ditto the *face pages* of important leases and similar documents, etc.

Length versus Pithiness

Before including appendices, CIMs usually run from 40 to 60 pages in length. Those running longer should be reviewed carefully to ensure they are neither excessively verbose nor prone to redundancy. Overly lengthy CIMs tend not to be particularly productive. Verbosity, redundancy, and the like too often result in minor and even major inconsistencies over the course of the too-long CIM. You confuse, you lose when it comes to prospective buyers/investors. The CIM is created as a somewhat extended resume of a company being presented for sale. It cannot begin to tell the entire story and history of a company, just as a resume cannot tell the entire life and employment history of a job candidate. The CIM is meant to summarize critical business information hopefully sufficient to engage several prospective buyers in an active negotiated auction. The prospective buyer who eventually executes a Letter of Intent (LOI) will be able to confirm the story[1] (and the CIM had better cover the whole story, albeit in shorthand, or else all bets are off) via final confirmatory due diligence.

Stick to 40 to 60 pages (outside of appendices), but only as a very general rule of thumb. The quality of a CIM has nothing to do with its length, be that short or long. Put in what is required, no more, no less, Ask the seller to help ensure that undue technical complexity is avoided. Prospective buyers need not understand particle physics or software source codes to buy most Middle Market enterprises; rather, they need to understand how to calculate their own investment value for the seller's company, based on its success in providing the goods and services to its clients in its industry.

Packaging the Business, Technology, and Mini-Conglomerates

Most Middle Market businesses require packaging or positioning. This is particularly true and often problematic of Middle Market businesses that over the years have become mini-conglomerates by providing a relatively wide variety of goods or services across a broad range of industry and/or customer groups. In point of fact, the sale of Middle Market enterprises that essentially operate as mini-conglomerates tends to be problematic at best. While it may look good in terms of top-line revenues, very few individual prospective buyers want a business that is the sum of many parts, involved in many efforts and industries. To the extent that prospective buyers prefer focused enterprises whose primary business activities can be melded with the buyers' own companies, sellers will be unlikely to realize anything beyond a de minimus investment value for extraneous business activities in which prospective buyers have no particular interest or fit. Prospective sellers considering a sale three to four years out would be well-advised to focus and rationalize their companies around a core business, perhaps by disposing of the noncore business. Barring that, sellers of Middle Market mini-conglomerates should make every effort to craft a CIM that focuses on the seller's main business lines to avoid confusing or driving away prospective buyers. In some cases, the seller and investment banker should consider preparing separate CIMs for different buyer groups, or at least separate the business lines into separate sections of the book.

The impetus for packaging and positioning also may be particularly acute among certain technology firms where the most logical prospective buyers may not necessarily be all that familiar with the technology, especially when it is new or disruptive. Once again, there remains a certain, inescapable "lead the horse to water" aspect to such efforts. The prospective buyer's entry point (this was also discussed in an earlier chapter) may be a critical factor in such cases. For example, when the seller's technology is particularly attractive to a prospective buyer at the operational level, the higher the buyer's division executive or possible deal champion approached the better. Closing a sale may prove significantly more likely than if the prospective buyer was approached through its M&A team/bean counters, who may not fully understand the seller's technology and especially its potential.

Setting the Agenda

The importance of setting and controlling the agenda may seem clichéd, but most clichés have a basis in truth. As I was, for some years, the chief executive officer (CEO) and chairman of a public company, I participated on several subsidiary-level boards of directors, attending all of the meetings of each (a circumstance I found most unfortunate). But those innumerable board meetings did teach me something about human nature that has proved useful to M&A investment banking.

For one thing, it is quite possible to set virtually the entire course of a conversation or debate by imposing one's ideas on others in subtle ways. But perhaps the least subtle and maybe most effective means of controlling a discussion is by preparing an agenda for it. One learns this by preparing agendas for discussion and, alternatively, by allowing others to prepare agendas and by observing how discussions evolve under each scenario. Very few directors deviated from agendas once they were established, and setting the agenda thus proved tantamount to establishing what was important and what was not. The same proves true even during intense debates. Any casual student of Roberts Rules of Order understands that the manner in which a question is framed will dictate the ensuing discussion.[2] The same holds true for the CIM, which essentially sets the agenda for the sale of a company while framing the proposition as to the company's operational and financial performances in a manner that tends to set the tone for the competitive auction that inevitably will establish the company's true investment value to at least one buyer.

As negotiations proceed, each successive draft of legal documents will be able to trace its origin, at least in part, to the CIM and related documents. In a very real sense, the CIM, created and distributed to a pool of prospective buyers by the seller and his investment banker, represents the first foreshadowing of the coming negotiation process. How can the CIM prove most effective in controlling the agenda in the sale of a Middle Market business? First, through its success in presenting the key selling points, strengths, and opportunities that the seller's company offers prospective buyers. Every prospective buyer will read a CIM differently, because every prospective buyer is seeking something unique in an acquisition suitable to his own requirements. Still, the CIM should address selling points, strengths, and opportunities clearly and directly: A CIM, like every other selling document, has only little place for subtlety.

The CIM also may address opportunities the seller would have addressed "but for" his decision to sell the company. These "but-fors" may include enhancing distribution channels, raising capital, or creating or hiring more intellectual capital to attain a higher level of corporate performance. The CIM's market and industry section can and usually should point to the universe of opportunities that remain out there for the prospective buyer intent upon taking strategic advantage of the potential opportunities of the seller's company.

Weaknesses in the Client's Business

A second way in which the CIM helps control the agenda is by readily identifying company weaknesses—a critically important objective of the most effective CIMs. The seller and his investment banker must do everything in their power to identify the company's weaknesses before prospective buyers have a chance to do so—and most especially before a Letter of Intent (LOI) is executed. Weaknesses discovered by the buyer after the deal has been largely negotiated and following the execution of an LOI offer the buyer an opportunity to aggressively renegotiate the terms of the deal at a most inauspicious time for the seller. On the other hand, weaknesses pointed out by the seller before the execution of an LOI can be discussed and negotiated more easily, while several prospective buyers remain interested in the acquisition, allowing the seller far greater leverage.

Clearly, there is a highly psychological component to every negotiation process, especially in regard to *when* weaknesses in the seller's company are raised and addressed. Once someone has agreed to pay a set price under specified conditions for the seller's company, the seller's failure to "deliver" the company as specified gives the would-be buyer cause to walk away from, or at least heavily renegotiate, the deal. The only way the seller can then keep the would-be buyer at the table (after having declined proposals by various other prospective buyers who are now scattered to the four corners of the earth) is by agreeing to concessions that may dramatically reduce the investment value of his company, not a pleasant thought to contemplate. Alternatively, weaknesses pointed out by the seller almost always can be framed as opportunities for the prospective buyer, glasses half full as opposed to half empty. If only the seller had had the capital, the distribution channels, the right chief information officer, and so forth, it could have achieved even greater things. In other words, the *buyer* who brings such resources to the table should be convinced that he or she very likely will realize significant gains in operational and financial performance as a result of the seller's weaknesses.

Post-LOI, buyer's remorse may (actually usually does) set in, especially when the investment banker has negotiated particularly well on the seller's behalf. Mild to severe symptoms of buyer's remorse will reflect the buyer's own sense of having been pushed to edge of his envelope, having committed more resources to the purchase than he would have liked, and possibly even wondering whether the acquisition makes as much sense as he once believed. The seller's admission of a previously unrecognized or unacknowledged weakness—or, worse yet, the buyer's discovery of it without earlier disclosure—provides a buyer with a chance to recoup as much as he can from a deal that is beginning to psychologically sour for him. With that in mind, even minor weaknesses later discovered may become major issues as the buyer consciously or subconsciously overreacts, given his own doubts and discomfort (see Chapter 15).

A Preliminary Due Diligence Document

The normal Middle Market M&A process results in an LOI that, when drafted and executed properly, very clearly stipulates all of the business terms before the buyer initiates the final confirmatory due diligence, during which he reviews all underlying books, records, contracts, legal and corporate documents, and other statements in the CIM to confirm that they are in accordance with the seller's representations. As noted elsewhere in this book, in the case of effective negotiated auctions, confirmatory due diligence is not usually not undertaken until the ultimate buyer and the seller have negotiated the basic business terms of the transaction and executed an LOI. Allowing several buyers to conduct confirmatory due diligence in advance of the execution of a LOI would prove cumbersome and would unnecessarily reveal the seller's confidential business information (e.g., names of major clients, key management, and/or sales personnel) to several companies, where only one is destined to acquire the seller's company.

A Securities Document

While some might debate the point, many Middle Market investment banking professionals consider the CIM to be a securities document, because while it is offering a business for sale, it does not necessarily specify whether the acquisition will be consummated by acquiring the stock (or equivalent) of the corporation owning the business or, in the alternative, by acquiring its assets. Selling a business by selling its stock to the acquirer is a technically a securities transaction and therefore subject to SEC regulations. With that in mind, the mere *solicitation* of a possible sale of securities through distribution of a CIM to prospective buyers may well be considered a securities representation, especially under the state securities laws codified under the Uniform Securities Act (historically known as Blue Sky laws).

Financial Statements in the Confidential Information Memorandum

Financial statements, the lingua franca of business, are a critical component of the CIM. But the person who prepares those financial statements can make a world of difference over the course of a Middle Market M&A transaction.

Financial data are usually prominently displayed in only three areas in a CIM (although it may be repeated in part elsewhere in miscellaneous charts, tables and graphs):

- The executive summary overview
- The recast or normalized financial statements
- The accountant- or company-prepared financial statements

In the executive summary, most CIMs provide a high-level summary of several years' operational data, usually on the first page or two. This high-level financial overview usually summarizes the recast or normalized financial statements included in the body of the CIM.

The second place financial statements ordinarily appear but in more detail is in the CIM's financial history section, presenting several years of (normalized and recast) profits and losses (P&Ls) and, at the very least, the seller's most recent balance sheet. While these normalized statements typically are prepared by the investment banker, they are based upon financials prepared by the company itself or by its accountant as a reference point. It is preferable, big time, to begin with the accountant-prepared statements, no matter how dramatically they may be transformed by recasting. Accountant-prepared statements go a long way toward establishing a credible *starting point* for the recasting of the financials that the investment banker will do. Starting with accountant-prepared statements also routinely eliminates any confusion about changes being made by the investment banker to the accountant-prepared statements; the accountant's statements are used as the starting point rather than themselves being modified. In other words, the investment banker starts with the CPA's bottom line (net income!) before demonstrating point by point, line item by line item, how he believes the financials should be recast and normalized. Sellers and their investment bankers start off on the wrong foot entirely when they fail to provide readily and easily understood reconciliations between company-prepared financial statements and the investment banker's recast financial statements. At best, this proves irritating to prospective buyers, who are then forced to undertake the necessary reconciliations on their own. At worst, it causes prospective buyers to lose confidence in the basis for or accuracy of the investment banker's recasting, raising skepticism that may prove a serious threat to the deal itself. Would-be buyers might simply balk at the prospect of undertaking reconciliations on their own and simply toss the CIM in question into the trash before moving on to the next CIM to review an opportunity that may be presented more clearly.

Even after Enron, WorldCom, Adelphia, and other recent accounting disasters, CPAs remain trusted figures—and their independence undeniably will make financials they attest to much more credible than those prepared and presented by the seller himself or his investment banker. The critical importance of realizing an optimal result in the sale of a Middle Market enterprise underscores an imperative: start off with a CPA's numbers, as in the example below:

Net Income as reported by Company or CPA $3,000,000
Adjustments made to recast and normalize the Income
  Income Statement (see below) $2,200,000
Normalized and Recast Earnings (EBIT, EBITDA, etc) $5,200,000

The third place that financial statements should appear is in the CIM's appendix, where the actual accountant-prepared or company-prepared statements are presented and where these financials provide a credible, easily understood reference point for the investment banker to modify and recast the financials in a manner that makes sense to prospective buyers.

Recasting Financial Statements

The starting point for determining EBIT and its variations (EBITDA, etc.) is the reported net income, as determined by the accountants. Recasting adjustments are then made to restate income to EBIT(DA) to add back (recast) Interest, (income) Taxes, Depreciation and Amortization. Hence:

Earnings *(before)* Interest, Taxes, Depreciation, and Amortization

---

Normalizing Financial Statements

Once EBIT(DA) is determined by recasting, the investment banker in turn will further restate EBIT and/or EBITDA to normalize it. Normalizing earnings is achieved by restating the financials of a client's company to reflect what would constitute *normal operations*. There are four broad categories of normalizing adjustments.

Category 1: The first category consists of one-time, *nonrecurring items* (usually involving expenses, but occasionally affecting revenues as well) that might arise from natural disaster or casualty losses, one-time (hopefully) embezzlement losses; litigation expenses and/or awards of an unusual nature, and many others that might arise in a particular business or business year.

Category 2: The second category of normalizing adjustments is undertaken when *expenses are overstated (sometimes understated)* as a result of tax planning, or when there is an inconsistency with normal marketplace costs and expenses, or when inventory costing practices may be inconsistent with Generally Accepted Accounting Principles (GAAP) or economic earnings. For example, two of the most typical expense adjustments made by Middle Market companies are when owners' salaries are paid more as a function of tax considerations than of the market-rate compensation that nonowners would receive for the same work, or when real estate rental expenses paid to the company owner (who also owns the real estate) are casually determined or calculated to minimize the company's taxable income. This second category would also include discretionary expenses, such as charitable contributions, personal travel, mistresses, etc. (Just kidding!). In addition, nonoperating income, such as interest income on excess cash, would be removed.

In regard to normalization adjustments, some areas will be less than clear to the inexperienced. For example, does a discretionary bonus (does not have to be paid) that has in fact been paid annually for a number of years constitute a proper add-back? The answer is probably not, as the last thing a new owner wants to do is to announce to the staff that from now on, this bonus will not be paid. Each decision about whether an add-back is legitimate or not will invite the application of some common sense and careful consideration.

Category 3: A third category of normalization adjustments is employed to reflect *economies of scale* that *most* prospective buyers would realize, typically including, for example, salary expenses associated with financial and personnel administration, the resources for which many buyers will already have. Chief financial officers (CFOs), other accounting personnel, and/or human resources personnel, for the most part, would not be required by larger buyers, who would merge an acquired company into their own. Discretion should be exercised here, because different buyers may or may not retain CFOs, other accounting personnel, and/or human resources personnel in companies they acquire. As a result, these types of add-backs should be presented separately as *"likely economies of scale"* or similar descriptions.

Category 4: The fourth and final category of normalization adjustments arguably is the most difficult to identify, but many successful deals have depended on the sellers' or their investment bankers' abilities to identify *synergies* a single particular buyer might realize. This last category of add-backs does not usually appear in the CIM, as that is prepared for all buyers. These tailor-made add-backs for particular buyers require an in-depth understanding of the buyers' financial and operational structures. This category of normalization adjustments falls under the "you can sometimes lead a horse to water" banner. Sellers and their investment bankers should not necessarily assume that prospective buyers recognize these opportunities for themselves; it is a mistake to assume that either horses or buyers see the water before it is pointed out to them. Where the buyer truly does not recognize special synergies peculiar to it, it can result from two causes: Large buyers, in fact, may be so heavily burdened by their own bureaucracies that they cannot recognize the trees for the forest. Small buyers, on the other hand, tend to have fewer available resources to do the research required to identify nonobvious synergies that the seller and his investment banker may point out. So "a little help from my friends" is called for. This involves real work, but it can generate significant returns where the investment value to a particular buyer of the seller's company is involved.

Having been led to the water, the horse or the buyer either can deny that it exists or acknowledge that it exists while claiming he should not have to pay for it. In either case, when the seller and his investment banker have done their work well, they and the buyer(s) will know it, and that can only improve their position during negotiations. In competitive auctions, this is precisely the kind of information that can encourage a prospective buyer to up the ante in order to win the acquisition.

Normalizing and Recasting Financial Statements: Summing Up

Primary categories for the recasting of CIM financials (see Exhibit 7.2) include adjustments to:

1. Convert or recast accounting net income to a cash flow proxy (usually EBIT, EBITDA).
2. Normalize EBITDA by eliminating nonrecurring costs and expenses and aligning costs and expenses with appropriate market levels.
3. Reflect possible economies of scale to most or all prospective buyers.
4. Provide a final adjustment category, rarely included in the CIM, that reflects synergies and economies of scale peculiar to a particular buyer.

Chapter Highlights

- The Confidential Information Memorandum (CIM) is:
  - A sales document
  - A preliminary due diligence document
  - A controlling-the-agenda document
  - A securities document
- The CIM is a highly collaborative document created by the client, the investment banker, and the investment banker's analysts.
- The CIM must describe everything a prospective buyer would want to know about a business before making an offer to buy it.
- In CIMs, pithiness is more important than length.
- A CIM need not be written in a one-flavor-suits-all-prospective-buyers style, but rather may be edited to suit different buyers.

EXHIBIT 7.2   Recasting and Normalizing Sellers' Financial Statements

TYZ Corporation

Net Income Reported by Company Accountants	**$ 5,000,000**

RECASTING ADJUSTMENTS

Adjustments to covert or recast accounting net income to cash flow proxies such as EBIT, EBITDA:

Interest on long-term debt	900,000
Income taxes	4,000,000
Depreciation and amortization	400,000
Nonoperating income	(100,000)
Total	5,200,000
Net Income recasted as EBITDA	**$ 10,200,000**

NORMALIZING ADJUSTMENTS

Adjustments to eliminate nonrecurring costs and expenses:

One-time litigation costs	250,000
Uninsured portion of hurricane damage to plant	100,000
Total	350,000

Adjustments to bring cost and expenses into appropriate marker levels:

Owner officers salaries in excess of market levels	300,000
Understatement of rent expense from seller-owned real estate leased to business	(75,000)
Owner's discretionary business expenses	25,000
Total	250,000

Adjustments to reflect economies of scale to all possible buyers:

Chief financial officer	225,000
Human relations officer	150,000
Other likely duplicate personnel	200,000
Total	575,000
Recast and normalized EBITDA (all likely buyers)	**$ 11,375,000**

Adjustments to reflect synergies and economies of scale peculiar to a particular buyer's investment value:

Duplicate plant costs for XYZ Corp.	1,250,000
Channel sales channel costs reductions	800,000
Total	2,050,000
Recast and normalized EBITDA (XYZ Corp.)	**$ 13,425,000**

- Weaknesses in a client's business should be addressed up front in the CIM while the client still enjoys the relative advantage of multiple prospective buyers and the opportunity to explain and/or correct the weakness.
- CIM financial statements should always begin with accountants' end numbers to establish credibility before being modified by the investment banker to communicate investment value.
- Normalization should be performed with great care in four major categories.

Notes

1. Confirmatory due diligence.
2. But when the board's issues became important and the going got rough, good board members were capable of "reframing" the question and the debate. They had not become directors by being pushovers, but it was clear nonetheless that agenda-setters and proposition-framers gained significant advantage because their agendas and propositions usually at least provided the foundation and direction for all ensuing discussions.

CHAPTER 8

Confidentiality While Doing the Deal

Seattle, WA—March 1997

I had to hold the phone away from my ear to avoid permanent damage to my hearing. Charles, my Seattle-based textile manufacturing client, was livid.

"Do you know that your (adjective deleted for decency purposes) analyst faxed us, without any kind of warning, a copy of the draft Executive Summary describing our business for sale ... and my manufacturing vice-president got the chance to read it before I even knew it was here? Damn it, how many times did I tell you and how many times did you agree that nothing was to be faxed to our offices without calling me first so I could get to the fax machine?"

Charles had told us this many times, we had agreed, and Eric (the analyst) was well aware of the client's reasonable request. I winced for Eric but, in the moment, my first thoughts were of salvaging this business relationship, which I did not want to lose. Needless to say, Eric was seeking employment elsewhere that very day, even as I hopped a flight to Seattle to offer as many mea culpas and apologies as the situation required, which was a lot. In the end, Charles forgave us and stuck with us, though it probably took him a while to forget the unnecessary unpleasantness. Within the year, we helped him sell his business for a fairly spectacular price.

Last I heard, Charles was spending his time cruising the waterways of the Pacific Northwest.

McLean, VA—October 2000

Kamran, one of our senior analysts, had been out to dinner the night before with his girlfriend and her father in a local, somewhat-renowned

81

Italian restaurant. He looked chagrined this morning and I asked him what was troubling him.

"Boss, I think I really screwed up."

"Okay, tell me about it." Damn it, it was only Monday, and I did not need anything this early in the week to screw it up. That would come later anyway, I thought, but let me get through Monday. I have always hated Monday in exactly the same proportion that I loved Fridays. I guess most of us do.

Apparently Kamran had casually mentioned a telecom deal he was working on, ostensibly in the privacy of a family (or soon to be a family, perhaps) conversation. The only problem: Kamran's girlfriend's father was an in-house attorney for a fierce competitor of the client, a point our young analyst did not realize at the time. Perhaps the girlfriend's father saw "son-in-law potential" in the young analyst, because he kept his counsel, both literally and figuratively, and no harm was done. Even so, Kamran, who subsequently became a junior investment banker, walked around for days on pins and needles. To his credit, he was honest enough to tell me about the incident and how much he had learned from it. Ever since that day, when speaking about deals or potential deals in public, he uses code names and he encourages his junior colleagues to do the same. In fact, our firm does this as standard operating procedure now.

Confidentiality in General

Confidentiality in market M&A transactions is a serious concern in four areas.

- First, with employees of the selling company
- Second, with customers and suppliers of the selling company
- Third, with competitors of the selling company and the public
- Fourth, in cases where a public company is involved on one side or the other of a deal, as possible insider information

Confidentiality may seem like a side bar issue to inexperienced readers but frankly I have had clients, and just as frequently nonclients, refuse to even have lunch with me in a public restaurant out of concern that if anyone sees them lunching with me (in at least my hometown I am fairly well known as an M&A guy) the observer will immediately assume my lunch partner is for sale. I am not sure whether I am flattered by this or not. I know it limits my public lunch companions for sure.

Employees and Confidentiality: Two Approaches

There are, broadly speaking, two approaches for dealing with employees in the face of a business sales process being undertaken. Although I recommend the *Controlled Disclosure* approach, I must admit that my clients over the years have fairly evenly divided their approaches to this issue between that and what I call the *Surreptitious* approach. I will explain what I mean.

The Surreptitious Approach

In this approach the Middle Market business owner may choose to tell as few people as possible of his plans to sell the company. Under such circumstances, very few individuals beyond the immediate owners of the business and their principal financial advisors are aware of the impending sale. The surreptitious approach has clear advantages: The fewer people who know about a prospective sale, the less likely it is that news of the sale will fall into the wrong hands, to the disadvantage of the seller.

Yet the surreptitious approach has drawbacks of its own. Veteran investment bankers will observe from punishing experience that the longer it takes to sell a business (and six to twelve months is a reasonably long time, all in all) the more likely it is that word will get out through rumor mills, the most destructive and demoralizing of all information channels, too often rife with half-truths and misinterpretations that, in a Middle Market investment banking corollary to Murphy's Law, invariably cast the impending sale in the worst possible light at the most inconvenient time—especially to employees who are caught off guard.

Rumor mills too often explode without allowing the principals any chance to attempt damage control, if the principals are even aware of the information leakage in real time. Employees who learn from rumor mills information about the sale that their Middle Market business owner(s) declined to share with them for any reason are likely to become angry, distrustful, demoralized, and fearful for their futures. The consequences to a company about to be sold can obviously prove problematic.

The Controlled-Disclosure Approach

Alternatively, Middle Market business owners may choose to release relevant information in a highly-controlled manner. Principals choosing the controlled-disclosure approach tell their key management people what they are doing and why, in a way that can help alleviate many concerns while possibly allowing those key people to look forward to new and better career opportunities that might result in the wake of the imminent changes.

While more people are aware of the imminent sale when principals choose the controlled-disclosure approach, the principals themselves have had the opportunity to frame the situation accurately, or at least on their own terms, while demonstrating a level of trust and confidence in their key people. The controlled-disclosure approach may even encourage key people to help the principals advance the sale and eventually to put their best foot forward when it comes time to inform the rest of the employees and, perhaps, key customers of the sale. If rumors do get out, especially to other employees, the "in-the-know" group can help relieve stress by explaining the possibility of a sales transaction or a recapitalization as just another step in the life of a business.

If this approach is taken, it may be desirable to indicate that the client has engaged an investment banker to explore alternative means to tap the additional capital and/or opportunities required to expand the business, whether via an M&A sale, a partial recapitalization, or other methods such as new strategic alliances. A seller's honest ability to take this approach reflects the fact that most Middle Market businesses grow in stages. Their resource requirements vary over time when it comes to finances and capital, management experience, distribution channels, etc. In this regard, key people are likely to understand that new ownership or new capital may be desirable, as it may provide cash infusions and/or other resources that will allow the company to grow and thrive. Larger organizations with greater resources are more likely to provide better opportunities for career advancement to key managers of the selling company who intend to stay with the business.

The Investment Banker and Confidentiality: Communications between Banker and Client; Preventing Premature Disclosure

Whether the seller chooses surreptitious or controlled-release approaches to information sharing, or some combination of the two, unintentional breaches of confidentiality are sometimes unavoidable. The seller and his investment banker can do several things to minimize the risks of such information breaches:

1. Create an exhaustive *written list* of all persons who have been advised of the impending transaction within the client's firm and among his professional advisors and family members. The investment banker's job is to ensure that such a list is maintained and consulted before any contact is made with any of the above groups by the banker or his staff.

2. Maintain a list of email addresses, fax numbers, snail-mail addresses, courier addresses, etc., that are permissible for client/investment banker communications, while establishing standard procedures under which those addresses might be used. For example, investment bankers and their associates should agree not to fax any documents, even to agreed-upon fax numbers, without first notifying the client to ensure that he is standing by the fax machine or otherwise has secured it so that no other parties might intercept the document being faxed.

3. Only the investment bank's senior investment bankers and analysts should be allowed to contact representatives of the client's staff that have been cleared by the client in advance.

4. Under no circumstances should any member of the investment banker's staff ever divulge the name of an existing client, or even the existence of a current engagement involving a company in a particular industry because an astute listener might well put two and two together and guess the identity of the client. We use and strongly advise the use of code names for all clients.

The Executive Summary and Confidentiality

The seller and investment banker should review the anonymous Acquisition Profile or Executive Summary very carefully before finalizing it and releasing it to prospective buyers. Here, as elsewhere, achieving the proper balance is imperative. Should the anonymous Acquisition Profile disclose too little detail (by relying too heavily on obfuscation to preserve client confidentiality), it may well prove less than helpful. On the other hand, should it disclose too much information, it will risk unmasking the seller's company before prospective buyers have executed nondisclosure confidentiality agreement(s). An anonymous Acquisition Profile might suggest that the seller's company is "located on the East Coast" or, more specifically, "is located in Maryland." There are tradeoffs to be realized in either approach. The client and the investment banker should decide together which approach is best suited to their circumstances. Furthermore, depending on the intended recipient, the Acquisition Profile may be crafted differently for different buyers in terms of disclosures.

Web Site Business-for-Sale Listings

Web site and/or broadcast email should be very cautiously approached when it comes to "publishing" or distributing even disguised descriptive materials. Generally speaking, this approach to selling Middle Market businesses is inappropriate anyway in most cases and is more of a business brokerage technique than one used by investment bankers. A good investment bank need not rely on such tools except in the very rarest of circumstances (e.g., as a last resort).

Nondisclosure Agreements

Nondisclosure and confidentiality agreement(s) are designed not only to prevent a reader from stealing the "secret sauce" of a seller's business (including employees, customers etc.), but also to provide *some degree of confidentiality*, so that a seller's business is not harmed by disclosure to outside parties when he reveals his company's actual name and business details in the follow-up Confidential Information Memorandum (CIM).

But do nondisclosure agreements (NDAs) really work? The answer to this most important question, as with so many others that must be addressed while selling a Middle Market business in an M&A transaction, is: "Yes and no. It depends." Yes, to a large degree, NDAs do work. That said, the longer it takes for a deal to be consummated (or for the deal to fall through after an extended period), the greater the likelihood a mistake will occur and confidential information will be released or improperly used. There is something about being an insider on a deal that causes people to slip up, mentioning something offhand, or even bragging about a transaction to someone who should not know anything about it. Loose lips sink ships ... and Middle Market M&A transactions. Veteran investment bankers will admit to having seen it the whole gamut, ranging from deals that were tight as a drum, with nothing being disclosed until the deal had been done, to deals in which information leaked out all too quickly.

One consolation to sellers, who quite justifiably can become very paranoid about leaks: Even when information does slip out prematurely, it only rarely does much harm in my experience. Slips only rarely cause sellers the harm sellers themselves typically anticipate with great dread. That said, everything that can be done to avoid leaks or interference with the clients business should be done. The best bet: Combine a strong Confidentiality/Nondisclosure Agreement with a clear conversation with the prospective buyer/investor as to the potential for significant harm to the client should leaks or misuse occur. Confidentiality agreements constitute a shot across the bow of the prospective buyer/investor; they really should make him or her think twice before violating them. It is also a fact worth mentioning that unauthorized disclosure or use of information may well give rise to legal recourse by the seller against the discloser or misuser. The biggest problem with such recourse, naturally, is proving that the disclosures or misuse occurred in violation of the agreement in the first place; that would be a matter for the lawyers to address.

Will Buyers and Investors Sign Nondisclosure Agreements?

Will prospective buyers and/or investors sign NDAs? Yes, the vast majority of them will sign (frequently though after some negotiation over the details), but investors in early-stage technologies may sometimes decline to do so. For example, in the late 1990s, venture capitalists received thousands of deal solicitations a year. Many of these were fairly harebrained, but the unfortunate VCs could never know when they might come across another "killer app" that sort of looked like the one that they signed a confidentiality nondisclosure agreement on a year ago. Think about it: if the VCs had agreed to sign nondisclosure documents for every last one of those deal solicitations, they might in fact have been signing away their right to do a more legitimate deal with a similar but more realistic technology or business. And what would prevent the authors of hare-brained schemes from claiming that their proposals contained an important kernel of insight that the VCs in fact found in another deal entirely? The VCs did not want to risk being sued, and so many of them simply refused to sign nondisclosure agreements. This situation still holds today. Many VCs will not sign NDAs, whereas later stage (buyout or recapitalization) funds have no problem with signing one.

Clients who really wanted a VC to look at a deal routinely were forced to waive nondisclosure and/or confidentially agreement provision(s). But most VCs and private equity groups (PEGs) do not exist for the purpose of stealing someone else's ideas; they are too busy for such shenanigans, too honest to consider doing so, or, last but not least, too fearful and reticent to risk extended litigation.

Confidentiality and nondisclosure agreements will, in any event, usually exclude information that is either already public, already known to the party, or came to the parties' attention in some other fashion.

Information That Cannot Be Disclosed until the Last Minute . . . Even with a Nondisclosure Agreement

Occasionally, circumstances arise in which the seller, with good reason, refuses to release the full details of the information the buyer requires to make a final decision until the seller is convinced beyond doubt that the deal will close. Such situations usually involve disclosures of key customer(s), employee(s), or similar information. As a rule, these situations should be fairly rare, occurring in less than one in five transactions.

These circumstances can be handled by supplying the buyer just enough information so that the buyer knows what he is getting, but not enough to do any damage should the deal fail to close. If an issue arises involving a government contractor's contract information, for example, the name of the government agency client and the general tasks to be performed might be disclosed early, while specific contract information is withheld as long as possible, especially concerning actual contact with the customer. Titles, job functions, and educational levels of key employees could and usually are released (in the CIM), while names might be withheld until the last minute.

One way or the other, the buyer will need to know this very final information before the final settlement. The seller and investment banker might decide to delay final disclosures until definitive agreements have been fully negotiated and executed, and then allow the buyer, say, 24 hours to repudiate his agreement if he does not like what he sees in the seller's final disclosures. Whether such disclosures are made just before or just after the definitive agreements are executed (or even in some cases after a dry settlement, in which no money changes hands or in which monies are escrowed) probably will not negatively affect final closure anyway. By the time settlement arrives, both parties tend to be emotionally and financially committed to the deal and have spent so much time and even more money on attorneys, accountants, and so forth that neither side is likely to indulge in any final game-playing. What would be the point?

Securities Laws and Confidentiality

When public companies are involved in Middle Market M&A transactions, special care must be taken to preclude premature and inappropriate disclosures of what might be insider information. A failure to do so can result in severe penalties for even a minor screw-up: criminal, civil, and regulatory penalties, as well as penalties to others outside the company who should have known better.

Chapter Highlights

- There are two basic approaches to disclosing to employees the impending sale of a business: the surreptitious approach and the controlled-release approach.
- The client and the investment banker should agree to strict rules regarding all transaction-related communications and should establish dedicated email and snail-mail addresses and an agreed-upon list of client management contacts as required.

- The anonymous Acquisition Profile must achieve a fine balance by adequately describing the business without prematurely disclosing its identity.
- Web site businesses' for-sale listings generally are not advisable or useful and may in fact risk disclosing the imminent sale of the business to the wrong people.
- Nondisclosure agreements (NDAs) are basically warning shots across the bow of signing parties, alerting them to possible liability from improper disclosure or misuse of the information learned about the client.
- Some VC parties will decline to execute NDAs (for good reason).
- Occasionally, confidential information should not be disclosed until the last minute. Information that is absolutely sensitive can be disclosed subject to and following a dry settlement.
- Disclosure of deal information may constitute a violation of securities laws when a public company is a party to the deal.

EXHIBIT 8.1 Sample Confidentiality Agreement

CONFIDENTIALITY AGREEMENT

This Confidentiality Agreement is entered into between _____ ("Company"), a ABC state Limited Liability Company organized under the laws of the State of _____, with a permanent mailing address of _____, Company being represented herein by The McLean Group, L.L.C., a Virginia limited liability company, and the Undersigned, and pertains to Company and any other entity in which Company owns a majority of all of the voting interests, ("Subsidiary Companies") as well as _____, an ABC state Limited Liability Company with a permanent mailing address of _____ ("Affiliated Company"), collectively referred to as the ("Subject Companies") or individually referred to as a ("Subject Company"), regarding certain confidential information pertaining to Subject Companies, including but not limited to financial information, project information, employee information, customer information, and patent information. The Undersigned is interested in reviewing the information supplied by Subject Companies regarding a possible acquisition of an ownership interest in Subject Companies. Said information which is communicated by Subject Companies to the Undersigned, with the exception of information in the public domain, or which may enter the public domain without the fault or negligence of either party, is hereinafter referred to as "Confidential Information."

For purposes of this Agreement the "Undersigned" shall mean _____, a _____ organized under the laws of the State of _____, represented herein by _____.

EXHIBIT 8.1   *(Continued)*

CONFIDENTIALITY AGREEMENT

1) <u>Confidential Information</u>. The Undersigned agrees that the information supplied is proprietary to Subject Companies and agrees that said Confidential Information will be treated as strictly confidential by the Undersigned. The Undersigned further agrees that its review of said Confidential Information is for the sole purpose of evaluating a possible acquisition, as referred to in the foregoing paragraph. The Undersigned agrees not to disclose, directly or indirectly, the Confidential Information to any third party without the Company's prior written consent; provided, however, that the persons described in Section 5, below, may be furnished such Confidential Information by the Undersigned under the terms and conditions and for the purposes set forth herein.

2) <u>Exceptions</u>. All of the foregoing obligations and restrictions do not apply to that part of the Confidential Information that the Undersigned demonstrates (a) was or becomes generally available to the public other than as a result of a disclosure by the Undersigned or the Undersigned's representatives or (b) was available, or becomes available, to the Undersigned on a nonconfidential basis prior to its disclosure to the Undersigned by a Subject Company or a representative thereof, but only if: (i) the source of such information is not bound by a Confidentiality Agreement with the Subject Company or is not otherwise prohibited from transmitting the information to the Undersigned or the Undersigned's representatives by a contractual, legal, fiduciary, or other obligation; and (ii) the Undersigned provides the Subject Company with written notice of such prior possession either (a) prior to the execution and delivery of this letter agreement or (b) if the Undersigned later becomes aware of (through disclosure to the Undersigned or otherwise through the Undersigned's work on the acquisition transaction) any aspect of the Confidential Information of which the Undersigned had prior possession, promptly upon the Undersigned becoming aware of such aspect.

3) <u>Disclosure by Process of Law</u>. Notwithstanding the provisions of this Agreement, in the event that the Undersigned is required by document subpoena, civil investigative demand, interrogatories, request for information, or other similar process of law or by any governmental action or court of competent jurisdiction to disclose any of the Confidential Information, the Undersigned will deliver to the Company timely notice of such requirement(s) so that the Company, at its sole cost and expense, may seek an appropriate protective order and/or waiver of compliance by the Undersigned with the provisions of this Agreement. If, failing the obtaining of a protective order or the delivery of such a waiver (in either case in a form reasonably satisfactory to the Undersigned), the Undersigned is, or as it determines in good faith, would be, compelled to disclose, disseminate, or otherwise communicate the Confidential Information, the Undersigned may disclose, disseminate, or otherwise communicate the confidential Information, but only to the extent so compelled or advised, without liability hereunder.

EXHIBIT 8.1 *(Continued)*

CONFIDENTIALITY AGREEMENT

---

4) <u>Return or Verification</u>. The Undersigned agrees to return all Confidential Information, including any photocopies, to Company or to destroy such confidential information in the event the Undersigned decides not to enter into an agreement with Subject Companies concerning the aforementioned acquisition. The Undersigned further agrees to make an independent verification of the Confidential Information in the event a decision is made to enter into an Agreement with Subject Companies.

5) <u>Examiners of Confidential Information</u>. The Undersigned agrees that it will restrict review of the Confidential Information, including copies thereof, provided by Subject Companies to (a) agents and employees of the Undersigned and its direct and indirect subsidiaries; (b) Board of Directors of the Undersigned; (c) legal counsel of the Undersigned; (d) accountants and financial advisors of the Undersigned; (e) insurers of the Undersigned; and (f) other advisors and financing sources assisting in the Undersigned's evaluation of the company, provided that the Undersigned shall use reasonable efforts to limit the class of such individuals to those persons directly involved in evaluating the acquisition for the Undersigned, and provided further that the Undersigned shall bring the obligations of confidentiality and nonuse set forth herein to the attention of such individuals.

6) <u>Noninterference</u>. The Undersigned agrees that it will not, without the expressed written consent of Company, for a period of two (2) years from the date of this Agreement:

   (A) Solicit or induce any person who is or was within the past twelve (12) months employed by a Subject Company to interfere with the activities or businesses of a Subject Company or to discontinue his or her employment with a Subject Company;

   (B) Hire any person who is currently employed by a Subject Company or was employed by a Subject Company within the past twelve (12) months into a business or enterprise which competes with a Subject Company; or

   (C) Make contact with any customer, lender, vendor, employee or agent that has been at any time within the past twelve (12) months under contract or doing business with a Subject Company, regarding any of the Subject Companies, without the consent of Company.

7) Breach of Agreement; Indemnity; Remedies. It is agreed and stipulated by the parties hereto that a breach of the Confidentiality Agreement shall occur upon failure of the Undersigned to observe any of the provisions contained in this Confidentiality Agreement including, but not limited to, the release of any Confidential Information by the Undersigned to any party without the prior written consent of a Subject Company and that the breach of this Confidentiality Agreement will irreparably harm a Subject Company. The Undersigned shall be liable for all claims, losses, and liabilities arising out of or in any manner predicated upon or contributed to by a breach of this Confidentiality Agreement

---

(Continued)

EXHIBIT 8.1   *(Continued)*

CONFIDENTIALITY AGREEMENT

by the Undersigned. The Undersigned further agrees that in addition to any other rights and remedies available to a Subject Company hereunder, injunctive relief is a proper remedy for enforcement of this Confidentiality Agreement.

8) <u>Notices</u>. All notices, requests, demands, waivers, and other communications to a party required or permitted under this Agreement shall be in writing and shall be delivered personally or sent by electronic mail, telecopy, or internationally recognized delivery service providing for guaranteed overnight delivery, addressed to such party, attention "President & Chief Executive Officer," at its address first written above (or such other address as is provided by such party to the other party from time to time). Each party shall be responsible for supplying the other with any changes in the postal addresses, electronic addresses, or telecopy numbers for notices hereunder. All notices, requests, demands, waivers, and communications shall be deemed to have been given on the date of personal delivery, or on the first business day after overnight delivery (or the second business day after international overnight delivery) was guaranteed by an internationally recognized delivery service, except that any change of address shall be effective only upon actual receipt. Written notice given by electronic mail or telecopy shall be deemed given when electronic or telephonic confirmation is received by the sending party.

9) <u>Miscellaneous</u>. This Confidentiality Agreement shall be binding on the parties hereto and on their affiliates, agents, employees, successors, and assigns. If any provision of this Confidentiality Agreement shall for any reason be adjudged to be void, invalid, or unenforceable, the remainder of this Confidentiality Agreement shall continue and remain in full force and effect. Unless otherwise stated, the terms of this Agreement and all rights and obligations provided herein shall terminate two (2) years from the date of this Agreement.

THE MCLEAN GROUP, L.L.C.
BY: _____
DATE: _____ NAME: _____
TITLE: _____

BY: _____
DATE: _____ NAME: _____
TITLE: _____

CHAPTER 9

Middle Market Investment Bankers and Intermediaries

Understanding What They Do and Picking the Right One

Baltimore, MD—August 1999
M&A Representation in a Nutshell

Larry, a transaction attorney and a friend with whom I had shared several clients, had just referred me to these telecom clients the previous Thursday. Larry also had made it clear the clients did not want me to sell the business. They just wanted a consult; the clients already had a buyer, after all, and a $9 million offer on the table.

"Dennis, the clients only want you to advise them on the valuation and negotiation process," Larry explained. "They already have the offer in hand." As a rule, I always make every effort to discourage clients from dealing with only one buyer. But when clients insist otherwise, as appeared to be the case this August morning, I am willing to proceed, advising them on an hourly-fee basis rather than for my normal contingent fee. And so the Monday morning meeting had been scheduled.

I arrived at the meeting that Monday morning in a warehouse-office industrial park. Larry introduced me to the buyers as the clients' investment banker. The buyers previously had offered to pay approximately $9 million for the clients' business, and were there to close the deal at least at the Letter of Intent stage. But within minutes that morning, the buyer raised the offer to $11 million, before I had a chance to do anything more than shake hands and sit down. Had my good looks alone sufficed to account for this 20% increase so quickly? My wife, a better judge of such things, doubts it.

The buyer, a group from Florida chasing the telecom explosion that was just then reaching its peak, immediately had assumed— incorrectly—that the presence of an investment banker reflected the likely interest of other prospective buyers. In an attempt to preempt a competitive auction for the seller's firm, the buyer immediately raised its offer by more than 20%. This was the buyer's first mistake, and it richly rewarded the clients; a $2 million windfall gained in mere minutes is not chopped liver!

Yet despite the fact that buyer's first mistake played out in favor—big time—of the clients, it also exposed a misperception on the part of the clients that otherwise could have proved quite costly. Up until that Monday morning, the clients thought they understood the value of their business in the marketplace. A $9 million offer on the table was more than they thought their business was worth, or they would not have asked me to limit my participation to negotiation formalities to close the $9 million transaction. But in just a few minutes, the buyer opened the clients' eyes. The clients realized now that, in fact, they had no idea how valuable their firm might be in the marketplace. And maybe the buyer had no idea either, but the buyer's eagerness to close a deal made one point perfectly clear to the clients: Their firm was possibly worth more than even $11 million.

After the buyers left the meeting, my new clients asked me what I really thought their business was worth. Having completed some preliminary calculations, I suggested that a preliminary valuation of $20 million seemed reasonable. The clients asked what my fees would be and readily agreed that, while the fees were not insignificant, they would be quite reasonable if I could get them another $9 million in value. In the wake of that meeting in August 1999, the clients decided to auction their business.

Eight months later, I assisted the clients in closing the sale of their firm for more than $38 million. In fact, the highest offers on the business exceeded the accepted deal price by at least $6 million more than even that.

Finally, I should add that within less than 90 days of the closing, the business could not have been sold for $5 million, much less $38 million. The telecom market imploded with the power and suddenness of an atom bomb. My client, by the way, is now fat and happy in a well-funded retirement. He plays golf most days now, and I admit that I am little jealous of that. His handicap dropped 15 strokes, too. I guess you can buy a golf swing if you have the time and the money after all.

The Telecom Deal

Our Middle Market telecom deal was illustrative of many aspects of Middle Market deals. It reflected the impact of even apparent auctions on the outcome, as well as the paradoxical need for and at the same time fallacy of preliminary valuations except as points of departure. Did I really screw up suggesting a $20 million preliminary valuation for a company that ultimately sold for $38 million? No. My preliminary valuation was accurate, as far as it went. The closing price reflected the orchestration of an auction among competing buyers.

This anecdote (true) also illustrates a concept we will address later: *deal terms* trump deal stated or *nominal prices* every time. The clients, in this case, entertained several offers that, expressed in terms of price alone, substantially exceeded the offer they finally accepted. The clients preferred the terms of the winning buyer to the some of the "nominal prices" offered because, quite frankly, it was worth more money in their pockets at the end of the day and after all that is what counts.

The story also highlights the dramatic impact of timing and business cycles on valuation (see Chapter 6). The clients sold their firm at the peak of the telecom industry bubble and got out just in time. Had they closed the transaction just a few months later, they would have been forced to accept a much lower price (probably not in excess of $5 million).

Using Professional Investment Banking Assistance and In-House Teams

I will address the external teams necessary to get a deal done later, but professional investment bankers will spend a fair amount of attention to organizing a team of in-house professionals that represents the client's needs and understands its business functions. For example, in my own firm, a typical team consists of at least five professionals, a lead investment banker, a second coinvestment banker, a senior analyst, a junior analyst, and a valuation expert. This is more or less critical to a successful outcome, just as the proper stance and grip are crucial to a great golf shot. Some say that it's all in the swing. But if your stance and your grip are wrong, your swing will be all wrong, too.

Professional Assistance in M&A Deals

In most cases, the cost of an experienced mergers and acquisitions (M&A) investment banker amounts to little more than a fraction of the economic gain realized by the client. Sorry, I know that sounds self-serving, but I have seen this over and over again. Every month, someone brings a done deal to us or a Letter of Intent on a not-yet-done deal, and it is obvious how much can be or could have been gained in terms of additional dollars to the client if the client had professional advice and representation. The gains are not minor nor difficult to see immediately, most of the time. Unfortunately, most "might-have-been" clients do not have a clue, and as it is often unfortunately after the fact, we usually leave it that way out of politeness. While it is difficult to corroborate statistically, clients who represent themselves in so complex an undertaking most likely will leave *exponentially* more money on the table than they save on fees paid to a good investment bank. One of my business associates recently conducted an informal study of a large number of Middle Market deals. He compared deals in which sellers were represented by investment bankers to those in which sellers represented themselves. The deals closed by sellers represented by investment bankers closed at prices 10% to 30% higher than those in which sellers represented themselves. The results—even of this informal survey—strongly suggest that paying an investment banker a 3% to 5% fee is a no-brainer.

Middle Market M&A transactions by definition are high-stakes deals with no second chance to make things right if they go wrong. They require expert knowledge in the use of emotion and tone by principal negotiators who are skilled and disciplined in an understanding of limits, custom, usage, and standard M&A conventions. Negotiators must understand the nature of Middle Market M&A negotiations to distinguish between posturing for position and standing one's ground, between when to push, when to fight, or when to call it a day. Some very fine lines must be navigated here, for sure.

Professional negotiators understand that every deal dies a thousand deaths, but can be actually born (consummated) only once. Sellers who decide to go it alone might well find all of this overwhelming, especially when selling a business for the first time. To be confronted by "the thousand deaths" that such deals die before they close—especially as regards the sellers' "babies," businesses they have built from scratch—and to be distracted from actually running those businesses during the final crucial months, during which their operational and financial performances play a major role in their ultimate selling prices is . . . well, not a good idea.

Nor is the value an experienced M&A negotiator brings to the table limited to the art of the auction. The sport of boxing may provide an insightful metaphor as well. When an investment banking professional represents one side of a Middle Market business transaction while a counterparty remains professionally unrepresented, one of two outcomes will transpire. The most likely outcome will be a one-sided battle, as when an amateur steps into the boxing ring to compete with a pro.

Ironically, though, in Middle Market M&A transactions, even the pros prefer not to "box" with amateurs, precisely because the mismatch itself can compound the potential for missteps, blind alleys, and detours that needlessly frustrate the dealmaking process. Another scenario is the unpleasant, unsatisfying spectacle of the professional dealmaker inelegantly pursuing the amateur around the ring without making any real contact in advancing the deal. In such cases, the amateur usually is aware (heaven help his client if he is not) of the mismatch and, in response, endlessly plays defense by running away from all advances. Given this scenario, nothing gets done in the ring or on the deal.

The ideal outcome, a successful deal believed to be fair and equitable to both sides, most likely will result when seller and buyer both bring professional investment banking representation to the table. This is because the pros routinely cut through maybe 90% of the BS that hobbles the dealmaking process and bedevils unrepresented sellers and buyers alike. Think about it: The pros have no reason whatsoever to prolong the sales/auction process. Their intent is to close a deal quickly and efficiently while maximizing their clients' outcome—and then move on to the next deal.

When pros representing sellers and buyers face off against one another, their respective understandings of each other's likely strategies and tactics and their common knowledge of M&A conventions allow them to advance their agendas professionally, impersonally, and expeditiously, even as they test each other's limits and/or general willingness to deal. When sellers and buyers are mismatched, the likelihood of either a slaughter or an undoable transaction increases: No fun in either case.

Preliminary Valuations by Investor Bankers

Excellent technical skills that come from deep formal valuation training and experience are, in my opinion, absolutely required when it comes to ferreting though often contradictory and inconsistent valuation indicators while establishing a preliminary business valuation. A competent investment banker always conducts a preliminary valuation estimate based on what he believes to be the approximate range of values for a company in its industry at any given time. His job is not to underestimate or overestimate that valuation, even though some unscrupulous M&A intermediaries may overestimate valuations just to sign a client. Investment bankers who have seemed to overestimate valuations to this end have faced a number of class action lawsuits in recent years. Other investment bankers may underestimate their valuations to lower client expectations, thus making their jobs easier later on. No honest, professional investment banker would endeavor to over- or underestimate a prospective client company's valuation. Prospective sellers can protect themselves from less scrupulous investment bankers by checking the references of any they would consider hiring.

The differences between a preliminary valuation provided by an *experienced investment banker* and the final purchase price achieved for his sales-side client are usually more correctly attributed to a successful negotiated auction rather than a bad initial valuation. The negotiated auction itself is the best and final arbiter of the value of a Middle Market company at any given point in time, because it reflects what buyers actually did pay for a company in competition with other buyers.

Expertise and Investment Bankers

"The lawyer who represents himself has a fool for a client." This famous quote also applies, without question, to sellers of Middle Market businesses. Sales-side (and buy-side as well) M&A is a technically complicated process requiring knowledge of business valuation, taxation, contract law, negotiation, business finance, securities laws, M&A financial conventions, and the M&A process itself.

And never forget the all-important emotional objectivity. Herb Cohen, the author of *Negotiate This*, may have put it best when he wrote that the best negotiators convey a strong sense of "I care—but not t-h-a-t much," to the other side. This attitude allows them to keep things on a professional and impersonal keel while maintaining steady progress. They allow the most effective negotiators to press on at just the right time and with precisely the right tone—a major distinction between inexperienced and experienced deal makers.

Investment Bankers as Process Expediters

I heard this story from one of the principals, and I do not doubt its truth. The CEO of a local $20-million Middle Market company was chatting with an acquaintance, the chairman of another Middle Market firm of similar size in a complementary industry.

"It would be great if we could merge our two companies," they mused, enumerating all sorts of synergistic benefits to each other in the glow of the first date. But even in the lust of first encounter, they were somewhat cautious. It is a lot like meeting a girl (or guy) that you want to impress but are little bit uncomfortable at the same time for fear of offending in some unintended manner so you become perhaps a tad *too* careful.

And so the dance began. The CEO and the chairman scheduled a lunch, continued to discuss synergies, expounded on mutual benefits. Everyone started getting even more excited. There is one problem, though: Nobody wanted to mention the big question (in the business case, price), even though both sides knew that price eventually must be addressed.

Fast-forward through three months of lunches: (This is getting expensive.) Someone finally mentioned price, at which point the CEO and the chairman realized that their respective valuations of each other's business were too far apart to proceed. Unfortunately, their refusal to address this critical factor at the start of their fruitless three-month courtship might have saved them both considerable distraction and wasted time. The CEO's and the chairman's mutual reluctance to name a price early on obviously reflected their uncertainty as to their respective corporate valuations. It also very likely reflected the difficulty of discussing so "personal" an issue involving firms they had founded and led. The CEO and the chairman simply could not bring themselves to address this critical factor dispassionately and candidly, and most especially early on.

DEALING WITH PRICING COMPATIBILITY EARLY   Had they engaged professional investment bankers from the start, the pricing issue could have been dispensed with in the early goings. Investment bankers could have provided a comfortable (let's call it a *chaperoned*) environment that would have allowed them to explore the divergence in their valuations up front. A good investment banker would have accelerated this outcome precisely because he is paid to succeed and would not be willing to waste three months of his own time, let alone that of his clients. Bankers are paid to expedite the process, to separate the wheat from the chaff, so that sellers and buyers alike may keep their options open.

Investment Bankers as Management Time Savers

Investment bankers will spend from 700 to 800 hours from start to closing on a typical M&A deal—a prodigious amount of time, indeed. These hours are divvied up among the internal team referred to early in this chapter, including analysts, valuation personal, junior and senior bankers, researchers, etc. Very few sellers are equipped to dedicate 700 to 800 hours to the sales process while continuing to run their businesses. Sellers typically spend 150 to 200 hours of their own time in the sales of their companies via management presentations; preparing and supplying data to be incorporated in offering memoranda and due diligence materials; and other related activities. Burdening management with another 700 to 800 hours (and it would actually likely be much more time due to their inexperience) of deal-related activities would be foolhardy in the extreme. Sellers simply are not in a position to take this kind of time away from their own businesses. I have never, ever, met a seller who represented himself who said he would do so again on his own. Do-it-yourself sellers tend to live and learn.

Investment Bankers as Sin Eaters and Emotional Firewalls

Many Middle Market transactions are far from over even when they have closed. That is because most business sales agreements allow or require the sellers to receive additional payments—earnouts and the like—if their firms meet or exceed postclosing financial and other performance targets agreed to at the time of the sale. Such agreements also may include continuing employment of the seller(s), either full-time, part-time, or as consultants or employees. The success of such postclosing relationships depends in good part on the goodwill of all parties, particularly in the face of at least some degree of the inevitable buyer's remorse.

Here again, transactions that are intermediated dispassionately and professionally by investment bankers are most likely to allow sellers and buyers to reasonably sustain mutual goodwill, because professional intermediation minimizes the inclination of either side to blame the other personally for the transaction's business outcome.

This applies to more than posttransaction earnouts and the like, as well. In M&A transactions that involve millions of dollars, it is not unlikely that some and perhaps a lot of emotion will be experienced by the involved parties during negotiations. It is crucially important that there be an intermediary to absorb this emotional outpouring, as there is no more certain deal killer then letting the expression of anger enter into exchanges between the buyer and seller. Frankly, it very often destroys the necessary trust required to get a deal done. At various stages throughout the lifecycle of a given transaction, the Middle Market investment banker may find him or herself very much akin to an old west stagecoach driver, with bullets whizzing by from behind and arrows flying fast and furious at him from the front. That's not the fun part, but for the good of the transaction going forward, it often is "safer" for seller(s) and buyer(s) to shoot at their messengers than to fire on each other. Experienced investment bankers understand this and will manage the process well. They are paid to do the work, and they are paid to suffer the slings and arrows.

Choosing the Right Investment Bank

Very few investment bankers become sufficiently seasoned and experienced to lead the sale of a Middle Market business in fewer than five years' intensive on-the-job training (OJT) deal experience, including substantial supervision and mentoring by their more senior colleagues. And even at that, it is unusual if any one individual investment banker—no matter how deep and broad his or her experience—can bring to the table *all* of the skills, both science and art, that are required. As a result, an investment banker must be capable of mobilizing a team of professional colleagues who together deliver all of the requisite skills. The seller must choose an investment banker with the ability to put together an internal team (much less the external team that I will discuss in Chapter 10) to optimize the seller's outcome. In this respect, size often matters: as a rule of thumb, investment banks with three or fewer bankers are unlikely to be able to mobilize a team and support a staff sufficient to ensure the engagement benefits from all the representational firepower it will require in the coming six to twelve months through closing. Veteran bankers who operate on their own or with very small firms may constitute the rare exception to this observation, but even so, the seller must consider quite seriously the limitations implicit in their reliance on a solo or small practitioner: Can he bring all the required resources to bear on the assignment? Is his perspective or bandwidth broad enough? What happens if he gets "hit by a bus," or becomes distracted by other deals? On the other hand, an M&A investment bank should be small enough to ensure that every deal is represented or at least supervised by a very senior investment banker in the lead role.

Park City, UT—February 2001

I was sitting in the family room of a 12,000-square-foot second home perched atop the highest mountain in the vicinity. My host and hostess—he in his 70s, she in her 50s—could open a door and ski right down the mountain from their castle in the sky. They invited me to join them here for a couple of days to discuss their plans to sell their main business. "Chemistry," apparently, is quite important to them, and I was invited to join them primarily, I think, to test that factor before they hired me to represent them in the sale of their company.

Jim and Margot, relying only on one another, built a $25 million business from scratch, and weathered serious trials and tribulations of entrepreneurship along the way up mountains both figurative and literal. Often, they found themselves within two days of missing a payroll. They staved off bankruptcy through sheer wit, guts, and extreme carefulness, but now they had finally built a winner.

They gave me the impression that they understood better than anyone that, in Middle Market businesses, anything could go wrong, and at any time, unless they held each other accountable and took every matter into their own hands. Not a bad philosophy, and most certainly one that had served them well.

A few days into my visit, Jim looked me straight in the eye and asked, "Dennis, do you have any experience doing sales-side investment banking for a company in our very specific niche industry?" While that very question was by no means unexpected, its timing nonetheless took me aback. Out of the corner of my eye, I saw Margot, watching me like a hawk, carefully studying my reaction while waiting for my response.

The time had come for the rubber to meet the road, or the skis to hit the slopes. Knowing it was coming eventually, on my flight out to Utah, I had pondered several alternative responses. There were so many ways to answer, yet each potential response seemed out of context, inadequate. The problem with context—and any conditionals I might apply in my answer—was the high risk that Jim and Margot dismiss it all as "hedging," as positioning myself to win the engagement. And from all I could tell, Jim and Margot had never "hedged" anything while building their business, and their innate BS-meters were attuned to trigger sirens should conversational hogwash exceed a few nanoparts per billion.

All of which left me with but one course of action: I had to tell Jim and Margot the unvarnished truth as I saw it, regardless of the consequences. In fact, the unvarnished truth pretty much always is the best of all possible alternatives, even when it costs you a deal from time to time.

"Jim, the answer to your question is no . . . and yes," I equivocated. (Truth even unvarnished is not necessarily straight lined). Margot seemed confused, if only for a moment.

"No, I never represented a business in your particular industry niche. But, at the same time, yes, I have indeed sold several companies in industries similar to and related to your own niche industry. Frankly, I believe that my experience with those sales-side clients is directly relevant to this assignment, were the two of you to hire me to undertake it." That answer reflected both my own commitment to never misstate my past experience on the one hand and my gut sense that I could deliver all that Jim and Margot would require in this transaction . . . and more.

Jim, Margot, and I discussed this further over the next day or two, but eventually they hired another niche banker (a sole practitioner) who, from what I understand, proved still unable to sell their business (a good one) three years later. I never regretted my answer or even the business outcome. No one wins 'em all.

Jim and Margot were highly successful entrepreneurs, great people, and fine hosts. In retrospect though, I remain no less certain that I could have easily closed a sale of their business that would have served their interests very well.

Specialists versus Generalist Bankers

Because almost any experienced Middle Market investment banker will have closed deals across a large number of industries, industry-specific experience can be highly overrated. Even so, one can always run the risk of underrating industry-specific experience, as well. Let me try to explain this paradox.

If a Middle Market investment bank has reason to believe it lacks the requisite industry knowledge to outmatch either an industry specialist or another generalist firm, it should say so up front and decline the assignment for two reasons: 1) to maintain its reputation for professional integrity and 2) because its shortcomings are likely to result in a deal closed poorly or never closed at all. A bad deal invariably costs the investment bank responsible and, even more importantly, its client.

Investment banks of any decent size will have access to broad, deep, and expensive proprietary and nonproprietary databases and research engines; analysts skilled at obtaining relevant industry information; and the ability to transform industry-related information into marketable business intelligence to advance the sale of the company quickly and efficiently. In certain particularly complex and usually esoteric industries, however, a banker's comprehensive knowledge of "all the moving parts" and, better yet, a wealth of close relationships with major players having decision-making authority at senior levels may prove advantageous in competition with a full-service Middle Market investment bank.

Yet therein lies the rub. By definition, such a banker's limited focus could prove useful to closing a deal but must be weighed against the lack of dealmaking facileness that only broad deal-making experience over a large number of industries may bring. I know some fairly successful self-styled investment bankers who transitioned into investment banking after establishing their reputations as business executives in a particular industry who subsequently closed on the acquisition or divestiture of one or more deals on behalf of their former corporate employers. Such M&A intermediaries often bring great interpersonal and social skills to the table as well. Unfortunately, this broad experience invariably leaves them lacking when it comes to the necessary training and broad experience in both the art and the science of sales-side investment banking. At least some of these guys would have trouble calculating compound interest. And, as to critical negotiations, they often prefer to introduce the parties, provide some basic background data and withdraw from the scene, leaving the principals to fend for themselves and have at it. More than a few so-called industry specialists with only minimal deal-making experience never get a deal done. They usually last a few years in the profession before moving on to something else.

How do I know this? My own firm has employed industry specialty investment bankers from time to time over the years, and an enormous amount of my or other senior bankers' personal time over the course of their first three or four years was required before these industry experts finally became deal makers. But when industry experts (in a very few truly esoteric industries, and there are some) succeed in becoming expert deal makers, it can be the best of both worlds for their clients. Probably 95% of M&A investment bankers are not industry-specific in their focus, as this would limit their opportunities severely. Specialists in the most esoteric industries would account for the remaining 5%, but even then, as I said, most investment banking generalists worth their salt can master industry-specific knowledge very quickly in the information age.

The misconception that industry-specific experience trumps deep general deal-making experience in most cases has led many clients to choose the wrong investment banker, especially when that "specialty banker" is a sole practitioner or a member of a small consulting practice without real M&A experience outside of the client's own industry.

Finally, even in the cases of larger firms, another issue to consider in dealing with specialists is that after a number of years of this type of narrow industry focus, assuming they are successful, a certain coziness can develop between them and the key industry buyers, not unlike that between lobbyists and politicians. They each rely on the other, possibly, in some cases, to the detriment of the client and/or objectivity. I am not saying for a moment that this always exists, but in some cases, it seems to, especially in an industry with a very limited number of key buyers. Choosing the wrong kind of banker based on a misplaced emphasis on narrow-niche expertise can prove very expensive in terms of lost deal value.

Investment Bankers as Matchmakers

A widespread misconception among sales-side clients is that Middle Market investment bankers are mainly responsible for providing matchmaker or "dating" services on behalf of sellers. Identifying and introducing prospective buyers arguably is among the least difficult and possibly (albeit counterintuitively) least important of the services provided to sellers by Middle Market bankers. This is another reason that the "specialty bias" is largely a myth.

In the vast majority of transactions in which I have been involved, the ultimate buyer has been identified within the first four weeks of the engagement. With Middle Market engagements for even excellent companies averaging six to twelve months in duration, or 180 to 360 days, the four-week buyer identification phase accounts for approximately 15% or less of the engagement cycle and, arguably, its overall importance in selling a

Middle Market firm. The other 85%, essentially, is about execution, structure, negotiation, etc.

Middle Market investment bankers most certainly do occasionally play substantial matchmaking roles—and quite effectively, especially in banker-initiated engagements where the banker senses the potential for a "deal made in heaven" that the prospective seller and buyer have yet to recognize. (See Chapter 30, *The Business of Middle Market Investment Banking for Consultants or Others Who Might Like to Do This Kind of Work*—*"The New York Style of Banking"*).

In summary, Middle Market investment bankers do locate potential buyers after being engaged to transact a sale, even though this aspect of their work usually remains among the least challenging and lowest value-added of the services they provide.

Securities Laws and Investment Bankers

Wall Street's Upper Market M&A deals are all but exclusively handled by broker/dealers and securities representatives licensed through the National Association of Securities Dealers (NASD) (and through its successor, the Financial Industry Regulatory Authority, or FINRA, as of 2008). This is not always the case in Middle Market M&A, although Middle Market investment bankers in increasing numbers are seeking to become licensed with FINRA broker/dealers as securities representatives. Prospective clients are well-advised to seek representation only from FINRA-licensed investment banking professionals and firms.

Since 1986, changes in the U.S. Internal Revenue Code necessitate the strategy that the sale of most Middle Market businesses occur through the buyer's acquisition of the seller's stock in the corporation being sold (to avoid severe double taxation). Owners usually risk disastrous taxation results should they fail to sell their firms as stock deals.[1] Engaging a FINRA-licensed investment banker to conduct the sale of a Middle Market firm via the purchase of the firm's securities minimizes the risk of violating federal and state securities laws that, if violated, might result in the rescission of the sale by the buyer, among other highly undesirable legal consequences.

Investment Bankers and Formal Valuation Experts

Independent, credentialed valuation experts rarely are required (or capable, unless they are also deal-experienced investment bankers) to represent sellers of Middle Market businesses; but on the other hand sellers' investment bankers should be quite capable of providing all necessary expert valuation services as part of their overall professional representation. As a rule, then, the investment bank should also provide formal valuation services to a large number of business not necessarily in M&A transactions, as that will ensure that there are adequate numbers of highly trained in-house staff to provide the type of preliminary valuation needed in the initial stage of an M&A deal. A Middle Market investment bank's admission that it cannot provide such expertise and/or services should constitute at least a significant red flag arguing against its proposal or pitch to a prospective sales-side client.

Prospective buyers—whether larger companies or sophisticated private equity groups—undoubtedly will bring a trained valuator to the table. Sellers are obviously well-advised to match, as best they can, the skills prospective buyers mobilize. A Middle Market investment bank that lacks embedded formal valuation knowledge is disadvantaged by prospective buyers that employ expert valuators, and that in turn disadvantages the seller. Investment bankers who rely solely on their command of the "art of the deal," at the expense of any particular focus on its scientific underpinnings (including valuation science)—bringing no more than a rudimentary grasp of multiples, rules of thumb, etc., to the table—are very likely to miss or to misstate financial values, especially when representing unusual sellers or transactions seeking capital for clients. There can be no substitute for formal financial and valuation skills at least somewhere in the bank's professional staff when it comes to establishing the value of product line sales, startup companies, balance sheets, working capital deliverables, and tax structure, among many, many other special situations.

Chapter Highlights

- Auctions real or perceived, represented by qualified M&A Investment banker, typically greatly increase the value to a client (as opposed to working with a single buyer).
- Most qualified investment banks will assemble a team of five or more professionals for each engagement.
- Nominal or stated deal prices are always trumped by deal terms and structure and what that brings to the bottom line for a client.
- Client self-representation is virtually always a very costly mistake in terms of the bottomline the real consideration received by them.
- M&A investment bankers, beyond deep expertise, provide technical client assistance in several areas:
  - Preliminary valuations
  - Conducting of well-managed auctions
  - Taxation
  - Contract law
  - Negotiation
  - Business finance

- Securities regulation compliance
- M&A financial conventions and process
- Investment bankers function in addition to the above by:
  - Expediting the deal process
  - Saving substantial amounts of management time
  - Acting as sin eaters and emotional firewalls to protect the deal
- Qualified investment banks should be large enough to offer the various technical services that are not usually embedded in only one or two people while at the same time small enough to be able to provide senior deal makers for each deal.
- Most, but by no means all, Middle Market transactions do not require specialty investment bankers or industry specialists.
- Matchmaking is widely perceived to be the most important task of an investment banker, but this is actually a myth.
- Formal valuation expertise is not sufficient to provide M&A representation, but nevertheless it is a critical skill in the best investment banks.

Note

1. An exception to this would be the sale of an S-corporation's assets. See Chapter 29 regarding taxation.

CHAPTER 10

The External M&A Team, and Using the Team Correctly

Richmond, VA—April 1996

"Tony, please—we asked you not to do this."

My cobanker was talking to Tony Bartelo, and he was barely able to keep his exasperation from boiling over. Tony, the chief financial officer (CFO) of our client, was a great guy. He loved people, conversation, good wine, and opera, and was a real delight to be around ... most of the time. But here he was, doing it again. He had just come from a meeting we did not know about with the private equity group (PEG) investor who was frothing to invest some $20 million in Tony's company on practically any reasonable terms. For what we could tell, Tony had managed to undo the last week of hard negotiations with the investor in a 30-minute meeting. Tony simply could not resist getting involved, especially if he received an invitation from the other side to debate some negotiating point, even after we had previously addressed it and thought it put it to bed. He loved people too much to say no to any request. The PEG investor had gradually become aware of this opportunity and so seized it every time he felt a need to. Tony's CEO was also a great guy, but a passive and somewhat nervous type who actually preferred no involvement at all.

"Damn it, Tony," my partner said "you have got to stop doing this if you want us to handle these things. You know it just gets us back to stage one and worse."

"Bob, I know; I am really sorry. This, well, this just kind of happened. I promise I will back off."

Bob and I looked at each other. By now, we knew as well as we knew our own names that Tony would not be able to resist the invitation to renegotiate some point we had already won if invited to do so again. Oh

well, we would just make the most of it. We did. The deal got done, but
probably at a cost to the client that did not have to be incurred.

The External M&A Team

I described elsewhere in this book (Chapter 9) the merger and acquisition
(M&A) investment banker's internal team. I would now like to devote some
attention to an equally important team, and that is the outside team representing the client on a business sales transaction. The outside team usually
consists of the investment banker, a transaction (M&A) attorney, and the
client's CPA. In addition, other experts can come into play as needed, such
as specialized legal or tax counsel, technology and subject matter experts,
and, on rare occasions, forensic experts. Yes, forensic experts ... there are
some bad guys out there, too.

The M&A Attorney

Middle Market business sellers should take extraordinary care in hiring an
M&A attorney to represent them. This is no time to hire a friend, or a personality, or the guy or gal who handled your last divorce, or any attorney who is
not a highly experienced specialist in Middle Market M&A transactions. Nor
should sellers automatically choose a "tough" attorney, who often special-
izes in litigation rather than M&A, because practitioners of these two legal
specialties tend to be polar opposites in both experience and temperament.

More deals are killed or seriously harmed by an inappropriately chosen
attorney than you can imagine. This is not to say that sellers should hire
their M&A attorney to be Mr. Nice Guy, either. The M&A attorney should
bring firmness, finesse, and deep M&A experience in equal measure to his
representation of sellers ... but the job never is about "making a killing"
in confrontation with prospective buyers. Most M&A attorneys and professionals out to make a killing tend to kill little more than the deal itself.
Defeating the other side is not what it is all about. Simultaneously advo-
cating the deal and the client's position is what it is about, and this is very
different from litigation. The most effective Middle Market M&A attorneys
successfully balance their clients' objectives and the imperative of sustain-
ing prospective parties' "will to transact" while protecting their client from
serious legal errors.

The CPA

Another very critical player on the seller's team is his accountant. All
Middle Market deals must employ Generally Accepted (Accrual Basis) Accounting Principles (GAAP) as the basis for their financials. Sellers' GAAP

misstatements, no matter how unintentional, are detrimental to their interests. The best way to ensure that the seller's financial statements conform with GAAP is to engage a reputable accounting firm to conduct an audit or, at the very least, a review of the books. Employing an accounting software package without expert accounting guidance simply will not suffice to do the job. Do not underestimate the importance of a rigorous review of GAAP conformity in advance of a sale. Should a prospective buyer identify accounting irregularities or other GAAP deficiencies while reviewing the seller's financials and/or conducting due diligence, the seller risks losing control of the deal, especially post–Letter of Intent (LOI).

Among the most common errors or omissions are improper revenue recognition, improper capitalization of such items as R&D, failure to record product warranty reserves, and improper inventory costing. All of these deficiencies and more can easily happen, even where a CPA is employed to provide compiled statements where the stricter application of the standards of GAAP as a practical matter are less observed then they might be in a review or audit-level engagement.

FINANCIAL STATEMENTS AND LEVEL OF ATTESTATION   CPA firms generally prepare three levels of financial statements for their clients or, rather, attest (or not) to their clients' financial statements in different fashions:

- Compiled (or compilation) financials
- Reviewed financials
- Audited financials

One might think that Middle Market companies with revenues beginning (at the low end) at $5 to $10 million would pretty much always have had audits prepared, but in fact this is not the case. I would say as a rule that in the case of companies with sales of $20 million and up, it is quite likely that their financials are audited; below those numbers, however, any level of financial statement attestation (or lack thereof) is possible—including, believe it or not, merely client-prepared (and often ill-adjusted) statements on Quick Books[1] or similar do-it-yourself software. I have observed $5 million business and larger whose books were no more than a series of Excel spread sheets. Ugh!

COMPILED FINANCIAL STATEMENTS   When dealing with complied financial statements, the CPA's primary role is limited to assisting the client in assembling financial statements in a manner that usually is consistent with standard financial statement presentation. The accounting firm does nothing to establish the veracity of the underlying numbers however. But even this level of overview is preferable to financials solely prepared by the client because if anything is *obviously wrong*—whether in presentation, accounting principles or the substance of the data—the CPA will or should correct it. Experienced investment bankers will pretty much universally agree that "compiled (by a CPA) financial statements" represent the extreme and *barely minimally acceptable* level of financial statement suitable for inclusion in a Middle Market M&A Offering Memorandum. Even here, however, real problems may arise subsequently during confirmatory due diligence because the Seller only minimally involved a CPA in presenting his company's financials.

REVIEWED FINANCIAL STATEMENTS   At the review level, the CPA performs certain tests that do not rise to the level of an audit but nonetheless increase his involvement significantly while reducing the likelihood that financials and related data will be misstated significantly. At the review level, the CPA authenticates to a great degree the underlying financial data or, at the very least, performs tests rigorous enough to minimize the likelihood of misstatements. This really should be the threshold level of involvement.

AUDITED FINANCIAL STATEMENTS   The higher the level of CPA involvement (the best bet: conduct a full audit), the easier it will be to consummate a transaction. Why? Because a full audit by independent CPAs will increase prospective buyers' confidence level in the financials they receive and, in turn, in the seller's company as a well-managed business. Perhaps even more importantly, a full audit by independent CPAs very likely will allow the seller's company to avoid accidentally misstating data, which can prove disastrous, especially following the execution of an LOI.

ACCOUNTING METHODS   Middle Market transactions are negotiated based on historic and/or projected financial results, and only GAAP, applied on an accrual basis, will suffice. Period!

Cash basis and accounting principles other than GAAP are inappropriate. Most M&A negotiations to establish investment value for a buyer are undertaken based on how the rest of the world calculates investment value when using comparable reference points—and virtually all such comparative data and reference points are based on accrual basis GAAP accounting.

Finally readers, and buyers, who are unfamiliar with the Middle Market might question the need for an emphasis on the accrual accounting method. How many of these not-so-small businesses would be using cash-basis reporting? Quite a few: Under current IRS regulations, fairly large businesses can use cash basis reporting methods for quite some time.

Tax Counsel

Specialized professional tax counsel can be no less crucial to the sellers than ordinary accounting and transaction legal advice, given the complexity of many M&A transactions. The seller's accountant or transaction attorney (or one of his partners) may provide this, depending on the complexity of the deal's tax issues. Sellers tend to seek tax advice at four critical stages as the deal progresses.

First, the seller may seek tax advice well before putting his company on the market. His objective at the very early stages—perhaps when the business is first being formed—is to establish the tax strategy, including his choice of business entity, to optimize his tax outcome. At a later point, for example, the seller, his accountant, and tax advisor may decide whether the transaction is better as a stock or an asset deal, and under what precise circumstances in accordance with tax law. Choices made at this point will determine how the business is sold and to a degree how its final price is negotiated.

The second instance when tax advice becomes important is during negotiations with prospective buyers. At this point, the seller's investment banker should have a command of his client's basic tax attributes, allowing him to be well-grounded in negotiations with prospective buyers while properly representing his client. The investment banker's own understanding of fundamentals of M&A tax law should allow him to collaborate with the seller's tax counsel and accountants throughout the process of the sale of the Middle Market company.

At the final stages of a sale, the seller's tax attorney may assist in the drafting and review of final definitive agreement documents because *precisely how these documents are drafted* often will have tax consequences for the seller for years to come. For example, the proper *drafting* of an earnout document or a transaction that is partially tax deferred under one of the Internal Revenue Code reorganization sections requires expertise that will go beyond the scope of even most tax specialist CPAs.

Finally, tax counsel (usually the CPA in this case) plays a particularly important role in the seller's post-transaction compliance with tax filing requirements. Middle Market M&A transactions may result in a range of reporting obligations, from ordinary, run-of-the-mill filings to quite complex ones (i.e., again when the transaction is governed by certain reorganization sections of the Internal Revenue Code).

Using the Team Properly and Sequencing the Professionals; Separating the Tasks and Single Negotiators

Carefully selecting an experienced, as opposed to dilettante, team of Middle Market investment banking and support professionals will make all the difference in a successful sale, because experienced professionals know how to collaborate with the seller and each other to ensure that nothing is overlooked in the crafting of a successful deal. Sellers should not compromise by hiring inexperienced professionals for *any* part of the team; it could cost them millions of dollars and endless difficulties with the buyer, tax authorities, and others.

Sequencing is important. The investment banker leads deal negotiations, through to the LOI, but does so in consultation where necessary with the seller's M&A attorney, accountant, and tax counsel. The attorney usually, but not always, reviews the LOI and may well suggest and/or make edits to the document. Because the LOI remains for the most part nonbinding, its creation is very important but not as absolutely critical as the Definitive Purchase Agreement will be in a legal sense (but not in a business sense; see Chapter 15). Even so, the more detailed, exacting, and accurate the LOI is, the less likely the seller or buyer is to be surprised by the Definitive Purchase Agreement. A good way to exert self-discipline here (that is at the point of preparing and negotiating the LOI) is to be prepared to live with the deal terms outlined, even if the LOI is nonbinding.

There are many ways a seller can fail to use his or her team effectively, which leads to disaster. Two classic failures deserve serious mention and should be avoided by sellers at all costs.

- First, it is critically important that only one principal negotiator represent the seller through the drafting of the LOI. Tasking multiple negotiators in the crafting of the LOI exponentially increases the risks that any one of them might overlook a key detail in the negotiation by assuming his legal, accounting, tax counsel, and/or investment banking counterpart was responsible for that. Multiple negotiators, plain and simple, are a recipe for disaster. Remember: Mistakes arising at the LOI stage and beyond always occur to the detriment of the seller while increasing the advantage—and leverage—of the Buyer. Multiple negotiators of an LOI and/or Definitive Purchase Agreement tend to inadvertently "divide and conquer" the seller's own team to the express benefit of the buyer. The seller may not know any of this, but most experienced M&A professionals understand all too well the importance of honoring an explicit division of tasks and responsibilities, because they have seen deals implode when too many cooks spoiled the broth. When experienced M&A professionals counsel sellers against using multiple negotiators, sellers overrule them at their peril.

  When, in spite of his professionals' advice, clients insist on a given course of action, investment banking and related professionals necessarily defer to them, even when the action requested appears to be wholly inappropriate in advancing the transaction. The client may not always be right, but when he's wrong—and insistent upon a given approach—investment banking and related professionals will do it his way, whatever the cost. He is paying the freight afterall and entitled to call the ultimate shots. But hopefully, as long as a seller retains confidence in each of his professionals, he should rely on them solely at the appropriate time and place to play their specific roles in the transaction at hand. Sellers who believe that involving the investment banker, M&A attorney, accountant, and tax counsel simultaneously in negotiations (or simply the banker and M&A attorney) may learn soon enough that bedlam will occur.

■ A second way sellers may misuse their investment banking and support professionals—often at great expense—is by initiating, or tolerating, "end runs." End runs usually are attempted by buyers seeking to deal directly with sellers in hopes of winning the deal and/or cutting a better deal than a negotiated auction might allow. When sellers allow buyers to approach with end-run proposals, they effectively isolate themselves from and undermine their professional representatives, often tipping the balance of power in the deal to the buyer. Sometimes sellers themselves initiate end runs, especially when they consider themselves to be better deal makers than the professionals they have hired to do the deal, and to whom they're paying big bucks, even at fees as low as 3% to 5%.

■ Confidential to Middle Market M&A business sellers: Trust your team's judgment and experience. They are there to protect you, to represent your interests by achieving the best deal possible for you in the marketplace, because that is what you are paying them to do. Sellers who are wowed by a particular buyer may be lulled into a false sense that "two nice guys—a seller and a buyer—can work anything out if they just sit down and talk." Not so! The seller/client is, of course, as he should be, always in control. His or her team, in the final analysis, is made up of his/her paid servants. It is up to the seller to seek advice, but when the rubber hits the road, the final decisions are up to him or her.

　　PS: When sellers are approached by buyers seeking to end run a transaction, they should smile to themselves while presenting the best poker faces they can muster to the would-be buyers. When prospective buyers attempt to end run the negotiation process, they are betraying their own desperation to win the deal. Sellers should thank such buyers graciously, reaffirm their confidence in the negotiated auctions being managed by their professional teams and immediately advise those teams of the nature and details of the attempted end run.

End Runs Revisited from a Buyer's Perspective

When buyers constantly violate normal protocols and insist on end-running the seller's intermediary and other advisors, they risk losing face with the seller, alienating the seller's principal advisors or intermediaries, or both.

When one buyer among several buyer/suitors attempts an end run, he risks looking amateurish in that other prospective buyers will be represented by professionals who know what they are doing. End runs by this kind of a buyer often eliminate that buyer from the deal if they are pushed excessively.

Summing Up End Runs

Sellers who confuse and/or undercut their own professional teams by misusing them or allowing or provoking end runs do so at their own peril and usually great expense. Even the best of clients may well be tempted by an end run at any given point in the lifecycle of a transaction. When tempted, they should do all they can do to resist the temptation. Only in the rarest of cases is a seller remotely prepared to achieve a more successful outcome than that team was likely to reach. Even sellers who have lost faith in the support provided by one or more professionals on his or her transaction team have a far superior option to the end run: hire another expert.

Chapter Highlights

- M&A transaction attorneys are not litigators, nor should they be. They recognize advocacy of the deal, careful representation of their client, and the will to transact.
- CPAs play a critical role on the seller's professional transaction team; their knowledge of a client's accounting subtleties and tax complexities is critical in providing the Seller a transaction and deal value that ultimately reflects the Seller's unique deal and tax profile.
- CPAs perform three levels of financial attestation (or lack of) to a clients' financial statements, beginning with the lowest acceptable and running to the highest (most desired) level, to avoid deal failure problems based on accounting misstatements:
  - Compilations
  - Reviews
  - Audits
- Attorneys may serve as special tax counsel where methodical and highly-sophisticated drafting of documents is required to preserve the seller's tax options under various scenarios. In these situations, the input of the seller's legal tax counsel is critical.
- CPAs once again should be tapped when it comes to conducting preliminary inquiries to ensure proper accounting and tax compliance prior to launching a transaction. CPAs also play an important role in providing post-transaction tax reporting and compliance advice.

- The professional transaction team, if at all possible, should meet as a group with the client before the transaction is launched to clarify and coordinate respective roles up front.
- The seller should ensure that his M&A team members are sequenced properly to ensure their proper engagement at the appropriate points throughout the transaction lifecycle, as follows:
  - The Investment banker usually serves as team leader through the drafting of the LOI
  - The M&A attorney assumes team leadership following the drafting of the LOI and through the completion of the Definitive Purchase Agreement
  - The tax attorney and/or tax CPA advise on deal structure tax issues while the investment banker continues negotiations leading to the LOI
- The client should coordinate the activities of his professional transaction team as above while refusing to instigate or allow end runs by a buyer.
- End runs can be just as dangerous from the buyer's point of view, as they may well (and usually do in my experience) put him in a bad light with the seller.

Note

1. QuickBooks is actually fine software for small- to medium-sized Middle Market businesses. My point is not that the software is inadequate to the task, but that it can be inadequate if it is not supervised to some degree by expert accounting assistance. I have observed any number of $10 to $20 million dollar business successfully using QuickBooks and other similar software.

CHAPTER 11

Anyone Can Do M&A—Right?

Never try to teach a pig to sing. It wastes your time and annoys the pig.
Anonymous

I refuse to have a battle of the wits with an unarmed person.
Walt Kelly, Pogo

A long habit of not thinking a thing wrong, gives it a superficial appearance of being right.
Thomas Paine, Common Sense

Anybody Can Do This?

I recently was told about a remark—adamantly expressed, apparently—by a professional in the business valuation field to the effect that mergers and acquisitions (M&A) cannot be taught. By sheer coincidence, I encountered him professionally a short while later in an M&A matter, and it was clear he did not have a clue. This made me think of a hypothetical and opinionated philosopher in the 18th century asserting that the Internet could not be taught. Well, of course it can not be taught if you do not know what it is or that it even exists or might exist in the first place.

Too often, it has been my observation that Middle Market M&A support consultants with training and experience in finance, legal, accounting, or business may assume they know just about everything they need to know about actually executing a Middle Market M&A deal. This also reminds me of the proverbial twelve blind men and the elephant. Each one thinks that the part he is touching is the whole creature. And of course these professionals would think that way. Often, the owners of Middle Market businesses themselves feel this way. These are not timid souls, and M&A deal making is just negotiation, something these executives do every day of their lives, is it not? But many years of teaching the subject and as a practicing M&A

banker has reinforced my convictions beyond any shadow of doubt that without training most would be practitioners or clients do not have a clue.

An executive is a person who always decides; sometimes he decides correctly, but he always decides.

John Patterson

McLean, VA—January 2001

Here we go again! *I was feeling really good about the presentation that my staff and I had just made to the chairman of a prospective sales-side M&A client, especially since the chairman is a well-known, highly sophisticated entrepreneur. An engineer by training with a technology background, "Craig" is a no-bullshit kind of guy who always seemed a step or two ahead of the conversation. But we had done our homework and our presentation had made that clear.*

Craig had agreed to fly into Washington, DC, to visit our offices in McLean with his CEO for the presentation in our main conference room—a good sign. And we definitely had deep deal experience with their industry. This was a slam dunk. We were highly recommended and a favorite of the CEO as well. I was proud of my guys and confident that we had a very, very, good shot at this trophy engagement, a deal so highly prized that our competition included several large regional investment banks that until the Internet crash of 2000 had looked down on hundred-million-dollar deals. Not any more, baby!

And then the hammer fell. The new chairman had just been brought in by the venture capitalists who had funded the business since its start up days, and while the business was a trophy engagement, it had its problems. They were the same problems that so many of these 1990s VC-funded wunderkind businesses had now. When its business model had not proved out as well as the VCs had hoped, the VCs grew tired and wanted out. So did management.

Despite the fact that this was a fundamentally good business for which there should exist several prospective buyers, its corporate governance was, to put it mildly, dysfunctional. The chairman was still enjoying a "honeymoon" with his board and management, and the continuing dysfunction all around allowed him a great deal more power and influence than he otherwise would have enjoyed.

By the conclusion of our presentation to the board and chairman which included a great deal of incisive industry analysis and insight, the chairman mildly observed, "You know, I actually sold my last business by myself, for $60 million, and I am very familiar with the process."

At that point, one of my partners glanced at me knowingly from the other side of the room—and not pleasantly, either. We now know who our real competition for this business was. It was the chairman, an expert in his own mind.

Here we go again, I thought, gazing out our large conference room window overlooking the parking lot adjacent to our building. (Memo to self: when our lease comes up for renewal, avoid office space with parking lot views. Oh, and tell building management that these windows are long overdue for a cleaning.)

The Deal the Client Never Got

Middle Market business owners who represent themselves in the sales of their companies will never know the offers they might have but never received or the deal terms that never were negotiated, even though they could and should have been. One of my fondest dreams always has been to play golf in an imaginary world in which my score for each round reflected my self-confidence rather than my actual skill. That par is irrelevant and unknown. Were this the case, I would find myself on the pro tour in no time.

Come to think of it, how hard can it be? After all, swinging a club at a ball is ... well, it's just swinging a club at a ball. How hard can it be for most of us not to play like a pro? Most of us have essentially the same physical and mental traits, as well as the ability to hone our techniques and our mental toughness. Most of us own essentially the same golf equipment and can seek out professional training to enhance our skills, to boot.

Barring some providential escape to a world in which we all get to play the golf game of our dreams, however, there is only one problem all the rest of us face when dreaming of facing off against the pros: the scorecard ... and par. The devil, as always, is in the details. Thousands of details come into play in a span of 18 holes and, maybe, three hours' time. The golf swing is but one of these details: As simple as it seems, it is also all but impossible for mere mortals to execute in a consistently flawless manner. Middle Market M&A transactions are complex in ways similar to golf. "The round" played by selling business owners routinely stretches over the course of months, upwards to as long as a year. The closing price of a completed transaction undoubtedly represents one's score at the end of the game, but as measured against what?

Furthermore while gentlemen's wagers in golf might set someone back a few dollars on a bad round, a round of Middle Market M&A sales, played badly, can cost an owner millions, even tens of millions of dollars. Most owners unfortunate enough to play the M&A game badly will walk away from the sales of their business with one consolation prize: They will leave the game *unaware* of how much they lost by assuming they were pros at the M&A game.

There are a few simple reasons so bright a line can be drawn between the golf pros who dominate the professional tour and the rest of us duffers:

- The pros pursue life-long learning, continuously working with other pros to refine their games, improve their stamina, and enhance their mental games.
- For pros, the game of golf is no game at all. It is work.
- The pros' successes reflect their singular commitment to the game of golf and to winning at it.
- Because these pros "make it all look so easy," we too often find ourselves deceived. "I can do that," too many of us think, without ever coming close.

For that matter, when's the last time we saw a uniquely accomplished athlete in one field chuck it all to head off to a different field in search of victory against pros in that field? Michael Jordan, one of the most accomplished athletes ever to set foot on a basketball court, not so long ago decided to play baseball in the Major Leagues. And fizzled. Case closed.

Admittedly, many successful Middle Market business owner/ entrepreneurs along the way have gained some experience in business negotiations, some experience in M&A, some experience working with accountants, lawyers, valuation experts, and so forth. And just enough experience to put their own best interests at risk by assuming that the smorgasbord of quasi-M&A–related insights they have picked up along the way offer the equivalent of a career dedicated to this field.

When an owner represents him- or herself in such a deal, one may be inclined to shrug it off, admitting that at least the owner/manager got what he or she deserved. But it is much more difficult to be so accepting when semiexperienced semiprofessionals presume to represent others in the sale of their businesses. This happens most frequently when a business consultant endeavors to be all things to all people by doing a deal he is ill-suited to consummate, as well as when the occasional CEO, officer, or accountant decides "I can do this."

Experience and M&A

Having worked with some incredibly bright and highly experienced junior deal makers over the years, I am confident that after just a few years of focused practice, such associates bring vastly more deal experience to the table than the one- or two-time amateur or semipro do-it-yourself deal makers.

Chapter Highlights

- A client who represents himself in the sale of his own business or engages inadequate professional services will never know value of the offer he never received, or the financial sum he left on the table.

CHAPTER **12**

Two Types of Auctions: The Informal Auction and the Controlled Auction

Auctions in General

- Since I use the term "auction" throughout this book, I want to take this opportunity to define that term further. A number of years ago, for pedagogical purposes, I began describing auctions to my students as being one of two types. By then the effective/informal/negotiated auction or the controlled/formal action

In reality, frequently auctions for the purposes of sales-side mergers and acquisitions (M&A) have elements of both of these approaches. Usually, though, and always unless I specifically indicate otherwise when using the term "auction" (ugh!, an ugly word I avoid using in the presence of buyers), I am referring to the "effective/informal/negotiated auction," more common in practice.

The Effective or Informal or Negotiated Auction

The effective or negotiated auction generally offers the best approach to the sale of Middle Market companies. It leverages the best qualities of an auction and a negotiation, as several—and sometimes many—rounds of offers and counteroffers are involved. The strong interest of several prospective buyers will allow sellers to initiate effective auctions of their businesses in a manner that maximizes their proceeds. A primary objective of sellers of Middle Market businesses and the M&A professionals serving them is to facilitate an effective auction of the business, gathering together as large an audience of prospective buyers as possible and encouraging those buyers to compete against each other at least implicitly.

While I make every effort to avoid using the "A" word in the presence of prospective buyers, only the least sophisticated among them will fail to recognize the inherent nature of an effective auction when they find themselves competing for the acquisition at hand. Experienced, professional buyers are not that much bothered by the prospect of an auction; they know how to play the game, and they know all too well the legitimate and appropriate devices they employ to avoid irrationality (i.e., consideration and terms trump nominal price, use of the Super Rule of Five in pricing a company, and being able to walk away, as discussed in Chapters 18, 23, and 16, respectively).

- This approach is *informal* in that it typically does not have the somewhat more rigid deadlines for expressions of interest and LOIs, etc., that are aspects of the more formal, controlled approach.
- This type of auction is *effective* is that it is not a pure auction (e.g., in the sense that there is an auctioneer at Christie's), but it nevertheless is an auction, at its roots, to see who comes up with the highest ultimate price. It is also more implicit (silent) than explicit as in the traditional auction.
- These auctions are *negotiated* in that unlike in a conventional auction, there is a constant stream of negotiation going on throughout the process.

The Formal or Controlled Auction

This approach, the formal or controlled auction, is more of both (formal and controlled) than the effective auction. In my experience, formal auctions in their strictest form are used primarily by public companies divesting smaller Middle Market divisions or businesses. Ironically, public companies at least occasionally employ this approach out of a lack of experience with less formal auctions (while often compounding their misjudgment by entrusting these divestitures to internal operations or to financial people who have only a modicum of M&A experience). On other occasions, public companies may complete divestitures via formal auctions simply to get the job done as quickly and expeditiously as possible without losing focus on their core, continuing businesses. Bureaucracies have a tendency, once a decision is made, to just plow on towards an end using the shortest means.

Controlled/formal auctions are also appropriate when the businesses being are unique or very special. Years ago, our firm was engaged to sell a very special mining operation that no more than half a dozen businesses worldwide would have had an interest in acquiring. The formality of the controlled auction process worked very well on behalf of the owners of the mine, because it created a sense of urgency among prospective buyers—which is, in fact, one of the greatest strengths of the formal auction from the seller's perspective. Everything about the formal auction is designed to keep things moving among a relatively small group of prospective buyers.

However, keeping things moving too fast can prove disadvantageous to sellers pursuing an effective auction, because a larger number of prospective buyers from any number of industries can be brought into play more gradually with the objective of maximizing the final purchase price. In effective auctions, urgency should be reserved for the later stages of the deal. While there infinite variations among auction types generally, the two respective approaches tend to be sequenced as shown in Exhibits 12.1 and 12.2.

Document Rooms and Sequencing in the Controlled and Effective Auctions

In the controlled auction, the seller invites prospective buyers to provide indications or expressions of interest, which constitute a preliminary bid/proposal as opposed to a LOI which is (or should be) more detailed and final. After selecting the finalists' expressions of interest, the seller makes a Document Room (which, these days, is posted electronically on a Web site with a password requirement) available to the prospective buyers that

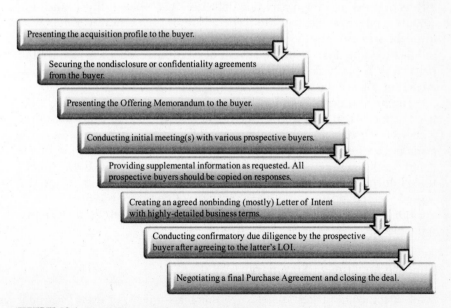

EXHIBIT 12.1 The Effective/Informal Auction Steps

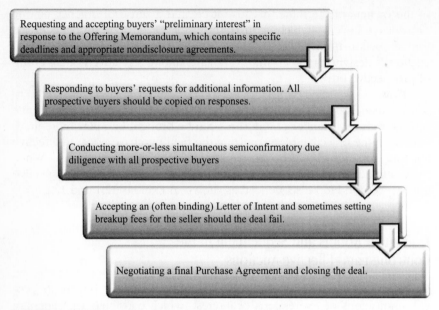

EXHIBIT 12.2 The Controlled Auction Steps

submitted the best preliminary bids/proposals. Seller information made available for review in the document room allows prospective buyers to conduct their due diligence, much of which is the equivalent of confirmatory as opposed to preliminary due diligence. Also noteworthy: Competing would-be buyers sometimes are made aware of each other by sellers who invite them to use the physical Document Room or adjacent facilities at more or less the same time. With the advent of electronic Document Rooms, the practice of a physical Document Room likely will not be used for much longer, in spite of the psychological negotiation edge it often provided.

The main difference in terms of Document Room usage in the effective auction is that in this case, there will now usually be only one buyer who won the right to confirmatory due diligence. In the case of effective auctions, confirmatory due diligence follows the actual negotiation of the complete business terms (into what becomes a nonbinding LOI). In controlled auctions, much confirmatory due diligence tends to more or less precede the negotiation and documentation of complete business terms in the LOI which allows more or less immediately then going to a Definitive Agreement.

Effective Auctions: A Summary

While it sometimes takes longer to consummate a deal (or even *because* it takes longer to do so), the effective auction is much more likely to maximize transaction value for sellers of Middle Market businesses. Effective auctions help interest build to a crescendo among multiple prospective buyers. They simultaneously allow the seller's investment banker much more leeway in using multiple initial offers submitted by prospective buyers to solicit better offers while gaining invaluable insights into the prospective buyers' individual and collective investment value calculations. An experienced investment banker can thus orchestrate the results to greatly improve the ultimate terms on behalf of the seller.

For example, if I have two offers, one for a total price of $20 million including $5 million in cash and the other for a total price of $18 million including $16 million in cash, I am in a position to truthfully tell the first buyer I already have an offer with $16 million in cash in it and the second buyer that I already have a $20 million offer. I have pointed out elsewhere in this book that honesty and integrity are key to negotiating transactions and I firmly believe that. In other words one should always tell the truth. But not the whole truth. Nobody in a negotiation is expected to disclose their whole hand. It is not in the nature of negotiating do that. The seller in this case is, in my opinion, under no more of an obligation to disclose all of the details of other offers than the buyer is to disclose his investment value limits. The negotiated auction is a fairly designed process that will ultimately determine where a buyer and sellers interests intersect (if they do).

Seller convenience and privacy is best served by the effective auction as well, because only one prospective buyer ever conducts confirmatory due diligence—after agreeing to the final business terms and after all other buyers have dropped out of the bidding process. Most sellers obviously will prefer to conduct confirmatory due diligence with only one prospective buyer than with seven or eight. In the latter case, a plethora of prospective buyers conducting due diligence very likely would prove most disruptive to the seller and the seller's ongoing business operations. Increasing the number of prospective buyers conducting confirmatory due diligence also increases serious disclosure risks of otherwise proprietary information. Having agreed to final business terms in advance of confirmatory due diligence removes a great burden of uncertainty and inconvenience on the part of the seller. With final business terms in place, the seller understands that the closing of the sale is hopefully just a matter of time.

Earnest Money Deposits and Breakup Fees in Auctions

Nonrefundable deposits and breakup fees are rare in effective auctions, because very few buyers would be willing to risk making sizable financial deposits against such deals without having been given opportunities to verify the underlying data in post-LOI confirmatory due diligence. To every rule, however, there will be exceptions. Deposits and breakup fees occur occasionally, particularly when:

- Deal terms have been thoroughly negotiated.
- Virtually all material confirmatory due diligence has been completed for one reason or another and it would somehow seriously harm the seller to further prolong exclusivity with a single buyer.
- The transaction requires little confirmatory due diligence (i.e., the purchase of something less than an entire business), and it would somehow seriously harm the seller to further prolong exclusivity with a single buyer.
- Potentially, if a new buyer appears at the last minute and is intent on having the seller walk away from an existing offer.

Computing Deposits in Breakup Fees

How should a seller compute deposits and breakup fees? In the past, I have used two approaches.

First: Compute the compensatory damages to the seller, should the buyer walk. Such a calculation generally is straightforward enough. It can be established by adding up nonrecoverable transaction and support costs to date (including both external consultants and internal payroll), the time value of money on the lost transaction value (i.e., it most likely will take months to consummate another deal with another prospective buyer), and a catch-all amount reflecting whatever else the market—and the balky buyer—will bear.

Second: When the seller really wants to prevent a prospective buyer from walking from the deal—either because the seller is convinced the perfect deal has been hammered out, or because a new buyer appeared at the last minute and is intent upon having the seller walk away from an existing offer—or where it would truly and materially hurt the seller by prolonging a settlement the second approach comes into play. In this scenario, the seller uses a deposit and/or a break-up fee (let's call this calculation punitive) to inflict more than just enough pain (which is usually a lot) on the walk-away buyer, to make him really think twice about dropping out of the transaction.

The Need for Auctions: What a Buyer Will Not Tell a Seller; How the Seller Finds Out; Is This Really Fair?

A Classroom in an MBA Course, VA—2007
Recently, I met with a new client (who also had been a student of mine when I was guest lecturing in an graduate course). She was then studying for her MBA. Among the other guest lecturers in her course on M&A was the senior M&A officer for a public company headquartered nearby.

The M&A officer had completed several acquisitions of smaller Middle Market firms in recent years. He proceeded to discuss in the classroom a specific transaction he had completed, including actual deal terms that at least already were public knowledge. But even so, I found myself somewhat surprised by the candor of the lecturer as conveyed by his student, my client. I was even more intrigued by the unfolding narrative, given the fact that my investment bank has done deals with the M&A officer's own firm—and we have found his firm to be a great and a highly-skilled buyer.

Apparently, in the scenario presented to the MBA class, the M&A officer's public company was the only buyer for the acquisition in question, despite the fact that the target was very attractive and quite easily could/should have found multiple prospective buyers. Why had the target not identified multiple prospective buyers? I had no clue, nor did my client, the MBA student.

In due course, the M&A officer-turned-guest-lecturer apparently disclosed to the class both the price it actually paid and the price his public company would have been willing to pay for the target. My client told me that she—and most of her classmates—practically fell out of their chairs when they realized the difference between those two price points. Many years of experience had taught me, on the other hand, to simply nod and shrug. I told my client that I hoped no friends or family of the selling owners had been present to learn how many millions of dollars they had left on the table. The public company, in fact, had been willing to pay nearly double the price it paid for that acquisition.

Single Buyers, Sharks, and Wet Chickens

Buyers, of course, are never under any obligation to reveal what they will pay. Investment value (unlike fair market value) inevitably is subjective and extremely confidential. For a prospective buyer to volunteer the slightest hint of a target's ultimate value (to the target) would be foolhardy in the extreme. The seller's only recourse is to do everything he or she can do to determine the highest value the target company could realize by gathering as many prospective buyers together as possible and initiating . . . you guessed it . . . an auction.

The seller who fails to identify two or more prospective buyers will find himself somewhat at a loss in negotiating with the lone prospective buyer he has been (usually) approached by. In fact, I have always considered the seller facing off against a lone prospective buyer to be almost as inconsequential in the process as a chicken flapping its wings, facing off against a great white shark. The buyer, just like the great white, is in heaven—and so, too, will the chicken be . . . shortly.

When the Shark Is Already in the Tank

Sometimes, despite best efforts, only one prospective buyer materializes. When the seller and his investment banker are forced to make the best out of the situation, some standard negotiating tools will apply. Among these are:

- Try to convey an ambivalence about the deal: You do not need to close it, nor do you care very much whether or not a deal is closed. (This is easy to say, but pulling it off convincingly but requires great constraint and self-control. It is also one of the most valuable things a negotiator can do, under these circumstances.)
- To understand, that conversely, the buyer more often than not also has constraints and time pressures, even if they are not apparent to the seller.
- Be patient because patience conveys confidence in one's own position.
- Never forget that the buyer only rarely is fully aware of a seller's vulnerabilities.
- Imply at the very least that others are interested in your business (there always would be the problem is you just haven't found them yet.)
- Set a minimum walk-away price, in advance, and stick to it.
- Engage an investment banker to serve as the intermediary with the buyer, even if you only pay him on an hourly rate basis; the investment banker's presence alone will imply that an auction is taking place.
- But do not fake the unfakeable or exaggerate your position to a point where it becomes obvious to the buyer that you have a very bad hand, because doing so either will destroy any prospects of a deal or shred what little leverage the seller has in the process. Just be cool. Any attempt by a seller to blatantly overfake an auction can be fraught with problems. First and foremost among them: If there is only one buyer, there is only one buyer and that buyer very likely will become aware, in time, that he is the seller's lone prospect. If, after best efforts, the seller still has only one prospective buyer, it probably would be best to mildly imply that there are other interested parties (of course there must be, whether or not you have yet identified them), rather than fake an auction entirely and risk a loss of credibility when the truth comes to light. Limiting the fakery to this light touch will reduce significantly the pressures of obvious inconsistencies that likely will arise between the actual pacing of the deal with a single buyer and the pacing in an auction.

Chapter Highlights

- There are two types of auctions, controlled and effective.
- Many Middle Market M&A deals have some elements of each as deemed appropriate for the particular circumstances.
- The effective auction is almost always the best choice for business sellers in Middle Market M&A transactions, as it allows more flexibility for the sellers and their advisors; therefore, it is much more prevalent in practice.
- The controlled auction is typically employed by public companies divesting subsidiaries or on occasions when very special/unique sellers are unlikely to have more than a very few likely buyers.
- The sequencing and effect of the two auctions differs:
  - In controlled auctions, the LOI *follows* the Expression of Interest and much confirmatory due diligence, may be binding, and may have a breakup fee.
  - In effective auctions, Expressions of Interest are less commonly used than LOIs for the initial proposal. LOIs tend to be nonbinding, thorough (as compared to Expressions of Interest), and usually involve no breakup fees. Most confirmatory due diligence follows the LOI.
- Effective auctions are more seller-friendly and convenient, since there is only one buyer doing confirmatory due diligence.
- The effective auction is more likely to maximize seller value, as there is more opportunity to use various offers, or at least elements of various offers, to improve others.
- Single buyers are not desirable, as a rule, because they give sellers little means of determining the buyers' actual investment value or walk-away price.
- Buyers can defend themselves in auctions by using such rules of thumb as the "Super Rule of Five" (See Chapter 23) and having a walk-away price.
- When absolutely necessary, sellers can defend themselves against single buyer—great white shark—situations by:
  - Not caring t-h-a-t much (Thank you Herb Cohen)
  - Implying an auction (very gently, carefully, and consistently)
  - Having a seller's walk-away price

Financial Services Agreements, Estimating Professional Fees, and the Importance of Integrity around Large Sums of Money

Help me to resist temptation, Lord, especially when I know no one is looking.

Anonymous

Always do right. This will gratify some people and astonish the rest.

Mark Twain

Financial Services Agreements, Broadly Considered

Some of this chapter may seem cynical at first blush, but this book was written to tell it like it is, primarily for the benefit of prospective sellers and investment bankers. Some readers may disagree with my perspective, here or there, but it reflects extensive real-world, real-life experience and any number of lessons learned the hard way, lessons that just may spare my readers, whether they are sellers or novice transaction professionals, one or more hard lessons of their own.

Over the course of my career, easily 95% of my clients have been wonderful to work with and for. In the case of the vast majority of those clients, we have remained friends years after the fact. But you have to factor in the remaining 5% to account for 100% of a career, and as to that other 5%, "Whoa!" They made life, and the deals themselves, very tough on all of us. The same 95/5 rule has proved true over the course of a career's worth of collaboration with other investment bankers. The majority epitomize integrity, professionalism, and genuine goodwill towards their clients and professional counterparts. In fact, life is too short, and the Middle Market community is way too small, to conduct oneself otherwise, because word gets around—and fast. But once again, that other 5% of investment bankers make life—and the transaction of Middle Market deals—needlessly difficult for sellers, buyers, and other professionals. And one must guard against them. Perhaps the best way to do that is to be forewarned which is one of the purposes of this chapter.

Lawyers and Investment Banking Financial Services Agreement Reviews

After a prospective seller and his chosen investment banker launch a transaction with a handshake, their agreement must of necessity be formalized in an investment banking Financial Services Agreement (FSA), which for the most part is a fairly standard document from firm to firm, at least in its substantive terms. But before the seller signs an FSA, he is well-advised, even when working with the most reputable investment banking professionals, to review it with his attorney. Having been a party to hundreds of FSAs over the years, I note with some bemusement that not a single one of them ever came back from its review by the seller's attorney without sporting one or more changes, usually of de minimis overall import but rarely the same from attorney to attorney. I once asked an attorney friend of mine why this was the case; he reflected for just a second and then said, "We have all been burned in different ways." Fair enough. But attorney-inspired changes to the FSA fall into either legal or business categories.

Legal changes that the attorneys suggest are usually acceptable, if usually minor, having been crafted by attorneys whose job it is to cross the legal *t*s and dot the legal *i*s. It's likely that the FSA itself was, in fact, long ago drafted as a template by some attorney, and if it was not basically fair, no investment bank would continue with an agreement that would tend to start every engagement off on the wrong foot.

However, proposed business changes by attorneys to FSAs occasionally quibble with issues of fees and, in such cases, are totally inappropriate unless (a big unless) the attorney has substantive real-world experience in the realm of Middle Market investment banking fees and finds something inconsistent with his experience and . . . he has a reasonably good understanding of any unique issues in this *particular* engagement.

In such cases, but *only* in such cases, a seller's attorney quite rightly advises his client as to proposed changes in fee structure. Unfortunately, some attorney-recommended changes in fee structure are inappropriate and gratuitous. Perhaps the attorney was just testing the waters to see whether a professional investment banker would back down from an often-standard industry fee schedule. Or he might simply be unfamiliar with fee ranges that can vary from bank to bank depending on the quality and experience of the bank and the peculiarities of the engagement. The attorney might believe that nothing ventured is nothing gained, or perhaps an inexperienced attorney will see this as a good way to impress his or her clients. But before virtually every last handshake launched hundreds of my own Middle Market investment banking engagements, the prospective seller and I had already agreed to a basic fee structure (often negotiated) that was to be only merely formalized in the FSA.

In short, gratuitously revisiting fee structures to which the principals have already agreed (unless it is appropriate to do so) is a sure-fire way to chill, needlessly, the attorney/investment banker relationship right at the starting gate. By the way, for my friends in the legal profession (and there are many), I never once have recommended that an investment banking client adjust his attorney's fee schedule downwards. I consider that a matter between the client and his lawyer.

So when are the times that fee reviews might be appropriate?

- When the client asks the attorney to do so because he has had second thoughts
- When the application of the fees to a particular definition of transaction value is inconsistent with the attorney's experience
- When in the attorney's *personal experience* the fees are out of line with customary fees—but only when the attorney is familiar with (has bothered to inquire) as to any special issues that might be inherent in this particular engagement

Large Sums of Money and Odd Behaviors

There is game called the Ultimatum Game that neuroscientists have carefully studied with MRI brain scans. In the game, a person indicates to a second person that he has received a sum of money (let's call it $50), but can only keep it on the condition that he shares some of it with the second person. So he offers the second person $10. Universally, it seems the second person will decline this offer, even though it is found money. Apparently studies done the world over indicate that most participants who are offered this will prefer to walk away and get nothing if they cannot get at least a third of the total sum. They are evidently offended and take umbrage at what seems like an unfair division. Now that is fascinating and instructive about our moral indignation (as measured by brain scans) when we think the other side is being unjustly rewarded even though we have nothing to lose. We see versions of this every day in mergers and acquisitions (M&A) negotiations.

Even more fascinating is what happens when, in a figurative game, the stakes go up to, say, $10,000 and the offer is, say, $2,000—or to $10,000,000, and the offer is $2,000,000. In this latter case (with a larger sum of money) it seems likely that at some point, the 20% would be eventually accepted. And in fact it usually is. There is no question that rationality depends on the size of the sums of money and is contextual.[1]

Montana—June 1996

As I picked up the phone, I was feeling really good about my client's transaction—it had been scheduled to close yesterday. My client's lawyer was on the line, and I immediately assumed he wanted to tell me that the deal closed so that we might gloat a little together. We had developed a very good relationship while working together. Attorneys and investment bankers usually do. This deal had been a hard-fought deal, fraught with challenges, that took more than a year to close. I was feeling very pleased that all that was behind us now, particularly because I really liked the client, too, and had enjoyed working with him so much. "Buzz McClellan," the client, was at least a vocationally a Montana cowboy, family man, church deacon, and more. Buzz rode and raised horses. And along the way, he had found the time, energy, and imagination to build a highly specialized government contracting business from scratch.

"Hey, Dick," I greeted the attorney. "How did it go yesterday?"

"Well, great, but ah . . . well. Buzz received your fee invoice yesterday and he does not believe he should pay it all, for various reasons," answered the attorney.

Phone calls like that tend to shock one. Over the course of the rest of that conversation, and several others that followed, Buzz's lawyer proceeded to advise me—and hang tough on point—that in the wake of closing a long, hard-fought deal, Buzz suddenly believed the investment banking fees agreed to in the FSA were too high. This, in spite of the fact that Buzz had been highly complimentary of my work throughout the deal.

It is safe to say that any attorney anywhere can always find a technical issue on which to threaten litigation or withhold payment. In this case, it had to do with the application and relevance of some obscure Montana real estate law to this transaction. That was the technical issue. The actual issue was that, in retrospect, Buzz thought he was paying too much in fees.

Dick and Buzz left me with two alternatives, neither of which was particularly attractive. I could accept their counteroffer of $250,000 there and *then. Or I could spend two or three years litigating to win the $310,000 fee stipulated in our FSA. I was advised confidently by my own legal counsel that I almost surely would have won. But Dick and Buzz knew as well as I did that the costs of litigation, the time value of money, and the basic distraction factor inherent in pursuing justice very likely would exceed the $60,000 they hoped to deny my firm. Buzz himself had just received a check for many millions of dollars, and it was a bet or bluff that he could easily afford.*

Dick's rationale for Buzz's apparent belief that a lesser fee was justified made no sense at all, either in the context of the FSA or of all of the work that had been done to close the deal. Frankly, I do not even think Dick believed this was right (actually, I know so, from after-the-fact conversations), but after all, the client had the right to his services.

All Buzz really wanted was to clip me of $60,000, because he believed he could get away with it. And, of course, he did get away with it, because I knew as well as he did that winning back that $60,000 inevitably would cost me far more than it was worth. You live and you learn.

Virtually all investment bankers will face such a disappointment somewhere along the way and will forgo fees legally agreed upon and earned, even through great effort, rather than waste time in pursuit of the amount disingenuously withheld. But once burned, twice shy: most investment bankers will respond to such an experience by tightening up their financial services agreements quite substantially to ensure that they are all but bulletproof.

Washington, DC—October 2003

I was interviewing an investment banker candidate who seemed really interested in "taking the plunge." This guy had a lot of financial services experience and some operating experience in the very hot aeronautics and space industry as well. We could really use this guy, *I thought.*

"Well," he said, "700 hours . . . that really is a lot of time to spend on a single deal."

"It sure is," I responded.

"Anyway," the young man said with a smile, "you get paid a lot."

"Most of the time you do," I answered.

"Most of the time?"

"Well, any number of things can happen that will keep a deal from closing, right up to the very last minute. I have seen it all. The seller can lose a major client, there could be heart attacks, serious business reverses,

new competition, you name it. Anything can happen at any time, and that deal you have spent 700 hours on just evaporates."

The interviewee's interest started to wane a bit. "Well, it must really piss you off when that happens."

I shrugged, then answered, "No, it disappoints the hell out of me, but it does not piss me off. It just goes with the territory—part of the professional risk."

He grabbed the arms of his chair. "My God. What does piss you off, man?"

"Well, I do get pretty upset when the deal is done, all went well, and the client still tries to find an excuse to shave my fee."

"So that 700 hours or part of that goes down the drain too? How do you avoid that?"

"Pick good clients, pray for the best," I answered.

Incidentally, I never saw that interviewee again, but I hear he took a job as an accountant somewhere with a reasonable and dependable monthly check.

Success or Contingent Fees Formulas (The Lehman Variations)

There are many success fee variations, but most sales-side investment bankers charge fees based upon some version of "the Lehman formula" (or something reasonably approximating it), which was developed in the early 1970s for large Wall Street investment banking activities. According to the formula, as the transaction value (sales price) goes up, the fee as a percentage of transaction value goes down. As the formula was developed for transactions that would likely occur only in the Upper Markets or upper reaches of the Middle Market and is some 30 years old, Middle Market investment bankers have adopted several variations of the formula as more realistic and fair. A common contemporary variation for Middle Market transaction fees is called the Double Lehman, which charges a 6% to 8% fee for the first $2 million of transaction value, then 5%, 4%, and 3% for each successive $2 million in transaction value, respectively, and then 2% of all transaction value exceeding $8 million. Sometimes, when the transaction is large enough, a 1% fee is charged for all transaction value exceeding $20 to $100 million. All of this is usually with a minimum success fee of something like $250,000.

Some Middle Market investment banks state their fees as a flat rather than scaled percentage of transaction value, but even then, the result usually proves more or less equivalent to a Double Lehman formula calculation. For deals generating less than $5 million in transaction value (these tend to be relatively rare), the $250,000 minimum fee protects the banker. In some cases the Double Lehman formula may well charge 10% on the first $2 million. This adjustment reflects the fact that Middle Market investment bankers know all too well they are likely to invest essentially the same 700 hours on a $5 million transaction as they would on a $50 million deal.

Other fee schedules include *blended rate* Middle Market investment banking fees for:

- *Very small deals* ($3 million or less) that rarely fall below $250,000
- *Small deals* ($4 million to $10 million) that range from 7% to 5%
- *Medium deals* ($11 million to $20 million) that range from 6% to 3%
- *Larger deals* ($21 million to $35 million) that range from 4% to 2.5%
- *Still larger deals* ($35 million to $50 million) that would range from 2.5% to 1.5%
- *Deals exceeding $50 million* in transaction value drop fairly rapidly to just over 1% and routinely are subject to prior negotiations between the seller and the Middle Market investment banker.

Alternative Approaches to Fee Formulas

The Double Lehman formula reflects an inverse relationship between transaction value realized and the fee percentage levied, because the ultimate transaction value of a deal has less to do with the amount of work involved than one might expect.[2] At the same time, Middle Market sellers and investment bankers know it is in their mutual best interest to reasonably compensate investment bankers to maximize transaction value. And the Lehman formulas' declining fee schedules ensure that investment bankers continue to realize somewhat higher fees in return for increasing transaction values, even as the fee percentage declines. Frankly, though, as a practical matter this is more about fairness to the client than motivation of the investment banker, and I will discuss that point further.

On occasion, a client will suggest a *baseline transaction value*, for which he proposes to pay a fee that is lower than the normal Double Lehman while agreeing to pay a fee that is much higher than the Double Lehman above the baseline. Various theories held by clients may drive such proposals, such as motivating the investment banker to get a higher price. In fact, it is highly unlikely that clients would influence the outcome of a transaction by adjusting its fee structure, except perhaps by adjusting it so low that no good banker would accept it. In the vast majority of negotiated auctions, prospective buyers drive the transaction value by competing to win the acquisition. Experienced investment bankers can and very much do influence the process, but they cannot determine the final outcome. In fact, in the heat of the deal, they do not have and should not take the time to calculate alternative fees arising from varying proposals. I can say that I am not usually at all aware of the precise fees involved when in the heat of battle, and I do not think many of my colleagues are either. Provided the basic fee agreement was fair, there is already a sufficient prize to the banker.

But insisting on a lower *floor fee* in return for higher fees paid at the upper end of the valuation range can prove very costly. This may emanate from the client's own human tendency to bluff from insecurity. When a client bluffs from insecurity, it usually reflects a certain defensiveness, given his unfamiliarity with a process he nonetheless feels he is supposed to control. He thinks if he bluffs by building a higher fee into a higher value, he will produce it. Sorry, but it does not and *cannot* happen that way.

This approach can have unintended and, from the client's point of view, unfortunate consequences. In an engagement I worked on a number of years ago, it happened, for reasons unique to the marketplace at that time, that a buyer on the verge of its own initial public offering wanted a company so badly that he paid almost 300% of the figure initially considered to represent the high-end of preliminary range of value. None of the other prospective buyers even came close to this extraordinarily motivated buyer's offer. Remembering that I had strongly advised him against the higher fee percentage on a higher transaction value approach, the client proved quite willing to pay me six times the fee that the Double Lehman equivalent would have allowed, for which I myself was much obliged. In short, though, this approach can backfire like crazy.

How Transaction Value Is Measured

Transaction value—what the company is sold for—is never quite so simple a concept as it might first appear. Determining transaction value often is very complicated, requiring enormous care. In financial services agreements, the language used to define transaction value tends to be very specific, complex, and extensive, in the interests of both client and investment banker. If proper care is not taken at the outset (and even sometimes when it is), it may prove all but impossible to calculate investment banking fees at closing that the client and investment banker alike find equitable and in line with their prior agreement. Should the client and the investment banker interpret contractual definitions of transaction value differently, they very likely will disagree as to fees due and payable. At all costs, all parties should avoid ruining the triumph of the successful sale of a company by allowing confusion to lead to differences over the investment banker's bill.

The complexities of transaction value definition arise from the painstaking care required to define all of the potentially discrete categories of value to be realized upon closing:

- *Contingent versus noncontingent transaction value*—transaction value that may or may not be realized following the closing of the deal, often in the form of an earnout
- *Escrow set-asides*—whether a closing fee should be paid on these, even though the client will not receive them until sometime in the future
- *Noncash, but noncontingent elements of transaction value*—such as stock and notes
- *Obscure or disguised transaction value*—arising from unique terms agreed to within the deal negotiations to accomplish certain tax advantages (e.g., special consulting fees)
- *Consideration included within the transaction whose value is difficult to measure*—such as stock in a privately held company or in a PEG recapitalized company
- *Transaction value to the client derived by an investment banker's intense negotiation*—to take certain assets out of the deal for the client, such as balance sheet cash or excess working capital.

Contingent versus Noncontingent Transaction Value

This one is easy. Because contingent consideration—often called earnouts—in transaction value (see Chapter 13) tends to be based on future business performance, it cannot be measured precisely in the present. As a rule, most investment bankers *do not* expect to be paid success fees based on earnouts until their clients actually collect the contingent portion of the consideration.

Escrow Set-Asides

This is a tough one, and I have seen it done both ways (attributable fees paid at closing, or fees paid later when the escrow is released). The two arguments, each favoring a different approach, go something like this:

- Escrow set-asides are for adjusting claims that are asserted later for events that often occur or become known postsettlement, and therefore investment banking success fees attributable to escrow set-asides should be paid at closing. Furthermore, the investment banker did his job and now has no control over these subsequent events and or claims, which is not entirely true of the client.

■ Any postclosing adjustment charged against escrow set-asides is a purchase price adjustment in effect, and therefore no investment banking success fee should be paid on escrowed amounts until the escrow is released.

There may be elements of truth on the side of either argument, depending on what the escrow is intended to cover. In the final analysis, each case should be evaluated on its own merits. One reasonable compromise is to pay fees currently on some portion of the escrow set-aside and defer fees on the balance until the escrow is released. In my experience, very few escrow set-asides are not eventually paid if appropriate due diligence was performed by both sides of the transaction before closing. A good compromise, then, is probably a formula that provides that 75% to 851 of the escrow set aside will result in an immediately attributable fee payable to the investment banker, with the balance of fees paid when the escrow is finally released. This constitutes a kind of escrow agreement within the escrow agreement.

Noncash, but Noncontingent Elements of Transaction Value and Their Effect on Fees

Noncash, noncontingent transaction value may include promissory notes, stock, etc. The consideration is fixed, having a stated and therefore knowable value upon closing, even though that value may change over subsequent time. Most investment bankers will want to be paid according to the stated or face value of such consideration at settlement. This should not usually unduly burden a client, given that Middle Market investment banking fees tend to average only 3% to 4% of transaction value. The client invariably receives more than enough cash (many multiples of that amount, in fact) in a transaction to pay investment banking fees in cash, based on the value of noncash consideration. Furthermore, the acceptance of noncash, noncontingent consideration is ultimately always a client's decision, not the investment banker's, and the total transaction value to a client is a much larger sum of money than the professional fee received by the investment banker. Sometimes, it is in the best interests of the client to take some of this type of consideration to get the deal done, or as frosting on the cake, but it should not be in turn imposed upon the investment banker's fees, which are merely for professional services. I have never seen, for example, a lawyer or an accountant paid in like-kind consideration for the services rendered in support of an M&A transaction.

When Mechanics of the Deal Obscure or Disguise Transaction Value

This kind of transaction value can take many forms. It often arises when the investment banker recommends using a mechanical device—often addressing tax, financing, or other imperatives of the seller or the buyer—in the course of a transaction negotiation to get the deal done for his client. For example:

- A lease agreement may be substituted for a promissory note as part of the consideration to be paid the seller.
- Substituting a very lucrative consulting contract for the seller in return for some reduction in the purchase price also might be acceptable (assuming all the rights and remedies remain identical, the seller may find 60 monthly installments of $10,000 equivalent whether they paid as a lease, a note, or a consulting contract). It may have been just this touch that allowed the deal to get done.

Transaction Value That Arises after the Deal Was Completed

Transaction value may be realized years after the deal has closed. This involves such post-transaction events as the buyer's acquisition of an asset that had been leased but not included in transaction value. It may involve equipment which the buyer had an option to buy, or a lease that was treated as an operating lease as opposed to a capital lease (in which the "lease" in effect is a financing device that was negotiated by the investment banker to facilitate the deal for his client, and the buyer subsequently decided to purchase the underlying assets). Should the banker be paid for the additional value or opportunity negotiated on behalf of his client? This is a fair question, and one that needs to be addressed in every financial services agreement, but there is no one-size-fits-all answer. It will depend on a number of factors, such as the passage of time between exercise of these options or events and the original deal closing. Then there is the double counting of transaction value that can sometimes come about in these cases and of course should be avoided and can be with good contract language.

Consideration Included in the Transaction with a Value That Is Difficult to Measure

What happens when a transaction involves the merger of two private Middle Market public companies? Such merger deals often involve relative rather than absolute transaction values. The seller may agree that the buyer's business is worth 133% of his own, while both parties decline to place an absolute value on either company. The relative value approach is not uncommon, because it sometimes is much easier for two Middle Market merger partners to agree on than absolute value. Establishing relative values requires a great deal of work, despite the fact that the results often remain more obscure in terms of actual values. Relative values may well be more intuitively apparent. For example, a review of revenues and net earnings may help establish the relative values of two companies operating in the same industries. So what is the transaction value in this type of situation? It will prove elusive, and may require independent appraisals or negotiations between the investment banker and his client. By closing, hopefully, the investment banker and his client should have established the kind of relationship that keeps such negotiations from becoming contentious. This has usually been my experience.

Extra Transaction Value Derived by the Investment Banker

A substantial part of most Middle Market transaction value negotiations will typically surround negotiating balance sheet targets (i.e., working capital and cash). The negotiations around these issues can be just as intense as those around basic transaction value and in fact can significantly alter the outcome of the aggregate transaction value for his client, sometimes by as much as 5% to 15% or more.

In general, investment bankers will want to include in transaction value those concessions won in a negotiation resulting in assets or cash retained by, or distributed to, a client that *otherwise would not have been retained and/or be removable* by the client in the normal course of events. The problem with this is measuring those extra concessions against what is otherwise normal. For example, one might safely assume that, since enterprise value is conventionally defined as cash free, any transaction value attributable to the cash retained by the client is not subject to an additional investment banking fee, and that would be correct.

But there is also working capital (which incidentally, and as discussed in Chapter 27, must also be conventionally determined on a cash-free basis, since to do otherwise would simply cancel out the effect of the basic cash-free enterprise value convention itself by adding cash back in when it comes time to establish the working capital target). There is no convention associated with working capital, beyond the fact that it ordinarily should be cash free and should in some way represent adequate[3] working capital to which the buyer is entitled. "Adequate" is usually determined by reference to the company's recent history of actual cash-free working capital, *provided that the company has had positive cash free working capital*. An experienced investment banker will do all that he can on behalf of his sales-side client to leave as little working capital on the balance sheet as could fairly meet the definition of adequate. To the extent he is successful, his client benefits, sometimes handsomely. But there is no standard way for the banker to be compensated for these negotiations unless working capital targets are established upfront between him and his client and then used as a basis to determine additional transaction value based on the banker's negotiating skills. In point of fact, it is not usually done this way, and some bankers may just throw this in as an additional benefit to their clients—which I suspect is rarely appreciated,[4] simply because it is not that well understood by them.

There is one clear instance, though, where such increments in value can be readily measured and the banker compensated for his efforts; that is when the banker is engaged after a Letter of Intent (LOI) has already been received. One way or the other, either by omission or commission, working capital and cash targets have been established implicitly or explicitly and therefore can be used as a basis for measuring additional transaction value on which the banker can and should be paid, since in this case he clearly, visibly, and measurably increased the net amount of transaction value received by his client.

Retainers (Commitment Fees)

Retainers, more appropriately called commitment fees, usually barely cover the start-up costs of an investment banking engagement, including the first month's work. Thus, they tend to be relatively inconsequential in financial terms to the investment banker. But commitment fees are important to investment bankers, as they tend to distinguish the serious sales-side client from those who always have a "for sale" sign out but are not interested in selling until the price is not only right but extraordinary beyond any reasonable expectation. In fact, they are often more curious about their value than serious about a transaction. Without retainers or commitment fees, most investment bankers could spend entire careers representing clients who turn out not to have been serious when a buyer makes an offer. There are plenty of these pseudo-clients around. Why not? They have little to lose. Investment bankers cannot afford to represent this type of client by any means, although novice or dilettante intermediaries will sometimes agree to do so. They soon learn, too late. With a commitment fee of from $35,000 to $50,000 in hand, most investment bankers can proceed on the assumption that their new client is committed to closing a deal under the right circumstances.

Finally, commitment fees may or may not be credited against the success fees, depending on the size of the deal and other concessions or special arrangements that have been negotiated between the investment banker and his or her client.

Basic Contract Period

Sellers typically engage an investment banker for a basic term of from six months to one year, usually automatically renewable thereafter for serial extensions of 60 to 90 days. Most investment bankers should find six-month basic terms sufficient to prove themselves to the client. The longer, 12-month basic term reflects the average time required in the United States to fully complete a Middle Market deal.

Richmond, VA—October 1995

Early one morning, Benjamin, a lawyer, asked me to review, as an expert consultant, a case involving a Middle Market investment bank in the southern United States that was claiming a $1 million (wow!) fee from a client, on whose behalf the investment bank had seemingly done little or nothing.

It seemed the investment bank had a clause in its financial services agreement stating that a fee would result in the event the client closed a deal within 18 months (of the termination of their agreement) with any buyer to whom the investment bank had introduced the seller. Allegedly, the investment bank, understanding the client was going to fire it in a couple of days, launched a massive mailer to all potential buyers it could imagine existed. A substantial number of buyers were undertaking roll-up acquisitions in the client's industry at the time.

After firing its investment bank, the client eventually closed a transaction with a buyer who, not coincidentally, had received a letter from the investment bank via its final mass mailing.

As despicable as it seemed that the former client would be obligated to pay $1 million dollars to an investment bank that had provided nothing of substance in support of the deal, the clause had been agreed to and might well have proved enforceable. I suggested a solution to the problem by advising the attorney that, under the circumstances, the investment bank in question probably had to be registered as a broker dealer with the National Association of Securities Dealers (NASD, now known as the Financial Industry Regulatory Authority or FINRA; see Chapter 30) to close such a transaction. In fact, the investment bank was not an NASD broker dealer. When confronted on this point, the investment bank backed off its claim, thereby avoiding significant issues with NASD and, quite possibly, the Securities and Exchange Commission (SEC) as well. I understand that the case was settled with only a nominal amount paid to the bankers.

Trailer Periods

Virtually all financial services agreements include a "trailer" that provides that if an investment banker "had contact (with a buyer) in connection with the engagement" and that buyer eventually closes a deal with the client—even after the expiration of initial and follow-on terms of the engagement—the investment banker will be entitled to a fee, as provided in the FSA. Most investment bankers and clients consider, and most agreements will provide, that 18 months is a fair term for the trailer, beginning with the termination of the base agreement (plus extensions) between the client and the investment banker. The investment banker very likely performed hundreds of hours of work on behalf of his client without a payday. Should a prospective buyer identified by the investment banker to his client eventually close the deal, it is reasonable to assume that the investment banker's own efforts played a role in the deal eventually consummated.

Problems nonetheless arise when the phrase "had contact with the buyer in connection with the engagement" is vaguely defined. What exactly constitutes contact? Simply identifying the buyer on a list of potential prospects certainly would not seem fair to the client, or to anyone else for that matter. Any number of databases would allow an investment banker to create a laundry list of prospects in the hundreds. Completing a mailing to 1,000 prospects at a cost of $1.50 or so per piece (or less, in the case of email) in order to "stake a claim" on the possibility that the eventual buyer is included among them would epitomize bad faith on the banker's part.

The best way to avoid such problems is by requiring *substantial* contact and by defining substantial contact in a manner agreeable to both client and investment banker. For example, substantial contact might be defined as having been achieved when a prospective buyer has executed a confidentiality agreement and received the confidential information memorandum. Such a buyer may be considered a serious prospect, one whom the investment banker not only identified, but also brought into the pool of likely participants in a negotiated auction. With the confidential information memorandum in hand, the prospective buyer essentially has in hand the basic information he needs to determine whether to buy the seller's company immediately or up to 18 or more months hence. He has been exposed to the target in a serious way.

Breakup Fees

Some FSAs also include a clause entitling the investment banker to a breakup fee if he is fired before the contracted engagement expires. In the Middle Market, breakup fees typically range from $100,000 to $200,000. Like retainers, breakup fees protect the investment banker under circumstances in which the seller gets cold feet. At the same time, investment bankers and clients alike may find breakup clauses both offensive and essentially unenforceable. A client who is disappointed in his investment banker need only wait the investment banker out through the expiration of their engagement. This may inconvenience the client, but most investment bankers, were they to stand in their clients' shoes, would reject breakup clauses in their own FSAs. Similarly, most Middle Market investment bankers worth their salt (and integrity) would not insist that the client agree to such a clause. In no way does it serve an investment banker's interests to penalize a client that has grown unhappy with him.

Carve-Outs and Approaches to Carve-Outs

What is fair when a client already has entered into a dialogue with a prospective buyer *before* hiring his investment banker? Under such circumstances, should the investment banker expect to receive his full fee? Most investment bankers will want to know how much dialogue or "traction" has been realized with the prospective buyer. A simple phone call inquiry from a prospective buyer should not count for much, but early negotiations extending over the course of weeks can hardly be ignored. However, simply introducing or mentioning a prospective buyer to the investment banker should not entitle the seller to automatically expect a carve-out or even a reduction in fees. It has been estimated that the client at least identifies if not introduces the final buyer to the investment banker in one out of three U.S. Middle Market deals.

If carve-outs were justified solely by naming names, sellers, too, could conduct a database search to create their own list of prospective buyers to carve out or expect to receive a fee reduction from their investment bankers. In the final analysis, simply naming names, or even a very uncomplicated meeting with prospective buyers, hardly qualifies as sufficiently "heavy lifting" in a Middle Market sales-side transaction to warrant a fee reduction. As noted previously, investment bankers invest the vast majority of their efforts in managing the negotiated auction, structuring an evolving transaction, advising through the drafting and execution of an LOI, and providing additional support in final negotiations through the close of the deal. M&A representation is less about matchmaking than the layman usually understands, at least until he actually been in and observed the myriad other issues that constitute a successfully completed deal.

But investment bankers should be willing to concede a fee reduction when the seller has generated significant traction in discussions with from one to usually no more than three prospective buyers. Alternatively, the investment banker might allow a "carve-out" of success fees for one or two prospective buyers while nevertheless arranging to charge the client on an hourly basis or a reduced success fee, often some combination of the two for services provided relating to those particular prospects.

But any carve-out or fee reduction arrangement may raise at least an unconscious conflict of interest for the investment banker. When one prospective buyer will generate a large success fee for the investment banker, while the other will yield no more than a limited number of hours billed at a set rate or a substantially reduced fee, even the most scrupulous of investment bankers may at least subconsciously hope that the higher-fee prospective buyer wins the day. It's only human nature. A way around this, and usually a fair one, is that the carve-out can be designed so that it expires at some point after the engagement begins. In my experience, about 30 to 45 days makes sense. If the carved-out buyer has not put an executed LOI on the table within that period, the chances are he is a full participant (in terms of time and effort by the investment banker) in the auction. And it is that auction conducted by the banker that will actually raise the likely offer from the carved out buyer.

One last observation that is hard to resist making: Ironically, and counter-intuitively, investment banking representations involving single buyer deals should in fact involve fee premiums, not discounts. Of course, it is not easy to convince clients of this fact, let alone get them to understand it, and therefore as a practical matter it is unworkable in most cases. Nevertheless, in single-buyer representations, the seller and the investment banker would do well to agree to a hybrid compensation package combining facets of hourly rate billing and contingency billing. Doing so would serve to acknowledge the additional challenges arising when the seller, for whatever reason, does not want the investment banker to conduct a sale of his firm through negotiated auction.[5] This type of hybrid arrangement is also a good approach from the client's point of view, as a pure hourly rate can run a up a very large fee quite fast without a deal ever closing. When a reduced hourly rate is combined with a reduced success fee, the client is somewhat insulated against the high-fee, no-deal situation. In turn, the banker in this type of arrangement shares the risk reward equation in perhaps a more balanced way with the client.

Compensation to the Investment Banker in Warrants, Options, or Other Equity

In most Middle Market M&A deals, the seller simply takes the money or other consideration and runs, at least figuratively, as a result of a total outright sale of his entire company. But in recapitalizations and equity-sourcing engagements, where the client retains a portion of the company, investment bankers not uncommonly ask for a warrant or an option to buy up to 5% of the stock in the refinanced company at the same price the company was valued at (the strike price) when the deal closed, or sometimes at a lesser price. In the alternative, the banker may just ask for an outright equity position, but probably at a much smaller amount than an option or warrant would provide. This recognizes the fact that the banker has to negotiate the value of the entire company, and both parties (investor and investee) at the close of the transaction now own a more valuable investment as a result. This also establishes the value for future follow on transactions. But the investment banker is typically paid only for the value that changes hands.

Warrants or options may be appropriate in other instances where for a small capital raise (say, $2 million), the investment bank's minimum fee (say, $250,000) may not make sense in terms of the net proceeds to the investees (especially from the point of view of the investor), but both the bank and the client nevertheless want to work together to do what is probably an A^6 round.

Equity positions with no exercise price, warrants, or options with an exercise price in lieu of some reduced fee may make sense. Reasons for wanting to work together could include a real expertise on the part of the banker in this industry, combined with his real confidence in the client and the fact that later capital rounds may be more in line with the bank's normal fees. For example, the investment bank's option strike price could be expressed in terms of the A round valuation . . . and then exercised later, when a B round causes the value to go up. This approach is not only a way to preserve cash for the client in the A round but also a way to really bind the investment bank to the client and vice versa in terms of goals.

Some investment banks and bankers ask for equity or options or warrants as a routine matter in every capital raise, recognizing the greater difficulties inherent in these engagements.

Integrity and Investment Banking and Large Sums of Money

Just as it is with clients, integrity is especially required when large sums of money are at stake on the part of the investment banker as well. But how does a seller ensure that he will receive that from his banker? Money encourages unpredictable behaviors in different people, sometimes highly unpredictable and distasteful ones. The best bet is for the client to do all the homework he can before engaging an investment banker. Check references with *several* of the investment banker's former clients. Consider using only an investment banker who has been around for a long while, completed a number of deals, and works for a reputable firm. The more transaction experience the better, and the more transaction experience, the *less fascination with large sums of money,* per se: Seasoned investment bankers will usually consider their own financial outcomes important, but secondary to obtaining the best deals for their clients. It is not that they are altruistic, especially. It is rather that they are more used to the high stakes and no longer fascinated by them or dependent on them, either—at least as to any individual transaction. And finally, a client should trust his gut; intuition often is invaluable in making such choices, especially if the client tends to value his intuition for good reason.

Another test of integrity is that when the investment banker weights alternative deal proposals with his client, the rankings generally should reflect the face value of the consideration weighted according to the net cash value or equivalent to his client, which often will result in a deal being recommended that results in a lower fee for the banker. There is usually much information available on the market values of noncash consideration offered. Most really good investment bankers present to their clients comparisons of alternative proposals in terms of their cash equivalencies, and they are not afraid to steer a client away from a deal that would otherwise produce a larger fee for the investment banker. I also discuss this briefly in Chapter 18.

After a banker is hired, a client can also observe how hard the investment banker pushes to improve prospective buyers' proposals to the client. Is the investment banker ready to accept the first deal that comes along? Does he point out the problems with specific offers and sometimes encourage his clients not to accept them? Is he patient, willing to collaborate with his client over the long haul at the expense of not generating a fee in the short run? If the banker does not seem to be acting this way (with integrity), the client can always fire him should he find his initial judgment erred, or simply allow an engagement term to expire without renewal.

Bankers Fees Paid at Settlement—More about Large Sums of Money

The deal is about to close. Along with everyone else, the investment banker is looking forward to getting paid the fees to which he is contractually entitled, having fulfilled all of his obligations to the seller. Sometimes on the seller's big day—and big payday—the seller unreasonably and groundlessly demands that his investment banker accept a lesser fee. Investment bankers can and should protect themselves from such day-of-closing nightmare scenarios by stipulating in the FSA that the settlement agent, at the time of closing, will pay the investment banker's fees by wire transfer, much in the same way (and for the same reason) that things are done in a real estate transaction. Such stipulations in the FSA will make the seller's contractual obligations to the investment banker unambiguous from the start. They also, quite arguably, will provide the investment banker with a powerful ally—the buyer—in ensuring that he or she receives the agreed-upon fee in full at closing, in accordance with the FSA. This is because in the case of deals in which the investment banker is denied fees contractually agreed to in the FSA, the *buyer* may incur transferee liability for those fees, particularly if the transaction involved the sale of a corporation through a stock transaction but even in the instance of an asset sale. This situation may be a concern on the part of the buyer if he has been put on notice of the fee due the banker in advance.

M&A Lawyers and Fees

I offer the following solely as guidance for sellers trying to estimate their costs for a transaction, and in no way mean to suggest what reasonable attorney fees are. That depends on each and every individual transaction, and they can involve very different issues of complexity. But a seller might preliminarily reasonably estimate legal fees of between 0.25% and 1.00% for deals generating between $100 million and $5 million in transaction value. Attorneys will typically charge an hourly rate, but this range in terms of percentages, will often in basic transactions be a good preliminary estimate of legal fees.

Fees more likely than not will prove to be larger as a percentage of transaction value in smaller deals and vice versa, just as with investment banking fees. It can take as much or more time for a transaction attorney to close a small deal as a larger one. All estimates should be taken with a healthy grain of salt, though. Complexities arising from securities or tax laws, complex entity structures, a particularly tough negotiation on representations and warranties, or fundamental inadequacies in the client's basic legal documents can dramatically affect billable hours.

Accountants and Fees

- At the risk of some redundancy as to earlier chapters in this book, CPAs normally play three roles in connection with sales-side M&A transactions: First, the CPA ensures that the company's financials are in good shape before the due diligence process begins. When deals fall apart (or are substantially renegotiated, to the seller's chagrin) following execution of a LOI, most of the time it is because of accounting inadequacies in the seller's financials. Such records must be in pristine shape—no surprises here. If the seller's business does not have a CPA, it should hire one.

- Second, the CPA closely collaborates with the investment banker concerning his client's tax issues, especially as they can be addressed by various alternative provisions in the imminent transaction.
- Third, the CPA performs compliance work once the deal has closed and tax returns must be filed on behalf the seller. Related CPA fees may well reflect this work.

All in all, a CPA might bill from $25,000 to $150,000 for undertaking an *average* amount of work required in support of a Middle Market M&A sales-side transaction.

Clients' Overall Estimate of Professional Fees for a Typical Engagement

Having addressed so many permutations and variations in the setting of fees may have left a reader somewhat confused. That was not the purpose, however understandable the outcome. As a rule of thumb, then, let's just create one "for instance" for a $20 million transaction, which probably would generate fees as follows:

- Investment banking fees: between 3% and 4%, or $600,000 to $800,000
- Basic attorney's fees: between .50% and .75%, or $100,000 to $150,000
- CPA's fees (assuming an audit or review was being undertaken anyway, regardless of the transaction): between .25% and .375%, or $50,000 to $75,000
- Total fees: Approximately $750,000 to $1,025,000, a very rough estimate for a $20 million sales-side transaction. Overall, a seller might estimate total fees of between 3.75% and about 5.12% of the sales price of his firm. Averaging out to 4.5% would work as an approximate early estimate just to get one's bearings.

Chapter Highlights

- FSAs (see Exhibit 13.1) are necessarily complex documents whose main features include:
  - A success fee schedule that usually resembles a Double Lehman formula or any of several variations:
    - A minimum fee (e.g., $250,000), but not a breakup fee
    - A sales-side retainer (commitment fee) of from $25,000 to $50,000 payable upfront, which may or may not be credited against an eventual success fee

- Provisions describing transaction value (including contingent and noncontingent, deferred and noncash) that allow the success fee to be determined
- A basic contract term of from 6 to 12 months with automatic 60- to 90-day serial renewals
- Trailers defining how the investment banker will be compensated for a buyer that he introduced to the seller when that buyer closes a deal after the expiration of the investment banker's engagement has expired
- Carve-outs and/or hourly rate agreements involving buyers with whom the seller already has initiated negotiations
- Attorneys' reviews of FSAs are usually helpful, but in rare and inappropriate occasions, they are not. Attorneys should limit reviews to legal terms rather than business terms except in special cases. Reviews regarding investment banking fees, especially those that are already agreed upon, are inappropriate except in certain defined cases.
- Wire-transfer fee payments at settlement are ignored at the peril of the investment bank.
- Client checks on investment banker integrity and experience are critical before and after the engagement agreement is established to select the right investment banker.
- Estimates of the M&A support professionals' fees (lawyers, accountants, and others) are likely ranges, because of the complexity of one engagement compared to another.

EXHIBIT 13.1 Sample Financial Service Agreement (FSA)

FINANCIAL ADVISORY SERVICES AGREEMENT

This Agreement is made and entered into as of the _____ day of _____, 200X, by and between _____ (the Seller), _____ (the Company), located at _____, and The McLean Group, LLC and its affiliate, McLean Securities, LLC, located at 1660 International Drive, Suite 450, McLean, VA, 22102, the foregoing collectively known herein as "The McLean Group."

WITNESSETH:

WHEREAS, the Company has or expects to have the need to raise funds and/or desires to sell a portion or all of the assets or equity securities of the Company and to conduct appropriate activities for those purposes during the term of this Agreement.

WHEREAS, The McLean Group has experience in advising clients in connection with raising funds for the benefit of businesses and conducting appropriate activities for the purpose of selling businesses.

WHEREAS, the Company is seeking advisory services and The McLean Group is willing to provide such services to the Company in connection with raising funds for, or selling all or a portion of, the assets or equity securities of the Company on the terms and conditions hereinafter set forth.

EXHIBIT 13.1   *(Continued)*

NOW, THEREFORE, in consideration of, and for the mutual promises and covenants contained herein, and for other good and valuable consideration, the receipt of which is hereby acknowledged, the parties agree as follows:

1. *Purpose.* The Company has the need to raise funds or to sell a portion or all of the assets or equity securities of the Company. In this connection, the Company hereby engages The McLean Group for an exclusive term specified in this Agreement to render business consulting and advisory services upon the terms and conditions set forth herein.

2. *Representations of The McLean Group and the Company.* The McLean Group represents and warrants to the Company that it is free to enter into this Agreement and the business consulting and advisory services to be provided pursuant to this Agreement are not in conflict with any other contractual or other obligation to which The McLean Group is bound. The Company acknowledges that The McLean Group is in the business of providing business consulting and advisory services to others and that nothing herein contained shall be construed to limit or restrict The McLean Group in conducting such business with respect to others, or rendering such services to others.

3. *Definitions.*

3.1 Sellers: shall mean the natural person(s) or legal entity(ies) named above as the Company shareholders and their Affiliates.

3.2 Affiliate: shall mean a person or entity that directly or indirectly, through one or more intermediaries, controls, is controlled by, or is under common control of the Seller(s).

3.3 Buyer: shall mean a natural person (including shareholders and/or employees of the Company) or legal entity that agrees to purchase or otherwise acquire all or a portion of the capital stock and/or assets of the Company from Sellers and/or the Company at any time during the term of this Agreement and whether or not such a person or entity has been introduced to Sellers or the Company by The McLean Group.

3.4 Client: shall mean the Company, its shareholders, the Sellers named above, and their Affiliates.

3.5 Lender/Equity Participant: shall mean any person or entity that lends or advance Funds, money, or other consideration to the Company or makes an investment in the Company in consideration of any equity securities, instruments convertible into or exercisable for equity securities, or assets of the Company during the term of this Agreement, whether or not The McLean Group has introduced the party to the Company or has made authorized representation to the person or entity on behalf of the Company.

3.6 Funds: shall mean the aggregate amount of money and other consideration that any Lender/Equity Participant or Buyer commits to lend to, invest with, and/or use for the acquisition of the Company, with terms and conditions acceptable to the Company.

3.7 Consummated Transaction: shall mean any consummated transaction in which a Lender/Equity Participant or a Buyer provides money or other consideration to the Company in exchange for ownership of all or a portion of the

(Continued)

EXHIBIT 13.1   *(Continued)*

assets or equity securities (including instruments convertible into or exercisable into equity securities) of the Company.

3.8 Transaction Value: shall include all Funds and shall mean an amount equal to the aggregate consideration delivered to the Company for all or any portion of the assets or equity securities (including instruments convertible into or exercisable into equity securities) of the Company, without regard to the form of such consideration, which consideration shall include, without limitation, all cash, promissory notes (whether made by Buyer or not), equity securities, instruments convertible into or exercisable for equity securities, assumed interest-bearing liabilities, accounts or notes receivable and other assets retained by Sellers or the Company, (but not earnouts, the fees attributable to which shall be paid as the earnout is collected), royalties, lease payments, and all deferred compensation payable to Sellers and other shareholders or employees of the Company for consulting services, noncompetition agreements and the like (except for salary, consulting, or commission compensation payable to such persons for services rendered as employees, consultants, or commission agents at rates not in excess of industry standards). If the equity securities (or instruments convertible into or exercisable for equity securities) of the Company are sold, exchanged, or otherwise transferred, or if the Company is a party to a merger or consolidation with or into a Buyer during the term of this Agreement, Transaction Value shall include an amount equal to the value of the aggregate consideration received by Sellers and the Company, and The McLean Group shall be entitled to compensation under this Agreement based on the Transaction Value as if the assets of the Company were sold. If any assets of Sellers or the Company are leased to the Buyer ("Leased Assets"), Transaction Value shall include, at the time of Closing, an amount equal to the present value, discounted at the prime rate of Citibank, N.A. in New York, at the time of Closing, of the aggregate sum of the lease payments over the full term of the lease, including any extensions, renewals, or replacements thereof. If any assets leased to the Buyer are purchased by the Buyer within sixty (60) months of closing, The McLean Group will be compensated under the same terms and conditions of this Agreement, except that credit shall be allowed for any Transaction Value and resultant fees previously paid pursuant to this paragraph for Leased Assets.

3.9 Offering Memorandum: A document that, for most engagements, is prepared to provide to prospective Buyers and/or Lender/Equity Participants. The document summarizes the Company's business and describes the offering. Although The McLean Group manages this effort and is responsible for finalizing the document, Company management is required to provide necessary information and, given their direct knowledge and experience with the Company's business, may need to write certain sections for the earlier drafts.

4. *Duties of The McLean Group.* The Company hereby appoints The McLean Group as its exclusive agent to represent the Company in an advisory capacity for the purpose of procuring Funds and/or selling the Company, and The McLean Group hereby accepts such appointment. Subject to the terms and conditions of this Agreement, The McLean Group shall advise the Company in connection with procuring Funds for the Company and/or selling the Company. The Company

EXHIBIT 13.1   *(Continued)*

agrees to reasonably cooperate and assist The McLean Group in providing information to the prospective Lenders/Equity Participants and/or Buyers as reasonably necessary or appropriate for the procurement of Funds or the sale of the Company. During the term of this Agreement, The McLean Group shall be available at reasonable times for consultations with the prospective Lenders/Equity Participants or Buyers or the Company in regards to this engagement.

5. *Term.* The term of this Agreement shall commence when the Agreement is signed by both parties and continue for one (1) year **after the day the Offering Memorandum is completed** and for automatic renewal terms of **ninety (90) days** provided that neither the Company nor The McLean Group has notified the other in writing of its intent to cancel this agreement thirty (30) days prior to the termination of the original term or any automatic renewal term hereunder.

6. *Fees.* The Company shall pay The McLean Group fees as follows:

6.1 Commitment Fee: A Commitment Fee payable with the execution of this agreement in the amount of **forty-five thousand dollars ($45,000).**

6.2 Transaction Fees. Transaction Fees as set forth in Section 8 of this Agreement upon the conclusion of a Consummated Transaction.

7. *Expenses.* In addition to the fees payable hereunder, the Company shall reimburse The McLean Group within thirty (30) business days of its request for any and all reasonable out-of-pocket expenses incurred in connection with the services performed by The McLean Group pursuant to this Agreement, including (i) reasonable hotel, meals, and associated expenses; (ii) reasonable charges for travel; and (iii) other reasonable expenses spent or incurred on the Company's behalf. Any single such expense in excess of $100 shall be preapproved by the Company.

8. *Transaction Fees for Consummated Transactions.* The Company hereby agrees to compensate The McLean Group as follows:

8.1 Sellers and Company, jointly and severally agree to pay to The McLean Group a Transaction Fee equal to the greater of **$250,000** (Minimum Transaction Fee) or a percentage of the Transaction Value of a Consummated Transaction as follows:

TRANSACTION VALUE	TRANSACTION FEE %
$2,000,000	6
$2,000,000	5
$2,000,000	4
$2,000,000	3
$8,000,000	

8.2 The Transaction Fee due The McLean Group, plus any unpaid expenses, shall be paid by the Company in cash, by wire transfer drawn on the account of the Buyer and/or Lender/Equity Participant, at the closing of the Consummated Transaction without regard to whether the Consummated Transaction involves payments in cash, in stock or in a combination of stock and cash, or is made on an installment sale basis.

8.3 In addition to the cash Transaction Fee, The McLean Group shall receive _____% of the Transaction Value in warrants to purchase Company stock for $.01 per share for a (10) ten-year period.

(Continued)

EXHIBIT 13.1   *(Continued)*

8.4 In the event that, for any reason, the Company shall fail to pay to The McLean Group all or any portion of the fees payable hereunder when due, interest shall accrue and be payable on the unpaid balance due hereunder from the date when first due through and including that date when actually collected by The McLean Group, at a rate equal to four (4) points over the prime rate of Citibank, N.A. in New York, NY, computed on a daily basis and adjusted as announced from time to time.

8.5 If, for any reason, the Company or Sellers terminate this Agreement prior to its expiration, other than for fraud, willful misconduct, or gross negligence by The McLean Group as determined by a court of competent jurisdiction, Sellers and Company agree to pay The McLean Group fifty percent (50%) of the Minimum Transaction Fee as written above. (USUALLY WAIVED)

8.6 Notwithstanding anything herein to the contrary, if the Company shall, within 18 months immediately following the termination of the original term or any renewal period of this Agreement, conclude a Consummated Transaction with any party introduced by The McLean Group or with whom The McLean Group had substantive communication (defined as the execution of a nondisclosure agreement and the receipt of an Offering Memorandum) in regard to the Company and the purpose described in this Agreement, during the term of the Agreement or any renewal period of this Agreement prior to termination, the Company shall pay The McLean Group the Transaction Fees determined herein.

8.7 Any definitive agreement describing a Transaction contemplated under this agreement and binding a Buyer or Equity/Lender Participant to consummate such transaction shall contain a written statement describing the fees payable to The McLean Group under this Agreement and the fact that such fees will be paid in cash, by wire transfer, from funds otherwise due the Company at closing.

9. *Authority.* The Company represents and warrants to The McLean Group that the engagement of The McLean Group hereunder has been duly authorized and approved by the board of directors of the Company, and this Agreement has been duly executed and delivered by the Company and constitutes a legal, valid and binding obligation of the Company.

10. *Display of the Company Logo.* The Company grants The McLean Group a nonexclusive, revocable right to use the Company's logo within The McLean Group Web site and/or on promotional materials for the purpose of announcing the engagement or any successful Consummated Transaction. The McLean Group may also use the Company logo to create a tombstone or other similar advertisement for the purpose of announcing the engagement or completion of a successful transaction. The McLean Group may not alter or modify the logo in any way beyond purposes of sizing. The Company reserves all rights in its logo and the associated message, images, trade names, trademarks, and all other related intellectual property rights.

11. *Use of Financial Advice by the Company.* The Company acknowledges that all opinions and advice (written or oral) given by The McLean Group to the Company in connection with the engagement of The McLean Group are intended solely for the benefit and use of the Company in considering the transaction to which they relate, and the Company agrees that no person or entity other than the

EXHIBIT 13.1   *(Continued)*

Company shall be entitled to make use of or rely upon the advice of The McLean Group to be given hereunder, and no such opinion or advice shall be used for any other purpose or reproduced, disseminated, quoted, or referred to at any time, in any manner or for any purpose, nor may the Company make any public references to The McLean Group, or use of The McLean Group's name in any annual reports or any other reports or releases of the Company without the prior written consent of The McLean Group.

12. *Securities Recommendations.* The Company acknowledges that The McLean Group makes no representations whatsoever as to making a market in the Company's securities or to recommending or advising its clients, or any other persons, to purchase the Company's securities. Research reports or corporate business reports that may be prepared by The McLean Group will, when and if prepared, be done solely on the merits or judgment and analysis of The McLean Group.

13. *Company Information and Confidentiality.* The Company recognizes and confirms that, in advising the Company and in fulfilling its engagement hereunder, The McLean Group will use and rely on data, material, and other information furnished to The McLean Group by the Company. The Company acknowledges and agrees that, in performing its services under this engagement, The McLean Group may rely upon the data, material, and other information supplied by the Company without independently verifying the accuracy, completeness, or veracity of same. In addition, in the performance of its services, The McLean Group may look to such others for such factual information, economic advice, and/or research upon which to base its advice to the Company hereunder as The McLean Group shall in good faith deem appropriate. Except as contemplated by the terms hereof or as required by applicable law, The McLean Group shall keep confidential all nonpublic information provided to it by the Company, and shall not disclose such information to any third party without the Company's prior consent, other than such of its employees and advisors as The McLean Group determines to have a need to know. The McLean Group will return or destroy all confidential information provided to it by the Company upon request.

14. *Indemnification.* The Company shall indemnify and hold harmless The McLean Group against any and all liabilities, claims, and lawsuits, including any and all awards and/or judgments to which it may become subject under the Securities Act of 1933 (the "Act"), the Securities Exchange Act of 1934 as amended (the "1934 Act") or any other federal or state statute, at common law or otherwise, insofar as said liabilities, claims, and lawsuits (including costs, expenses, awards, and/or judgments) arise out of or are in connection with the services rendered by The McLean Group or any transactions in connection with this Agreement, except for any liabilities, claims, and lawsuits (including awards and/or judgments), arising out of willful misconduct or willful omissions of The McLean Group. The Company also shall indemnify and hold harmless The McLean Group against any and all liabilities, claims, or lawsuits arising out of errors or omissions occurring as a result of The McLean Group's reliance on information and representations made by the Company. Finally, the Company shall indemnify and hold The McLean Group

(Continued)

EXHIBIT 13.1   *(Continued)*

harmless against any and all reasonable cost and expenses, including reasonable legal counsel fees and expenses, incurred relating to the foregoing.

The McLean Group shall give the Company prompt notice of any such liability, claim, or lawsuit which The McLean Group contends is the subject matter of the Company's indemnification and the Company thereupon shall be granted the right to take any and all necessary and proper action, at its sole cost and expense, with respect to such liability, claim, and lawsuit, including the right to settle, compromise, and dispose of such liability, claim, or lawsuit, excepting therefrom any and all proceedings or hearings before any regulatory bodies and/or authorities.

The McLean Group shall indemnify and hold the Company harmless against any and all liabilities, claims, and lawsuits, including any and all awards and/or judgments to which it may become subject under the Act, the 1934 Act, as amended or any other federal or state statute, at common law or otherwise, insofar as said liabilities, claims, and lawsuits (including costs, expenses, awards, and/or judgments) arise out of or are based upon services rendered by The McLean Group, except for any liabilities, claims, and lawsuits (including awards and/or judgments) arising out of errors or omissions occurring as a result of The McLean Group's reliance on information and representations made by the Company. In addition, The McLean Group shall indemnify and hold the Company and Seller harmless against any and all reasonable cost and expenses, including reasonable legal counsel fees and expenses, incurred relating to the foregoing.

The Company shall give The McLean Group prompt notice of any such liability, claim, or lawsuit which the Company contends is the subject matter of The McLean Group's indemnification and The McLean Group thereupon shall be granted the right to take any and all necessary and proper action, at its sole cost and expense, with respect to such liability, claim, or lawsuit, including the right to settle, compromise, or dispose of such liability, claim, or lawsuit, excepting there from any and all proceedings or hearings before any regulatory bodies and/or authorities.

15. *The McLean Group as an Independent Contractor.* The McLean Group shall perform its services hereunder as an independent contractor and not as an employee of the Company or an affiliate thereof. It is expressly understood and agreed to by the parties hereto that The McLean Group shall have no authority to act for, represent, or bind the Company or any affiliate thereof in any manner, except as may be agreed to expressly by the Company in writing from time to time.

16. *Entire Agreement.* This Agreement between the Company and The McLean Group constitutes the entire agreement and understanding of the parties hereto, and supersedes any and all previous agreements and understandings, whether oral or written, between the parties with respect to the matters set forth herein.

17. *Miscellaneous.*

17.1 Any notice or communication permitted or required hereunder shall be in writing and shall be deemed sufficiently given if hand-delivered or sent by facsimile and postage prepaid by certified or registered mail, return-receipt-requested, to the respective parties as set forth below, or to such other address as either party may notify the other in writing.

EXHIBIT 13.1   *(Continued)*

If to the Company: ———————————

If to The McLean Group: **Partner Name**
                                     The McLean Group, LLC
                                     1660 International Drive
                                     Suite 450
                                     McLean, VA 22102

17.2 In the event that any provision of this Agreement shall be held to be invalid, that same shall not in any respect whatsoever affect the validity of the remainder of this Agreement.

17.3 This Agreement shall be construed and enforced under the laws of the Commonwealth of Virginia, without reference to its choice of law provisions. The parties agree that any action brought by any party against another party in connection with any rights or obligations arising out of this Agreement shall be instituted in a proper federal or state court of competent jurisdiction with jurisdiction only in the Commonwealth of Virginia. A party to this Agreement named as a defendant in any action brought in connection with this Agreement in any court outside of the Commonwealth of Virginia shall have the right to have the case dismissed, requiring the other party to refile such action in a proper court in the Commonwealth of Virginia.

17.4 If it becomes necessary for any party to this Agreement to institute litigation to enforce or construe any of its terms, then the prevailing party in such action shall be entitled to recover an award of reasonable attorney's fees. Any aggrieved party may proceed to enforce its rights in the appropriate action at law or in equity.

17.5 The parties hereto covenant and agree that they will execute each such other and further instruments and documents as are or may be reasonably necessary or convenient to effectuate and carry out the purpose of this Agreement.

17.6 This Agreement shall be binding upon and inure to the benefit of each of the parties hereto and his or her respective successors, legal representatives, and assigns.

17.7 This Agreement may be executed in any number of counterparts, each of which together shall constitute one of the same original documents.

17.8 No provision of this Agreement may be amended, modified, or waived, except in writing signed by all of the parties hereto.

           *   *   *   *

This Agreement has been duly authorized, executed, and delivered by and on behalf of the Company and The McLean Group.

IN WITNESS WHEREOF, the parties hereto, upon proper corporate authority, have caused this Agreement to be duly executed, as of the day, month, and year first above written.

THE McLean GROUP, LLC   **COMPANY NAME**

By: —————————————————   By: —————————————————

PRINCIPAL NAME   **NAME**
Principal   **TITLE**

Date: ———————————————   Date: ———————————————

Notes

1. Once again, I am indebted to Richard Restak's *The Naked Brain* (Harmony Books, 2006). The whole book is an incredible read about the way we think.
2. Most experienced Middle Market investment bankers would argue that very small deals often involve more work proportionally. Smaller deals also tend to be harder to do, because they are less attractive and to fewer potential buyers. Furthermore, the parties involved—both sellers and prospective buyers—often are less sophisticated and less experienced with mergers and acquisitions. As a result, they tend to require a great deal more education and hand-holding along the way, often making them considerably more difficult and time-intensive where investment bankers are concerned.
3. "Adequate" in this context is from the sales-side point of view, as it defines the convention, meaning what a buyer is entitled to but not necessarily what he needs. The buyer will compute needed working capital, especially where a lot of future growth is contemplated, in his own private and subjective calculations, usually in some form of a discounted cash flow analysis. But if this is a calculation of additional working capital needed to expand as opposed to maintain the business then this working capital conventionally would come from the buyer and not the seller.
4. A discouraging outcome, especially for new investment bankers, of a client's innocent unawareness of the sometimes herculean efforts to add millions of dollars to his transaction value is that the client will be very quick on occasion to quarrel about some other amount of transaction value that is relatively minor while unwittingly ignoring the free transaction value his banker has extracted for him.
5. Often, this reluctance is associated with the client's confidentiality concerns which, while understandable, usually tend to be exaggerated. (See Chapter 8).
6. Subsequent rounds of capital raises are usually characterized, starting with the initial round as "A," "B," "C," etc.

CHAPTER 14

Investment Banking Representation on the Buy Side

Some Further Thoughts for Buyers

If you see a snake, just kill it—don't appoint a committee on snakes.

Ross Perot

Bethesda, MD—June 1990

Having rather abruptly arrived without a prior appointment, Steve sat himself in my office and told me (more accurately, he insisted) that he will know a good acquisition target when he sees one. Yet he had been pretty vague thus far when I asked him to describe for me what he thought his ideal acquisition would look like—and how it would fit into his company and his strategic plans. Steve's been all over the waterfront, in fact, on this point. This is not to suggest that Steve was operating totally in the blind. He knew his own fairly large Middle Market business as well as the back of his hand—and he knew the industry in which it flourished equally well.

Steve doubtless would recognize a perfect fit when he saw one, or when one was presented to him. There lies the rub. There really are no perfect fits out there, even though there are a lot of close but "imperfect fits" that come pretty close to the mark. Did Steve understand that? I was not so sure. And if Steve did not understand that point, it is even less likely that he would accept the fact that imperfect acquisition fits are one rule to which there are virtually no exceptions.

Steve then suggested that if I could not generate a sales-side fee from parties I introduced to him, he might *pay me a buy-side fee.*

165

Hmmm, he "might." Hmmm, again . . . I wonder how many prospective customers have told Steve they "might" pay him for the goods and services his firm would provide them—if he could not find someone else to pay for them instead. I wonder how many times—or how seldom—Steve has accepted such proposals? I strongly suspect I know the answer. Here, in my offices—where real clients pay the rent, my employees' salaries, our database expenses and so forth—Steve did not inspire me much to seek out his "perfect" acquisition. Nor did he appear to have considered paying a suitable retainer to cover the substantial up-front work required to plan and execute a buy-side engagement, as in this case: serious strategic planning to define a target, identifying and researching candidates and their potential fit, and addressing financing and integration issues, among many other considerations.

So I gave Steve my standard short-form lecture, attempting to be polite and politic at the same time:

"In fact, all our clients agree, up front, to pay us our success fee (at least if we go on to negotiate and execute the transaction), but at a minimum to provide us with a reasonable monthly engagement retainer up to that point. I thank you for your interest, but so much time and effort would be involved simply in identifying and researching suitable acquisition candidates for you that we could not undertake this assignment without a retainer and a success fee when an acquisition was closed. Thank you very much for stopping by."

Steve appeared altogether unfazed by my remarks as he stood up and headed for the door. Turning back before disappearing, he suggested, "Well, at least let me know if you come across anything that you think I might be interested in."

"You have a deal, Steve," I said with a polite wink, without mentioning that if could, I would present any such candidate to another two dozen or so would-be buyers with whom he would have to compete.

The Buy Side

This book focuses primarily on the sales side of Middle Market mergers and acquisitions (M&A) transactions for two reasons: 1) space limitations make it difficult enough to address the sales side alone in a book (heck, maybe a buy-side sequel down the road could finish off the subject), and 2) most Middle Market M&A advisory work is undertaken for sales-side clients, because most buyers are large enough to have in-house M&A and corporate development staffs to identify acquisition candidates and to pursue and close transactions. Even so, most investment bankers do some buy-side work, which involves its own unique set of challenges and considerations, some of which I will address here. And if sellers and new bankers gain an understanding of some of the buy-side point of view, it can only help them better prepare themselves and their companies for sale, and all that the sale involves.

Buy- versus Sales-Side Representation

Representing the buy side is frankly more problematic than the sales side. On the sales side, a banker is representing something other people want (always an advantage), whereas when I represent the buy side, I am trying to acquire something some else owns and perhaps others are also interested in acquiring . . . not quite as good a negotiating position, obviously. On the other hand a sales-side client, a serious prospective seller, sooner or later, will usually sell to someone. He cannot take the company with him, and over the course of a negotiated auction (however extended), at least one prospective buyer is likely to make an offer the seller is loathe to refuse or at least is reluctantly willing to accept as he or she gradually faces the reality of the marketplace.

As a buy-side client, a prospective buyer, on the other hand, need not buy at all. Ever! He or she may be quite willing to drop a line and hook (the investment banker often playing the role of the fishing tackle) in the water while refusing to seriously bait the hook. A prospective buyer may even reverse course in the middle of the engagement (it has happened to me several times) and decide to sell before he buys, if another buyer approaches him with an attractive offer.

Investment bankers representing sales-side clients know that if they do their homework and collaborate with clients in the identification of prospective buyers, someone in the pool of prospective buyers will likely make an offer. Additionally, if the auction is well run, the seller will have the luxury of several competing bidders. On the other hand, buy-side parties usually focus all their efforts on one would-be seller (one at a time anyway). They most likely will walk away from the deal if a negotiated auction drives the seller's value above the investment value to the buyer—and/or beyond the terms—they are willing to pay. And of course they should walk.

So buy-side representations arguably involve more risk at least where Middle Market investment bankers are concerned. Of course the real risk is the likelihood that the investment banker will drill a dry hole, identifying acquisition candidates for which the buyer is unwilling to pay sufficient or reasonable consideration to close a deal. As I said, the odds against succeeding are far more daunting on the buy side than on the sales side.

Put slightly differently, an investment banker representing a buy-side client is likely to do a great deal of work identifying, valuing, and approaching a potential—but not necessarily committed to this particular transaction—seller. Once approached, that potential seller very likely will (and should) consult with his own investment bank to evaluate the offer. This, in turn, may well lead to the potential seller's acquiescence to initiating a negotiated auction engagement in which the buy-side firm finds itself competing among, say, ten prospective buyers. By that point, as one of ten buyers, the buy-side client and his Middle Market investment banker face a 10% chance of success, all other things being equal.

Buy-Side Fees

Given the inherently greater risk on behalf of buy-side clients, the fees that bankers charge for such representations tend to be structured differently than sales-side fees, despite the fact that both transaction types ordinarily involve a retainer and often a success fee. In cases where the investment banker is not only engaged to locate targets and to value or evaluate them (preliminarily perhaps) for the client, but also to negotiate and execute the transaction and even perhaps to find financing for it, there will be a success fee.

For starters, buy-side retainers usually are paid monthly, whereas sales-side retainers typically, but not always, consist of a one-time lump sum. Buy-side retainers typically range between $7,500 and $30,000 a month for a minimum of four to six months. Buy-side retainers usually are not creditable against a success fee (although some Middle Market investment bankers may chose to credit them if the success fee itself is large enough). In addition, buy-side success fees may vary widely. They need not reflect, Double Lehman–type fee structures and other variations described in this book (see Chapter 13). They may or may not, depending on circumstances mainly pertaining to the amount of work involved, tend to be as low as approximately two-thirds the size of Middle Market investment bankers' sales-side fees in recognition of the larger monthly retainer and especially if the retainer is not credited towards the success fee.

Another approach to buy-side success fees is to not base the success fee on transaction value. Basing the investment banker's fee on transaction value can be an obvious and inherent conflict of interest, given that the banker's role is to logically reduce his or her client's purchase price to the extent possible. When the success fee is based on transaction value, the clients actually *pay more* to the banker for the higher purchase price. A sensible alternative may be to base the success fee on "revenues acquired"—of course, at a substantially lower rate than if based on transaction value—which is a rule about 50% to 60% of the revenues of the acquired company.

But again, there is no one size fits all.

It's All in the Planning

You will recall from an anecdote earlier in this book (Chapter 10) that too many cooks in the kitchen make a mess out of the meal. Public companies, especially very large ones, tend towards this error. Having 50 people in a firm constitute the buy-side committee, at least the working committee, usually leads to no results or at least to results that are so compromised as to be ineffective. Rule number one if a buyer needs to have a committee, keep it small. Ross Perot had it right in the quote above, leading this chapter.

Buy-side engagements do require substantial up-front planning. An old saw goes: "prior planning prevents poor performance." In a similar vein, when you take the wrong stance when approaching a golf shot, and you are not lining up with the target, it will not matter a damn bit how well you swing the club; the ball will likely be heading somewhere other than where you intended. Buy-side up-front planning at the very least should address the following issues:

- The buyer's primary objectives in making acquisitions (see Exhibit 14.1), potentially including:
  - Attaining or maintaining a geographical advantage
  - Expanding or enhancing existing product and/or service offerings
  - Entering into new or related product and/or service offerings

EXHIBIT 14.1   Synergies—Survey of Desired versus Achieved

	Sought	Actually Achieved
Access to new markets	76%	74%
Growth in market share	74%	60%
Access to new products	54%	72%
Access to talent	47%	51%
Enhanced reputation	46%	48%
Reduction in operating expenses	46%	39%
Access to distribution channels	38%	60%
Access to new technologies	26%	63%
Reduction in number of competitors	26%	80%
Access to new brands	25%	92%

Source: PWC

- Reducing manufacturing, distribution, or other costs
- Generating additional distribution channels
- Gaining new clients or customers
- Realizing staffing improvements by gaining new professional and/or technical staff
- Eliminating, or at least neutralizing, competition (to the extent that is an objective)
- A rigorous buyer's self-analysis, including an assessment of the buyer's corporate culture, to determine what target company types would be most consistent with the buyer and which would be most likely candidates for successful postacquisition integrations.
- The manner in which the acquisition will be integrated:
  - Allowing target to remain intact and under current management
  - Integrating the target rapidly and thoroughly into the buyer's operation
  - Integrating the target gradually into the buyer's operation
- A comprehensive analysis of the buyer's financial war chest, vis-à-vis alternative acquisition candidates; does the buyer have access to:
  - Sufficient cash to consummate the deal(s) being contemplated
  - Other available financial resources
  - What the buyer can afford in the way of targets (e.g., by revenue size or similar considerations), based on the totality of available financial resources
- A financial model and action plan created by the banker or the buyer (typically after the target(s) has been indentified) that:
  - Incorporates a well-analyzed financial/integration plan that brings structure and discipline to the review of prospective target acquisitions
  - Estimates postintegration growth rate expectations, assuming the buyer's acquisition strategy is well-executed
  - Deals specifically with postintegration earnings and dilution arising in the case of public companies
  - Creates an initial target list while conducting sufficient research on each target to allow the buyer and his Middle Market investment banker to assess the target's suitability and overall "fit" as an acquisition candidate
  - Establishes a buy-side team whose members have specifically-identified and assigned tasks divided among operations management, M&A deal management, and legal management

Only after all of the above has been completed should the execution phase of the buy-side engagement be initiated. The tasks outlined above represent a very significant investment in the process—and the prospective success—of a buy-side M&A undertaking. When undertaken professionally and thoroughly, the likelihood that a suitable acquisition candidate will be identified should increase dramatically.

But homework alone will not close the deal: Even so, a prospective buy-side acquirer who is committed to closing an acquisition and who has done his homework may well approach the target with an offering price sufficiently close to the prospective seller's own hoped-for price that the seller might do the deal without pursuing a negotiated auction.

A *major warning* to buyers is that even when the calculation of their offering price is a generous and accurate one, the LOI is not the place to get cute with vagaries or one-sided stipulations. That is the way to lose the deal as the seller's investment banker will likely seize these issues as further justification for going out to auction. Buyers should offer what they truly believe the target is worth (or very, very close to it) and in a straightforward manner.

How Many Targets at One Time?

Oddly enough, many highly experienced Middle Market investment bankers have observed that the more successful the buy-side investment banker is in identifying and introducing potential acquisition candidates targets, the less likely the prospective buyer he represents will be to make a decision. This observation may have its corollary in the poorly thought out and therefore merely casual "I will know it when I see it" fallacy: too many targets very likely will lull prospective buyers into a false sense that a perfect acquisition candidate eventually will materialize. Middle Market investment bankers representing buy-side clients can confront this issue in three ways:

1. As I have already said, conduct thorough, up-front planning to ensure that investment banker and buy-side client are "on the same page."
2. As a corollary to number one, introduce only the most suitable and the most likely acquisition candidates to the buy-side client.
3. Consider slowing the rate of acquisition target introductions to no more than two or so per month over the course of four to six months, to ensure that the buy-side client can be provided, and perform, an in-depth analysis of each target in turn.

The Platform Philosophy versus the Financial Approach to Acquisitions

A number of public companies over time have won negotiated auctions in which they participated with great consistency. Were they paying too much? Not at all! They in fact were trading on excellent track records as operating companies with exemplary stock market performances to boot. Such buyers as these pursue a platform philosophy or approach while other buyers who consistently lose negotiated auctions tend to employ a financial approach. Platform approach buyers approach prospective acquisitions with a view to buying the *future results* from the acquisition of the acquired entity, properly merged and properly exploited. To that end, the platform approach buyer conducts substantial research and analysis up front to estimate the additional synergies and financial outcomes to be realized. Such buyers then engage their in-house M&A personnel to negotiate and execute the transactions while allowing appropriate operating division executives to champion the deal.

Financial approach buyers, who never seem to win the day (or as frequently tend to overpay), tend to focus on what the company is worth in the immediate moment, on a stand-alone basis, without thinking sufficiently of its postacquisition future within the acquiring firm. Unfortunately for them, as the investment value of the acquisition candidate rises over the course of the negotiated auction, financial approach buyers either are outbid or withdraw from the auction because they have focused upon the company's current value rather than its future value as part of the acquiring enterprise. Or even worse, since they have not done the real homework (sure, there is often lots of busy work) connecting and maximizing future opportunities realistically to the present, they can just as easily be led to overpay in the auction process. Preparation and information rule. Financial approach buyers, who cannot see the acquisition candidate as a platform on which to build the merged enterprise, would do well not to even involve themselves in the negotiated auction, as they are most unlikely to prevail one way or the other.

You would think that the above contrast between a platform and a financial approach should seem obvious and elementary, but in practice it is not, as any sales-side banker can testify from having observed certain buyers who just do not get it, time after time, and wonder why their acquisition programs are so unsuccessful.

Who on the Buy Side Should Negotiate?

Buy-side clients' division executives, while they should be deal champions and identifiers of synergies and opportunities should not usually be allowed to directly *negotiate* an acquisition. In-house M&A staff or the buy-side client's investment banker should undertake the negotiations, both on the basis of their substantial experience and because they are more likely to remain highly disciplined as acquisition terms are hammered out. Ideally, in the best acquisitions, there is always a strong dialectic, a healthily stressful one, going on between the visionaries (division executives or deal champions) and the bean counters and the negotiators (M&A staff). This type of dialectic, if not too biased toward one side or the other (the bean counters versus the visionaries), is a reasonable approach to the platform philosophy.

Orchestration (or Art) versus Science

Sales-side investment banking tends to be 50% orchestration (art) and 50% science (valuation, structuring, negotiations, etc.). Buy-side investment banking tends to be 90% science and 10% orchestration (art).

Buy-side valuation science (the 90%) is not meant to develop fair market value, though. In buy-side M&A transactions, the valuations of an acquisition candidate may vary widely according to each prospective buyer's own unique purposes in closing the deal and are almost universally based on Discounted Cash Flow Analysis (see Chapter 24). By definition, the wide variations in valuations established by prospective buyers reflect their very subjective nature. Subjective valuation involves the modeling of a price range, as opposed to a specific price point, that makes sense to the prospective buyer. As I said this range generally is estimated based upon a discounted cash flow (DCF) model, one that takes into consideration the present value of all future cash flows to be realized from the acquisition, including the target's current cash flows plus future cash flows from postacquisition growth and synergies.

However, objective value (recent similar deals in the market place) clearly offers a point of reference that is worth some consideration. Buy-side investment bankers and their clients should rest assured that sellers and their investment bankers will be highly conversant in objective comparable transaction value and its influence on their own companies' values. Objective valuation data may serve as a wake-up call to prospective buyers whose own unique valuations are either too stingy or too rich alongside those of their counterparts.

The issue of "too rich," though, needs to be carefully considered and not assumed if it is not reflected in the buyer's own DCF analysis. If it works for that buyer, "too rich" is an irrelevancy and may simply be a reflection of a platform philosophy pursued well. If the valuation is too stingy when compared to comparable transactions, it should also cause buyers to rethink their valuations to ensure they did not overlook something. No buy-side M&A client ever pays an exact "objective comparable transaction value" for an acquisition candidate. But very few ever will ignore such data while conducting their research. Even when companies similar to a prospective acquisition target are selling at a multiple of six times trailing EBITDA, a buy-side client may run the target's financials through his discounted cash flow model and conclude that a five times trailing EBITDA multiple reflects an entirely appropriate offering price. But if the buyer hopes to compete in a negotiated auction, his offer of five times trailing EBITDA will offer him little prospect of success. As a result, to justify a six times trailing EBITDA offer—or higher—the buyer necessarily will reconsider such potential synergies as economies of scale, cost cutting, and so forth, as illustrated in this chapter. Even though the buyer may prefer not to pay for prospective synergies that he may feel should be his, but this is a dangerous approach. The buyer who intends to win a negotiated auction must bring to the table a competitive offer, and this may be one way to justify it, that is by a willingness to pay for synergies that he feels he brings to the table. After all is it really important, where these synergies come from, if the deal makes good sense?

Who Does the Investment Banker Represent? Possible Conflicts of Interest in Buy-Side Representation

As I have said more than once, for most seasoned M&A practitioners, sales-side representations constitute 75% of their business and buy-side work 25%. But Middle Market sales-side investment bankers do represent buy-side clients frequently. Occasionally, a sales-side investment banker will find himself involved in an engagement in which two of his clients—one from the sales side, the other from the buy side—are interested in closing a deal between themselves. As a rule, it would be an obvious conflict of interest for an investment banker simultaneously to represent both the seller and the buyer in an M&A transaction. The investment banker necessarily should recluse himself from one side of the deal or the other.

This is painful, especially with investment bankers who believe that they forthrightly can negotiate an equitable transaction between the two parties. But any investment bankers proceeding with the representation of both clients put themselves at great risk. A seller or the buyer may emerge from a transaction believing himself to have been ill-served by his investment banker. If the investment banker has represented both sides under such circumstances, litigation could possibly result. In short: Representing both parties to a single M&A transaction is a lose/lose proposition to the Middle Market investment banker.

Which client should a Middle Market investment banker represent when both seller and buyer have been his clients in the past? The investment banker may choose to represent the party who has been his client for the longest period of time or the party with whom he has enjoyed the most rewarding business relationship (on any number of levels) tact is called for in making—and in communicating—the investment banker's ultimate decision as to whom he prefers to represent. It is also critically important to secure well-documented releases from the client he will not represent, as he may have come into possession of information regarding that client that would not otherwise not be available except for the confidential relationship they have had. In some cases, it is possible that a banker faced with such a situation will have to relinquish both clients for that particular negotiation.

It is not unheard of for Middle Market investment bankers to be paid as "mediators" when both sides are agreeable and both sides clearly understand the investment banker's role as mediator. In such cases, after securing the necessary written agreements with both parties, the Middle Market investment banker's fees should be paid by both parties for obvious reasons.

Finally, even where a Middle Market investment banker declines to represent one party to an M&A transaction in favor of representing the other, the first party might propose that the investment banker assign a colleague from his or her own firm to represent the first party in the transaction. This option has been suggested to me several times over the years, but it is highly problematic: Putting an investment banker and another of his investment banking colleagues from his firm on the other side of an M&A engagement would still raise serious conflicts of interest questions and should be avoided. A second fee (or any fee) is never worth that kind of long-term risk.

Chapter Highlights

- Sales-side representations generally are more easily consummated than buy-side engagements.
- Buy-side investment banking fees tend to be weighted toward larger monthly retainers and possibly additional success fees, in cases where the banker is expected and engaged to also negotiate and execute the transaction; this reflects the fact that buy-side representations are somewhat more akin to consulting assignments than are sales-side engagements, and unfortunately less likely of consummation.
- Buy-side engagements should be initiated with comprehensive strategic planning to identify the types of acquisition candidates that are most suitable based on fit, culture, likely ease of integration, available financial (and financing) resources, and so forth.
- Buy-side investment bankers (ironically) should limit the number or at least the frequency of suitable targets they present to ensure that the buy-side client has sufficient time to properly evaluate each opportunity as it is presented.
- Successful buy-side clients tend to use a platform philosophy in tandem with creative deal making when seeking to acquire a company in highly competitive Middle Market negotiated auctions.
- Buy-side deal executions tend to be more scientific than their sales-side counterparts, involving discounted cash flow and similar methodologies

in the calculation of their subjective investment value; on the sales-side, by contrast, deal executions are much more dependent upon the orchestration of the negotiated auction and with reference to comparable or similar transactions.

- The two aspects of subjective buy-side valuations, which together may be used to establish a bidding range and a walk-away price for the transaction, are:
  - The target's stand-alone value (objective or comparable transaction value)
  - The target's stand-alone value plus the estimated value of prospective synergies that may or may not be realized (subjective or investment value)
- On the buy-side:
  - Division executives or operations people should champion the deal.
  - Corporate development or M&A personnel or outside professionals should negotiate the deal.
  - Both groups should collaborate closely as a team while respecting their separate roles within the team.
  - The buy side group teams need to be sufficiently small to be effective.
- A Middle Market investment banker should not (except perhaps as a mediator) represent both sides of a transaction, even where both parties agree to such an arrangement.

CHAPTER **15**

The Letter of Intent: The Most Critical Document?

I t would seem counterintuitive that serious parties would spend months negotiating a Middle Market acquisition only to conclude by executing an agreement that is not really that much of an agreement, at least in a legal sense but more of a menu that will list the main ingredients for getting to the ultimate goal line which is the Definitive (Closing) Agreement. All that the usual Letter of Intent (LOI) does legally is to bind the seller and the buyer by virtue of a few significant but essentially peripheral clauses (exclusivity and confidentiality). Yet executing an LOI constitutes a critical juncture in the merger and acquisition (M&A) process. In fact, I will go out on a limb by flatly stating that it is the *single most important document* in an M&A transaction, because if it is not done right, nothing else will matter.

So why is a LOI for the most part nonbinding? A seller pursued by several prospective buyers simply cannot afford the distraction, time, and expense involved in having multiple prospective buyers simultaneously reviewing seller documents while performing all the audits and reviews required in the course of confirmatory or final due diligence. Furthermore, neither the Middle Market seller nor the eventual buyer gain anything whatsoever by providing several failed suitors such extraordinary access to the seller's most confidential business information. Not surprisingly then, it is usually in the best interests of the seller to allow only one prospective buyer to proceed to the point where the buyer is entitled to conduct confirmatory due diligence in furtherance of a likely acquisition.

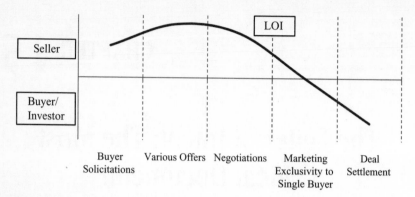

EXHIBIT 15.1 Do Not Hide Problems/Issues: Letters of Intent Are Not Invitations to Further Negotiations

Content and Precedents of a Good Letter of Intent

The fact that LOIs are nonbinding gives rise to three very serious considerations on the seller's part:

1. The need for thoroughness of the business terms
2. The need for disclosure of any weaknesses during the preliminary due diligence period and prior to confirmatory due diligence
3. The critical importance of accuracy of the data or premises on which the preliminary due diligence and LOI are based

The Buyer/Seller Advantage Curve

A seller should make sure he or she understands and agrees with all of the LOI terms before signing it. In the absence of serious changes in the context of a deal, attempts to change LOI terms after signing reflect poorly on the seller's business acumen and integrity. This is equally true for buyers, I might add.

But especially in the sellers case his failure to give proper attention or care to LOI content and/or precedents can be disastrous. Prior to the executing the LOI, especially in an effective, negotiated auction that is going well, the seller has most of the advantage. The buyer wants the business and knows he must compete with other buyers to win it, while the seller, sometimes with multiple offers in hand, is confident and in command of the high ground in the negotiations at that point. The balance of power changes dramatically as soon as the seller grants a single buyer exclusivity, during which for 60 days or so, the seller and his representatives agree not to talk to other buyers. That effectively takes the business off the market. While the affirmative response clause discussed later in this chapter can mitigate this to some extent, other prospective buyers may turn their attention elsewhere and never look back. Should it come to that, seeking to re-ignite the interest of former prospective buyers in the seller's company may prove difficult to impossible or at the very least problematic when those former buyer prospects learn the seller's post-LOI negotiations with his chosen buyer have collapsed. In short, as soon as the LOI has been executed, the advantage shifts to the buyer, because the seller has more at risk should the deal collapse. Should the buyer walk away, the seller essentially must start over.

Preliminary versus Confirmatory Due Diligence

Preliminary due diligence begins as soon as a single buyer accepts a series of seller stipulations and/or premises as the basis for formalizing a business deal in the LOI. For the most part, these stipulations and premises are contained in the Offering Memorandum (see Chapter 7) and supplemental information provided to the buyer by the seller and his investment bankers. Preliminary due diligence precedes the prospective buyer's preparation of a final *business terms* offer—the LOI.

Having executed his LOI, the buyer proceeds to complete final or confirmatory due diligence (often conducted in an electronic due diligence room, a Web site of sorts) to establish that in fact all of the seller's representations are true and accurate. As thorough—and as representative of preliminary due diligence—as the properly executed LOI may be, it is not usually, except as noted, binding until confirmatory due diligence has been completed to the buyer's satisfaction and the final purchase agreement is executed.

Exclusivity, Confidentiality, and the Letter of Intent

While the LOI is nonbinding as to substantive deal terms, it usually is binding—and quite necessarily so—in two critical respects: confidentiality and exclusivity (the latter also being known as the nonmarketing or no shop clause). The agreement to respect the seller's confidentiality, as initially established in the nondisclosure agreement or NDA (see Chapter 8) typically is reaffirmed and possibly expanded upon in the LOI. It remains legally binding for obvious reasons.

The seller, in turn, agrees to an exclusivity or nonmarketing or no shop clause to protect the buyer's interests during the confirmatory due diligence period (he is spending a lot of money and time at this stage), during which period definitive purchase agreements are also being prepared and negotiated simultaneously.

As a rule, and without being overly rigid, sellers and their investment bankers should decline exclusivity periods exceeding 60 days. Once an LOI has been signed, there is usually no good reason why confirmatory due diligence and the preparation of definitive sales agreements cannot be completed within that time frame. Longer exclusivity periods will serve only to encourage foot-dragging and potentially endless haggling over legal points in final negotiations. Longer exclusivity periods also may needlessly subject the seller to risks of a business turndown that could materially reduce his company's selling price. The LOI should make very clear the exact duration of exclusivity, the date when exclusivity expires, and the fact that exclusivity may be renewed only with the seller's express written consent.

Affirmative Response Clauses

Since the late 1990s, I have started to regularly insert affirmative response clauses on behalf of sales-side clients into LOIs submitted by prospective buyers. I have since noticed a few other bankers doing the same thing. The affirmative response clause was designed to allow a seller to, in effect, preemptively terminate the exclusivity period if he suspects that the buyer is preparing to materially change deal terms agreed to in the LOI.

Some investment bankers might prefer to insist on an affirmative response clause only if they have reason to believe they are dealing with a buyer likely to agree to terms solely to take the seller's company off the market before proceeding to change the deal terms without justification, especially at the last minute. The nature of negotiations preceding the LOI may sometimes provide the seller and his investment banker with a gut sense that they are dealing with just such a buyer. A buyer who constantly and unilaterally changes terms already agreed to while the LOI negotiations are taking place, may also take unfair advantage of seller exclusivity. It is very difficult to discern buyer characteristics and/or behaviors suggestive of such bad faith negotiations once the exclusivity period has begun, because the seller and his representatives will not necessarily receive daily reports on changes in the buyer's thinking. The affirmative response tactic can help here a lot.

Insisting on an affirmative response clause not only gives sellers a possible out before the exclusivity period expires but to some degree also places the buyer on notice that bad-faith behaviors will not be tolerated. Here as elsewhere, in the crafting of LOIs, the slightest wordsmithing nuances in an otherwise nonbinding document may have a significant impact on the end result. Investment bankers may also find it especially advantageous to invoke the affirmative response clause when they have a buyer in the wings offering a fall-back deal nearly as or even more attractive as the one already on the table, should the current deal collapse. Under such circumstances, it enables the seller and his investment banker to minimize the risk of losing the second buyer by preemptively ending exclusivity when evident bad-faith buyer behaviors justify so doing.

In my experience, most buyers and the attorneys representing them accept the clause as a part of the LOI, at least eventually, when it is explained. It in no way changes the essentially nonbinding nature of LOIs. Furthermore, buyers or attorney representatives who protest too vociferously may serve only to raise serious questions as to their own sincerity.

Affirmative response clauses may be written in a manner similar to this:

> *Without changing the fact that this Letter of Intent will be, except as otherwise provided herein, nonbinding on the parties, the seller reserves the right to request on one/two/three, etc., occasions during the exclusivity period a written affirmative response from (the buyer) stating that (the buyer) contemplates no material changes in the deal terms outlined in this Letter of Intent. Buyer's failure to so respond will automatically terminate the exclusivity provisions of this Letter of Intent.*

While the LOI itself is nonbinding, a lawyer likely would be required to determine whether or not a buyer's violation of the affirmative response clause had given rise to damages to the seller, if the seller claimed damages. But most sellers and their investment bankers should find this entirely satisfactory, because affirmative response clauses primarily serve to avoid bad faith behaviors by threatening an "early out" to exclusivity, which itself will tend to minimize the risk of damages to the seller. And it tends to keep the buyer on track.

Weaknesses and Opportunities—Disclosure and Accuracy of Preliminary Due-Diligence Data

Sellers should disclose company weaknesses as soon as possible while they can do so on their own terms. As I mentioned in Chapter 7, typically this is done in the Offering Memorandum. Failing to do so makes it all but inevitable that those weaknesses will be exploited when they are later discovered in confirmatory due diligence. When prospective buyers believe they have discovered material undisclosed or inadequately disclosed business weaknesses during post-LOI confirmatory due diligence, the consequences to the seller and the deal invariably prove difficult. I often use this as kidding example that I do believe, if somewhat trite, sufficiently illustrates the way to change a weakness into an opportunity:

> *You know the chief technology officer in our technology company is 82 years old. Yep, think what we could do with this company if you hire your 26-year-old techie nephew.*

The point being made is that when an otherwise good company has one or more weaknesses, they can usually equally be portrayed as opportunities that have not been exploited thus far, for one reason or another. At least the seller is seizing the agenda and dealing with these on his own terms and early in the process. It makes a big difference.

The "Honey, I Did the Deal" Rule . . . Thoroughness of Business Terms

The importance of executing LOIs that absolutely and thoroughly address all relevant business terms cannot be overstated. The LOI should not be an *invitation to further negotiation* of issues it does not explicitly or thoroughly cover. Rather, it should be the culmination of the business terms negotiation, leaving no additional important business terms unnegotiated. While final definitive sales agreements invariably involve some negotiations between the attorneys for the seller and the buyer, these should as far as possible be restricted to legal issues.

Let's repeat that once more for effect:

> *All negotiations of significant business terms must, must,* must *be completed in advance of the LOI and documented fully and unequivocally within it in advance of the LOI's execution.*

Buyers, public company buyers, in particular, often view the LOIs they issue and then execute as little more than an invitation to themselves (should the seller be so foolish as to agree to their terms) to "hop in and kick the tires" via a thorough-going confirmatory due diligence. Their LOIs often will suggest ranges of purchase prices the public company buyers would be willing to pay, "depending" on what they "discover in due diligence or further examination." Once such LOIs are executed and confirmatory due diligence has begun, sellers realize all but immediately at which end of the price range the buyers' final offers inevitably will fall. The lower end . . . always!

The "loosey-goosey" LOIs preferred by many buyers—and agreed to by sellers at their extreme peril—offer myriad avenues of attack by the buyer, post LOI. Balance sheet adequacy in various modes (when targets or clear formulas for establishing targets are not defined in the LOI) is attacked routinely. These formulas and targets should be agreed upon in pre-LOI negotiations and memorialized in the LOI.

Buyers may also insist that "Sellers transitional or ongoing employment compensation and its major terms will be established during due diligence." These and other issues proposed by many buyers as a rules should not be allowed to be negotiated after an LOI has been executed. One way to deal with the employment or similar important "but not quite so important" issues is to shorten the 60-day post-LOI period as it deals with these or similar specific issues, for example:

> *Seller's employment compensation and major terms pertaining thereto will be established during due diligence but no later than (fill in the desired number of days) days from the execution of this Letter of Intent.*

Any type of LOI, in any form, that allows any prospective buyer such postexecution latitude in revisiting and renegotiating business terms must be avoided at all costs and whenever possible, even when the seller has few prospective buyers on the horizon. Only under the most difficult of circumstances—the availability of virtually no other prospective buyers, or the seriously weakened and/or deteriorating circumstances of a seller's company, for example—should such LOIs be entertained, because they otherwise offer little upside to sellers.

In sum, every substantive business term ranging from exact purchase price; form of the transaction (stock or asset deal and compensation mix); any contemplated buyer's tax elections of potential concern to the seller; exact formulas for earnouts and balance sheet targets, interest rates, and other payment terms; possibly the main terms of post-transaction employment agreements (where and to the extent these are material or critical to the basic deal); and so on should be covered in the LOI prior to its execution.

When executing an LOI that is as thorough as possible, the seller should be able to go home and say, "Honey, I did the deal," fully confident that he knows virtually all the terms of the soon-to-be-consummated transaction and essentially the exact bottom-line dollar value of the deal to him. If the seller cannot go home fully confident of most of these details, he has not completed a thorough LOI and he has violated—or is at serious risk of violating—the "Honey, I did the deal" rule.

Use of Subtlety and the Effect of Precise Words in Letters of Intent: What the Definition of "Is" Is

Among the inherent paradoxes of the LOI, however nonbinding it may be for the most part, is the kind of psychological negotiating history it creates, depending upon the very often subtle shadings of meaning in word choices used to hammer out business terms. Sellers and their investment bankers should take extreme care to only execute or if necessary recraft LOIs that are as direct and clearly written as possible. They should eliminate all terms, phrases, and word choices that are vague, qualified, confusing, or that offer multiple alternative interpretations. Language that seem broadly qualified or equivocal, like:

- This is an expression of our possible interest in acquiring your company. (This means that this is no LOI, it is simply what it says it is, an invitation to negotiate.)
- We are offering seven times your trailing EBITDA, depending on due diligence. (This should read that we are offering $14 million. Even if it is based on a seven multiple, there will be ample opportunity for due diligence, and it does not need to be stated. When stated like this, it suggests that for every $50,000 of EBITDA in disputed minor differences, the offering price will go down $350,000. They are either buying a $14-million company or they are not. Obviously, big changes to EBITDA will make a difference but the LOI should discourage or at least not encourage nickel and diming.)
- We are offering $14 million for the company and will determine in due diligence whether this will be a stock or an asset deal. (Whoa, that could make a 30% difference or more in the net proceeds to the seller).
- We will pay $4 million in an earn out, with targets to be negotiated and agreed upon during due diligence. (Again, whoa. This could make the difference between an earn out that can actually be collected and one that cannot).

While there are many other examples, I think you will get the point here.

Negotiating Protocol and the Letter of Intent

The ideal protocol for negotiating the LOI is by exchanging reciprocal red-lines of successive proposed drafts (e.g., using Microsoft Word's Track Changes option or its equivalent in other word processing software programs). The buyer submits his LOI in both hard copy and electronic format. The seller edits it with his requirements, while ensuring that all recommended changes can be reviewed by the buyer in both hard copy and electronic formats. This allows for continuous redrafting, as well as precision vis-à-vis each party's positions. Seller and buyer alike should save each successive draft separately before saving the electronic version under a file name reflecting the new draft and proceeding to update it. This will provide a negotiating history that could prove very useful later if the parties dispute or recall differently how or the order in which positions were developed, particularly regarding tradeoffs and concessions in earlier negotiations.

It is worth noting that, sooner or later, multiple layers of changes may degrade the clarity of a draft-LOI-in-progress, sooner rather than later. While retaining hard copy and electronic format versions of each successive draft, seller and buyer might agree to launch every other round of proposed LOIs with a "clean" document on which no traces of past edits can be found.

For convenience purposes, the final draft LOI should be saved, separate from its predecessors, with a unique file name clearly indicating it was the executed version. This final electronic draft LOI should obviously precisely match the printed version (give or take letterhead or stationery issue distinctions). I recommend the use of PDF format copies as opposed to alterable copies.

I also highly recommend that sellers, their investment bankers, and buyers use the telephone to review proposed changes amongst themselves with each separate draft, to help all parties clearly understand the others' motivations behind requested changes and to maintain good faith all around. I refer you to Chapter 16, *Some Thoughts on the Psychology of M&A Negotiations*, particularly in regard to use of email for negotiations as opposed to its use for simply exchanging deal documents.

The Reverse Letter of Intent

Occasionally, the buyer's LOI is so inadequate or so far off the mark that the seller's investment banker and/or other representatives actually prepare a completely new draft version, at least as to the style of buyer's LOI, that they (the sellers) find acceptable. While no seller can impose his terms on a buyer capriciously, the seller's recommended LOI format can help the buyer understand early on the basic business terms and, most especially, the form (e.g., the lack of qualifiers or vagaries) of an LOI the seller would find acceptable. Should a seller and/or his investment banker decide to rewrite the whole of the buyer's proposed LOI, the investment banker should talk with the buyer before forwarding it. The investment banker should gently explain that he has drafted the alternative LOI for clarity's sake, while providing the buyer with a sense of the business terms that are of greatest importance to the seller. The investment banker also will advise the buyer that he is free to edit to incorporate changes that are important to him as the negotiation of the LOI proceeds.

LOIs from the Buy Side Point of View

So what does a buyer want in an executed LOI? Essentially the exact opposite of the seller's ideal document. The buyer would prefer an LOI with few specifics that is open to broad interpretation and renegotiation during confirmatory due diligence—a period in which the leverage and the initiative shift in the buyer's favor. The more imprecise the LOI, the more the buyer will enjoy disputing and renegotiating the meaning of business terms to reduce the investment value of the seller's company and the price he must pay to close the deal. The buyer can then take full advantage of the fact that the seller has removed his company from the market, turning away and possibly alienating other prospective buyers for as long as 60 days.

Chapter Highlights

- The "Honey I did the deal" rule—The LOI should be as thorough as possible while defining all business terms as specifically as possible. No "loosey-goosey" LOIs allowed, unless the seller wishes to lose serious leverage during the post LOI period.
- All weakness should have been disclosed before the LOI is executed.
- Vague or nonspecific language must be avoided at all costs in LOIs.
- LOIs in effective auctions are usually mainly nonbinding.
- Usually, exclusivity periods should not exceed 60 days.
- An affirmative response clause should be included in most LOIs.
- Seller Beware: The seller/buyer advantage curve flips to the buyer's advantage as soon as the LOI is executed.
- LOIs usually are usually negotiated through sequential red-lined mark-ups.
- When the seller receives a really vague or otherwise inadequate LOI, the seller should not hesitate to create a "reverse LOI" that eliminates the original's vagueness and/or inadequacies.
- Confidential to: buyers and investment bankers representing buyers alike: when you are preparing your LOIs, you should operate in accordance with a set of LOI rules that reverse each and every one of the preceding rules, if at all possible.

Don't play dumb. You're not as good at it as I am.

                                                                                          Colonel Flagg-Mash

CHAPTER 16

Some Thoughts on the Psychology of M&A Negotiations

Fairfax, VA—January 2004

Some damned fool (unfortunately, I think it was me) once said with great resolve, "I will never *move south to live, because I would miss the change of seasons." That is not exactly how I feel at the moment. The Washington, DC, metropolitan area has been in the grip of a cold snap for more days in row than I can remember in 50 years of living here (thankfully, memories can be short). The only saving grace to this meteorological misery is that it will allow me to make some progress on this book, because it is too damned cold for golf.*

I love golf, except when I am annoyed by the game, which I am quite often. Obsessive pursuit of this stupid game becomes all but inescapable as one tirelessly seeks to achieve each incremental improvement. Hope springs eternal, even in the dead of winter.

They say that, in the arc of an amateur's swing, a club head moves at about 95 miles per hour in the nanoseconds before it strikes the ball. How can a mere amateur control such speed, momentum, and eye/hand coordination in such an explosive moment? The amateur's untrained brain is neither fast enough nor focused enough, and he is probably overconcentrating on technique. *They say the secret to golf is to let it happen, but to which "it," precisely, do "they" refer?*

Do you have to know what "it" is to let it happen? Yes, you do.

Golf is a subtle game. It is a great deal like learning the game of Merger and Acquisition (M&A) negotiation which, like learning golf, puzzles, flummoxes, and flat-out makes you crazy for a few years before you get the feel of it, especially when you concentrate too much on technique.

Most golf pros will tell you that more than one swing thought at a time is probably too much. Just ground yourself in some basic fundamentals and let it rip in M&A negotiations, too. I admit, I have yet to get the "feel" in golf though. Oh, well.

A Few Preliminary Thoughts on Negotiation

There are hundreds of books on negotiation out there, and several great ones. Middle Market investment bankers just launching their careers would do well to read a few of them. Among the very best are several by author Herb Cohen, including *Negotiate This: By Caring, But Not T-H-A-T Much*, and James C. Freund's *Smart Negotiating: How to Make Good Deals in the Real World*. These guys are excellent, and their books tell it like it is. However, for the most part I do not like courses and workshops that teach negotiation techniques. I believe that, as in too many sales training classes, many students become obsessed with technique and miss the bigger picture, which has more to do with honesty and integrity, sincerity, making a friend (trust), preparation, feel, and a few other fundamentals.

In his recent book *The Naked Brain* (Harmony Books, 2006), Richard Restak, M.D., a neuroscientist, confirms what every experienced negotiator has sensed intuitively and experientially: trust counts. "Economic decisions...involve people not only interacting with other people but also trusting them. There is an additional reason why it pays to cultivate trust. According to recent brain research, distrust is dangerous, because it increases the likelihood that the distrustful person...may take aggressive action."

Restak also explains the results of experiments that indicate larger sums of money will change behaviors as well; I have addressed that elsewhere.

Preparation

Nothing but nothing surpasses thorough preparation for a negotiation: knowing everything about your counterpart that you can and having a firm grasp of all of the facts. This starts with industry and buyer research and a thorough knowledge of the M&A intermediary's client's business. It is frequently even possible to research the negotiating styles of your counterparts. Talk to other people with whom they have done deals. It helps a lot.

Ironically, though, veteran bankers can be particularly vulnerable to too much casualness about preparation. After several hundred deals, an investment banker can develop overconfidence in his ability to rely on his skills—to wing it, if you will. This is a major disservice to the client and the negotiations that will follow. No one is that good.

To begin with, seasoned investment bankers know that negotiations begin the very second that the buyer and the seller and/or their representatives make their first introductions and shake hands. Right there and then, posturing and positioning begin, whether consciously or subconsciously. All parties attempt to reveal themselves in the most favorable terms to their counterparts, adjusting their body language and communication styles and sizing up the other team. It's fascinating to watch—and the investment banker in the group had *better* be watching, and listening, closely. Well before this, the banker or his/her staff will have done the initial research spadework that makes such a difference. To enter into a negotiation for many millions of dollars without through preparation would be the equivalent of a boxer entering the ring without sufficient prematch physical conditioning. No matter how good that boxer is, even if he is a world champion, he is likely to get soundly knocked out of the ring if he has not prepared.

Clients and Negotiation

None of the observations raised in this chapter (or elsewhere throughout this book) are intended to criticize clients. Even so, some of the situations recounted will appear to do so. That Middle Market M&A clients, and sellers in particular, almost always are complete novices in the realm of M&A is a point quite worthy of repetition throughout this book. And regardless of the successes, however unique and extraordinary, they have achieved as entrepreneurs, the fact remains that the vast majority of them will be complete neophytes in the Middle Market M&A negotiations.

Sellers in particular are further handicapped by the fact they very often are too fully invested in their companies to be sufficiently detached when it comes to establishing the value of the company, let alone negotiating its sale. Detachment is a big issue, as author Cohen says in *Negotiate This: By Caring, But Not T-H-A-T Much.* He does not mean that one should be a cavalier or careless negotiator. He does mean that the ability to achieve a certain amount of detachment is a powerful strength in any negotiation.

Politicians and Honesty

An argument, at least in the sophistic or rhetorical sense of the word, is initiated with a desired end result in mind. It proceeds to its fulfillment by providing supporting reasoning that listeners can "buy into." Sometimes, a proposition is supported by reasoning that is inapplicable, inauthentic, incomplete, or all of the above—it's held together by a false proposition in logical terms, bailing wire and bubble gum. Too many politicians tend to be renowned for hype, spin, and false propositions, and people view them with extraordinary skepticism in return.

Hype, spin, false propositions can only take one so far before shredding one's credibility. "Fool me once, shame on you; fool me twice, shame on me," goes the old adage. In Middle Market M&A, investment bankers understand that hype and spin might win a single battle—perhaps even closing a deal under extraordinarily favorable conditions and even unjustifiable terms—but very likely that single win will come at the expense of their reputations and long-term business interests. Usually though these single battle wins will come at the expense of losing or derailing the whole war, which is closing a deal.

The risks are too great. Hype, spin, misrepresentation, and worse can destroy the will to transact, which is so critical to successful M&A deal making. I only hesitatingly use the war and battle metaphors in the preceding paragraph. It is the will to transact that lies at the heart of all M&A activity. The parties to the deal want to consummate a transaction. The objective should not be to "kill the other side." This is not to say that there is no place for small doses of rhetoric in negotiations, for putting one's best foot forward, but the best negotiators place reasonable limitations on the positions they take and equally on the way and style that they present them.

A good listener is not only popular everywhere, but after a while he gets to know something.

Wilson Mizner

Honesty and Integrity Are Still the Best Policies . . . Making a Friend

Honesty is the best policy, not simply for some moral reason but also because it's the far more pragmatic and sustainable course in the long run. In the final analysis, it's all but impossible for a seller and his investment banker to misrepresent the facts, no matter how subtly, all the way to a successful sale of a Middle Market company. Think about it: However much control a Seller may have over the presentation of the company through the Confidential Information Memorandum and the supplemental documentary representations of the company and its performance through their courtships with various prospective buyers, sooner or later they must settle on one buyer with whom they will execute a nonbinding Letter of Intent (LOI). And after the LOI is executed, the representations made inevitably face the acid test of confirmatory due diligence, in which the buyer is given access to virtually all of the company's financials and other related documents. Misrepresenting the company into an executed LOI and then confirmatory due diligence to be completed over the course of a 60-day exclusivity period could not possibly be more contrary to the interests of the seller. And I am not talking just about the avoidance of obvious fraudulent misrepresentation here. I am talking about tendencies or temptation to overly spin facts in seriously misleading ways even if not actually fraudulent. As they say "things are what they are" and you might as well speak the truth as everyone knows it anyway.

Honesty is the best policy because in the final analysis, it is inescapable. The best mantra a seasoned investment banker could share on the art of negotiation would be: "Come from a position of honesty and integrity." Counterparties may disagree with your valuation; with the price you put on your client's company, with how you managed the negotiated auction, and all the rest. But if you come from a position of honesty and integrity, they will respect you nonetheless, and they will trust you. And without respect and trust, it is all but impossible to convince a buyer to consummate a transaction on terms favorable to your client.

Beside which, as people come to respect your consistent honesty and integrity, they will also come to like you. You are making a friend, and that is the best person to negotiate with, even for high stakes. I have seen more than one dying deal resuscitate because I and the negotiator on the other side were able to establish a bit of an offline relationship, even if only for the duration of that deal, as we came to trust one another and respect each other's positions, even when we differed. At some point in most negotiations, it is critical to be able to put yourself in the other party's shoes. Many, many deals can be sustained when the negotiator has an ability to empathize with the other party. It should not be surprising how, when one is able to do this, solutions to dilemmas will quickly arise.

Dangers of Written Argument

The Internet, email, instant-messaging, and the astonishing acceleration they have facilitated in our lives and in our businesses have increased the volume of written communications exponentially, especially in business. Merely 35 years ago, electric typewriters and carbon copies on onion-skin paper constituted cutting-edge technologies in business communications. But however easy email makes communications—without carbon-paper–smudged hands as a price of cc:ing—there is a downside to it that can tend to surface in every transaction among the unwary.

Email allows the parties to a Middle Market M&A transactions to answer their own team's and counterparties' communications rapidly, short and sweet, with bullet points, attachments, and more. But the downside is that those responses are tonal—or atonal—and are rooted in the coldness and often abruptness of the electronic word. Way back when, in the days of carbon paper, the sheer unwieldiness of written communication favored face-to-face interactions. Even when written responses were crafted, they took days to draft and more days to deliver (in those lazy, hazy, crazy days). Doubtless, the sometimes negative impact of atonal written communications in those days was dampened by the face-time that often occurred between volleys and frankly because of the lack of alternative media the writing was usually better and more carefully crafted then in today's email world.

These days, electronic responses may fly nearly as fast as punches in a boxing ring. But the electronic communiqués arrive without the benefit of intonation, body language, or myriad other interpersonal signals that aid in their proper interpretation while assisting in crafting an appropriate response. Even in phone calls and conference calls, participants can discern meaning "between the lines" and among the silences punctuating a conversation. Not in email. The absence of tone in electronic communications can make them appear harsh, abrupt, and dismissive—all the more so when the response is succinct and direct in an effort to communicate clearly so as to avoid misinterpretation. This often causes the recipient of the electronic correspondence to project upon it either his hopes or his fears, or more likely, his suspicions, the latter of which usually involve misperceptions. As a result, it is critically important that sellers and their investment bankers recognize the strengths and the weaknesses of written, and especially fast electronic, communications when selling their companies. Two rules of thumb concerning written communication:

- DO use written communications to exchange drafts of legal documents.
- DO NOT use written communications when presenting an argument for one's own position regarding a transaction—rely on person-to-person communication, even by telephone, instead.

Never forget the communications corollary to Murphy's Law: If a written communication of any sort, and in particular the rapid electronic variety, can be misinterpreted, it will be. And each and every serious misinterpretation forces the seller and his/her investment banker to backpedal frantically to save a deal and/or keep a prospective buyer on board. Sooner or later, one too many misinterpretations will leave credibility shredded, with a frustrated prospective buyer or seller who will shrug in confusion and/or anger and simply walk away.

Cheer up; the worst is yet to come.

                                                                    Philander Johnson

Every Deal Dies a Thousand Deaths

Fairfax, VA—September 1996
An Anxious Client and a Door Opened Too Soon

I was sitting in my home office in Fairfax, happy to see that this deal was almost done. It had taken nine long, tedious, off-again, on-again, months, but we were almost there. I was feeling particularly relaxed, as I always do when pondering the grain and tones of the mahoganies in my study. When I get really pooped, I find gazing for a minute at the beautiful garden my wife has lovingly tended particularly mind-clearing. I really wish I could work here more often. This deal reminded me that, even after so many years doing this work, it still can be very stressful.

Just an hour before, I had hung up the phone after completing an only somewhat tense conference call with the South American buyer of my client's company. The tension reflected the fact that, as close as we were to doing the deal, it still might fall apart, like a putt for the championship that refuses to drop into the cup. We had addressed—and agreed to—a few final negotiation points. The buyer and the seller now were separated by no more than $350,000 of transaction value in a deal worth $12 million. My client, the seller, clearly was entitled to that $350,000, no doubt about it—a point the buyer eventually willingly conceded. (After, of course, making the customary noises about what a grand concession he was reluctantly making).

The phone rang again. I answered it to find my business partner and co-banker on the deal, Jean, on the line. "Dennis, you will not believe what just happened. Paul (the seller, our client) just gave in on the last point."

"Jean, I got the buyer to concede that point to us not an hour ago," I answered in disbelief.

"I know, but Paul was freaking out. For some reason, he could not reach me and I could not reach him to tell him we had won the point. And he was so panicked at the prospect of losing the deal, he called the buyer himself and conceded. He told the buyer that he was instructing his investment bankers that there would be no further negotiations on the final point, that he conceded it."

Not only is Paul's story true, albeit fictionalized somewhat to preserve the client's anonymity, it or something similar is one that occurs scores of times and memorializes the misadventures of clients who panicked and jumped the gun even when everything was going their way. This is both exasperating and completely understandable. Every veteran M&A intermediary has experienced firsthand, more times than he would care to admit, the truth of the old cliché: "Every deal dies a thousand deaths, but is born (closed) only once." Middle Market investment bankers are well-advised to remind their clients of the old cliché and its significance, where appropriate, throughout the course of the deal negotiations.

It even takes a while for most investment bankers to internalize, and to fully understand, the "thousand deaths" cliché. But until they do, they tend to operate in panic mode, because a thousand deaths in the course of a seven-month deal require a thousand and one apparent resuscitations.[1]

So less experienced investment bankers and their clients second-guess themselves at every step, fearful of being too aggressive, or not sufficiently so. Ironically, second-guessing oneself and always playing defense only compounds the impact of the cliché. The deals usually rise again, because the seller wants to sell and the buyer wants to buy. It took many months of arguing in Philadelphia among the delegates to complete the first draft of the United States constitution. Time and time again, any number of delegates was ready to pack the horses and go home, because various positions seemed so extreme that there appeared no hope of reaching common ground. But the delegates persevered, "slugged it out," and discovered common ground just as their forbears had discovered a New World in spite of the many times they thought they were about to sail off the end of the world.

Cutting a Middle Market M&A deal is nowhere near as complex as creating from nothing a national Constitution: Infinitely fewer "moving parts" are involved. But both processes require the passage of time, or competing parties will not be able to reconcile their positions. Should "take it or leave it" attitudes be allowed to prevail, failure is certain. The "will to transact," when allowed to run its course, is marvelous.

The best way for investment bankers to represent their clients is by decisively and professionally acting in accordance with their best judgment and their clients' best interests, and letting the proverbial chips fall where they may. (Detachment, again.) And, when a deal dies one of its many deaths, the investment banker steps in with the business equivalent of the cardiac paddles used in television emergency rooms, charges the paddles, yells, "Clear!" and resuscitates the deal.

Investment bankers should reiterate the cliché of one thousand deaths to their sellers, perhaps with greater frequency and emphasis, in the final negotiations of the deal. It is precisely because this end-game is not one to be played by the inexperienced or the faint of heart that clients must be encouraged to trust their negotiators and step back from the final negotiations of price and terms to a great degree. But the client is always in control ultimately. It is his deal and his money.

Clients should respect the importance of their investment bankers' professional specialization (and their banker should earn it) and resist the urge to assume they are equal to the task of closing the deal. This is asking a lot of a client, and all intermediaries need to respect that. What a flattering thing to have so much trust and confidence placed in one. The obligation back to the client on the part of the banker is even greater under those circumstances, for obvious reasons, and all good intermediaries feel that obligation deeply.

Water Torture Approach

Some negotiators bring what could be called a water torture approach to the business of negotiations: They simply, and usually calmly, repeat over and over again a particular position. This can prove very effective when the negotiator either is so confident of his position that he is certain it eventually will sink in and be agreed to by the other side, or when there simply is no other position to be taken, but that is rare.

The danger arises if neither of these conditions apply and this approach is simply a strategy or technique or inflexibility for its own sake. The risk is that this drip approach can prove annoying in the extreme and likely destructive of the relationship that has developed between the negotiators, especially in cases where it is obvious that these are not deal-killer level issues. When either the seller or the buyer has reached a point where either side simply is repeating, over and over, a position, a log jam arguably has been encountered over a transaction term that may prove to be a deal killer.

When log jams and/or potential deal killer impasses do arise, negotiators must stop, look, and listen. They should carefully re-examine their transaction positions to determine whether or not alternative approaches exist. And they must consider, carefully, the increasingly likely prospect that the other side has a rational basis for remaining stuck on a point (rather than mere obstinacy or game-playing). Negotiation should be seen as a process seeking convergence, not submission.

Incremental Deal Making and Laddering

Laddering the other side up through a series of concessions is a closely related and equally dangerous and distasteful approach. Here, one of the parties will seek concessions sequentially. "Well, I won that one, but here is another one I want to win." This is usually done after the other side thinks the last concession was sufficient to close the deal; the counterpart keeps introducing brand new issues. This is not to say that negotiations cannot be sequential, but at certain stages of a negotiation, new issues should simply not be introduced unless they are introduced as solutions.

Sometimes, requiring both sides to present their entire positions, or better yet their goals (as opposed to terms), at either an earlier stage or at a later point if negotiations break down is a great way to avoid or subvert incremental deal making or laddering and get the parties back on track. This approach will perhaps allow each side to understand more clearly the other side's real goals and wants and, in turn, to start trading-off "not-so-important" terms for "must-haves." Both sides can keep one eye on balancing their respective positions and the other on closing the deal.

Avoid having your ego so close to your position that when your position falls your ego goes with it.

Colin Powell

Negotiator, Know Thyself: Sometimes the Intermediary Is the Problem—Avoiding the God Complex

Columbia, MD—September 1993
Who's Got the Stick?
All hell, it seemed, was breaking loose in our rented hotel meeting room. There were 12 people present, 10 too many to conduct the reasonable, rational negotiation of a deal involving very large sums of money, at least from my perspective.

I was the senior banker for the sellers in a Middle Market transaction in an industry that was anything but high tech. The sellers operated a very large retail business in an industry sector where only the fearless were willing to tread. The clients were both reasonably bright and fortunate enough to have inherited the business (and its culture) from a close relative. Their business had been targeted by a major strategic roll-up party. The clients had wisely decided that the time had come to take the money and run.

The primary suitor for their business was a strategic acquirer operating in the same industry. At a certain point in the negotiations, my banking partners and I agreed that getting the parties together would be good for chemistry. For the most part, the terms of the deal had been laid out in broad-brush terms. That's when all hell broke loose.

I will forever remember my great frustration as bedlam ensued in a particularly cacophonous meeting of nearly intolerable confusion and lots of yelling. I had not encountered anything like this before, having had the great good fortune of representing clients who, for the most part, trusted me to do the dirty work. But this seemed to be going nowhere.

I recently had read about a "parliamentary procedure" among certain aboriginal tribes that granted a "talking stick" to each participant in a tribal gathering when it came time for him—and him alone—to talk. The person in possession of the "talking stick" had the right to speak for a certain interval without risk of interruption. A "talking stick" quite clearly was required in this particular meeting, or so I thought.

Rather abruptly, I stood up and spoke loudly (one had to in this group to be heard), and quickly recounted the tale of the talking stick as a potential means of restoring order and sanity to the proceedings. My contribution was received with all the enthusiasm that would have greeted my lobbing a highly agitated skunk into the middle of the room. Nothing ever was the same with the client after that, even though the deal eventually was consummated and even though it proved to be a very good deal indeed.

Is there a lesson here? Absolutely! These clients and the buyer, who, as I said, was in the same industry, had long since had grown accustomed to doing things their own way. They operated in a rough and tumble culture that celebrated stubborn independence and refusal to cede much authority even to trusted (but mere) advisors.

Business intermediaries often make serious mistakes when assuming in a rigid God-like manner that they and only they know what is best for their clients. Good intermediaries offer advice because that is what they are paid to do, but they also acknowledge that clients may choose to ignore that advice and pursue an entirely different course. When the client decides to "go his own way," assuming the way is at least ethical and legal, the intermediary needs to demonstrate sufficient flexibility to go along. Back in that noisy meeting room, the author's younger self apparently had not had enough investment banking experience to adapt to clients who seemed to him to be doing everything wrong. And interceding to bring a stop to the apparent chaos only succeeded in compounding the clients' lack of respect for this investment banker who just did not "get it." Life is a learning experience, I guess.

Looking back over the years, it seems clear that these clients, in fact, were particularly well-suited to representing themselves in negotiating the sale of their business (and the author was just along for the ride in support mode). These clients were so effective, in fact, that I find it all-but-impossible to claim that I could have negotiated a better final financial outcome than they had done for themselves in closing the deal. These clients had needed nothing more than technical advice. They had become excellent negotiators in their own right because negotiation played a significant role in their industry, where survival required great shrewdness in the face of narrow margins. What I failed to realize was that it was my job (with this particular client) to provide certain technical advice and then to bow out to a degree, while remaining fully cognizant of all proceedings should the clients signal further need of advice with other technical issues.

A little humility, one eventually learns, can take an investment banker a long way. When a client appears to insist that he can "drive" the transaction and demonstrates most of the requisite skills to do so successfully, let the client have the keys and get in the passenger side of the car. There's plenty of work to be done as the co-pilot. And, of course, the fees for riding along already have been agreed upon.

An investment banker's job is to collaborate with clients while playing a role that very likely will change from deal to deal. This is why the investment banker checks his ego at the doorstep of each new transaction engagement. It is, of course, his obligation to determine whether and to what degree his client can or cannot "drive the deal" and communicate his best advice accordingly. In the vast majority of cases, the best advice I can offer a banker will be to convey, mainly by demonstration, that the investment banker brings broad and deep M&A experience on which the client can rely and most clients do. But over the course of a single transaction, investment bankers may fill the roles of psychologist, coach, priest, or rabbi, even drill sergeant. They must bring to these roles patience, good will, good humor and the good judgment to discern exactly what role to play at each inflection point from the launching of a deal to its closing.

One M&A attorney, a good friend, prefers to practice a sort of golden rule; suggesting alternative approaches—and the likely outcomes of each—to his clients while declining to tell them what to do. This works for him. Most investment bankers, however, will find such a course difficult to totally follow. It can be difficult to stand by when the client stops listening and starts making some major mistakes. Sticking with the client through thick and thin is important, but so is guiding him and suggesting alternative approaches when the client's own decisions appear to be contrary to his own interests. It's a balance.

Communicating with Clients Up Front: Forewarned Is Forearmed

But even better is discussing all of this with a client at the beginning of the engagement. Usually, this discussion can be handled humorously and without offense. Just after agreeing to work together, maybe over dinner or drinks where things are relaxed, make some humorous comments along the lines of: "You will not believe how stressful these deals get at the end," "Every deal dies a thousand deaths and that cliché is about to take on new meaning for you," "Prepare yourself for a roller coaster ride," and so on. Point out to the client that there will be times when he will be tempted to accept provisions that probably should not be acceded to, especially in the final stages, just out of sheer exhaustion; that he might expect, at least somewhere in the negotiations that the other side will try to negotiate with him directly. In return, try to seek assurances from the client or at least recommend that he not accede to a buyer's proposal without at least first discussing it with you. One inappropriate change in deal terms, however seemingly small, can sometimes have a cascading effect on many other terms already negotiated. Reassure him at the same time that all final decisions are his, which of course they are and should be.

Keeping Buyers and Sellers Apart?

So does this mean that clients should not talk to the other side during the process of deal making? The answer is a resounding NO! There are many important positive reasons for contact between the parties, ranging from the simple need for information exchanges to the development of the all-important personal chemistry that will often catalyze the deal. Investment bankers should never try to keep the seller and the buyer apart throughout the transaction, *except during the serious financial negotiations.*

When the Deal Starts to Fall Apart: Getting Credit for Concessions

During really heated negotiations, three simple rules to survive by apply:

1. Wait a bit.
2. Allow the parties sufficient time to process the latest round of counter-proposals, no matter how strongly—and/or how emotionally—one or both sides insist that all or part of the latest proposal is a deal killer.
3. If it is still a total deal killer (it usually will not be, after some time to reflect and absorb positions), try another approach.

Okay, maybe waiting a bit did not work after all; let's try something different. At this point, investment bankers who excel by persevering step back and decide whether another approach might be appropriate. They may revisit the last round or two to present alternatives, or they may even go back to the beginning to start over virtually from scratch, despite investing months of work so far. They might save the deal either way; it has happened for me more than once.

Hmmm, that last approach did not work either? Oh, well: nothing ventured, nothing gained. When one side cries out, "deal killer," and refuses to relent over some reasonable period, well, maybe you should take him at his word. It is what it is. But is the provision that will kill the deal so important to your side after all? If it is walk, walk, walk. On the other hand, putting things in perspective, does your client really want to start over from scratch (seeking new buyers) after coming this far? Nope?

Okay, then call the side that called you out on the killer provision. "Okay, we can do it your way, but I need you to give me this in return." And this is an important concept in M&A negotiations, always get something in return for *very reluctantly* giving up something. This is a negotiation tactic that is fair and in no way flies in the face of integrity; in fact, it is usually expected by the other side. In a certain sense, especially in the later stages, negotiating an M&A transaction is a zero sum game. You take a piece, I take a piece, but the total pie remains the same, as it will be split between us.

Successfully executing each of these rules (especially regarding getting credit for concessions) requires exquisite timing. Act too quickly, and one undercuts the purpose of the client's original position (the one so vociferously challenged by the other side) while signaling a lack of confidence in one's own position. But wait too long to act, and the deal might well die (a final death) as the other side gives up on the deal, having been pushed one provision too far.

Bricklaying and Negotiations

St Louis, MO—August 1994

I was tired, my partner was tired, and so was the other side's attorney, although you could hardly tell it through the tough New Jersey demeanor she continued to maintain. Two flights in one day and a long drive to a midwestern town ending in a depressing hotel meeting room. This day was probably it: the deal stage where everybody was ready to throw their hands up in desperation and move on if we could not get this done.

I was in the Midwest with Sheila, another partner in my firm, negotiating a very tough deal on a client's behalf. That client had been trying to obtain financing from a strategic investor in the financial services industry, a deal the client really needed. The deal involved many complexities and trade-offs but the final negotiations were intended to be handled in a single day session, or it looked like the parties would walk. In a real sense, this whole meeting was a "Hail Mary pass." It had been a fast-moving negotiation for various reasons unique to the client's and the investor's respective situations.

Doug, the client's CEO, has accompanied us. Obsessed as he is with the smallest details, Doug has no sense of the big picture. He had somehow earned a Ph.D., a biographical detail that has left him altogether overwhelmed with himself ever since. Sheila and I both wished we could have left Doug somewhere back on the side of the road and returned for him only after the negotiations had been completed.

But we were stuck with him, no matter what. Our only consolation—and greatest hope—was that the numerous cell phone calls that distracted him, allowing him to revel in his perceived self-importance, would keep him out of the conference room while we got our work done. Unfortunately, Doug insisted on re-entering the conference room at the conclusion of each call, interrupting the progress and growing ever more annoying with each departure and return. The deal took three steps forward during each of Doug's absences and two and three-quarter steps back with each return.

Things deteriorated so badly that my partner, I, and the New Jersey attorney for the other side decided, during yet another of Doug's urgent phone call absences, that the time had come to take up a collection and send Doug off somewhere for a nice, long, leisurely lunch.

That did not work either, and desperate times call for desperate measures. Sheila and I agreed that she would quietly step out of the room, call the chairman of our client firm, and see if he might call the CEO and get him under control or risk losing the deal he really needs. The chairman agreed, and his CEO no longer interrupted the proceedings. The deal was consummated but, understandably perhaps, Doug the CEO, his ego bruised, later exacted revenge when it came time to pay our fee. Life is a bitch sometimes.

To some degree, negotiation is an art and a craft, much like bricklaying. Imagine two bricklayers cooperating from opposite sides of a wall they are laying. Each is doing his own thing, but their common wall rises. They establish a rhythm and a style for their wall. Should a new bricklayer arrive and begin work from either side without coordinating his efforts or matching the established style, his work could force the original bricklayers to tear down all that they had achieved and start from scratch.

Usually, involving others in a negotiation that is already substantially underway, except to offer off to the side support (as one colleague might offer a partner), is very counterproductive. Negotiations are subtle, intense, and transpire through the course of many rounds over time. During the course of these negotiations, each negotiator hopefully gains a sense of trust and confidence in his counterpart and in their respective styles and approaches. Their mutual knowledge of each other eventually speeds the negotiation, though it very likely remains quite competitive. Interjecting other negotiators into the middle of this process invariably upsets the pattern and confuses and frustrates the original negotiators. It puts everything at risk for little gain.

I feel so strongly about the "lack of history" issue that I refuse to enter directly into any negotiation my younger or less-experienced partners already have launched, because doing so would prove so disruptive. Alternately, I offer to be of assistance from the sidelines.

A Lead Negotiator

Atlanta, GA—December 1993

It had been a typical closing up to that point—frankly boring and tedious, but we were almost through. It took many hard months of negotiation to get this high-end mill working company to the closing table. It was one of those single-buyer situations that I hate so much, but so be it. Both sides hung in. The deal had died the customary thousand deaths and it was about to be finally born. I really liked both parties in this deal, although I represented the seller this time. My client, Frank, was down-to-earth and sharp (if a little high-strung); he was the third-generation owner of the business. It was time for him to get out. In fact, he wanted to devote the rest of his life to charitable work. As a last-minute sanity check, he had put the deal before his accountant apparently, the day before settlement, and that is when all hell broke loose.

The CPA, Tom, was a conscientious guy. I had known him somewhat for years. He only wanted to make sure his client got all that was coming to him, even if the deal had been actually finally negotiated a month earlier and was just waiting today's settlement. And then Tom, who was invited to the settlement by the client, announced that the purchase price would have to change. We all kind of looked at each and waited for the bomb to drop. As a recovering CPA myself, I already knew how little Tom actually knew about M&A conventions, although like most accountants he had been around a few deals as an accounting and tax advisor and he was good at that.

"Well, I have to tell you guys," Tom said, "that there is about $350,000 of previously expensed tools on the balance sheet that Frank is not getting paid for in this deal, and he should."

This was a $12 million dollar deal. Tom did not understand the M&A convention that the buyer gets the balance sheet (see Chapter 27). It did not matter that whether the tools were reflected on the balance sheet or not, the purchase price, based on a earnings multiple, would not at all be affected. Tom was not to be dissuaded from what he thought was logical. The client who had been following Tom's good advice for years was now in an awkward and confused position. It took another several hours to get over that one and get the deal closed. Ouch! We almost lost that one, as the buyer was already paying a top price.

Middle Market investment bankers should ensure that there always is a lead negotiator and that his authority as "point man" (but not as decision maker, necessarily) throughout negotiations is absolute. He may be supported by colleagues but he must serve as principal business negotiator throughout the process. On the other hand, real cooperation with the other team members leads to new insights and better deal making, for sure. The client's investment banker should lead the business negotiation; a transaction attorney should handle the negotiation of legal terms; while accountants, engineers, and the like handle appropriate technical issues within their scopes.

Experienced M&A transaction attorneys overwhelmingly agree with this approach. There may be more room for confusion between the investment banker and the client's accountant than between the investment banker and the attorney. I think this is largely because accountants usually serve as the main business advisory role for their clients through much of their client's business life cycle. They are usually eminently qualified to play this role, especially with smaller Middle Market businesses who might be able to afford a controller but cannot afford the luxury of a chief financial officer (CFO). In the final analysis, though, the client's accountant should serve as a technical advisor rather than as a lead negotiator role unless he is functioning—based on his own extensive experience—in the equivalent role of an investment banker.

Sellers and investment bankers should not ever forget how frustrating multiple negotiators are to the buyers, too (no less frustrating than multiple buyer negotiators would be to a seller). Here I am not talking about new negotiators, as I was earlier, just the existence of simultaneous multiple negotiators. Multiple negotiators all too often cause deals to collapse, as sometimes the inconsistencies among them build confusion in the other party. Ironically, though *and this is very important*, when a buyer can and does tolerate a seller's multiple negotiators (or vice versa), it often reflects his interest in capitalizing on inconsistencies among the various negotiators' approaches to win the most favorable transaction terms. Avoid involving multiple lead negotiators in any business negotiations. This usually means up to the LOI and even afterward, if business issues resurface again while the definitive agreements are being negotiated by the transaction attorney.

When to Walk Away from a Deal

A Golf Course in South Carolina, an Office in Paris—August 1995
There was a bit of a joke going around the office, although I did not find it humorous at all: "If we want to close a deal, let's just send Dennis off on a golf vacation." I cannot begin to count the number of golf rounds I have played with a cell phone glued to my ear. Or how many rounds of 18 holes were derailed by a deal before I had finished the front nine! C'est la vie! This is neither a point of pride nor resentment: It's what my clients pay me for.

I was in Hilton Head, South Carolina, with my wife and friends during the summer of 1995, attempting to play a round of golf without interruption for the first time in four days. I had two transactions in hypercritical states, but the trip had been arranged many months before, and these hypercritical states are totally unpredictable in terms of timing and duration, so I and my clients made liberal use of my cell phone once again.

My co-lead investment banker was visiting the Paris offices of the buyer on a trip that was scheduled immediately after my departure for South Carolina, or I would have been there as well. The Paris deal seemingly had been in its final stages for many months of a negotiated auction process, and I had spent the better part of many a round of golf advising my partner as to how to deal with the Parisians: "Speak their language!" (Ba-da-bump! He spoke fluent native French, but I could not resist the corny joke.) I was imagining my partner forcing a grin...or was it a grimace? Though he was an industry expert, he was fairly new to M&A investment banking at that time and was very reliant on my counsel.

The deal was not going well. The buyer was altering terms continually and seemed all too obviously intent upon gaming my partner and clients while demonstrating abysmally bad faith all around. My partner and clients had booked a very expensive flight, with virtually no advance notice, in support of the deal. They were worn out, wrung out, and—though they refused to show it—angered by the arrogance and belligerence of the buyer. I felt every bit of their frustration through our transatlantic cellular connection, and it made me angry, too. I had an easy putt for a birdie on the beautiful 18th hole at The Ocean Course, but this was too much. I shrugged, swung my putter forcefully at the ball and sent it flying toward my golf bag, away from the cup. Then I picked up the phone again.

"Brian," I said into the receiver, "Tell our client that it's over. Then tell the buyer, 'C'est fini!' and both of you, pick up your bags, head to the door, and no looking back!"

"Okay, boss!" answered Brian, revivified somehow. "That's fine with us."

Maybe that sounds like a deal out of the movies, but it happened in real life. I have never wanted to walk out of a negotiating room as a tactic (too theatrical), and I have done so only rarely. There comes a time when you realize you have no alternative and the act is not one of contrivance. There comes a time when the seller and his investment banker must realize there is no deal to be made with the buyer before them. When that time comes, it's always best to have a back-up, but if there is no back-up available, then you are starting all over again. Sometimes that is the way it is.

But a funny thing happened on the way back to Orly airport. Brian and the client got no further than the lobby of the buyer's headquarters (this was a decent-sized multinational European firm) when the buyer's CEO chased them down, apologized, and said, "No one ever walked out on us like that before." The games pretty much stopped that day, and the deal eventually closed after things calmed down.

Over-Strategizing, Over-Scripting, and Over-Analyzing

By the way, as a novice investment banker, Brian was wont to over-strategizing and over-analyzing, a trait common to relatively inexperienced investment bankers (and consultants). This often reflects an inability to relax and take things as they come. With experience, all that changes. Over-strategizing and excessive posturing are never advisable. For one thing, they look dishonest.

As to over-analyzing, no matter what one infers from the other side's actions, no matter what one infers of their motivations, all that is pure guesswork and therefore pointless and, in my opinion, a big waste of time. Leave that to trial attorneys and litigators who are paid to expect the worst from their opponents. Relying on guesswork and conjecture about motivations (especially when the conjecture tends towards cynical) to negotiate a deal is at best an act of financial masturbation that accomplishes nothing more than allowing the conjecturer to blow off some steam.

The End of the Middle Part of an M&A Negotiation . . . Just Before the Letter of Intent

Virtually every offer on the proverbial table can be improved in some way right up to the conclusion of the deal making phase. Rational, incremental (but not laddering, see earlier in this chapter) counter-offers can be pursued longer than most of us would assume, provided they are handled tactfully, supported reasonably, and addressed within a rational context. Knowing when one has reached the conclusion of deal making is, admittedly, an art in itself; but as they grow more experienced, Middle Market investment bankers come to discern reliable signs that "the end is near."

One important signal is time. How much time has passed? Every deal stands on its own, because each incorporates a unique mix of seller, prospective buyers, and the target company. Successful transactions can be negotiated within a few weeks or over the course of four or five months. (On average, it takes four to six weeks overall from the execution of a confidentiality agreement to the LOI.) The amount of time spent on intense negotiations—without a break—is arguably two weeks or so . . . the end game. Sellers and investment bankers alike should not consider it unusual, especially in the auction process, for prospective buyers to take a breather but once intense unbroken negotiations resume, another two weeks can be spent without unduly straining the patience and tenacity of all parties.

To get a sense of "where they are" in the lifecycle of the final negotiations, investment bankers also observe the process closely for a combination of negatives and positives. On the negative side, the buyer gradually will squeal louder and louder for negotiations to be concluded and the deal to be done. Such buyer "noises" should be scrutinized carefully: is the buyer just testing the seller in hopes that the seller will fold (a strong possibility in the early goings) or is the buyer communicating genuine frustration that should be taken very seriously? Then again, the larger the pool of prospective buyers remaining, the less "troublesome" the squeals of the one complaining.

Of course at such critical points as these, we are talking art more than science. Following three or four rounds of offers and counteroffers, both sides will believe themselves to have reached late, if not final, negotiations. On the positive side, investment bankers should watch for signs of endurance on the part of the buyer. Positive, continuing endurance is reflected routinely in the level of creativity demonstrated by buyers in their offers and counteroffers. The tone remains positive.

Inexperienced buyers may also tire too early of offers and counteroffers and remove themselves from the auction. Investment bankers may attempt to explain the importance of this phase of negotiations, but if such buyers cannot be swayed, it is very likely all for the best. An alternate approach to such buyers: Leave them alone for awhile, allowing the auction to continue in their absence until the very end when a final valuation of the seller's company appears to have been reached. At that point, no harm can be done advising the balky buyer of the near-final terms of sale and giving that buyer a chance to offer a better deal. And do not be surprised if the balky buyer does that, more often than you would expect in fact. Investment bankers who preserve their credibility with balky buyers through dealing fairly and with honesty and integrity from the early stages throughout the auction process may find that the balky buyer had just taken another break from the action. While remaining fully willing to do the deal, the balky buyer preferred having the investment banker call when the negotiations had concluded to name a price so he might counter and close the deal.

Just Say No

I have almost never had to do this, but just saying flat out "no" or the equivalent, especially at the very end stages of negotiation, even when a client critically needs the deal, is not as risky as one might think. Say no on Monday. The deal fails. Call back a week later and indicate you have reconsidered . . . very few deals will not come alive again, provided the time interval is not too long. Nothing ventured, nothing gained. What is too long a time interval? I wish I could tell you, but it is mostly feel. Stay at it long enough and you will have it (feel), just like a golf swing. But a week or ten days is probably a good average interval in which the deal can still be resuscitated.

The Difficult or Unreasonable Negotiator

All of us, at one time or another, have confronted the truly unreasonable, difficult, or hostile negotiator. This is frankly fairly rare (in my experience maybe one in 25 negotiators), and when it happens, while initially it is likely to take you aback, it will also be fairly obvious, I hope, having called your attention to it. Do not make the beginner's mistake of being worried that this is about you.

I am not talking about tough negotiators here. I am talking about angry negotiators. Hallmarks of this type are hostility that is inappropriate for the situation, usually accompanied by colorful vocabulary that could not be printed in a family newspaper but that they use while, ironically, they are still trying to carry on a negotiation of sorts. This is the kind of guy or gal who wants to start a fistfight over a traffic dispute. This is also the easiest negotiator to deal with.

Most of the time, if you have other options (e.g., an auction), simply recognize him for what he is and just walk. I only take the time to mention this type as new negotiators need to be aware that these are infrequent and never last long in the negotiations world, and to let new negotiators know *how to distinguish the type from simply tough negotiators*. You will know the difference. Their problems typically are rooted in something in their lives that goes way beyond the immediate issues. Their style is rarely simply technique.[2] If you have to deal with one to some extent, due to the context of the deal, just ignore their ranting and ravings is my suggestion. It tends to nullify and even calm them. Because they are also typically unsophisticated, if the context demands (in other words this is all you have to work with), you can often accomplish a lot with them as well because of their typical lack of any real technical acumen. You can only go so far with them, but it may be worth a try. Picture yourself as a matador in a bull ring with a very stupid bull and work this to your advantage.

One Last Thought on Negotiations: A Confession

I think I am pretty good at negotiating M&A deals for large sums of money. In fact, unless you have as much experience as I do, you are likely at a strong disadvantage if you find yourself on the other side of a deal from me, and why not? This is my career. I would be ashamed if it were otherwise. This is not to say you will find dealing with me an unpleasant experience. You probably will not, as that is not my style.

But successful negotiation requires certain ingredients, especially the expertise and dispassion that I have written about in this chapter. So much for that, but the rest of life is negotiation, too (with wives and children and partners and so on). When I am out of my realm, such as negotiating with a loved one about who takes out the trash this week or with a partner on a financial matter, where my personal involvement does not allow detachment? Well, I am as bad if not worse than anyone. A real pussycat, some who know me would say. Unfortunately, I cannot find anyone to represent me with my wife, so I guess I will just go on carrying out the trash.

Chapter Highlights

- Negotiation is an art, mastered over time.
- Incremental (laddering) deal making and "water torture" techniques should be avoided.
- Up front and sensitive discussions with some humor with new clients about what to expect in the ups and downs of negotiating (roller coaster rides and the thousand deaths) for very large sums of money are very useful to have *before* the going gets rough.
- The art of not caring t-h-a-t much is fundamental to successful M&A negotiations.
- Professional negotiators must maintain self-awareness, particularly when it comes to dealing with the almost infinite variety of clients they will represent and be prepared to adjust for each unique engagement.
- Negotiation is an iterative process, much like bricklaying. How each course is installed will determine the manner in which the next course is laid, in turn; thus clear focus is required. Avoid introducing new negotiators to the process.
- Every deal should have no more than one lead negotiator addressing its business terms.
- Walking away from a deal may prove successful strategically, but only as a last resort; this "nuclear option" must be carefully and dispassionately considered before it is acted on.
- It is quite easy to over-script and over-strategize deal making negotiations. The first often results in perceived phoniness, while the second frequently results from mistaken assumptions about the other side.
- End-game negotiation is the most critical stage and needs to be addressed with careful observations, monitoring, and listening, to gauge the likely possibility of a negotiation surviving. Sometimes, allowing a buyer to "rest a bit" can often successfully keep him in the game.

Notes

1. The point here is that the need for resuscitation is usually only apparent. The deals are usually not dead but people posturing.
2. Although it can be confused with what is in actuality a cultural style. Certain cultural (country) negotiating styles can seem harsh but that is just the way they do things. Experienced negotiators who do deals cross border will come to recognize these styles for what they are and to be no more than what they are. For that matter other cultural or national styles can be vague and with sometimes annoyingly inscrutable negotiators. Frankly I would prefer if necessary to have the harsh but usually more candid style to deal with. At least you know where they are coming from.

CHAPTER 17

Initial Meetings with Buyers, Pricing the Company, and Pacing the Negotiations

Savannah, GA—1988
The Perennial Question
In the middle of one of our quarterly partner meetings, I was making people crazy, I suppose. My question was not a particularly difficult one, but I could not seem to get a straight answer to it, even now though I already could sense why the answer was a tough one.

"How the hell do you announce the asking price of the company you are trying to sell?" (I am still learning my new trade). I look around the table of my more experienced peers, and sooner or later, they take turns answering it.

Each one has a different take. Gerald suggested that the best approach is to name the highest conceivable price you can justify and then hang on for dear life. Dunn, a more easygoing type, believed expert valuations are the answer, and he always got one before proceeding with a deal. "An expert valuation takes the guesswork out of it," Dunn suggested.

Philip, of course, said, "Let the buyers go first, suggesting a price and then attack." Philip, admittedly, a bit of a cynic, believes that prospective buyers always will lowball a price but, once they have done so, the seller and his Middle Market investment banker will have a baseline and things can only get better from there. I admit there is merit to Philip's position, but there are problems with it too. What if the buyer simply refuses to "go first?" Somebody has to go first, right?

I suspected that each of these answers is problematic, but what did I know? Gerald, Dunn, and Philip had been doing deals fulltime.

Strange Role Reversals and First Meetings

After having been identified and contacted, the buyer has executed the non-disclosure agreement (NDA), received the Information Memorandum, and is looking forward to a first meeting. Typically, first meetings take place in the investment banker's offices, in deference to confidentiality concerns. These meetings will sometimes involve other members of the seller's management team, and maybe a more or less formal seller's management presentation . . . and that is okay too, even especially desirable, provided the seller has included his team in the knowledge that the business is for sale or seeking financing, which he almost always should do if they are important to the transaction.

The role reversals at these first meetings never fail to amaze me. One might well assume that the buyer does the buying and the seller does the selling. But more often than not, the prospective buyer does most of the selling, pitching his firm as the ideal acquirer of the seller's business. This probably reflects a sort of anticipatory negotiation, an attempt at "softening up" the seller, and an attempt to gain an edge in the auction (perceived or real) at the outset. We all quite naturally do all in our power to make a good first impression in business interactions of all types. Why should it be any different for prospective buyers in their first meetings with the seller? And there is much to be gained from this situation.

First Meetings: A Friendly and Professional Seller

There is a certain irony in the fact that the prospective buyer's interest in "selling" himself and his company should actually encourage the seller and his investment banker to refrain from their own "selling," at least in any obvious fashion. The seller's demeanor in this first meeting should be open, honest, and very friendly, but it also should be reasonably reserved. Any overt attempt by the seller to sell his company risks being interpreted as anxiousness, while signaling to the buyer that he may as well stop selling himself (e.g., the seller seems maybe a little too desperate or needy). It likely will throw the buyer off balance in the midst of his own "pitch," and if they interrupt that pitch prematurely, the seller and his investment banker run the risk of not fully understanding the buyer's motivations to acquire.

Every prospective buyer knows he would not be in the meeting with the seller unless the seller was interested in being acquired. That goes without saying. Thus, the seller need indicate little more than that. He should listen, mostly. And answer factual questions, and of course be friendly, and present the company in a factual and best light—but that does not mean overt selling.

Even in these very earliest moments of the overall auction process, impressions are being made that will inform the parties throughout the proceedings. The first meeting, in essence, constitutes a preliminary negotiation, no matter how you cut it. Sellers also should avoid any response that appears contrived, stiff, or disingenuous; these will only put prospective buyers on guard. Advice to sellers: Be relaxed above all. Being open and forthright, albeit reserved, may seem discomforting at first. Take comfort in a paraphrased dictum of legendary GE CEO Jack Welsh: "You might as well tell the truth, since everyone knows it anyway."

The Potted Plant Investment Banker

And what is the role of the investment banker in these first meetings? It is principally to be polite, observant, and above all, quiet. Investment bankers should do their level best to shut up in these first meetings, because these meetings are about the prospective buyer and the seller, not the investment banker. An investment banker who attempts to demonstrate his brilliance by dominating, upstaging, or "selling" his client is at best annoying and at worst, quite often, very destructive of his client's prospects. In fact, in these first meetings, investment bankers would do very well to impersonate an attractive potted plant. Be polite, of course, and facilitate the introductions, as required. Be willing to make friendly small talk. But that is generally quite enough! There will be plenty for the investment banker to do later. In the meantime, he best serves his client's interests by remaining highly observant. He is likely to learn a great deal more by actively listening to and observing the interactions of prospective buyer and seller in these initial meetings than by being a full participant in them.

Investment bankers should pay particular attention to the prospective buyer's body language: Does it reaffirm or contradict what the buyer is saying? The prospective buyer very likely will be more forthcoming in introductory meetings than at any subsequent time as negotiations heat up. The prospective buyer's "selling points" in the introductory meeting will prove quite useful later in negotiations, as the seller and his investment banker recapitulate and re-emphasize back to the buyer the virtues he or she extolled in acquiring the seller's company and the likely benefits he or she perceives in doing so. So the investment banker will pay particular attention to what the buyer tells the seller about his own company.

- How useful is that information to the seller and the investment banker as they consider how well—or not—the seller's company might meld with the buyer's own objectives?
- What does the buyer's presentation of himself and his company say about his personality, leadership, and managerial capabilities?
- Of equal concern: what kind of negotiator is he likely to be: bombastic, hard-nosed, or fair-minded?

The initial seller/buyer introductory meeting offers one of the single most important opportunities to gain insights into the buyer. We all, always, can listen more, and listen more effectively, not least investment bankers representing sellers in transactions of singular significance in their financial lives. Be an effective listener, a simple observer.

Pricing the Company: The Inevitable Question

There comes a time in this first meeting between the seller and the buyer when the inevitable question arises in one form or another. "How much do you want for the company?" the buyer will ask, in those words or something like them. The question usually comes up near the end of the meeting. Middle Market investment bankers would do well to position themselves close enough to the seller to "kick the client in the shin," by prior arrangement of course. Under no circumstances should the seller answer the "How much?" question.

The investment banker who prefers not to kick clients (an awful thought) will advise his clients in advance of the first seller/buyer meeting how to answer the "How much?" question:

"I prefer to leave those discussions to my bankers. That is why I hired them and paid them these outrageous fees. They should do something to earn their keep." Well, there's no need for that to be the literal response. But the substance of it offers a reasonable and humorous and polite approximation. The client-seller should not allow himself to be drawn into a discussion, however preliminary, about pricing. Humorously demurring from an answer without over-scripting things is best, establishing that the seller is not a wimp, is in control, and is a "good guy" with a sense of humor, to boot.

Pricing the Company: The Right Answer

Even a professional investment banker who is a valuation expert should avoid the temptation to place a price on the company. Most of the time, pricing the company would be a mistake, because a buyer will pay investment value for a company, an amount that reflects what the company is uniquely worth to him and only to him. There is simply no way to determine maximum investment value of a particular buyer in the absence of a real or perceived auction process. In the absence of an auction, it is all but certain that any price the seller or his investment banker would put on the company would over- or under-shoot, perhaps substantially, the value an individual buyer would place on it. In other words, nothing whatsoever is to be gained by pricing the company.

That does not change one critical fact: once the "How much?" question has been raised, an answer of some sort must follow. When the question is posed to the investment banker,[1] the investment banker's sincere, "I do not really know," should be followed by quick explanation that investment bankers, like the sellers they represent, have no way of knowing investment value when a company is first put up for sale. Although I would not suggest actually using the corny phrase, he is simply a "seeker of the truth," and it is hard to argue with that, for sure.

But a prospective buyer may balk at, "I do not know." In fact he may very well say, "I am out of here. There is no way that I am going to participate in an auction," or something to that effect. The object now is to keep him in the game, and an approach that is fair and relies on the truth—and is almost always successful with less experienced buyers (experienced buyers already know they are in an auction)—is to point out to him that the highest price rarely wins the deal, because a multiplicity of possible consideration types, deal structures, and miscellaneous terms will make each offer very different from the next for reasons having little to do with "price." The investment banker might also point out that his clients, having invested considerable effort in building their companies, undoubtedly will factor "chemistry" and "fit" into their decisions, which usually is true, at least in the early stages. Almost always, these answers will keep prospective buyers in the game. Who does not think in their hearts that they are creative enough to offer a deal that is the best one out of a group? Reassurances from the investment banker that the buyer will have several bites at the apple in that the banker will work with him in developing alternative creative offers can go a long way too towards quelling buyer anxiety.

So how much does the seller really want for the company? As I have said several times, he and his investment banker will not actually know at first, (other than a broad range) because they cannot know the value buyers individually would place upon it—and that is the simple truth. As a result, the seller and his investment banker should not price the company, at least not rigidly; they may suggest ranges based on comparable transactions. As a valid method of priming the pump, the investment banker may share with a buyer a suitable range of transactions involving companies similar to the seller's own to justify a range of valuation, as long as this in no way limits an upper value to the deal at hand. And why should these transactions not reflect the best of the bunch?

The above pricing conversation exchange accomplishes several things if done well. First it establishes both seller and investment banker as "good guys"—flexible, straightforward, and, possibly, easy to deal with when actual negotiations commence. And even though the existence of an auction initially may perturb a buyer, he very likely understands that he would demand no less, were he the seller. Furthermore, the auction process presents an infinitely superior alternative to a seller's arbitrary demand for an unsupported price.

A QUICK DIGRESSION FOR BUYERS ONLY   From the buy-side point of view, the opportunity—and challenge—to present a creative offer with a compelling structure and mix of considerations actually does benefit buyers in competitive auctions, precisely because sellers cannot *precisely* compare the value of multiple qualitative and to a degree quantitative deal points presented across several offers. When experienced sales-side investment bankers represent a buyer in a Middle Market negotiated auction, they often welcome the chance to encourage the buyer's creativity. For example, more creativity routinely "trades off" for fewer deal dollars, especially when tax structure is an important deal element.

Should a Company Ever Be Priced, and to What Degree?

As there are exceptions to every rule, there are occasions when a business should, indeed, be priced. Pricing the company *may be warranted* when selling a technology or a business for which few suitable bidders are likely to emerge. In the end, perhaps only one suitable bidder will materialize. Investment bankers strongly dislike such scenarios, but they do arise nevertheless.

When an investment banker cannot launch an auction, despite his or her best efforts, she should attempt to establish a valuation based upon whatever comparables and company-specific factors are available. In addition, in the case of early stage companies or possible recapitalization transactions with private equity groups (PEGs), where much of the value is put on future performance, he or she should establish a value for the company based upon its discounted cash flows, or DCFs (see Chapter 24). This is one of those rare occasions when the use of DCF methodology on the sales side is appropriate.

In addition, and this is usually very difficult, the investment banker also should attempt to establish what the investment value of the company might or should be to the lone buyer, by attempting to quantify the synergies that the acquisition will produce for the buyer. There are occasions when there is enough information to do this. This approach is called "leading the horse to water," to use yet another cliché. An investment banker who wishes to establish the potential investment value of the company from the buyer's perspective must do substantial intelligence-gathering and rigorous analysis concerning the buyer's business. In some respects, the seller's investment banker is "doing the buyer's work for him," but sometimes this is necessary. The buyer may not have done that kind of detailed homework. Should the investment banker present a rigorously-researched and analyzed investment value of the seller's company to the buyer, the buyer himself may prove unwilling to acknowledge (at least *overtly*) the merits of the argument—this being, of course, a negotiation. Even so, when this work is done thoroughly and conscientiously, both the buyer and the investment banker will know it, and the result inevitably will influence the negotiation process. Furthermore, the buyer will now be compelled to explain why the bankers assumptions are wrong and that in itself may provide even more useful intelligence that the banker might use in another round.

Encourage All Offers, No Matter How Low . . . Getting Them into the Tent

Job number one for sales-side investment bankers is to set things in motion. This includes eliciting every potential offer from buyers, no matter how low that offer may be. As soon as the investment banker has two or more offers in hand, he or she has something to work with. Any buyer's first offer establishes a reference point for the seller and the seller's investment banker as to where the company's value might stand with that buyer. Only rarely will that first offer not be able to be improved. With offers in hand, the parties start talking, and the auction takes on a momentum of its own.

Neither the seller nor the investment banker should take umbrage against a lowball offer. In fact, they should be delighted to get all offers. On a really lowball offer, a good response is, "Thanks, we really appreciate your interest, and we will present this to our client, but we think this may very low based on what we know and what we think we will see from other offers."

Any offer is useful. Perhaps it is an all-cash offer? Perhaps it incorporates a particularly generous earnout or royalty, potentially providing excellent post-transaction compensation to the seller? But the most important fact is that any single provision in an otherwise unacceptable offer can be used by comparison to improve the terms of competing offers and can be incorporated into developing a final purchase price from at least one other buyer. The object is to get the buyers into the tent. Once in, they will either aid the improvement of other offers or begin to get serious about winning the deal.

The Truth, the Whole (?) Truth, and Nothing but the Truth

Successful negotiations are predicated upon the credibility and trustworthiness of the negotiators. But while I have discussed this before in an earlier chapter let me address it again in the context of this one. Sellers and their investment bankers should understand that there is a difference between the truth and the "whole" truth. In every negotiation, seller and prospective buyers alike have the right to withhold certain critical information. The prospective buyer, obviously, is not under any obligation at any time to disclose his or her top-line offer, unless and until he/she chooses to do so. On the other hand, when an investment banker discloses different deal elements from competing offers for the purpose of encouraging prospective buyers to improve their terms, the banker is under no obligation to disclose in their entirety the offer or offers in which those terms were contained.

For example, when a seller receives a fairly low $10 million all-cash offer from one prospective buyer, his investment banker quite rightfully can advise another prospective buyer (who has offered $15 million, including $7 million in cash) that an offer with $10 million in cash in it already is on the table. The investment banker might tell a third prospective buyer that he already has a $15 million offer in hand. Each one of these is an accurate representation of fact within the negotiations process.

Timing, Sequencing, and Pacing the Deal while Pricing the Company

When an early and aggressive prospective buyer becomes active right from the start of the auction process, investment bankers do have mixed feelings. Such buyers can raise timing problems. The effectiveness and the success of the negotiated auction depends upon several buyers competing over time, thereby proposing deal terms that are increasingly favorable to the seller. When aggressive prospective buyers actively seek to speed up the process for their own purposes, or accidentally threaten to short-circuit it in their eagerness, investment bankers should do all that they can to manage the negotiated auction so that the most potential buyers will have time to participate to the fullest.

Sometimes sellers and their investment bankers are admonished by prospective buyers to maintain *a sense of urgency* in doing the deal. Actually this (a sense of urgency) is also the common and rather clichéd advice typically offered by less-experienced investment bankers, as well. In every transaction, there will be a time to go slow and a time to move fast. In general, though, the early stages tend to be best handled at a slow pace, and only the later stages at "sense of urgency" pace.

But again, it is true that prospective buyers who come early to the table may become discouraged if—in their estimation—the process drags on too long. But if remedying this entails accelerating the process past the point of allowing most of the field of prospective buyers to participate fully in establishing the investment value of the company, do not do it. Again, admittedly, investment bankers are confronted by a balancing act; that's why sellers pay them big money. How should one slow down prospective buyers demanding greater urgency at the expense of the auction? Once again, try honesty. Communicate to such buyers the seller's appreciation of their early proposal and of their patience as other prospective buyers put together their own bids. All squawking aside, such buyers understand that sellers are within their rights to give all prospective buyers a reasonable amount of time to submit an offer.

Once all buyers have had a chance to submit their respective offers, the seller and his investment banker may choose to "dial up" that sense of urgency a few notches to speed through a few rounds of offers and counteroffers to the end game. As I said, sometimes urgency is appropriate (usually in later deal making stages) and sometimes it is not. But be prepared for things to take usually much longer than you would expect. Deals for large sums of money and major elements of inherent uncertainty happen that way. Fits and starts, speed followed by slowness followed by speed.

Chapter Highlights

- Do not price the seller's company initially, but do provide a range of potential values for it.
- Emphasize to prospective buyers that the highest "price" rarely wins so as to encourage buyers to be creative participants in the negotiated auction, pricing, and establishment of terms of sale.
- Avoid using the term "auction" when dealing with prospective buyers; "auction" is a "bad" word, however implicit in the nature of the proceedings.
- Pricing is actually a function of the negotiated auction.
- Politely accept all prospective buyers' offers to get everyone in the tent.
- Combine elements of different offers to create optimal terms for the sale of the business.
- Auction pacing is usually slow in the beginning. Toward the end of negotiations, the pace may well quicken, but every deal is different.
- It always takes longer to consummate a deal than one expects going in. Investment bankers need to manage the seller's, the potential buyers', and their own expectations throughout the process.

Note

1. The prospective buyer generally will pose the question once again, to an investment banker directly, after the client has left the room. Having the opportunity to do so again, and to talk with the investment banker directly, can make things less awkward for everyone. It also more or less establishes the investment banker as an intermediary through whom the buyer must work from the launching of the sale through the conclusion of the negotiations.

CHAPTER 18

Consideration and Deal Structure

Price is what you pay. Value is what you get.

Warren Buffett

It's the Terms, *Not the Price*, Stupid!

Buffett had it right, of course. All too often—most of the time, in fact—clients think in terms of the nominal purchase price of their business, rather than the precise terms or nature of the actual consideration (its cash equivalent value). This is not so surprising, really; once the deal has closed, the financial press reports a number—the total purchase price—and very rarely any further details. Merger and acquisition (M&A) financial databases, in turn, mostly report deals by recording and publishing the nominal purchase price and in some cases additional, but very limited and usually inaccurate, information that relates nominal price to other factors like revenues or supposed EBITDA.[1] The problem is that on Middle Market deals, most of the really pertinent information is simply not available outside the deal room.

The public buzz in the wake of a deal also focuses on the nominal price. After a deal has closed involving a company in an industry they cover, investment bankers often receive phone calls from clients and prospective clients, noting the transaction price and asking, "What did you think of the ABC deal?" In the absence of any further details, the best answer would be, "Damned if I know...."

Chapter 9 related an investment banking representation that resulted in the client receiving offers ranging as high as $44 million. The client ultimately accepted a $38-million offer. Why reject a $44-million deal? Because the terms and the structure of the $38-million deal were much more favorable to the seller than those of the $44-million deal. The seller made his decision based on the nature of the weighted consideration and the deal structure, not the nominal offering prices—in other words, the net equivalent cash to himself.

EXHIBIT 18.1   Weighting Comparative Offers

	Buyer 1		Buyer 2	
	Nominal Value	Cash Value	Nominal Value	Cash Value
Form of Consideration				
Cash	$20,000	$20,000	$20,000	$20,000
Rule 144 stock	5,000	3,000	—	—
Earnout	50,000	25,000	40,000	32,000
Secured promissory note, market interest	—	—	5,000	5,000
Unsecured promissory note, below market interest	5,000	2,900	—	—
Purchase price paid as compensation	5,000	2,800	—	—
Escrow hold-back	9,000	—	7,000	—
Total consideration before tax adjustment	$94,000	$53,700	$72,000	$57,000

Consideration and Consideration Types

All consideration offered by the buyer in an M&A transaction should be weighted to its equivalent value in cash (see Exhibit 18.1). Otherwise, it is virtually impossible to meaningfully compare one offer to another so as to allow a seller to make a rational, informed decision.

As another old saw advises, "Cash is king." Buyers offering Middle Market sellers cash provide those sellers with instant, 100% liquidity. Money they can take to the bank. Few buyers make all-cash offers, however, because they often prefer to offer any number of alternative forms of considerations.[2] In order of likeliest preference to sellers, these alternative consideration forms include:

1. Cash
2. Highly-secured promissory notes in the form of negotiable instruments (interest rates vis-à-vis market rates will be an issue with this alternative)
3. Highly-secured promissory notes or non-negotiable instruments (once again, interest rates will be an issue, as above)
4. Moderately-secured promissory notes as negotiable instruments (ditto with regard to interest rates)
5. Moderately-secured promissory notes as non-negotiable instruments (ditto with regard to interest rates)
6. Unsecured promissory notes as negotiable instruments (ditto with regard to interest rates)

7. Unsecured promissory notes as non-negotiable instruments (ditto with regard to interest rates)
8. Freely tradable public company stock (float—average shares traded in a day or a week—is an issue, as well as how large or small the company issuing the shares)
9. Nonfreely tradable pubic company stock (rule 144)
10. Minority interest private company stock that includes a put option
11. Minority interest private company stock that does not include a put option
12. Secured, short-term earnout
13. Poorly-secured short term earnout
14. Other longer term earnouts (unless they are simply more frosting on the cake of an otherwise great deal)

The three major qualitative elements of consideration that should be considered and weighed are: (i) relative instant liquidity as compared to cash, (ii) time (the fixed term over which it is payable, including attendant market risks during that period), and (iii) seniority, vis-à-vis other financial obligations of the buyer.

Deal Structure

Other factors playing a pivotal role in determining the ultimate value of the buyer's consideration include:

- Tax consequences, such as:
  - The choice of a stock or asset purchase deal, with the former resulting in capital gains taxes and the latter sometimes generating ordinary income taxes
  - Buyer-favored elections that the seller might agree to: For example, buyer 338 h 10 elections under certain circumstances may require the seller to pay tax on the buyer's stepped-up basis in a stock deal as 338 h 10 allows a stock deal to be treated as an asset deal for tax purposes
  - Tax-deferred stock or asset exchanges transacted in the course of reorganizations
  - Ordinary income compensation, including post-transaction consulting contracts and noncompete agreements that arguably may be considered part of the buyer's purchase price
- Balance sheet targets (see Chapter 27), whether resulting in give-ups or add-ons to the purchase price, usually specified as:
  - Cash
  - Working capital
  - Net asset value

Frequently Offered Consideration Types—Overall

While a comprehensive discussion of each alternative consideration type cannot be undertaken within the constraints of this book, a brief overview of a few major alternatives may prove worthwhile. (Earnouts themselves will not be addressed here, but rather in Chapter 19, while the tax and balance sheet ramifications of various consideration alternatives will also be discussed in Chapters 29 and 27, respectively.)

- *Promissory deferred payment notes.* These are offered relatively infrequently to Middle Market sellers within a buyer's overall consideration mix, because most Middle Market companies are sold in return for cash and an earnout arrangement with occasionally a stock component too. When the buyer does, in fact, offer promissory deferred payment notes (usually only in smaller transactions of under $5 to $7 million) as part of his overall consideration, the prospective seller should evaluate their underlying terms very carefully to calculate a cash-equivalent value. Among other factors, the seller should consider carefully:
    - The credit worthiness of the issuer, because the prospective seller, in effect, will be lending that issuer money
    - Whether or not the interest rate on the note is set at the market rate for similar securities types being offered in the debt market (e.g., a well-secured first trust note on real estate arguably should bear the same interest rate that first mortgage rates bear, while a second trust note on subprime real estate should carry a significantly higher interest rate)
    - The cash equivalent value of the note, based on the time value of money (as it relates to above- or below-market interest rates) and whether or not the note is negotiable and, if so, the note's market value to third parties (a word of caution: many take-back notes accepted by Middle Market sellers indeed are negotiable on the open market but often at discounts of up to 40% off their face value)
- *Public company stock.* A rose may be a rose may be a rose, but not all public stock is equal when offered as partial consideration for a Middle Market M&A transaction. Most public companies issuing stock to sellers as part of the consideration mix while closing a Middle Market transaction in fact are issuing unregistered stock pursuant to SEC Rule 144. But unlike freely tradable public market counterparts, Rule 144 shares are by no means liquid, because they do not become freely tradable until six months (at the date this is written) after they are issued. Should the seller wish to sell those shares in the interim, he must identify private investors willing to purchase them at steep discounts of from 25% to 40% and possibly more off of the shares' market value,

given their market restrictions. As a result, investment bankers should advise their sales-side clients that the cash-equivalent valuation of Rule 144 shares should be calculated as, say, 60% of the current market value of the publicly tradable shares. Public company buyers offer Rule 144 unregistered stock because it is cheaper for them to do so than it is to hold already-registered stock (shelf registrations) with which to do deals.

When sellers accept Rule 144 "restricted" shares from buyers, they may well—and should—hedge those stock positions against any drastic market downturns, even though hedging simultaneously may "cap" the upside potential of their new stockholding. Sellers pay fees to hedge their Rule 144 shares, and hedging is often available only to those holding restricted shares in very large public companies with a substantial float (the average daily or weekly number of shares traded in the stock market).

- *Dribble rules.* These rules also must be considered, although they usually come into to play when a fairly small public company buys a fairly large private company in a transaction, with substantial shares exchanged. Should the seller become either a major shareholder in the buyer's company (owning 10% or more of the buyer's shares) or a member of the buyer's senior management team, additional restrictions on his ability to sell his shares may be triggered. Major shareholders and/or members of a public company's senior management cannot simply dump all their shares in the public market at once. Consider what would happen to Microsoft shares one day if Bill Gates instructed his broker to sell his entire position in the company. Rather, they may be limited to dribbling out their shares for sale over time. The dribble rule prohibits the sale of more than a certain number of shares during certain time periods, depending on whether he or she is a control party, which in turn depends on the number of shares he/she owns and his/her position in management.

  Sellers whose shareholdings in the buyer's company trigger dribble rules may want to also discount the value of those shares from their face value to establish their cash value equivalency.

- *Lock-up agreements.* Sellers who accept stock in a pre–initial public offering (IPO) company as part of a roll-up very likely will find themselves subject to lock-up agreements that prohibit their sale of such shareholdings for six months or more following the imminent IPO. Again, establishing a cash value equivalency for such shares sometimes requires a substantial discount from face value.

- *Financial decisions.* The aforementioned issues notwithstanding, sellers considering taking back stock in a transaction should ask themselves the question, "If I had sufficient cash to buy the shares I am about to accept from the buyer, would I invest it in these shares?" If the seller's answer to this question is "Yes," he should proceed. If the seller's answer is "No," he should decline the offer. Sellers will be all too aware that various buyers' offers constitute the largest amount of money they ever stood to receive in their lives, and a very large part of their (the seller's) net worth. As a result, sellers should proceed with all of the caution they would muster when evaluating the merits of any investment opportunity that might be presented to them. How much stock the buyer offers, and in what context, also must be considered. If the buyer's offer is a superior one, including mostly cash and cash equivalents along with a relatively small amount of stock, taking the plunge and accepting the shares might be advisable.

Sellers might seriously consider all deals offering 10% to 15%—*or less*—of their consideration in stock. On the other hand, when a buyer offers a seller 60% or more of a deal's total consideration in stock, the seller definitely should think twice. He is in effect being asked to invest that part of his net worth in the public company stock.

- *Private company stock*. One of my former partners, a bit of a jokester, used to advise audiences he addressed that the rule book of minority stockholders rights was more than three inches thick. Pause. The only problem was that all of the book's pages were . . . blank. My former partner was right on the money on that point (pun can be disregarded). Sellers should never forget that, 99% of the time, there simply is no market whatsoever for minority interest stockholdings in privately-held companies. Minority shareholders cannot cause dividends to be paid; block salary increases for executives and/or employees, etc.; or in any material fashion direct the company by themselves. Minority shareholders find themselves consigned to limbo, especially if that's where majority shareholders intend to keep them. The minority shareholder's most likely—and doubtless, only—market for their shares will be with other company shareholders—in most cases, at a steep discount (when markets are not liquid and a shareholder wants out, why should the prospective buyer do him any favors?). A sales-side client might find it advisable to become a minority shareholder in a privately-held company, though, or only, when:
  - All of the shareholders will be minority shareholders (and, ideally, not related to each other; when two or more minority shareholders are related, they may come to constitute a de facto majority or voting bloc) and he acquired his shares as part of a business combination in which he preferably will remain active
  - A put option (liquidity guarantee) at an acceptable strike price allows him to sell his stock back to the company for cash (never forget,

however, that put options lose all their value if the issuing party loses the financial wherewithal to redeem the "put-able" shares)

- The time period for exercising the put would normally correlate with some future intended event, like a resale of the business or an intended IPO of its shares
- *Escrow hold-backs.* Any consideration "held back" in escrow—and virtually all Middle Market M&A transactions involve escrows intended to protect the buyer against unforeseen future claims arising from events preceding the company's sale of the business—constitutes deferred consideration, which should be viewed as such and discounted to its cash equivalency value. Different buyers will require that sellers agree to different escrow amounts. The typical escrow range, though, is between 10% and 20% of the cash purchase price.

    In most cases, I estimate for my clients, somewhat arbitrarily, that consideration placed in escrow is worth approximately 95% of its face value (less a discount for the time value of money) if it is held in escrow for one year or less; and approximately 90% of its face value (less a discount for the time value of money) if it is held in escrow for more than one year but no more than two years. Most escrows are held back for only one to two years.

In Summary: Weighing and Comparing Offers

Multiple offers involving disparate forms of consideration must be analyzed quantitatively and objectively in order to establish cash equivalent values among them. Only by so doing can sellers—usually with the assistance of an investment banker—choose the most favorable offer, based on its specific terms and consideration mix. Elements of consideration should be weighted in accordance with two rather simple standards: the time value of money and the probability of collection. The investment banker should present a weighting protocol to his sales-side client that allows the seller to create his own estimates by using these two weighting factors or, at the very least, according to the probability of collection.

The investment banker and his seller would do well to calculate, separately, the respective cash equivalencies of the multiple offers placed before them. Having done so, the investment banker and seller should review their separate estimates to rank the offers, thus identifying the best offer among them. Even though the investment banker, with his own hopefully extensive experience, is likely to generate the most accurate cash equivalency valuations, sharing the responsibility with the seller for establishing cash equivalency valuations will enable a robust discussion between them, *especially in regard to earnouts*, where the seller's input can be more acute than the banker's. See Exhibit 18.1 for an illustration of the process.

Recommending Against Deal Consideration

Washington, DC—June 1993

As many years as I have lived in this city, I still love its beauty, especially around the National Mall, with the Smithsonian and so many other monuments to the nation, its history, and its people. Jim and Carol's small but highly specialized textile business was headquartered near the Mall.

I was really pleased with myself for successfully recommending that Jim and Carol reject an offer to acquire the company that they only recently received. While the prospective buyer had offered what appeared to be a fair price, the consideration mix would have been too heavily weighted to take back promissory notes from the buyer. In my opinion, the buyer, in turn, had way too much debt on its balance sheet. It took me some time to convince Jim and Carol to decline the offer even though closing that particular deal would have brought me a $300,000 fee. That made me feel rather good about myself, despite the months of hard work I had done on this deal. There would be another offer, a better offer for Jim and Carol, on another day. And when I arrived home that night, I celebrated what was not to be—and what was to come—with my customary end-of-the-day scotch. In the meantime, I drove out of the District, with the sunset gilding the Washington Monument, I could not help but remind myself, yet again, that Washington, DC, was a beautiful city, to be sure.

That's when my cell phone rang.

"Hello, this is Dennis."

"Dennis, this is Jim."

"Hey, Jim."

"Listen, buddy, we want to cancel the financial services agreement we entered into with you," Jim ventured, at once both tentative and determined.

Silence from my end. I listened intently.

"We just think you are not bringing us the right kind of deals," Jim continued.

Ironically, they had wanted to do the deal—it would have been so easy to do what they all but insisted upon and earn my fee. Frankly, they would have not known the difference between a good deal and a bad one when it came to this type of structure. I sure did think about that. But I did what I thought was right at the time.

Yes sirree! I went home and had two scotches.

One of the most valuable services an experienced investment banker can offer his sales-side client is advice on not accepting a deal. And that is very hard to do. Advising a seller, "No deal," when a deal of one sort or another might prove just passable, if not entirely in the client's interest, requires a particular type of integrity and professionalism, and it comes at a price. Even when "No deal" is the right thing to do, most Middle Market investment bankers will more than wince if they have to say "Leave it" to an offer that could generate a $300,000 to $500,000 fee. The investment banker's evil twin, right there on his shoulder (mine was certainly hanging around that day), very likely will yell, "What the hell are you thinking, big guy? Are you insane?" Well, yes, sometimes. But bad consideration in a deal is worse than no deal usally.

For Buyers: Creative Uses of Consideration as a Deal Making Device

I also discuss this elsewhere in this book, but this chapter should have made no less clear to buyers than to sellers the importance of offering a consideration mix within the context of creative deal making. Perhaps the seller expects to receive $10 million for his business, for whatever reason, yet the buyer has stretched his investment value walkaway price practically to its limits at $9.7 million. In such a case, the buyer might offer the seller a bullet promissory note due in 20 years at 0% interest for the $300,000 difference in a market where the interest rate on this type of note should be say 10%. The present value to the buyer will be a relatively small amount—and it may well close the deal. If such an arrangement cannot be made, and if a few thousand dollars on a $9.7 million to $10 million deal would keep a buyer out of the game, then the buyer does not belong in the game in the first place.

Stock and When It Is Priced

Should a seller accept buyer public stock in a deal, at what point in time should the stock be valued: on the date of the letter of intent, at settlement, or when? Usually, it is valued according to an average trading range of bid and offered prices posted over the course of a week or two immediately preceding settlement, with the average price being multiplied by the number of shares to be issued in order to constitute the value of the stock previously negotiated. This is intended to protect both parties from sudden and temporary spikes, at least as much as possible.

A Final Thought on Consideration Mixes

So what is the typical consideration mix sellers might anticipate in a Middle Market deal? The answer:

- Cash, at 50% to 100% of total consideration (larger deals should be *all cash* plus earnouts)
- Earnouts amounting to 10% to 20% of total consideration
- Sellers take back promissory deferred payments worth approximately 10% to 25% of total consideration (very small deals, usually under $5 to $7 million, are more likely have a seller take back notes)

One major reporting service has indicated that M&A transactions most broadly fall into three categories: all cash deals, all stock deals, and mixed deals, each accounting for one-third of the total. This can be reconciled to my observations in the list above by understanding that in the one-third of cases that involve mixed transaction consideration, the cash element is still typically 80% to 90%, with the balance being in earnout and/or stock. The one-third of the cases where stock is the only consideration are typically large public company mergers. So in most cases in the Middle Market, the predominant consideration used is cash.

Chapter Highlights

- To compare multiple deal offers effectively, each element of consideration must be weighted in accordance with its cash equivalency as a baseline.
- The time value of money and the probability of collection are the two principal elements to consider in weighting elements of deal consideration.
- Investment bankers and sellers should collaborate on the weighting of elements of consideration, and in particular *on earnouts*.
- Additional structural terms can affect elements of consideration materially, especially with regard to tax treatment and balance sheet targets.
- Rule 144, the dribble rule, very likely will restrict the tradability of public company stock received by the seller in a Middle Market M&A transaction, depending on whether or not he is a control party—which in turn depends on the number of shares he owns and his position in management.
- Lock-up agreements for stock to be received in an IPO will often prohibit trading for about six months, again necessitating a cash equivalency discount.

- The conditions under which a seller should accept stock in a deal are contextual (relating to the overall quality of the deal) and quantitative (relating to the value of the stock offered as a portion of the seller's net worth).
- In taking back deferred promissory notes, negotiable instruments are preferable to non-negotiable promissory notes.
- Deferred payment promissory notes basically are loans to the buyer; they should be considered only in light of interest rate, the issuer's credit-worthiness, security, degree of subordination, and the note's market value.
- Escrow and indemnity hold-backs (typically 10% to 20% of the cash purchase price) should be weighed against cash and perhaps discounted by 5% per year escrowed, plus the time value of money.
- Sellers should accept private company stock only rarely, and then only in combination with a realistically enforceable put option.
- Buyers may offer creative mixes of consideration to close what otherwise might be unclosable deals.
- When stock is part of the consideration mix, its pershare value usually is determined based upon a trading averaged over the course of one or two weeks immediately prior to settlement.
- Elements of consideration may be very mixed, but Middle Market stock and earnouts rarely should exceed 15% to 25% of total deal value in each case, with the balance being provided in cash; that is, unless the earnout is a bonus over and above a very fair purchase price.

Notes

1. The problem with reported EBITDA (or its equivalent) is that in the actual deal room, these cash flow equivalents are usually recast significantly to reflect normal operations, and the resulting EBITDA on which the transaction is *actually based* is not available to the reporting services or the press.
2. Having said this though most middle market deals above $5 million in value or so will tend to be composed of only two elements: cash and earnouts and occasionally stock from a public buyer. Usually cash will amount to 75% to 85% of the offer price and the balance, stock, and/or earn outs, 15% to 25%.

CHAPTER 19

Earnouts

Fredericksburg, VA—August 1996

I was heading south to Richmond, a Civil War burg that is a nice day-trip from Washington, DC, including ample time for touring the town.

Fredericksburg's historic downtown is a pleasant oasis, rich in history that withstands the tacky strip malls, edge cities, and most of the gridlock of greater Fredericksburg, which stands at least at some distance from the historic area. Fredericksburg's downtown, all six blocks of it, remains little changed since Generals Grant and Lee rode their respective horses through town—on different occasions, of course, as they were not exactly on speaking terms at the time. It still remains very much a southern town, with the muted and softer accents of Virginia as contrasted to the clipped accents heard just 40 miles north. That August afternoon was particularly beautiful, although more than a few tourists were there to enjoy it. But, I thought, I guess I can share.

We were sitting in Beau's office, discussing what seemed to be the best offer he had yet received for his distributorship, a very reasonable offer for a firm with $28 million in sales.

"I like the deal, but this earnout is ridiculous," Beau told me.

"Beau, what are you saying to me, man? You repeatedly insisted to these people, not to mention me, that achieving next year's projected earnings was a slam dunk."

"Yeah, but you know as well as I do that that was while we were negotiating . . . right?"

"Beau, you cannot have it both ways."

Be careful what you ask for, deal for, or pray for. Clients should always be aware that too great an emphasis on future prospects might result in earnout offers that say, in effect, "Okay, if you say you can do it, then do it and we will gladly pay you for it."

Sometimes, it is better to accept a more basic deal for less nominal transaction value but a more certain and immediate collectability.

Why Earnouts Are Dreaded but Very Frequently a Deal Component

After cash, earnouts are the most frequently used form of consideration in Middle Market mergers and acquisitions (M&A) transactions. Earnouts amount to an estimated 15% to 25% of deal value in probably 75% of Middle Market deals. But earnouts may be dreaded for any number of reasons, including a kind of post-transaction performance anxiety. In fact, they often prove to be real deal catalysts, a means of closing a deal that otherwise would not close. Via earnouts, buyers set aside a portion of their purchase price for a business to be paid if and when the business meets one or more financial performance targets following the consummation of the transaction.

Negotiating earnouts tends to be an awkward process, and committing them to paper is no less so, because earnouts are potentially quite susceptible to different interpretations or misinterpretations and, sometimes, to conscious or subconscious manipulation by buyers . . . and even sellers. Furthermore, earnouts very likely will frustrate sellers, because invariably, the sellers' ability to drive the business performance that will generate earnouts is minimized or entirely eliminated once the deal closes. Earnouts can also frustrate buyers, as well, by inhibiting their ability to integrate the seller's business into their organization.

Middle Market M&A transactions are driven by initially a convergence and eventually a divergence of interest. A would-be seller and a field of prospective buyers have very different interests at the start of the M&A process, but as the negotiated auction advances, less interested parties drop out and ultimately, there is a seller, a buyer and an executed Letter of Intent, or LOI (convergence). During confirmatory due diligence and final negotiations, the seller and the buyer are committed to a common goal: closing the deal. But once that deal has closed, the interests of the seller and the buyer once again diverge, often for good. Most sellers want to take all the consideration due them, ASAP, and run. Most buyers intend to hold back what they can in the form of earnouts and escrows as long as possible. The time value of money alone makes this understandable, but it has more to do with uncertainties about future performance.

The once-shared motivations of seller and buyer all but inevitably will be lost with the passage of time. A sense of buyer's remorse may arise and, to varying degrees, usually does, reminding one of the proverbial employee who, while with the firm, was considered among its best and brightest, but whose mistakes and human frailties gradually become more obvious after his departure. To some degree, the departing seller is very like that employee. Confirmatory due diligence and final negotiations are conducted at precisely the point that the enterprise the seller created holds its greatest attraction for the buyer. In the cold light of a post-transaction morning, shortcomings and disappointments will be inevitable. The buyer may blame the seller for developments quite beyond the seller's control, or for issues that the seller was under no obligation to disclose to the buyer or that were equally unknown to the seller. Industry changes that came up abruptly (disruptive competitive or technology changes) are an example of the latter. The buyer may blame the seller for the buyer's own failure to do his homework over the course of the negotiated auction, confirmatory due diligence, and in final agreements.

Postclosing, most buyers will believe that the businesses they now own are not exactly the ones for which they negotiated. The buyers thought they were buying a more loyal client base, a more committed workforce, stronger vendor relationships, a better business environment, and so forth. What they now own is different, diminished, at least in their minds. And with that, buyers very likely will recollect the slings and arrows of tough pretransaction negotiations (especially if the principals were involved) with more than a little resentment. All of this negativity may coalesce to make sellers' hopes of actually collecting their earnouts somewhat diminished. So real caution is called for when negotiating these necessary but painful provisions.

Whose Earnings Are These Anyway?

Buyers buy future earnings, not past earnings. But buyers also buy earnings growth rates, at least implicitly, by paying higher EBITDA multiples on trailing earnings for faster-growing businesses. Sellers are well aware of what buyers buy and as a result, sellers demand premium valuations for companies that have strong future earnings prospects. Inevitably, then, M&A transaction prices, consideration, and terms reflect future earnings estimates and growth rates.

Additionally, sellers and buyers forever have debated the question "Who owns next year's earnings?" If the buyer owns the company next year, then why should he pay for next year's earnings when closing the deal today? While this book will not put that debate to rest, buyers pursue one acquisition while declining to purchase any number of others based on the comparable performances—*and financial prospects*—of all the acquisition candidates before them. The ultimate acquisition will offer the best fit and performance potential among the businesses the buyer considers. Its EBITDA multiple inevitably will reflect its superior potential earnings and future earnings growth rate to a greater or lesser degree, even though it may be (usually is) stated as a higher multiple of recent historic earnings. But compromises on this issue (who owns the future) are commonly reached in the form of an earnout.

Avoid Confusion: Understand the Differences between Two Types of Earnouts

It is not my intention to split hairs when I prefer looking at earnouts as either of two types. It simply makes earnouts easier to analyze and structure if one makes the distinction between these two forms. The main differences are driven by the motivation behind the earnout in the first place (i.e., either achieving comfort or incentivizing growth). There also may be different tax consequences between the two, whether desired or unintentional.

Investment bankers, when analyzing any offer that incorporates an earnout, should begin by separating the wheat from the corn. Comfort earnouts often are confused—sometimes quite intentionally by buyers—with *incentive compensation* payable to sellers, in return for their remaining with the company in some capacity to grow the business and make it more successful. This latter type of earnout (incentive) is most likely to be offered when:

- The seller remains in the employ of the buyer after the deal closes, usually in a senior management capacity with future revenue responsibility.
- The negotiated purchase price of the business "as is" on the closing date is appropriate and not in dispute and not contingent on future performance.

Such earnouts should be thought of as incentive earnouts—not really earnouts at all, but more like a sales commission or the equivalent.

The second form of earnout (a true earnout) is intended to bring a level of comfort to a deal that is partially based on the company's future earnings. Comfort earnouts allow a deal to get done that otherwise might not get done. Every buyer, appropriately enough, will be somewhat anxious as to whether or not the company he acquires will achieve next year's earnings targets, as the seller said it would.

During negotiations, sellers, in an understandable attempt to maximize the multiple of trailing earnings paid by the buyer, will usually all but insist that the company can meet or exceed those targets. After all, they have been running the business umpteen years, they know it and its industry inside out, and they are on track.

Comfort earnouts are designed to bridge the gap between the seller's certainty and the buyer's anxiety when doing so is necessary to close the deal. Comfort earnouts allow sellers to "put their money where their mouth is," for buyers who are not, as yet, fully convinced. For example, both the buyer and the seller may be quite certain that the business will generate at least $15 million in sales at a 10% EBITDA margin in the year following its acquisition. Its track record over the course of the past several years makes that highly likely. The seller furthermore strongly believes the business will generate $16 million in revenues next year, while maintaining its EBITDA margin. On this point, the buyer is not so sure. But both parties agree on a 6 times EBITDA multiple, based their negotiations.

Value of business based on past earnings	$9.0 million
Value of business based on next year's earnings	$9.6 million
Suggested comfort earnout	$600,000

Elements of Negotiation in a Comfort (True) Earnout

The main elements to be negotiated in a comfort earnout include:

- The metric on which the earnout is to be based (sales, EBITDA, gross margin, etc.)
- Who controls events, or at least their measurement, throughout the earnout period
- Whether earnouts will:
  - Be all or nothing, or proportionate and scaled to achieved performance
  - Allow peaks and valleys in performance to offset each other
  - Be upside limited
- The time duration of the earnout

Bottom Line Earnout Metric (EBITDA, etc.)

Once the seller and the buyer have agreed to an earnout in concept, the question arises of how to measure the performance by which it will be earned. On first glance, this might seem simple enough. If, in the above example, the seller's company generates an additional $100,000 in EBITDA, then the buyer will pay an additional $600,000 in purchase price, or six times the gain in EBITDA up to a maximum $600,000 earnout. In the final analysis, though, the seller must understand that the buyer usually will be in control of all of the profit and loss (P&L) and management decisions that will drive the company's EBITDA postacquisition. In that regard, the buyer might "manage" the company's earnings by investing heavily in future expansion or property, plant, and equipment, or in sales or other personnel.

Earnings and EBITDA can be managed or even manipulated in innumerable ways by a buyer disposed to do so, while the seller usually has virtually no say in the matter and no actual influence on the results on which the comfort earnout will be granted or withheld. And the buyer essentially will be justified in any decisions he or she may make: he/she has bought the company, now owns it, and calls the tune as to how it will be run. The buyer may, for a legitimate reason even, decide to substantially modify the business emphasis as to certain sales or product categories in a way that harms the seller's earnout.

Top-Line Earnout Metric (Sales)

Should an EBITDA-related earnout metric prove too prone to "management" or "manipulation" by the buyer to be acceptable to the seller, it may be reasonable to go back to the drawing board and create a comfort earnout metric based on hitting a $16 million sales target (continuing with the prior example). A revenues-based comfort earnout metric should prove far less susceptible to manipulation or management by the buyer.

Revenues-based comfort earnouts may prove problematic, however, when the seller contractually continues to run the company during the comfort earnout period, as sometimes happens in Middle Market M&A transactions. Given this scenario, we may well find ourselves counseling, "buyer beware," because a seller intent upon maximizing a revenues-based comfort earnout might decide to focus on increasing company sales with little or no concern as to the impact of those sales on EBITDA-related performance metrics. The buyer could see a few "fire sale" signs appearing.

Middle-Line Earnout Metric (Gross Margin)

Buyers are likely to be most comfortable having EBITDA-related "bottom line" metrics driving comfort earnout calculations. Sellers—especially those who continue to run the company for an interim period—in most cases would prefer a top-line-revenues metric. Is there a possible compromise between the two? Yes, there is, at least somewhat.

Many investment banking professionals advise buyers and sellers alike to consider using gross profit margins as a comfort earnout metric. The gross profit margin metric constitutes possibly the best comfort earnout compromise buyers and sellers will find—*assuming the use of a single metric*—and they frequently agree to it. Surprise: The gross profit margin metric, like its revenues- and EBITDA-related counterparts, *is not perfect*. But it is clearly the most neutral *single* metric among the options available to the buyer and the seller. It is not perfect, because it neglects to consider bottom-line earnings performance—which is, of course, what the buyer thinks he is buying.

Mixed Earnout Metrics

Comfort earnouts based on mixed metrics also may be considered and are frequently the best solution, as both parties receive a good degree of protection. For example, an earnout agreement may stipulate that the seller will be entitled to a comfort earnout according to an agreed-upon formula, "provided the company generates at least $3 million in gross margin and at least $1 million in EBITDA during the earnout period." These "at least" phrases, of course, may be proportionately scaled in some way to determine the actual earnout due. Understandably, mixed-metric earnout agreements are even more difficult to develop and think through in a manner that makes total sense to all concerned. Mixed-metric earnouts also remain somewhat, but certainly less, vulnerable to the same problems (manipulation) arising from sales- or EBITDA-based comfort earnout metrics.

Royalty Earnout Approaches

Royalty-based earnout metrics are simply based on a "unit of product," etc. They are paid to the seller in the form of a royalty, a process that does not overcome the "fire sale issue" inherent in revenue-based comfort earnouts. Their main advantage may be that they are a little easier to measure, in that the point of measurement is a product, not revenue. In the case of revenue, the question can always arise: revenue from exactly what? This is especially true when the products and service of the seller and new owner are mixed; the royalty approach may somewhat alleviate this concern.

Effective or Legal Control

No matter what form of earnout proves acceptable to seller and buyer alike, a salient question will be, "Who controls the company?" From an ownership point of view, of course, the buyer will control the company while being responsible for the decisions driving earnout metric performances. Once a deal has closed, the company no longer belongs to the seller, and the buyer is entitled to make all of the decisions related to its management, no matter how brilliant or how ill-advised they may be and regardless of their impact upon the metrics driving the seller's comfort earnouts.

The only way around this—from the seller's perspective—is through legally binding agreements specifying the *precise way of measuring* the earnout metrics, any actions the buyer may take notwithstanding. For example, during the earnout period, any administrative salary increases initiated by management could be ignored by contract, thereby giving the seller effective control at least over that aspect of the earnout measurement.

Other Earnout Issues

- Is the earnout all or nothing, or proportionate and scaled to performance?
- Does the earnout allow peaks and valleys in performance to offset each other?
- Is the earnout upside limited?

Most earnouts are paid proportionally as a simple percentage or as different performance thresholds of the established earnout metric are reached, as opposed to being paid on an "all or nothing" basis. Virtually no seller ever should agree to "all or nothing" earnouts, as it is obvious that they simply do not usually make sense. However, I have seen then in practice, so I mention them.

When the seller and the buyer have agreed to multi-year earnouts, spikes (overachievement) and valleys (underachievement) and related cumulative or offsetting provisions may be incorporated into the agreement. In some deals for multi-year earnouts, if the company handily outperforms the metric or target by which the seller would maximize his earnout, the excess might be carried over to the following year in a manner that allows the seller to receive his second-year earnout even if the company falls short of its second-year metric (sometimes referred to as "carry forward" provisions). Or, just as easily and with similar effect, multi-year earnout agreements also might include provisions allowing the buyer to "carry back" to and against prior years' deficiencies, should the company exceed following-year performance targets.

What if the company exceeds the performance target(s) that maximize the seller's earnout? Should the seller's earnout payment be increased beyond the agreed-upon cap? The question comes up in many earnout negotiations and the answer is ultimately derived from negotiation. In this regard, earnout payments, exceeding a preset "cap," might be characterized as incentive earnouts and calculated differently, again more like a sales commission.

In the final analysis, multi-year earnouts tend to be determined on a deal-by-deal basis, with no one standard approach being generally accepted for Middle Market M&A transactions.

The Likelihood of Earnout Collections and the Time Factor

A seller's likelihood of collecting multi-year earnouts tends to decline proportionally—or even exponentially—with each passing year following the closing of the transaction. Much will depend on the quality of the earnout terms, the clarity with which they are committed to paper during final negotiations, and the expertise of the seller's own investment bankers and attorneys working in collaboration with each other. Most sellers will have essentially no practical firsthand experience with earnouts upon entering into final negotiations for the sale of their companies. As a result, their close collaboration with their investment bankers and attorneys will be critical, as their intermediaries should advise them what to expect and what not to expect.

As I have said before, investment bankers should especially invite their sales-side clients to estimate their own earnout expectations, based on a reasonable range of post-transaction performances by their companies (see Chapter 18). This has the very positive effect of getting a client to focus on what he really believes the outcome will be.

- How do such performance ranges and resulting earnouts affect the sellers' sense of the ideal earnout arrangements?
- What, then, is their preferred earnout arrangement?
- Can they "sell it" to the buyer? If not, what should be the sellers' fall-back position?

To the extent that M&A investment bankers can educate their sales-side clients as to how earnouts work in the real world, the sellers will find themselves much better prepared to negotiate or provide valuable input into the negotiation and accordingly will be much less likely to be unpleasantly surprised in the long run. Experienced intermediaries will ensure that sellers understand that buyers' remorse, buyers' interpretation of earnout provisions, and buyers' "management" and possible manipulation of financial results all may dramatically affect earnout compensation.

Somewhat arbitrarily, but based on real-life experience, I recommend that sellers (when weighing relative offers) should assume no more than an 80% to 90% likelihood of receiving a first year earnout, with the odds falling by another 20% with each passing year. Favorable exceptions to this rule are not infrequent, and the resulting checks should be welcomed with great enthusiasm and taken to the bank joyfully. I still regularly receive fees from clients arising from earnouts for five or six years after a deal has closed.

When an Earnout Is Simply Frosting on the Cake

Sometimes the stars all align. Some lucky sellers, of course, can be so satisfied with the noncontingent consideration they receive upon closing the sale of their companies that the earnout provisions are just frosting. For them, the deal terms proved so favorable that the earnout, in essence, becomes a bonus. These types of earnouts are often lumped with the rest out of a lack of understanding. They are, as I said, just frosting on the cake and should be viewed and relished as such. The cautionary warnings that accompany *normal earnouts*, where uncertainty is a real issue of concern, are not applicable here, at least to any great extent.

Earnouts and Taxes

The tax treatment of earnouts is also a major consideration. Are earnouts taxable as capital gains or ordinary income? Court rulings are mixed on the issue. For the most part, though, tax law and precedent tend to recognize installment payments in uncertain amounts emanating from a business sale as part of the purchase price, reportable as capital gains income.

In any event, it is critically important that sellers engage experienced tax counsel, especially when drafting the earnout agreement, to preserve sellers' options. Unless they moonlight as tax attorneys, investment bankers are not qualified to serve as tax counsel to their sales-side clients on complex deal-related tax matters, especially matters requiring very careful drafting of language. Without presuming to be (or capable of being) tax counsel, I will offer some rough tax guidelines on earnouts:

- When an earnout is absolutely conditioned on the seller's continued post-transaction employment by the buyer, the earnout is in danger of being characterized as ordinary income for tax purposes (while arguments supporting its treatment as capital gains would prove more problematic).
- Consistently characterizing the earnout as an element of the purchase price in the various closing agreements would tend to support capital gains treatment for it.
- When the earnout is structured as a deferred payment note of some sort, reducible in the event of the company's failure to meet earnout

targets, it arguably may better support a better argument for capital gains treatment.

Again: Under all circumstances, the *drafting* of earnout agreements by highly experienced tax counsel is absolutely critical.

Chapter Highlights

- A large number of Middle Market M&A transactions incorporate earnouts as a useful, if problematic, closing device.
- The likelihood of collection and the difficulty of measurement are the principal problems raised by earnouts.
- The likelihood of collection may be reduced dramatically by:
  - Postdeal buyer remorse
  - The slings and arrows of predeal negotiation
  - Miscommunication and misinterpretation of earnout agreements
  - Buyer "management" or outright manipulation of the company's post-transaction financial performance (among other things)
- There are two earnout types:
  - Incentive earnouts
  - Comfort earnouts
- Critical earnout negotiation elements include:
  - The metric (Top-Line, Bottom-Line, Middle-Line, Royalty, and/or Mixed) by which the post-transaction company's performance will be measured
  - The absolute financial performance(s) that must be attained to receive earnouts
  - Whether the buyer or the seller will be in control—either legal or effective—of decisions or of the measurement of the consequences of decisions driving the company's performance against earnout targets during the earnout period
  - Whether the earnouts will be cumulative or offsetting
  - The duration of the earnout period
  - How target-exceeding performances will be treated
- The tax treatment of earnouts—whether as capital gains or ordinary income—will depend upon careful and consistent drafting of earnout agreement and related transaction documents by highly experienced tax attorneys.
- Sellers always should participate in estimating both a potential range of earnout payments and their likelihood of collection, so as to better understand their role within the overall transaction itself and to inform the negotiations of the earnout agreement (see Exhibit 19.1).

EXHIBIT 19.1   Example of a Complex Earnout Agreement

"Schedule B Earnout Covenants"

Section 1. From and after the Closing through the completion of calendar year 2006, ABC [Buyer] shall maintain, or cause XYZ [Seller] to maintain, a financial reporting system that enables ABC or XYZ, as applicable, to separately account for the items of revenue and expense necessary to make the calculations required by this Section for each of calendar years 2007, 2008, and 2009. ABC shall maintain XYZ as a subsidiary during calendar years 2007, 2008, and 2009 ABC shall, and shall cause XYZ to act in good faith with respect to the operation of XYZ during calendar years 2007, 2008, and 2009 (including, but not limited to, using commercially reasonable efforts to maintain and increase existing levels of business and to obtain new orders and contracts for XYZ's products and services at reasonably acceptable margins). To the extent consistent with its good faith judgment regarding whether such action is in the best interests of ABC and XYZ, and allowing for changes resulting from the acquisition of XYZ by ABC as a subsidiary of ABC, changes in the administrative operations of XYZ as a result of such acquisition, and other changes reasonably related to XYZ being a subsidiary of ABC, ABC shall cause XYZ to operate XYZ's business in a manner reasonably consistent with the lesser of (a) practices of the business of XYZ prior to the Closing and (a) reasonably prudent business practices.

Section 2. Without limiting the foregoing, during calendar years 2007, 2008, and 2009, ABC shall use commercially reasonable efforts to, and shall use commercially reasonable efforts to cause XYZ to:

(a) operate in compliance, in all material respects, with applicable Laws and XYZ's contracts;

(b) keep XYZ's assets and property in satisfactory operating condition, ordinary wear and tear excepted, and make or cause to be made all repairs, renewals, replacements, and improvements thereto which are necessary so that the business can be carried on in the ordinary course of business;

(c) maintain sufficient staffing levels to operate XYZ in the ordinary course of business, and increase such staffing levels as necessary to perform under XYZ's contracts; and

(d) maintain and hold in full force and effect all material licenses, permits, certificates, authorizations, security clearances, and qualifications necessary to own and operate its properties and to carry on its business in the ordinary course of business.

Section 3. In addition, and without limiting the foregoing, during the first 18 months after the Closing, without the prior written consent of the Shareholders' Representative, ABC shall not take, and shall cause XYZ to refrain from taking, any action (or omit to take any action) that results in XYZ terminating without Cause (as defined in the Key Employee Employment Agreement) the employment of any of the Key Employees, or reassigning or transferring the Key Employees such that their full-timed

EXHIBIT 19.1 *(Continued)*

services are not available to XYZ and in the performance of XYZ contracts provided, however, that during calendar years 2007, 2008, and 2009, without the prior written consent of the Shareholders' Representative, ABC shall not take, and shall cause XYZ to refrain from taking, any action (or omit to take any action) that results in XYZ terminating without Cause (as defined in the Key Employee Employment Agreement) the employment of Elmer Jones.

Section 4. In addition, and without limiting the foregoing, during calendar years 2007, 2008, and 2009, without the prior written consent of the Shareholders' Representative, ABC shall not take, and shall cause XYZ to refrain from taking, any action (or omit to take any action) that results in XYZ:

(a) purchasing an equity interest in, or a portion of the assets of, any corporation, partnership, association, or other business organization or division thereof, except for any such purchase that would not reasonably be expected to have a material adverse impact on XYZ's EBITDA results;

(b) making any reclassification of assets or liabilities, except as may be required by Law or GAAP;

(c) terminating or breaching the Abramson Consulting Agreement for a reason other Abraham Abramson's breach of such agreement; or

(d) entering into any agreement or transaction with an Affiliate of XYZ on terms and conditions other than arm's-length terms and conditions.

Section 5. If, during calendar years 2007, 2008, or 2009, XYZ is sold (whether by a sale of all or substantially all of XYZ's assets, a sale of a majority of XYZ's equity securities, merger, consolidation, or otherwise (a "Transaction"), but not including a reorganization among ABC or its Affiliates other than XYZ) to a Person other than an Affiliate of ABC, then upon consummation of the transaction, ABC shall make a final Earnout payment to the Shareholders' Representative on the closing date of such Transaction, by wire transfer calculated as follows:

(a) The Actual EBITDA for the calendar year in which the consummation of such Transaction occurs shall be calculated as follows:

(i) If such Transaction is closed prior to June 30, Actual EBITDA for such year shall be presumed to over perform (or underperform) Target EBITDA for such year by the same percentage as Actual EBITDA for the prior year over performed (or underperformed) Target EBITDA for the prior year; and

(ii) If such Transaction is closed after June 30, Actual EBITDA for such year shall be presumed to over perform (or underperform) Target EBITDA for such year by the ratio determined by dividing (x) the Actual EBITDA achieved through the date of closing of such Transaction by (y) the Target EBITDA through the date of closing of such Transaction as calculated on a straight-line basis. (For clarity and by way of example, if Target EBITDA for a year is $7.2 million and the Transaction occurred at the end of the ninth month, straight-line monthly EBITDA of $0.6 million would be multiplied

(Continued)

EXHIBIT 19.1   *(Continued)*

times nine to arrive at the factor used for (y) in the above formula.)

(b) The Actual EBITDA for any calendar year following the year in which the consummation of such Transaction occurs (if applicable) shall be calculated by (i) multiplying Target EBITDA for such year by (ii) the average of the percentages by which Actual EBITDA (including Actual EBITDA calculated pursuant to clause (a) above, if applicable) exceeded (or was less than) Target EBITDA for the preceding calendar years.

(c) The Earnout payment shall otherwise be subject to the limitations in and calculated and paid as provided in Section 2.2(c) of the Agreement. Upon making such payment, ABC shall have not further Earnout obligations.

The Referenced Section in the Above 2.2

Purchase Consideration

As payment in full for all of the Shares and termination of all of the Options, ABC shall pay, in accordance with the terms and conditions of this Agreement, the amount equal to the Estimated Closing Cash Purchase Price, adjusted in accordance with Sections 2.3(c) and 2.3(e), plus the Stock Consideration, plus the Earnout (to the extent earned and subject to setoff and deductions as provided under this Agreement) (the *"Purchase Consideration"*). Payments shall be made in accordance with the Flow of Funds Memorandum, which will be signed by the Shareholders' Representative and ABC and delivered at the Closing. ABC shall pay in accordance with the terms and conditions hereof (a) at Closing, the *"Base Consideration"* that shall consist of (i) the Closing Cash Consideration (as defined and calculated pursuant to Section 2.3(a) below) and (ii) the Stock Consideration (as defined in Section 2.2(b) below); and (b) after Closing, the amount of any adjustment under Section 2.3(e) and the Earnout to the extent that the Earnout is earned pursuant to Section 2.2(c) below.

CHAPTER 20

The Proof Phase, or the Final Days

Confirmatory Due Diligence, the Definitive Agreement, and Closing

Confirmatory Due Diligence

Confirmatory due diligence (as opposed to pre-Letter of Intent (LOI) preliminary due diligence), drafting and negotiating the Definitive Agreement and finally closing the deal generally transpire over the course of some 60 days following the seller's acceptance of the successful (thus far at least) buyer's LOI. This chapter will address that process while avoiding becoming unnecessarily technical, but by necessity will repeat certain points made elsewhere in this book.

Confirmatory due diligence during the final 60 days before the a deal closes tends to fall into three major areas:

- Financial
- Legal
- Operational

Financial Due Diligence

Financial due diligence is conducted by the buyer's accountants as they carefully review the seller's financial records. Financial due diligence is pretty much that simple. The buyer essentially is taking advantage of his last opportunity to confirm that the company's actual financial performance "track" with the seller's representations of that performance as communicated throughout the negotiated auction period. I know I am repeating myself, but this is a point well worth repeating: Dangers lurk in the buyer's confirmatory due diligence if the seller has failed to complete a comprehensive audit (or at least a review) with his own CPA, or possibly another CPA, in advance of confirmatory due diligence. At the very least, the seller should ensure that a review is conducted of all his financials and accounting practices before the buyer issues an LOI and starts even his preliminary, much less confirmatory, due diligence to address and correct problems before the buyer happens upon them.

Legal Due Diligence

Legal due diligence involves a review of seller's documentation of legal agreements with customers, suppliers, landlords, lenders, taxing and licensing authorities, employees, subcontractors, and health and safety regulators, etc. While conducting legal due diligence, the buyer's attorneys and advisors also will ensure that patents, trademarks, copyrights, titles, and so forth are in good shape. Legal due diligence usually is conducted simultaneously with the drafting of the definitive sales agreement, because these relationships and contracts usually are incorporated within the Definitive Agreement (while the seller affirms that they are what they have been purported to be), and are all-inclusive. A good part of legal due diligence is simply aggregating much of the legal documentation supplied to the buyer by the seller as schedules and appendices to the Definitive Agreement.

Operational Due Diligence

Operational due diligence includes:

- Reviews of the seller's important technologies and processes and fixed assets
- Meetings with key customers
- A review of the accounting systems that the seller has created and their overall effectiveness (as opposed to the content of their financials)
- Meetings with executive management and sometimes key customers
- And more

The Definitive Agreement

Also known as the Asset Purchase Agreement or Stock Purchase Agreement, among other names, the Definitive Agreement is the final binding agreement of the Middle Market merger and acquisition (M&A) transaction. In terms of its preparation and content, the Definitive Agreement tends to become fairly lengthy, given all of the documentation referred to and incorporated within it, as well as its various appendices and schedules. Other legal issues would include:

- Incorporating previously agreed-to business terms in a legal format that satisfies counsel's concerns that they are easily understood, agreeable to both parties and enforceable.

- Establishing the seller's limits on the indemnification of the buyer, in the event of post-transaction surprises or discoveries that otherwise might be considered the seller's responsibility following settlement. The *maximum* amount of indemnification most buyers would request would cover the total purchase price; for various reasons, seller indemnification limits usually though are much less than that.[1] Furthermore, indemnification limits should be related to the actual conditions and risks in a particular deal, not arbitrarily assigned because of custom or tradition or because that is ("the way we have always done it"). This is equally true for the issue immediately following.
- Establishing categories of potential buyer claims and estimating a minimum dollar value per category, as well as an agreed aggregate dollar value of those potential claims, before any can be asserted, often known as "buckets or baskets."
- The degree of certitude—whether "absolute knowledge" or "to the best of the seller's knowledge"—with which the seller states that his representations and warranties, or certain of them, are correct will make a great deal of difference subsequently, should problems arise as far as what the buyer can claim is concerned.
- Whether all liabilities are included in the balance sheet. (Unlikely they will or can be).
- Whether the financial statements present everything consistently with past reporting practices or with GAAP or both.
- Provisions for settling differences.
- Jurisdictional establishment.
- Rights and remedies of seller and buyer, respectively, in the event of default.
- Escrow agreements:
  - Standard hold-backs range from 10% to 20% of total deal consideration before earnouts.
  - One to two years constitutes a standard duration for most escrow hold-backs.
  - While most escrow hold-back agreements are set at a 12- to 24-month period, sellers often may be better off seeking a shorter hold-back duration than a lower hold-back percentage, because statutes of limitations for civil claims often do not expire for two years. In other words, sellers may tend to be more exposed by time than amounts escrowed, but a highly experienced attorney's counsel is absolutely critical on all such decisions.
  - Whether or not interest will accrue—and if so, at what rate, etc.—on escrow accounts also must be negotiated; the funds escrowed belong to the seller, after all, and there is without doubt a time value of

money attached to escrowed funds. Even so, many escrow agents will not pay interest on escrowed funds.

- Sometimes, it may be suggested that the seller accept a promissory note from the buyer in lieu of separately escrowed funds. This is rarely acceptable to the seller, as it eliminates some of the formality and impartiality of a third-party escrow agent, but should the seller in fact find such an escrow note acceptable for any reason, the seller should be entitled to receive interest on it.
- Escrow agreements arise in both stock and asset deals; in stock deals, however, escrow agreements tend to involve larger hold-backs for longer durations, as the transferee's potential liability to the buyer may be greater when the buyer acquires the seller's business entity as opposed to simply the assets of the business.
- Confirmatory due diligence should be complete when the Definitive Agreement is signed. Closing should not ordinarily be subject to further due diligence.

The Final Days: Investment Bankers and Attorneys

Most of the issues that pop up during or prior to closing are legal in nature. Should business differences arise during this period, an experienced transaction attorney who was uninvolved in negotiating the original business terms will defer to the investment banker, and then they likely will collaborate on how the matter should be addressed.

As I have said often in this book, during the final days, the transaction attorney is the team leader. The investment banker, if necessary, ensures that the transaction attorney is apprised of the business terms (and context) negotiated by the investment banker up through the executed LOI.

This is where the services of an experienced transaction attorney are so critical. Inexperience will tend to lead to either overkill (usually as a result of relying on standard templates and static rules rather than the practical application of experience and knowledge on an issue by issue basis) and deal problems as a result, or in the alternative missing important provisions.

The Critical Importance of Speed in the Final Days

This book has argued for deliberation and orchestration at the expense of speed throughout most of the negotiated auction. Successful Middle Market M&A transactions take time if an optimal number of prospective buyers is to be identified and courted throughout the auction. In the final days prior to closing, however, all due haste should be taken to close the deal. Keep people moving! By the time a deal closing is imminent, nerves on both sides tend to be frayed and minds may change quite quickly. Sellers anticipating their big payouts grow anxious to be done with the deal and take their cash to the bank. Buyers, reviewing every last detail, actually may begin to worry: "Have I done the right thing?" Nor will the world around the seller and the buyer stop revolving to allow them to close their deal. In fact, experienced investment bankers may wonder whether or not the world lies in wait for precisely such moments so as to throw huge wrenches into the gears.

Evidence of major industry downturns affecting the seller, the buyer, or both may be reported in the final days before a deal has done. The seller—or the buyer—might lose one or more major clients, or gain some. A world-changing incident such as 9/11 can occur. Anything can happen, and as Murphy's Law reminds us again and again, anything that can happen will happen, and at usually the worst possible time. Everything can change overnight. The author has experienced far too many "near-death experiences" in the final days prior to closing, where a moderate delay would have imploded the deal. Occasionally, a transaction has closed within weeks of a crash in the seller's (or the buyer's) industry. In such cases, a slight delay would have resulted in a deal that was deader than the proverbial doornail.

The Closing and the Surprise at Closing

West Palm Beach, FL—December 2000

My client Bob's complexion grew more and more gray as the interminable day proceeded.

We had been shuffling settlement papers since 8:00 A.M. in the offices of the buyer's attorneys; it was now 3:00 P.M. Our conference room looked over the Intracoastal Waterway and Palm Beach. Out there, a beautiful afternoon unfolded as if to exponentially increase the torment and the tedium we were experiencing in the room. I suspected that Bob really, really wanted to scream. I know I did. Luckily, we were too tired to give in to our impulses.

"We're just about finished here," said the buyer's attorney, "but where is your counsel's legal opinion that the seller is in good standing with the state of Maryland with respect to all filings and business licenses at the state and county level?"

For reasons I cannot recall, my client's attorney was not in attendance at the settlement. Perhaps he was out there, in another stultifying conference room, deliberating issues arising from hanging chads in the presidential election.

After a few minutes, we tracked down the seller's attorney. Thankfully, he was not in Florida but back in Maryland on standby in case we needed any help. And we do. We explained our predicament and ask for a copy of the attorney's legal opinion on the matter.

"Legal opinion? Sorry, Dennis, but we're just the seller's transaction attorney, not its general counsel. We can't do a legal opinion. And besides, this is the first time the buyer's counsel has even asked for one."

Bob was looking really, really gray now. I knew he had high blood pressure and a heart condition, as well as a truly intense disposition, and he was not feeling particularly well at this point. I scanned the conference room, wondering if there were any portable defibrillators nearby.

Somehow, we got through it all. We completed the settlement, and color and life returned to Bob's face by the time we sat down to a settlement dinner that night. I wonder, sometimes, how many years a closing takes off one's life—but, then again, I have been to too many to be here today if somehow we did not survive despite it all.

P.S. Bob's doing great these days, wealthily retired, exercising his way back to nearly robust health, and enjoying his grandkids, farm, and yacht.

If only closings were noneventful confirmations of all the six or eight or longer months of concentrated effort that went into the deal at hand. Some closings do seem anticlimactic, but many of them are far from it. There is always something that comes up at the last minute that seems like a deal-killer, engenders all the posturing that is associated with deal-killers (people stomp out of the room, etc), but usually isn't. Unless something really drastic comes up at the last minute, the sheer momentum of emotional commitment (the parties never admit it, but it is powerful and always there) will carry the day. And if something important enough to actually put the deal in real jeopardy does come up, then some advisor has probably dropped the ball.

This is not to say closings are easy. They aren't. They are more likely to be boring, exhausting, and time consuming—and the indirect cause of the deaths of several small-sized trees necessary to provide paperwork that probably no one will ever look at again. Closings remind me of the way I once heard an FBI agent describe his career. He described it as years of sheer boredom interspersed by moments of pure terror.

I don't mean to make light of settlements. The closest times I have ever consistently come to actually, and I do mean actually, seeing clients suffer from apoplexy or worse, have been at this point when, from their inexperienced point of view, it looks like it could all blow up. It sometimes does, of course, but not usually. However, if the client has already mentally started his new life in Arizona or wherever and some young attorney says there is no way we can close because your lawyers can't give a legal opinion as to whether you are in good standing with the state, since they aren't your general counsel, he might just be a little upset.[2]

Chapter Highlights

- The 60-day or so exclusivity period following the buyer's execution of the LOI allows the buyer to undertake confirmatory due diligence, draft the final binding agreement and the Definitive Agreement, and prepare for final negotiations.
- Through a comprehensive final review of seller financials and other relevant documents, confirmatory due diligence addresses:
  - Financial issues
  - Legal issues
  - Operational issues
- Legal due diligence principally entails a careful review of:
  - All contractual relationships
  - Seller representations and warranties
  - Escrow agreements
  - Indemnification limits and buckets
  - Business terms as translated into "legalese"
- Escrow agreements parameters generally:
  - Specify a 12- to 24-month escrow duration (though sellers may prefer to limit such periods to 18-months or less, in light of statute of limitations issues)
  - Involve set-aside amounts ranging from 10% to 20% of the total transaction value price (wholly independent of earnout arrangements)
  - May be negotiated in either stock or asset deals
- The seller's Middle Market M&A investment banker and transaction attorney each bring a discrete and complementary expertise to final negotiations and the closing of a transaction; however, during the deal's final preclosing days, the seller's lawyer most definitely is the team leader.
- Going through this process with an inexperienced transaction attorney is like being guided up Mt. Everest with somebody who has never been there themselves.
- Speeding the process is critically important during the transaction's final days.
- Almost inevitably, one or more surprises will surface at the closing.

Notes

1. In certain industries, conventions have apparently been developed for indemnification maximum. For example, in government contracting, over the last few years the norm has tended to be around 25% to 50% of the total purchase price. I suspect this has as much as anything to do with a small community of lawyers who do these deals over and over again until what is initially random eventually becomes convention. The American Bar Association, by the way, has published a detailed analysis of transaction norms and statistics dealing with percentages of indemnifications and many other worthwhile reference points (it can be found on their Web site), and that is a document that should be in the library of every transactional attorney and investment banker.
2. It should be noted here that the settlement and execution of the closing documents may or may not be simultaneous, although in my experience they usually are.

CHAPTER 21

After the Nuptials: Postmerger and Acquisition Failures
A Very Brief Chapter, Mainly for Buyers

Dulles Tech Corridor, VA—May 1998

The first thing to catch my eye as we walked into the lobby of the northern Virginia technology company was a doubles match being played quite aggressively on the ping pong table, and 15 or more electronic games commanding the undivided attention of employees wearing cutoff jeans and ragged tee-shirts.

My client Elliot and I approached a receptionist, who was dressed as though she had just returned from the Woodstock rock festival, circa 1969. I introduced myself and Elliot, adding that we were scheduled to meet with the tech company's CEO, "Mr. Andretti," in 15 minutes. Elliot and I had scheduled the meeting because Elliot's old-line government contracting business was trying to become more deeply involved in the technology space in order to expand its product and service offerings to the U.S. government agencies it worked for.

"Mr. Who?" asked the receptionist, momentarily puzzled. Then a light-bulb seemed to go on and she brightly exclaimed, "Oh, you mean surfer guy? Let me get him for you, dudes."

Later, after we left our meeting with Surfer Guy/CEO, I delicately ventured to Elliot, whom I never had seen wear anything but a white shirt, dark navy or charcoal suit, and a subdued, consummately professional necktie:

"Do you think that maybe the cultures of your company and that one might be, well, a tad out of sync?"

Elliot turned to me with a somewhat vacant look in his eyes—he clearly was still trying to take it all in. "Well, we could always just approach it from a decentralized management point of view and avoid mixing the two companies' cultures. That should not be much of a problem," he said, rather unconvincingly.

In that moment, I knew that Elliot already had "bought" the tech company in his own mind. Though I repeatedly, albeit gently, suggested that he reconsider, Elliot would not be dissuaded from closing a transaction that inevitably proved to be an unmitigated disaster.

I have to admit this story has been colored up a bit (at least the characters), but I have experienced something very close to this, for sure.

A Brief Honeymoon, Perhaps; A Successful Marriage, Less Frequently

This chapter probably will be shorter than most post-transaction honeymoons, albeit not by a very large margin. Integration planning should begin as far in advance of the closing as possible and should involve close coordination between sellers and buyers management teams.

It goes without saying that post-transaction integration of the seller's company into the buyer's own platform is no less difficult than it is critically important. Entire shelves of books have addressed this topic. Having focused its efforts on Middle Market sales-side mergers and acquisitions (M&A) transactions, this book will not address post-transaction integration in detail. Why not? Two reasons: First, as soon as a deal closes, the seller and his Middle Market investment banker ride off into the sunset (although some sellers may choose to remain with the company for a transition of short to middling duration), and second, having virtually no experience whatsoever managing in post-transition integrations, the author believes it to be in his readers' best interests that he in fact claim no particular expertise on the subject other than as observed phenomena on various occasions. That said, an old saw states, "Opinions are like, er . . . belly buttons. Everybody has one." And on the subject of post-transaction integration, the author does entertain more than a few opinions, some of which warrant brief discussion, and while his experience has not been deep, it has been wide.

A perennial and perhaps somewhat pseudo-statistic floating around "out there" cites any number of surveys that conclude that from 75% to 80% of all mergers and acquisitions fail. Faithful readers of any given business periodical or any major metropolitan daily newspaper's business section cannot help but have read this or similar factoids a half-dozen times in the past twenty years. In fact, the reported 75% to 80% failure rate of M&A transactions has remained essentially constant for 25 or 30 years, at least.

These reported M&A failure rates do not reflect, by any means, the kind of business failures that wind up in bankruptcy court (even though, from time to time, a particularly ill-starred M&A transaction may, in fact, go bust). The 75% to 80% of "failed" M&A transactions are so characterized because they did not achieve their intended outcomes.

When M&A transactions fall short of their intended outcomes, the root cause tends to be one of two key errors (and frequently both) made by buyers along the way. The buyer's first error often occurs well in advance of the closing, when projected (and, subsequently, *expected*) post-transaction synergies to be realized from the deal are overestimated—sometimes grossly overestimated.

The second error seems to be a failure to execute the postdeal integration. In my opinion, a good set of rules to follow during integration are:

- Start managing the transaction immediately upon deal closure and then tighten up time frames steadily. Be aggressive, but set priorities and set them with due care.
- Communicate constantly: what, why, where, how. This is a particular obligation of top leadership.
- Do not stand by and hope. Immediately train the appropriate staff on immediate issues and approaches to integration.
- Anticipate and manage staff turnover.
- Pay close attention to productivity issues; keep the focus on clients.
- Consider, estimate, and measure the economic impact of all major decisions.
- Pay careful attention to cultural issues and "who gets corner office" people issues. They can get out of hand rapidly and be very destructive.

Such errors are by no means limited to Middle Market transactions, either. Books have been written about the AOL/Time Warner merger, a failure of near-mythic proportions that resulted from a combination of astonishingly overhyped synergies that never materialized on the one hand and an apparently very poorly executed integration that might never have been practicable given the incredible divergence of the merger partners' respective corporate cultures on the other.

In the AOL/Time Warner merger, though not for the first time, 1 + 1 equaled . . . well, less than 2. Literally! When AOL and Time Warner announced their merger on January 18, 2000, Time Warner stock closed at $59.02 (all stock quotes adjusted for subsequent splits and dividends: see finance.yahoo.com). When AOL/Time Warner completed their merger on

January 12, 2001, the stock closed at $45.67. Time Warner's (AOL was expunged from the company's legal name already) closing price on December 11, 2006 was $21.33. The AOL/Time Warner merger established, in spades, that there are deals where virtually no synergies will be realized and where the misfit between two respective corporate cultures is too massive to be bridged under any circumstances. Old-line media married high-tech Internet media and simply imploded.

Prospective buyers must guard against too great an enthusiasm for a given transaction (even as sellers and their Middle Market investment bankers admittedly strive to nurture and harness the enthusiasm of prospective buyers to maximize the value of the sellers' companies). The Super Rule of Five (see Chapter 23) notwithstanding, Middle Market investment banking M&A deals sooner or later demonstrate an inertial momentum that becomes hard to resist after a certain point, even when all signals point in the wrong direction.

Consider the division executive who champions a "must-do" deal to his CEO as a "great opportunity for us." A moment inevitably arrives when that executive becomes so committed to selling the deal to his CEO and others that he cannot objectively and critically reconsider his position, let alone admit that the deal may no longer be appropriate, given a pricing premium achieved via the negotiated auction, changes in underlying market conditions, or even the executive's vague second thoughts as to the original merits of the deal. Stopping short, or reversing course, on the deal at hand would force the executive to admit a mistake or a misjudgment and risk losing face, or worse.

Originally, the objective driving the proposed acquisition was to do good business. In the end, the objective too often morphs into doing the deal for the deal's own sake, long after circumstances no longer support closing the transaction on the merits.

The buyer's second error, committed both pre- and post-transaction, involves a failure to integrate the two companies effectively and thereby achieve what synergies may be realized. While AOL/Time Warner once again comes to mind, failures of this type are legion among Fortune 1000 companies and Middle Market enterprises alike. Integration failures may arise from integrating the two firms too aggressively and too quickly, or from managing the integration in so lackadaisical a fashion as to essentially communicate to the merged companies that the integration "will happen of its own accord." Or not.

To playfully adapt a famous old saying: buyer be wary. Once the deal has closed, the seller's company, for better or worse, belongs to the buyer and the buyer alone. The buyer's company, the acquired company and the combined enterprise all will suffer if the buyer fails to take ownership in full of the combination and all of its inherent challenges and opportunities.[1]

There are many arguments for "going slow," but buyers who properly identify their acquisition candidates and successfully close transactions tend to know precisely why they did so. And such buyers also know well ahead of closing their plans for the new acquisition, starting well before they open for business the day after consummating the deal. When going slow involves taking time to act decisively, fair enough. But when going slow reflects uncertainty, indecision, or a default to laissez-faire management, trouble invariably lies dead ahead for the buyer and his business.

Chapter Highlights

- Some 75% to 80% of M&A transactions historically fail to meet their objectives, due to:
  - An overestimation of potential synergies
  - A failure to anticipate cultural differences and related consequences
  - A failure to integrate the merged businesses effectively once the transaction has closed, because the buyer:
    - Went too slow (more typically)
    - Went too fast (less frequently)
    - Took a laissez-faire attitude to post-transaction integration (didn't take control)
    - Failed up well upfront to do the homework required to have any strategy whatsoever in place for integrating the enterprise starting on the first business day following the closing

Note

1. I sometimes like to imagine what would have happened if Jack Welch had been the acquiring CEO in the Time Warner deal. I suspect the acquired company (and there always is one, in fact) would have been made his on the day following the merger. I have little doubt, as that was his style, a pretty decisive and action-oriented one.

CHAPTER 22

Does a Sales-Side Client Need an Appraisal before Going to Market?

An economic forecaster is like a cross-eyed javelin thrower: they don't win many accuracy contests, but they keep the crowd's attention.

Anonymous

Arlington, VA—July 1992

I was in another meeting in another Arlington high-rise office building, but this time, happily, it was a building with a great southern barbecue and jazz bar downstairs, where we had just eaten a terrific lunch, maybe too much lunch. The restaurant was abuzz with discussions of the presidential campaign: Bush, Clinton, or Perot? The campaigns were heating up, getting ugly, and the perceived wisdom of inside-the-beltway crowds was tipping toward big changes at 1600 Pennsylvania Avenue come January 20, 1993. Throughout all my business travels over the course of many presidential campaign years, I never have found another American metropolis remotely as consumed by political debate—especially about presidential politics—as the denizens of Washington, DC, northern Virginia, and the District's Maryland suburbs. Then again, the District is the seat of government, when administrations change hands here, everything seems to change. But that is another story.

My lunch partners that day, Michael and Izzy, were an odd couple if ever there was one: an Irish Catholic and a son of Russian Jews who fled to America following the Russian Revolution. Both of them were brilliant, and both were quite happily settled into what seems to have been a very successful business partnership, lasting 25 years to date, while constantly squabbling with one another. Along the way, between their brilliance and the squabbling, Michael and Izzy had managed to build a consulting business that was admired the world over for its

*professionalism and business excellence. One or the other routinely was
quoted or cited in most of the literature dealing with their specialty. Even
the Japanese came to them for advice.*

*The firm Michael and Izzy had offices on three continents and served an
international array of clients, so Michael and Izzy traveled constantly,
in separate directions, which might well have kept them from killing
each other. Each had—but never boasted of—an Ivy League education.
Michael was a Princeton undergrad who earned his MBA from Harvard.
Izzy went to Yale (Michael never let Izzy forget it, either) and on to
Harvard Law for his JD. Somewhere in Cambridge, their paths crossed
and they had been arguing and building a business enterprise with a
sterling global reputation ever since.*

*By the summer of 1992, however, Michael and Izzy were ready to con-
sider cashing in and exploring their options while they were still way
ahead of the curve.[1]*

*I had known Michael and Izzy for a number of years and throughout the
course of several of my own sequential career trajectories, from public
accounting to entrepreneurial commercial banking to, ultimately, investment banking. I was pleased that the two would think of me when it
came time to put their firm on the market. Over lunch at the barbecue
restaurant, Michael lingered over small talk until Izzy interrupted: "Let
me get right to the point, Dennis." (He always did). Michael and I sat
back in our chairs as Izzy continued: "What's the company worth?"*

*Well, when you want to come right to the merger and acquisition (M&A)
point, I suppose there's no better question than "What's it worth?" But I
also was smart enough to know I was dumb enough on that issue, at this
stage, not to have a clue as to how to answer the question on the fly. And
I pretty much figured they knew that, too.*

*"Izzy, let me be frank with you. There's no way I can do that question
justice with an answer here and now that would be anything short of
sheer speculation. If you would be willing to give me a few days to get
back to you on that, I would be glad to do some research and share my
thoughts on the matter."*

*Izzy and Michael gave me the time and, a few days later, I did get
back to them after having conducted substantial market research on
their company and its industry. I told them that their consulting firm
probably was worth between $30 and $40 million.*

*Izzy, true to form, harrumphed in Michael's direction, saying, "See,
I told you your HBS professor had his head up his . . . ahem." Izzy
laughed at Michael's astonishment. Prickly as Izzy was—and we became*

great friends over the course of the eight months it took us to close the deal—he turned out to be a pussycat beneath his crusty, sometimes caustic persona. Turning to me while nodding (gloating?) at Michael, Izzy explained, "My partner, here, suggested that we ask one of the HBS geniuses who taught him finance to conduct a business valuation of our firm, and the guy came up with a $20 million figure which I knew right off the bat was way, way low."

Michael shrugged. "And, Dennis, if only you had been there to hear how Izzy communicated his skepticism to my former professor. It was bloody ugly."

"That's not uncommon in my experience," I answered (Meaning the professor's conclusion, although I could equally have meant Izzy's bluntness). "The professor's conclusion probably was far less than my own because it reflected standard P/E valuations in a static market (fair market value), rather than the investment value a firm like yours might bring in a negotiated auction involving prospective buyers competing to do the deal."[2]

This was by no means my first nor my last experience with business valuations conducted by formal valuators (and, especially, economists) who in the final analysis had nary a clue as to the dynamics driving Middle Market M&A. Yet all too many such experts stand ready, willing, and able to charge a hefty fee for bad advice presented quite confidently and no less obliviously. When formal valuators do their work, the figures they come up with may be right on paper for certain purposes but are often very, very wrong in the real world, where Middle Market M&A transactions are done. Seller beware!

By the way, do not get me wrong—I am a trained and credentialed formal valuator and a national instructor in the subject, and I certainly am not bad-mouthing my colleagues here, just the misapplication of good science to poorly understood subject matter. My own firm (collectively The McLean Group), runs a very substantial formal valuation practice through a separate entity with separate staff. As chairman of both firms I am equally proud of each and the guys and gals that make up the professional staff of each. But this has given me a unique perspective into how these two professions relate to each other very well at some points but amazingly distantly at others.

Four Basic M&A Marketplace Valuation Contexts

There are four valuation types or contexts in Middle Market valuations, and understanding the differences is critical to an understanding of M&A

valuation. Except by rare statistical quirk none of these are ever the same. They are:

- Fair market value (pretty irrelevant)
- Preliminary estimate of value in the marketplace (always useful and recommended)
- Investment value to particular buyers (different to different buyers)
- Final transaction (dynamic) value (the actual value paid in a deal that is consummated)

Formal versus Preliminary Valuation in the Marketplace

All of this talk about valuation might lead prospective sellers of Middle Market firms to ask, "Okay, but would it be wise for me to seek at least some kind of an appraisal of my company before attempting to sell it?" The answer to that question would be a qualified "Yes." A major caveat must be offered, however.

Most formal business appraisers (also known as valuators) focus their practices on conducting the kind of appraisals generally undertaken for such nontransactional work such as estate, income, and gift tax planning or litigation support. These are usually cases where the Fair Market Value (FMV) of a business (or some derivative thereof) is important.

And there lies the rub. FMV first and foremost, is a hypothetical construct that implies the existence of a sort of "invisible hand" in the marketplace. It suggests that there is, more or less, a single central dollar value that a very large group of buyers and sellers would likely assign (determined more or less by averaging) to a given business if each one of them had perfect, or at least equal, knowledge and none of them was under any compulsion to transact. Furthermore, FMV assumes an all-cash transaction. It is, in other words, a carefully defined "term of art" for use under and only under particular circumstances.

Experienced Middle Market investment bankers (especially those who are trained in formal valuation) will advise that FMV is to Middle Market investment banking as unicorn is to quadruped. The author himself has never, ever seen the hypothetical concepts described above as being explicit in FMV come into play over the course of hundreds of real-life transactions. In other words, the value a Middle Market business realizes in an actual transaction often is markedly different from the value an appraiser would estimate for the business using Fair Market Value as the standard.

Even then, and possibly to make matters worse, if you hire ten appraisers to estimate one company's FMV, then sit back and wait for the results, ten different estimates most likely will result. But that is a complete other story that deals with the relative inexperience in valuing sizable Middle Market businesses and, therefore, the qualifications of much[3] of the valuation profession in the United States today . . . and finally that unfortunately too much of formal valuation, which is supposed to be the objective opinion of an expert, is simply biased towards some client objective. Anyway I digress.

Furthermore, in the formal appraisal field, professional valuators are commonly termed *business valuators*, when in fact they usually are not doing that. What they typically appraise is the equity and the securities interest in *entities*, typically corporations. These entities may own businesses but they are not businesses.

Every business is like a watch (the business) inside a box (the entity). To determine the value of the business or watch, you have to remove the box so you can look at the business or watch separately. That is what M&A bankers do. Eventually, the business might be put back in the box (or not) when it gets delivered to the new owner (the buyer) and some transaction adjustments (tax-oriented entity adjustments e.g., getting the business out of the box or putting it back in) may be necessary to the purchase price, but initially the business needs to be valued as if the box (entity) did not exist.

Investment and Dynamic Value

Dynamic value is the *actual final transaction value* in a given transaction. Take a look around: In the real world of Middle Market investment banking, all the prospective buyers for any given seller possess unequal knowledge of the business and other relevant information on the one hand, while experiencing unequal (or at least different) forms at least of compulsion (e.g., self-knowledge) to complete a transaction. This is why dynamic valuation is one of a kind, never to be repeated. "Beauty is in the eye of the beholder," say the Romantics. "Investment Value is in the eye of the various prospective buyers," advise the Middle Market investment bankers. Establishing the final dynamic transaction valuation (actual transaction value) of the seller's company through a negotiated auction among several motivated and competitive prospective buyers (or even with only one buyer) constitutes the essence of sales-side M&A.

The Answer

Would-be sellers of Middle Market business, therefore, should not seek a formal appraisal by a business valuator, at least by one with little or no transaction-based valuation experience (M&A expertise). Having participated in one or five transactions in a supporting role does not, in my mind, qualify as legitimate, sufficient experience to provide a preliminary appraisal that is appropriate for an actual M&A transaction. The mere and likely lack of understanding of M&A conventions (see Chapter 27) is alone enough to make this a bad idea.

Appraisal Costs

The costs of a preliminary valuation appraisal will vary widely, but they should not necessarily. One self-described national Middle Market "M&A" firm for years charged $35,000 to $50,000 (way too high a price for most Middle Market business appraisals) for an "Appraisal" that the firm pitched as a prerequisite to putting the Middle Market business up for sale. The firm then subcontracted most of the appraisals to formal valuators with seemingly very little transaction experience. The firm ultimately sold no more than one in ten of the businesses whose sellers it represented, but it made a very handsome living on the appraisal fees. By the way, I saw many of these so-called appraisals, and most competent trained valuators would have charged $10,000 for the same work that was being billed for almost $50,000 in many cases.

A Preliminary Valuation in the Marketplace

Should a prospective Middle Market business seller decide to obtain a preliminary valuation of his company before selling it, any experienced investment banker (especially one with formal valuation training) should be able to advise a client as to a general price range within which the client's business would likely sell, plus or minus 10% or so (see Exhibit 22.1). Unlike Fair Market Value, this range will encompass strategic values recently paid in an industry, and experienced investment bankers will be able to interpret the data and the range when advising the seller. Furthermore, many investment bankers will provide this inherently more accurate data gratis, as a business development effort. In cases where a client may be several years way from selling his business, the investment banker may charge as much as $10,000 to 20,000 for this service (but for a much more extensive engagement, which involves very detailed analyses of extant positive and negative value drivers as well as suggesting desirable drivers yet to be obtained). Not uncommonly, they may credit the fee against a future retainer should they be hired by the client within a reasonable period after conducting the preliminary valuation. As I said, such elaborated preliminary valuations usually will identify positive and negative value drivers that should prove invaluable to the seller in improving his business so as to maximize its ultimate investment value.

EXHIBIT 22.1 Formal versus "M&A Street" Valuations: Why Formal Appraisals Do Not Really Work

	Formal (the Courtroom)	"M&A Street" Value
Standards	Usually fair market value	Always investment value
Circumstances	Usually hypothetical	Actual transaction
Situation	Static (calculation)	Always dynamic (negotiation)
Knowledge/Compulsion	Equal/invisible hand	Unequal/different
Consideration	Cash/noncontingent	Mixed/often contingent

Why bother with a preliminary estimate of value? First, a seller's understanding of the basic valuation range of his company is helpful to seller and investment banker alike. The seller will benefit by having a baseline below which it might make more sense to pursue such alternatives to sale as a refinancing, waiting for growth or profit improvement, or waiting for an improved M&A market. From the investment banker's point of view, the work involved in developing preliminary estimates should prove quite useful in the subsequent preparation of the Confidential Information Memorandum or CIM (see Chapter 7) he will prepare on the company's behalf.

Equally important, the seller benefits from knowing a baseline valuation range, because if the client and the investment banker's respective ideas of valuation diverge significantly, then they might not relish the idea of working together. The seller may feel underrepresented by an investment banker who fails to estimate what is in the seller's mind a desirable range of offering price. The investment banker in turn may be frustrated by what he or she believes to be unreasonable expectations on the part of a seller who may refuse to accept reasonable offers (even really good ones) that the investment banker otherwise would bring to the table. When the seller and the investment banker are likely to have very different expectations, the seller at the very least should consider obtaining a second opinion from another equally (or more) qualified investment banker.

As a final comment here, I hope it is clear that these preliminary valuations are not shown to buyers.

Bethesda, MD—May 1989
. . . a bluff?

I was in my job and in my first office as a sole practitioner investment banker in Bethesda, MD, an upscale city in an upscale county bifurcated by the infamous Washington, DC, beltway. My prospective client, Peter, looked me right in the eye. Full of self-confidence, without a hint of self-doubt, he said, "I just want you to know that I will not take anything less *than $20 million for this business. That's it. If you can get more, fine, but that's my floor."*

"My God," I thought. "Where the hell did he get that number?"

Actually, I knew where he got it: somewhere between pulling it out of his ... uhm ... "hat," his dream scenario, and the place in his cerebellum where he believes aggressive insistence alone will achieve the desired result by motivating his investment banker to work harder.

Chapter Highlights

- Understanding the distinctions among four basic valuation methodologies is critical to understanding the M&A marketplace:
  - Fair Market Value (mostly an irrelevancy)
  - Preliminary estimate of value in the marketplace
  - Investment Value to particular buyers
  - Final transaction (dynamic) value
- Sellers of Middle Market companies do not require a formal valuation of Fair Market Value.
- Middle Market investment bankers who have at least some formal valuation training generally are the best estimators of preliminary value in the marketplace.
- Preliminary valuations are, at best, estimates as to the Investment Value that one particular, buyer ultimately will establish for the seller's business when the deal is closed. Such estimates can sometimes vary widely from the final result, even when they are expertly done.

Notes

1. Their decision, in retrospect, turned out to be timed as perfectly as so many others they had made along the way: They sold their firm to a roll-up group for a very substantial sum of money soon after the 1993 presidential inauguration of Bill Clinton.
2. A roll-up promoter eventually bought the business founded by Michael and Izzy at a 20% premium over my own estimates, providing yet another illustration of why preliminary valuations conducted by formal valuators with little or no "Street" experience often are a waste of time and money and sometimes, catastrophically, encourage a seller to consummate a transaction for far less than his company's likely investment value. Even experienced investment bankers (with extensive valuation

credentials) often can provide no more than a baseline investment value range that the dynamics of a negotiated auction may very well eclipse.

3. By no means all of the profession. A substantial number of valuators who are in practice full time provide very high quality formal valuations. Even then their results will differ from each other to some degree because valuation is art and judgment and not purely science by any means.

CHAPTER 23

The Rules of Five and Ten and the Super Rule of Five in M&A Valuation

Salt Lake City, UT—September 2005

I never could figure out just what it is that people like about this city, except as a lifelong avid skier I knew that it was the gateway to some of the best skiing in the United States, just 30 minutes away. But it was September, no snow up there yet, and I was teaching mergers and acquisitions (M&A) investment banking all day anyway. The Salt Lake Valley is stunning, with it's surrounding Wasatch Mountain peaks, and that is clearly what people like about it. That and the other outdoor sports that are abundant here year round.

I guess I would have to get used to the fact that there was not that much to do here at night . . . and even if there was, I was not sure I would have had the energy for it. It was going to be a long week. But I love teaching this stuff. I was in the first hour of the first day of a weeklong training course.

One of my students, Larry—a great guy, but somewhat of a skeptic— raised his hand for a question. "Dennis, I have to tell you, I am not exactly a neophyte when it comes Middle Market M&A deals, and I rarely read about a deal that is priced at your so-called Rule of Five multiple. I just read in the paper the other day that company (ABC) bought company (XYZ) for an estimated eight times EBITDA multiple. Are you crazy, or are they crazy?" Larry was a business broker studying to climb up the ladder to Middle Market M&A transactions.

I checked my watch and then cleared my throat. This was going to be a good, if long, week after all. Curious students make it all worthwhile.

Larry eventually became a believer, and I hope you will too.

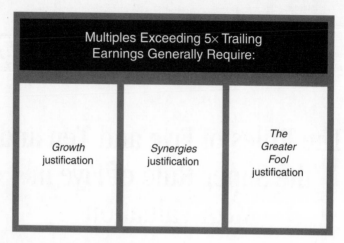

EXHIBIT 23.1 The Super Rule of Five

A Foundation for the Valuation of Middle Market Businesses

There is a rule of thumb, actually two rules that we will combine eventually, that are invaluable in Middle Market investment banking and business sales—and not bad rules for buyers, either. I am referring to two variants: the *Rule of Five* and the *Super Rule of Five* (see Exhibit 23.1). In addition, there is the *Rule of Ten*.

The foundation Rule of Five is not very technical, but it is not devoid of finance theory either, as opposed to most of the rules of thumb used in Mom-and-Pop business transactions. When combined with the Rule of Ten, it is very useful as a starting point, whether I am launching a complex formal business valuation for an expert opinion or simply getting my arms around the preliminary value of a client's Middle Market company for the first time.

The *Rule of Five* holds that any Middle Market business will be worth approximately five times its cash flow before interest expense and income taxes (EBIT, EBITDA, etc.), until demonstrated otherwise. The fun, of course, is in the "demonstrating otherwise" part.

A review of Middle Market M&A transactions closed over the course of many years substantiates the argument that the majority of Middle Market businesses sell for between 4.5 and 5.5 times their normalized EBITDA cash flows. Were one to plot cash flow valuation multiples on the traditional bell curve, two-thirds or so of the time, the correct multiple is approximately five. All other Middle Market transaction multiples can be understood as constituting deviations from the standard. Understanding this point—and why the deviations occur—provides a gateway to powerful insights into transaction valuation. By the way, when discussing valuation in this way, we are usually referring to Enterprise Value (the cash-free, debt-free value of the business), which has little to do with valuing the entity that owns the business. Businesses are not entities, although they are owned by them. Sorry to have to keep repeating that but it is important, especially in this context.

The Rules of Five and Ten, Cocktail Party Conversation, and . . . Quick Calculations

Sometimes at cocktail parties and other social gatherings, Middle Market investment bankers often are asked (free advice? . . . well, no problem there), "What do you think my company would be worth if I sold it?" I really do not have much time to spend on the question—as if it were even possible to come up with such a figure on the fly, with no particular points of reference! When someone presses the question, I usually tell him about the Rules of Five and Ten. And I certainly reference it in my answer, especially if I want to go get another glass of Scotch and/or meet the attractive blonde (my younger bachelor years) across the room.

Two Bell Curves

The first bell curve (Exhibit 23.2) indicates that most Middle Market M&A businesses, especially those in the lower one-third of the Middle Market

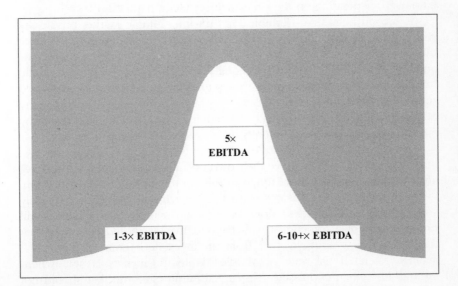

EXHIBIT 23.2 Bell Curve—Rule of Five

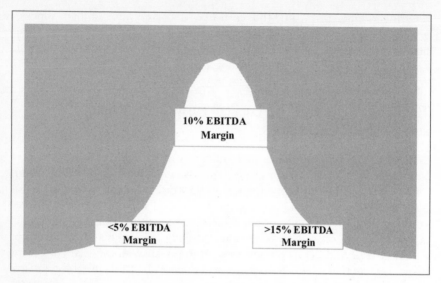

EXHIBIT 23.3 Bell Curve—Rule of Ten

(i.e., values of $5 million to $150 million) sell for more or less a five times EBITDA multiple. While this book often refers to EBITDA for convenience, other variations on pretax cash flow proxy figures like EBIT also might be employed, depending on the circumstances (see Chapter 24).

A second bell curve (Exhibit 23.3) tracking Middle Market businesses would establish that normalized EBITDA (or other cash flow proxies) most often equals approximately 10% of sales—actually, somewhere between 5% and 15% as a rule. So 5 times 10% equals 50%. These are not plotted on the same bell curve, just overlapping ones to some degree, but as combined rules of thumb they provide a pretty practical first estimate, and many Middle Market business owners can multiply their business revenues by 50% to arrive at a ballpark Enterprise Valuation for their businesses.

But rules of thumb, like rules of spelling ("I before E, except after C, that is so w*ei*rd. . . . "), do have their own peculiar and frequent exceptions, and the exceptions are more fun, as a rule. In the world of M&A valuation, the exceptions are the businesses that for one reason or another (usually some combination of stand-alone growth and synergies to a buyer) will produce multiples sometimes way beyond five. It should be noted that the Rule of Five suggests that from an investment point of view, the average tolerated risk rate of Middle Market businesses is somewhere around 20% when expressed as a capitalization rate, and that should not be particularly surprising to those knowledgeable about capitalization rates when compared to the returns on investment of other asset classes into which one might invest money.[1]

The Super Rule of Five

The tendency towards five times EBITDA multiple valuations of Middle Market businesses over the years reflects an average stand alone Middle Market business, assuming a fairly flat growth rate and without any significant synergistic values to the particular buyer. But remember, very few prospective strategic buyers consider acquiring a Middle Market business unless they perceive significant synergies or growth that may be realized in the transaction, such as a broader client base, new product and service offerings, cost savings, new distribution channels for the buyer's own products, and so on.

As I said, at any given time (and for obvious reasons), the most interesting Middle Market M&A transactions—the ones that make prospective sellers, buyers and Middle Market investment bankers stand up and pay very close attention—are the deals that close at substantially richer multiples than the standard five times. The key lies in understanding the reasons why particular businesses realize an EBITDA multiple higher (or lower) than five. Sellers and Middle Market investment bankers who find the key may well be able to transform the sellers' companies, over time, to maximize their selling multiples. There are several reasons (not counting "irrational exuberance") why Middle Market companies may realize selling prices significantly higher than five times EBITDA multiples. All of them involve aspects of the *Super Rule of Five.*

Stand alone Growth Rates

In general, if a Middle Market business's earnings are growing at a rate that will make the multiple paid today, whatever that multiple is, appear to have been a five times multiple when compared to the business's EBIT earnings *approximately eighteen months*[2,3] *to two years from now*, then that multiple is probably justifiable. For example, if a buyer pays an eight times multiple for a Middle Market business earning an EBIT of $10,000,000 this year, *and those earnings are growing at a 25% annual compounded rate*, then the projected earnings for the business two years out will be approximately $16 million.

The buyer's purchase price today was $80 million, or eight times the company's trailing $10 million EBIT. But that $80 million also reflects "only" a five times EBIT multiple of the projected $16 million EBIT earnings two years out.

In other words, the company's earnings grew into the purchase price. The eight times EBIT multiple was a reasonable multiple to have paid, given the company's projected EBIT growth rate based on stand alone, nonsynergies incorporated growth (see Exhibit 23.4).

This makes perfect sense when considered from another perspective (a negative, in this case) as well. Assume that a company is expected to

EXHIBIT 23.4   Illustration of the Super Rule of Five Stand alone Growth

	At Acquisition	2 Years Post-Acquisition
Announced Price	$ 80,000,000	$ 80,000,000
Earnings (25% forecasted annual growth)	10,000,000	15,600,000
Implied Earnings Multiple Paid	8,00×	
Real Multiple Paid		**5.13×**

Rule of thumb:

If the growth rate is fast enough (or synergies compelling enough) that the effective multiple paid one or two years out is 5×, the deal may be priced right:
- Current EBIT is $10 million (and 8× multiple) = an $80 million valuation
- EBIT two years from now is $15.6 million for an effective 5× multiple ($80MM/$15.6MM) assuming a 25% annual growth rate

generate the same EBIT next year and the year after that (zero growth) as it did this year and last year. Assume that the company is properly valued at a five times trailing EBIT multiple. That same multiple is likely to reflect its value next year and the year after that: no change. The company may be somewhat attractive to certain parties, but its performance is average, middle of the road, middle of the bell curve. And it is unlikely to command higher than a five or so or less multiple.

But consider the aforementioned Middle Market business, with its 25% compounded annual EBIT growth.[4] One of these two companies (flat growth or substantial growth) is going to attract far greater enthusiasm among prospective buyers than the other. And those prospective buyers, aggressively competing in the negotiated auction, will identify the premium they are willing to pay for the company with strong earnings growth prospects *over* the company with no earnings growth potential. It is not because the prospective buyers want to pay a premium EBIT multiple but because they *have to pay a premium* or lose an attractive acquisition to a likely competitor.

Synergistic Growth Rate of Target Business

But suppose a buyer knew he could acquire a business with a flat growth and achieve a 25% growth rate between the time he closed the deal on Friday and the time he opened the doors for business on Monday?

If, between his own company and the new acquisition, the buyer could theoretically eliminate enough duplicate costs or find other synergies over the weekend, he could do just that. That is the second reason a seller's

EXHIBIT 23.5　Illustration of the Super Rule of Five Synergistic Growth Rate

Objective stand-alone value as a function of trailing earnings ($10,000,000 × 5)	$50,000,00
Objective stand-alone value as a result of projected annual growth rate of 25% over 2 years ($15,625,000 × 5)	$78,125,00
Subjective value as a result of synergestic growth in earnings of $1 million over 2 years ($16,625,000 × 5)	$83,625,00
Implied subjective and retrospective multiple of trailing earnings that can be paid, consistent with the super rule of five	8.36×

company may generate an EBIT multiple substantially greater than five. Projected earnings growth will be realized not only from the acquisition's stand-alone growth (or lack thereof) but also, or perhaps rather, from the synergies the buyer will realize by acquiring the company. At the simplest level, these synergies might be merely economies of scale. But if a buyer can eliminate 15% of the acquisition's overhead over that first weekend (or even the next two years), the cost savings increase earnings by that same amount. Of course, the synergies to be realized may encompass much more than the reduction of expenses via economies of scale, including access to new customers and distribution channels and so on. (see Exhibit 23.5)

Synergistic earnings growth increases earnings just as effectively as stand-alone growth (though prospective buyers are less likely to want to pay for kind of that growth). And although one buyer's synergies may be utterly meaningless to another, synergistic growth is just as likely to intensify competition among prospective buyers in a negotiated auction as stand-alone growth. See Chapter 22, on Auctions.

In the actual M&A marketplace, real-world earnings growth in an acquired company usually comes from some combination of stand-alone and synergistic growth. It is up to the prospective buyer to carefully calculate the value of both and to pay as small a premium for both as possible when competing with other prospective buyers in the negotiated auction. Conversely, it is up to the seller to know the value of his business based on its own stand-alone growth and—with his Middle Market investment banker—to try to orchestrate a negotiated auction that will maximize the investment value his company will generate based on the combined stand-alone growth and potential synergies it offers the prospective buyers. This is what the auction does.

A Possible Third Exception to the Super Rule of Five: The Leveraged Deal

Assume that the buyer purchases the seller's business for cash. The seller's company has no existing long-term debt. Its earnings (EBIT) are $5 million, and the buyer paid a five times EBIT multiple (for a total purchase price of $25 million). The buyer can anticipate a 20% pretax return on his investment, even if there is no earnings growth.

But what if the buyer purchases the business using equity ($18.75 million) for some portion of the purchase price and using debt ($12.5 million) for the remainder, paying a total for the business of $31.25 million (or a multiple of 6.25)? The buyer pays 10% interest on his debt.

Under this scenario, the buyer might choose to pay more for the target acquisition while still realizing a 20% ROI. With $3.75 million in net earnings after interest expense ($5 million less $1.25[5] million in interest), the buyer can put up his own equity $18.75 million ($3.75 million times 5) for the target acquisition and still achieve the 20% ROI. And it would look like the buyer actually paid a 6.25 times EBIT multiple ($31.25 million/$5 million).

Alternatively, the buyer might pay the five times EBIT multiple ($25 million) while using half debt ($12.5 million). In that case, his ROI would be 30% ($5 million less $1.25 million = $3.75 million; and $3.75 million/$12.5 million = 30%.)

Such leveraged transactions do bear greater cash flow risks and leverage risks. Interest on the debt, and the debt itself, must be paid. But private equity groups (PEGs) use this approach in leveraged buyout transactions, and their offers may prove quite attractive to sellers.[6]

The Greater Fool Theory (Buyer Beware)

An acquisition candidate's stand alone growth, or its synergistic or investment value, or its potential for leverage may justify paying an investment value greater than a five times EBIT multiple. Nothing else should.[7] Yet every day in the Middle Market M&A world, irrational exuberance (hence, the greater fool theory) makes its delightful (at least from the seller's perspective) presence known, and a prospective buyer, somewhere out there, loses the discipline and judgment necessary to making good decisions and offers an entirely unjustifiable EBIT premium for a target acquisition. Buy-side use of the Super Rule of Five can be a reasonable sanity check against irrational exuberance.

Negotiated auctions are quite effective not only for sellers, but also for careful, judicious buyers who have done their homework, carefully think through the process, and studiously avoid impulsive decisions to do (or not to do) the deal for the wrong reasons.

When multiple companies in an industry begin selling for prices that suggest irrational exuberance, any number of factors may be involved. Some, in the final analysis, will come down to the "Greater Fool Theory" so buyers beware. But when Middle Market business in a given industry routinely seem to be selling for prices that violate the Rule of Five (not the Super Rule of Five), sellers and their investment bankers should take note: an extraordinary opportunity to do a deal may be close at hand (see Chapter 6, *Crystal Balls and Timing the Market*).

Chapter Highlights

The Rule of Five and The Super Rule of Five provide a useful frame of reference for both buyers and sellers in constructing a rationale for a given purchase price.

- Briefly restated, if an earnings stream (EBIT, etc.)—with the exception of startup companies, where growth rates are frequently automatically exponential because of the low starting point of earnings and revenues—will grow at such a rate that the price paid today will be five times the earnings stream of the target in 18 to 24 months, then the deal probably made sense, everything else being equal.
- An inherent irony in the Rule of Five is that if a deal will command only a five times earnings multiple, it probably is not a very interesting deal: five times multiples suggest that there is no stand alone growth rate or synergistic growth, which reaffirms the unattractiveness of the target.
- In most transactions, price is determined by some combination of the stand alone growth rate of the target and the value of expected synergies to the ultimate buyer in the negotiated auction. That is, in fact, the application of the Super Rule of Five in practice, especially it applies to the lower Middle Market.

Notes

1. Assuming that the approximate nominal annual rate of growth for many Middle Market business is 5%, then the implied discount rate is 25% (25% − 5% = 20%, which of course makes even greater sense when comparing the risk profiles of Middle Market compared to other investments under the theory of substitution).
2. At eighteen or so months, the earnings run rate of the business will be fairly well established, so reasonable estimates can be made of its second full year's earnings at that point to test compliance with the Super Rule of Five.
3. One might reasonably enquire as to why "two" years is selected as the measurement date. The reason is that inherently the Super Rule of Five in practice requires up front estimating and projecting not just after the

fact measurement. In the M&A world very little credence is, or probably should be associated with projections that extend beyond two years.

4. I am excepting here the obvious first several years of growth in startups, which is likely to be exponential but only because of starting from a very low point in either revenues or earnings—or, more usually, both.

5. I am intentionally ignoring the tax savings effect of the deductible interest here in order to more easily demonstrate the calculation. If the tax savings are included the picture is even rosier in terms of the results to the buyer.

6. There is one caveat: sellers must very carefully analyze such transactions if they intend to retain a residual interest in the business, because the indebtedness invariably winds up on the balance sheet of the seller's business and earnings hiccups among highly leveraged companies too often prove catastrophic.

7. Keeping in mind that the Super Rule of Five is merely a sanity check or a useful rule of thumb, as opposed to a formula that can be used for precise results, there is also the question of the size of a company. As a rule, studies have demonstrated that the larger the company, the higher the transaction multiple. This is in not inconsistent with the Super Rule of Five, in that larger companies are more likely to offer synergies to their acquirers and are more likely to have something beyond nominal or flat growth rates. The other element a larger company may possess is greater stability due to its size and, therefore, lower risk; this last factor, independent of growth rates and synergy, may contribute something to the overall higher multiples seen on larger companies. In general, though, most of the difference is likely to be seen in synergies and growth rates.

CHAPTER 24

An Introduction to the Basic Art and Science of Valuation (Sales-Side versus Buy-Side) as Applied to M&A Transactions, and Flavors of EBITDA Explained

Chicago, IL—June 1996
A Disconnect

I was looking around the room, somewhat awed by the valuation experts nurturing their hangovers from a bit too much partying the night before. My awe was that I was even sitting here with these guys. Some of them, at least, are household names in the valuation field. One guy in particular is a kind of Irish Moses who somewhat singlehandedly parted the valuation seas so the rest of us could make sense out of them. This guy's books were considered the bible of the Church of Valuation, and they were good, too.

This group of bleary-eyed valuation rock stars had been gathered together by one of the largest CPA foundations in the United States to provide and critique the canon that would be used to first train many CPAs in the valuation sciences. As I massaged my temples and chugged coffee, I thought that many people do not realize how young this so-called science really is.

I was aware that I was there as the token mergers and acquisitions (M&A) guy. These were good guys; I like them and was flattered to have been invited. I guess these people felt that if they were going to provide the Ark of the Covenant for business valuation principles, they might at least acknowledge there was a world out there where the businesses were actually bought and sold and deals were really done, although I imagine that many of them are somewhat skeptical about the relevance of that. Go figure. I tried to maintain a low and polite profile, though.

Trying to make the point that maybe there was a disconnect of sorts between formal valuation and what goes on the real market place for Middle Market businesses, I offered the suggestion that perhaps the rules of formal valuation might be kind of hard to apply to the local body shop chain. The Irish Moses, with the irreverent heart of a true Leprechaun, took right off on several double entendres about exactly what I might have meant by "body-shops." Anyway, I deserved it for selecting such a lousy example, and I certainly was not representing body shops in my deals at the time—that is, unless they were fairly large chain establishments.

So How Much Is It Worth? Valuation 101[1]

As a recovering CPA and an accredited valuation expert with years of experience, I am well aware of the disconnect among many of my colleagues about the techniques in the actual M&A deal world, as compared to the world of formal valuation (where business are valued for courtroom, litigation, tax planning, and so forth). It sounds strange, perhaps, but until the early 1990s, even those of us who did this kind of formal valuation work from inside the CPA profession were mostly in the dark about techniques used by other professionals. We were pretty much operating on the very limited suggestions offered by the Internal Revenue Code, of all things, which dated back decades (but Revenue Ruling 59-60 still provides the conceptual basis for much formal valuation) and, in one prominent IRS discussion, all the way back to Prohibition.

When I got into the deal business, I was swiftly made aware that I did not really have the tools to value businesses and that those tools might prove useful in the deal world as well as in the courtroom world. I got up to date pretty quickly: I took all of the courses, read much of the literature, even became an instructor—and this was at the same time that I was actually doing deals. I became even more aware, in time, that there was often a disconnect between the two worlds. Even though they both used some of the same reference data and terminology, neither seemed to be as aware of what really went on in each others' worlds as I thought they should have been. Being as always pretty vocal about my views, I somehow got invited to participate in the illustrious group I mentioned above, albeit right at the end of most of their deliberations about what the body of knowledge was and how it should and could be taught.

Let me try to clear a number of misconceptions about valuation and how it really works in Middle Market M&A, as a practical matter. I realize that I will be covering material here that is quite basic for many readers, but is new to others. I do not have the scope in this book to write what would amount to another text on valuation, and there are plenty of good ones out there. So I will keep pretty much to narrative, as opposed to a mathematic demonstration of the differences and similarities between M&A and formal valuation; that will be more than sufficient for my purpose here. I hope this material will be useful even to more experienced readers, even those with some or a great deal of training in formal valuation, in understanding the deal world.

I do think the approach of contrasting two different but related approaches (M&A and formal valuation) is especially useful as a pedagogical device for teaching M&A. One could equally accurately say sales-side and buy-side valuation, as the latter tends to be more similar to formal valuation, to the extent that it uses discounted cash flow methods frequently.

The actual art of deal making and the science of formal valuation are like two brothers on a teeter-totter. They relate and depend on one another more than either realizes. But unfortunately, they each think they know what the other does. They usually do not, at least entirely and when they occasionally try to switch sides, the results can be disastrous. In fact, the brother that can easily sit on both sides of the teeter-totter is the more skilled of the two. He is going to be the guy or gal I want representing me in an Middle Market M&A transaction.

Valuing Economic Assets in General and Business in Particular

A business, of course, is an economic asset. The value of an economic asset is its ability to produce earnings or return on investment to its owner in the future. So basically, business valuation *in an M&A context* is a combination of six steps, a mix of art and science: The science is very similar to that in formal valuation, for that matter, with one big exception which I have made over and over in the book: M&A bankers value businesses, and formal valuators usually value entities that own businesses. The six steps of M&A business valuation are:

1. Determine the (normalized) earnings of a business (including its stability and its growth rate) both before and after the acquisition (historically and projected).
2. Determine the estimated degree of risk involved in operating the particular business/industry (when compared to other investments, a.k.a. the principle of substitution), usually expressed as a *multiple of trailing*

earnings on the sales side and a *present value of future earnings on the buy side*. In either case, one is determining the return on investment (ROI) that will be required to justify the risk and therefore the value of the target.

3. Determine any hidden asset values in the business that go beyond, or should be added to, the value of its ability to produce earnings.
4. From the M&A seller's point of view, by use of an auction where possible, determine the buyer's Investment Value, which, of course, is peculiar to individual buyers.
5. From the buyer's point of view, avoid auctions if possible; whether that is possible or not, use of skillful negotiating and deal structuring as well as discounted cash flow analysis to determine his Investment Value in order to pay as little of that Investment Value, as possible, that he/she might otherwise be willing to pay.
6. The result of all of this is transaction value in the M&A world.[2]

M&A and EBIT(DA)

E—*Earnings* Are Actually Cash Flow

Here is another disconnection, at least in part, between what the M&A world does and the world of formal valuators does. In formal business valuation, the expert is likely to use any number of types of earnings, ranging from net income after taxes to operating cash flow. Furthermore, they may use earnings and cash flows to the equity owners or both the equity and debt owners. If the formal expert does use cash flow, he may likely use a version of it that is also different from that used by the sales side M&A valuator, in that it will be after income taxes (operating cash flows).

When these approaches are used by a formal valuator, he is usually valuing an entity (typically a corporation), not a business. An entity may pay income taxes and may incur interest expense on its long-term debt. The M&A valuator, however, is usually valuing a business, often known as an "enterprise"—hence M&A's references to Enterprise Value, a concept I more fully explain elsewhere. This is a big difference in approach and should be kept in mind. In the M&A world of the Middle Market, businesses are valued irrespective of the entities that own them. Hence, as I will demonstrate, terms like EBIT, EBITDA, and so forth come mainly from the M&A world, especially sales side, as they are applied to business earnings as opposed to entity earnings.

I will explain. Earnings are actually measured in terms of the approximate cash flow of the business to the owner before his income taxes. *E* for Earnings is just a starting point, as in EBIT, EBITDA, etc. (By the way, the *B* in all of this is simply Before.)

As long as we are discussing earnings (cash flow), I should comment that the reason for this (the use of cash flow) is the principle of substitution mentioned above. "If I do not invest in this business, how else might I invest my money?" is a question that all business buyers ask themselves, at least implicitly. To consider alternative investments in alternative economic assets (stocks, bonds, large public company securities, etc.) it is obviously useful to use the equivalent earnings stream (cash flows, before taxes to the prospective investor, not to the entity). For example, it would not make a lot of sense to value a bond at its after–investor tax earnings and a stock investment alternative at its before–investor tax earnings.

I—Cash Flow Is Before *Interest Expense* . . . the Effect of Long-Term Debt

Whether or not an investor borrows money to make an investment (or buy a business) is his personal decision, which has nothing to do with the investment. If your real estate agent agrees to sell your house, she may not even ask you what the mortgage is on it. The value of the house is what it is, regardless of the amount of a mortgage. You can count on the fact that the agent's commission will be based on the value of your house, and not your equity in it. Likewise, your local real estate tax assessor does not care about your mortgage, either. And so it is in M&A; no one cares about the long-term debt on a business. It is simply disregarded when valuing the business. You will have to pay it off eventually, but that is of no concern to a buyer. This is why the *I* (interest expense) on the long-term debt on a business gets ignored (added back to cash flow) in valuing the business.

T—Cash Flow Is Before *Taxes*

A great deal of information is readily available, not only about current investments and their potential returns, but also about historical investments. In both instances, contemporary and historical, the earnings streams to the investors are always measured in terms of the earnings before taxes to the investor. Call this EBT. Ibbotson Associates has accumulated investment return data since 1926. It is always reported on the basis of the cash flows before the *investor's* taxes. There would not be any other way to compare alternative investments, would there?

DA—Cash Flow Is Also (Usually) Before *Depreciation* and *Amortization*

Keeping in mind that both the stock return and the bond returns are stated in terms of cash flow, when we refer to EBIT we need to make a slight adjustment to make sure it is, in fact, cash flow. *DA*, depreciation and amortization, is normally an accountant's simple bookkeeping entry, having no immediate impact on cash flow (as in a service business where there is little capital equipment investment and therefore is a small and insignificant number). If DA is more significant, it may not be added back to earnings, as it may actually be a good proxy for actual capital expenditures that would reduce owners' cash flows. In this case, the acronym would be properly EBIT instead of EBITDA.

CAPX—Capital Expenditures (EBITDA-CAPX), a Buy-Side Methodology

If depreciation and amortization are really large numbers, it is an indication that the business may be dependent on recurring and heavy capital expenditures that may need to be further accounted for by deducting average capital expenditures (CAPX), in which case the best proxy for cash flows may be EBITDA-CAPX. In these cases, CAPX better represents average annual capital expenditures than does DA. Capital expenditure in any one year is not as important as CAPX over some reasonable average time—approximately five years. Future CAPX, for that reason, is usually an estimate ... *but* ... this is typically a *buy-side calculation*, as on the sales side, deals multiple are usually reported and executed as EBIT and EBTDA multiples, so those are the sales side's natural reference points. Of course these multiples will in turn may reflect the heavy capital expenditure burden if there is one.

Working Capital (EBITDA-CAPX +/− Changes in Working Capital)—One Last Flavor of EBTDA

Hang in there. This is a tough as it gets, and we will have finally parsed all of the flavors of EBITDA. If heavy investment in working capital is required to support a rapidly growing business (such as in businesses that hold increasing amounts of inventory or accounts receivable and/or on credit from vendors), it is possible that cash flow will be measured as EBITDA-CAPX, minus changes in working capital, as that portion of the cash flows will not be available to the buyer/investor. It can be a plus to cash flows though, because if working capital needs are declining, it could mean a possible increase in the cash flow available to the buyer and be a positive as opposed to negative adjustment to cash flows. As in CAPX, though, this is typically a *buy-side calculation*, because again, on the sales side, multiples are reflected when deals are usually reported and, as I have said, executed as EBIT and EBTDA multiples. Again, those are the sales side's natural reference points. Furthermore, as discussed in the next paragraph the buy-side is more likely to make CAPX and working capital change adjustments in a DCF model than in a simple capitalization (multiples) approach.

Another Approach to Valuation: The Discounted Future Earnings (DFE) Method versus Multiples

But there is another approach common both in formal valuation and buy-side M&A valuation. The reason for this is that a *multiple* is simply a convenient term used in lieu of more formal terms in finance for more or less the same thing, which are *ROI* or *capitalization rate*. If I promise to give you $1 million per year *for the rest of your life*, and you perceive that you need a 20% ROI, then you will in turn give me $5 million. So the multiple (as used in M&A) of what you get (the $1 million) that is necessary in order to determine what that amount is worth is five times what you will receive.

But it assumes that it is what you will get "for the rest of your life." You see, capitalizing earnings assumes they will go on forever, to infinity, even longer then the "rest of your life." I wonder if anyone really believes this?

In the real world of transactions (from the buy side, usually), we see a number of instances where making such an assumption would be obviously wrong. Let's say I am buying the earnings from an individual contract that is only for five years, or a single piece of technology that is expected to ramp up for three years and then level out and even fall off over several years thereafter. Or I am considering investing in a new business that will grow like Topsy for three or four years and then level off.

The crux of the problem is that if earnings (cash flows) are at anything other than a *steady constant amount and forever*, it is impossible to use a capitalized (multiple) of earnings approach. Buyers need to find another approach. Most of them are trying to anticipate increases in earnings from synergies and what not when they determine how much to pay. What is the value today of those fluctuating earnings? They are not, as a rule, interested in just acquiring an ongoing flat earnings stream. Fortunately, there is a well-developed approach called the discounted future earnings (DFE) or sometimes the discounted cash flow (DCF) method.

I will refer to it as the DFE method. Its usefulness comes into play when earnings are erratic or short-term or growing steadily and we need some way to estimate their "present value." Fortunately, everything you need to know about it you learned in fourth grade, when you learned that principal (P) times time (T), times rate (R) equals interest (I):

$$P \times T \times R = I$$

Try this on for size: If I need to earn 10% on my investments, and you promise to pay me $110 in one year, then the present value to me of the $110 that you will give me one year from now is $100.

Simple enough, as 100×1 year $\times 10\% = \$10$, so in a year it will be $110. Using the DFE method is simply turning the old fourth-grade formula of interest on its head by determining first what we will need to, or will in fact, receive in the future at a particular interest rate (the discount rate) and thereby determining what we need to invest today (the present value). So if a business's (or a product line's or a contract's) earnings/cash flow are lumpy or go only for a finite period of time or are really growing, we can simply apply this DFE method to what we project each of the years to be in terms of cash flow/earnings until earnings level off and then simply capitalize (use a multiple) for the remainder.

Valuing Product Lines, New Technology, or Contracts

I hope it is also apparent how the DFE method is useful in valuing separate product lines, technology, or contracts that likely will have a finite life. This case is the one where even *sellers* need to apply the approach in valuing their assets of these types, as using a multiple simply will not work for something that does not go on forever and flatly.

The question that may well arise is, "But all businesses are merely an aggregation of separate contracts, product lines, and maybe technology, right? And if so, why not use the DFE method on all elements (product lines, etc.,) of businesses?" The answer is that we do not really need to, because a business, as opposed to a separate product line, has a critical mass that is kept intact by the constant churning of various product lines, contracts, etc. In other words, when one or several of these are winding down, more are in their middle or beginning phases, so we can operate at the macro business level in terms of valuing a business. We do not usually need to visit the micro level to get good valuation data. We assume as I said that things will just go on regenerating themselves for ever. Formal valuators call this "into perpetuity." As I said, oncelumpy or rapid growth stops we just capitalize (use a multiple) the future earnings.

Valuing Rapidly Growing Businesses for Venture Capital and Similar Investments: Is This Valuation?

You will recall that in the section of this book that deals with buyer types (see Chapter 3), I mentioned early stage private equity investors, commonly known as venture capitalists. I include this type of investment in Middle Market M&A because it should be included. It is an equity investment in a Middle Market or would be Middle Market business, just like any Middle Market business purchase, except that is an investment. It differs only in that it is usually for a minority interest and is usually for a business undertaking that has to go a long way to prove itself. But it does explicitly or implicitly use a DFE approach.

This raises the question of whether or not this is really valuation or negotiation. If you are a lawyer, and I am an investor in your law practice, we might agree that I will put up $5,000 to get you started for a 50% interest in your law practice's future earnings. Under the venture capital approach, this would suggest that your law practice is worth $10,000 before you have your first client. Well, it might be to you and me, but it is not likely be worth that if we tried to sell it right away. Whether or not this type of investment establishes true value will of course be a function of the age and stage of the (law practice) business.[3]

DFE Methods Summed Up

DFE approaches are predominantly *buy-side* approaches to M&A valuation and deals. Of course, as the M&A issues for buyers are different from the issues for sellers. One might say that the seller is simply focused on creating an auction (where he can) to sell his business, and this does not require excessive amounts of calculation (beyond looking at comparable transactions) so much as it does orchestrating the auction (see Exhibits 24.1 and 24.2).

Buyers, on the other hand, employ widespread use of DFE-present value of future earnings streams-methods, as they are trying to determine the current value (to themselves, i.e., investment value) of the future business earnings they are buying. To consider the effects of the target's growth and the synergies perceived by the buy side, buyers by necessity have great

EXHIBIT 24.1   Simplified illustration of the use of the DCF/DFE Methods with Rapidly Growing Earnings as in Technology Companies and Similar Situations

	Year 1	Year 2	Year 3	Year 4	Thereafter
Earnings or cash flows	$ 10,000	$12,000	$15,000	$19,500	$20,475
Growth rate	—	20%	25%	30%	5%
Discount rate (ROI)	20%	20%	20%	20%	15%[1]
Present value of earnings	$ 8,333	$ 8,333	$ 8,681	$ 9,404	$11,707
Sum of present value of earnings: Years 1, 2, 3, and 4	$ 34,751				
Capitalized value of earnings thereafter	11,707				
Present value of all earnings including "thereafter" earnings as capitalized	**$46,458**				

[1]20% less 5% growth rate = 15% or 6.7 multiple

EXHIBIT 24.2 Use of the DCF/DFC Methods with Product Line or Contract
Acquisitions

	Year 1	Year 2	Year 3	Year 4	Thereafter
Earnings or cash flows	$ 10,000	$12,000	$15,000	$10,500	$ —
Growth rate	—	20%	25%	−30%	−100%
Discount rate (ROI)	20%	20%	20%	20%	NA
Present value of earnings	$ 8,333	$ 8,333	$ 8,681	$ 5,064	$ —
Sum of present value of earnings: Years 1, 2, 3, and 4	$30,411				
Capitalized value of earnings thereafter	————				
Present value of all earnings including "thereafter" earnings as capitalized	**$30,411**				

need of the DFE method. This is not to say that a skilled investment banker
should not be equally capable of using this tool. In fact, he can use them
in various ways, among which are:

- Calculating preliminary values for product lines, groups of contracts,
  and early stage businesses for his sales-side clients
- Defending against, by understanding, the buy side's use of these methods in a negotiation

Chapter Highlights

- Sales-side M&A valuations are done and reported predominantly by the
  use of multiples applied to normalized trailing EBITDA or EBITDA (or
  a similar proxy for cash flows), which do after all take into account
  growth, but by applying an appropriate multiple (higher or lower) to
  trailing EBTDA earnings.
- Buy-side M&A valuations are largely done by DFE approaches.
- Both sides may use the DFE methodology to determine the value of:
  - Product lines
  - Separate contracts
  - Early stage businesses or new technology

- EBITDA is a proxy for cash flows: Among the flavors are:
  - EBIT (*sales side*)
  - EBITDA (*sales side*)
  - EBITDA-CAPX (*buy side*)
  - EBITDA—Changes in Working Capital (*buy side*)
- Long-term debt on a business has no relevance to its value; its only effect is to reduce the value of the equity in the business.
- Investment bankers should be knowledgeable abut DFE methods for many reasons—if nothing else, to defend against them in negotiation.
- Businesses do not pay income taxes. *Only the entities that own them do.* So taxes are ignored in computing the value of the business (M&A Enterprise Value).
- Present-value calculations used in the DFE methodology are as simple as fourth-grade arithmetic. The value of $110 million one year from now, but today at a 10% rate of return, is $100 million.

Notes

1. I want to again remind my readers that this and other sections of this book on valuation are directed to M&A investment bankers and others with only slight training in formal valuations although even trained professionals may find something of value here.
2. There is of course the issue of taxes and how they impact deal value, but I am discussing businesses here. Businesses do not pay taxes; only entities do. I have long recommended a two-step approach to deal structuring. The first is to determine the value of the given business. The second is to further impact the deal value by any income tax considerations that might arise as a result of the fact that businesses are usually owned by entities separate from them. By extension, from the formal valuator's point of view, at a minimum all valuation conclusions should be reality-checked against the implied EBIT(DA) multiples on the operating businesses owned by the entities they are probably valuing. I am tempted to write more developed article on formal valuation that would employ this two-step process from the ground up, by first valuing the business and then and not until then considering income tax effects at the entity level. This article might have cut through a lot of the debate about tax effecting S corporations a few years ago. I touch on this again in Chapter 32.
3. I need to point out that this example is for pedagogical purposes only, as in most states, a nonprofessional would not be allowed to be a partner in a law firm.

CHAPTER 25

A Brief Discussion of Multiples and Multiple Realities

Tyson's Corner, VA—1997

While Charley was practically shouting at me (mergers and acquisitions, or M&A, is a noisy business, but I suppose that is reflective of the stakes involved), I looked out of the window of the Tyson's Corner, Virginia high rise his offices were in. I remember from the days I was raising money for a new bank that Tyson's was something like the eleventh largest city in the United States (and that was in 1984) in terms of office space. Well, I was thinking, that might be great, but so far they had really made a mess out of it, at least in terms of people friendliness. It is basically a high-rise canyon without any charm at all. But it is also a power center for the Northern Virginia Tech corridor. It was the height of the dot.com boom and everybody was feeling fat and happy—invincible, in fact.

Charley, the proprietor of an Internet service provider (ISP), was telling me I was badly mistaken (his words were perhaps a little more colorful than that) with my initial preliminary valuation of his company. He considered himself a competitor of AOL, another Tyson's area business, but I seriously doubt they had a clue about him. There were dozens of these little ISPs starting up at the time.

The one consolation I got between Charley's yelling and the ugly and inefficient mess at Tyson's is that we were high enough that I can look east about 10 miles and see much of the skyline of Washington, DC, my hometown (I have to admit it, even as a native Texan). In my opinion DC is one of the most beautiful cites in the world.

Charley, calmed down a little (I found he did that when you let him vent) and still tried to explain to me that if the value of AOL per Internet subscriber customer was about $1,400, based on AOL's total market cap, then Charley's business with 10,000 subscribers logically was worth about $14 million, and I was having a hard time explaining why the mere fact that AOL was a much larger public company with quadzillions of subscribers would make a difference.

Multiples in General

Let's explore the term *multiple* a little further in the context of this book, since there are so many widespread misconceptions among lay people about their appropriate use. A multiple is simply a convenient term used in lieu of more formal terms in finance, for more or less the same thing, which are return on investment (ROI ... a form of) or capitalization rate.

To demonstrate as I have previously: If I promise to give you $1 million a year for the rest of your life, and you perceive that you need a 20% ROI, then you will in turn give me (invest with me) $5 million. The *multiple* of what you get ($1 million) is five times what you will receive. For example, a multiple of four, is equivalent to a 25% ROI, and a multiple of six is equivalent to a 16.7% ROI.

By now, you will have perhaps noticed that by dividing the multiple into 100 you get the ROI or capitalization rate, and conversely by dividing the ROI or capitalization rate into 100 you can derive the multiple. They are simply arithmetic reciprocals of each other or two ways of arithmetically saying the same thing. Pretty simple so far?

Businesses are economic assets. As also discussed previously, economic assets are valued based on the income they will produce to the owner or buyer. By using a multiple of, say, five or six or whatever, or alternatively a cap rate or ROI of 20%, 16.7%, etc., I can determine the value of the underlying asset (more specially the value of its earnings) at that given rate of return. For example, the following illustrates the value of an income stream (think a business) at different multiples, assuming the income continues in perpetuity:

Earnings	Capitalization or ROI Rate	Multiple	Computed Value
$2,000,000	20%	5×	$10,000,000
$2,000,000	16.7%	6×	$12,000,000
$2,000,000	14.2%	7×	$14,000,000

Risk and Multiples

These rates or multiples are directly correlated to the degree of risk perceived by the investor. An investor, according to the theory of substitution, could choose to buy a Middle Market business or invest in a ten-year treasury note. As a ten-year treasury note is about as safe as you can get, you would usually expect to get an ROI of around 4% to 5%. There is a ladder of choices and risks, ranging from the notes at 5%, to large public stocks at, say, 12%, to less-than-investment-grade bonds at, say, 16%, to Middle Market businesses at 20%. For example, (keeping in mind again that all of these rates of return are before the investor's taxes, although the cash or the equivalent (capital appreciation) returns themselves are after the payers' taxes, if any):

Investment Category	Rate of Return	Multiple
Ten-year treasury note	5%	20×
Commercial real estate rentals	11%	9×
Large public company stock	12%	8.3×
Small public company stock	17%	5.9×
Middle Market business	20%	5×

Note: Another interesting way to look at the multiple is to consider how many years one would be willing to wait to get the original investment back. Note that the riskier the investment, the less one is willing to wait (and the higher the required return).

The *Rule of Five* (see Chapter 23) suggests that a Middle Market business (not an entity that owns one) will be valued at a five-multiple of its before investors tax cash flow earning stream until there is reason to do otherwise. This is a very useful starting point, as I pointed out in that chapter, and, as I also point out, many Middle Market business sell for and are valued at substantially more or less than multiples of five (or 20% ROIs). It also assumes a going concern, in the sense that the earnings will be received in perpetuity (at least in theory).

Derivative Multiples versus Actual Deal-Driving Multiples

It is not uncommon to pick up the financial press or an M&A reporting service and have a Middle Market deal reported as having been for a multiple of almost anything that the reporter chooses to state it as. For example, in the late 1990s it was not uncommon to have the purchase price of a business expressed as a multiple of some pretty strange and exotic things, like discrete Web site visits, or the number of network engineers employed. Well, folks, these are not what deals are actually (or should be anyway) based on. What they *are* based on are multiples of cash flow earnings (EBITDA, etc.). Any other multiple is a multiple derived *after* the transaction was done. And while it was being done, you can be assured that the parties, especially the buyer, were thinking in terms of earnings multiples. If there were not any current earnings, you can bet earnings were at least being projected. (See the DFE methodology in Chapter 24). Furthermore, important aspects of the deal like normalized EBTDA and precise deal terms are usually not known by the reporting service.

While not quite as far-fetched as some of the multiples used in the late 1990s, revenue multiples frequently cited are also ... derivative multiples. They are calculated *after* the deal is done, but do not drive the deal.[1] Once the purchase price is determined as, say, $10 million, it is easy enough to divide that number by the revenue of $8 million and report that the deal was for a multiple of the sellers revenues of 1.25 to 1.

Well yes, it is a true statement, but it is just arithmetic, not deal making. My advice in general is get your mind off of revenue multiples. They are misleading, except for limited purposes, and then only in the hands of experts and negotiators, and are otherwise pretty useless.[2]

Public Market versus Private Market Multiples

Another aspect of multiples that needs attention is the difference between public company valuation multiples and private Middle Market company valuation multiples. I have heard some very sophisticated people discourse on the valuation of their private Middle Market companies, while totally misapplying public company multiples to them and, as a result, drawing some very wrong conclusions about their company's value. I have mentioned elsewhere the phenomena of the roll-up industry, which resurrects its ugly/pretty head periodically. In that phenomenon, which is based really on financial engineering and arbitrage (a price difference for an identical asset in different markets), sponsors go about buying privately held Middle Market businesses, repackaging them, and then reselling them as public companies in the form of IPOs (initial public offerings). Understanding this is a big step to realizing why public multiples really cannot be used to determine the value of a Middle Market company for transaction purposes.

I do not deny that I and other experts use the guideline public company method (essentially using public company multiples) for formal valuation purposes in courtrooms and so forth to value private companies, but even there it is used with great care, with a number of necessary transformation equations applied (one example is a discount to account for the difference in liquidity between a public and private company), and as only one of several methods. Furthermore the guideline public company method is one that is, in fact, frequently discarded after all the work is done as being not particularly useful, even by formal valuators.

Private Middle Market companies are valued on their earnings, generally modified to a proxy for their cash flows, but which is nevertheless close, as a rule, to the *before tax, before interest* net income (EBIT) that an accountant comes up with when he does the audit or the company's tax return. As discussed elsewhere in this book, these earnings are usually multiplied by somewhere between 4.5 and 5.5 (although the multiple can be quite different). And that is how private Middle Market companies are valued (at least on the sales side), but it is not the way public companies are valued.

Public companies are most commonly valued on the basis of *after tax* earnings, and the multiple that is known most commonly in this market is the price-to-earnings ratio (P/E ratio). This is essentially a derivative multiple that results from the collective votes cast every minute by the shareholders buying and selling stock in a public company, and it reflects the value of the equity alone (market capitalization) rather than the entire enterprise.

Arbitrage and Roll-Ups: A Practical Example of Public versus Private Company Valuation and Multiples

Let's take a quick look at Company A (see Exhibit 25.1), which is valued as if it is a privately owned Middle Market company on the one hand, and as if it is a publicly owned company on the other. This is particularly revealing regarding the possible arbitrage between buying this company from its private owners, repackaging it with a number of similar companies, and then selling the package to the public market as an IPO. It points out nicely the benefits of price arbitrage, but my main reason for including it is to illustrate the important distinction between valuing a company using private market multiples and public market multiples.

You simply cannot take public multiples as indicative of what a private business is worth for many reasons, including size, similarity (degree or lack of) of the businesses, etc., but a fundamental reason is that the multiples are extremely different in their application, one (private businesses) being a before-entity tax cash flow multiple and the other (public entities (P/E ratio)) being after entity taxes.[3] They are usually also very different in magnitude. The private multiples are usually in the five or six range. The public multiples, in the 15 to 25 range, reflect the value of the equity alone (market capitalization) rather than the entire enterprise.

EXHIBIT 25.1   Example of Private to Public Pricing Multiple Arbitrage

	Privately Owned	Publicly Owned
Earnings	$ 10,000,000	$10,000,000
Taxes	—	4,000,000
EBIT/after-tax earnings	10,000,000	6,000,000
Multiple	5×	15×
Valuation	$ 50,000,000	$90,000,000
Difference in valuation (arbitrage)	**$40,000,000**	

It takes just a telephone call (or a keystroke on your computer if you trade online) to sell your pubic company shares, and three days until you are paid. In a Middle Market company, it can take seven to twelve months and longer to liquidate your investment. The difference attributable to this illiquidity advantage is typically around 30% to 40% of the value of the equivalent public shares.

I have seen the misapplication of (or at least confusion in applying) public P/E multiples to private company EBITDA from time to time by laypersons. I also not infrequently see it in studies purporting to reflect M&A multiples based on EBITDA, when actually what is being reflected are public stock prices as a multiple of EBITDA.

Chapter Highlights

- Multiples in Middle Market M&A transactions for private companies are described in the press and reporting services based on very limited information (e.g., normalized EBITDA and precise deal terms are usually not known) and, which affects and limits their usefulness significantly.
- Revenue and second-order or derivative multiples should not be considered very seriously.
- Cash flow (EBITDA, etc.) multiples are first-order (deal-driving) multiples.
  - But these are only a referential starting point in M&A deals that are good for:
    - Preliminary value in the market place estimates
    - Negotiating, in some cases
  - And these are the equivalent, mathematically and reciprocally, of a capitalization rate or ROI
- Multiples for private businesses are not comparable to multiples in public companies, because:

- Public company multiples are generally applied to the after tax income of the entity owning the business, and private business multiples are generally before the income taxes of the entity owning the business
- Public company ownership interests are extremely liquid

Notes

1. There are a very few exceptions, particularly in certain few pure professional service business like accounting practices and some consulting firms (but not many others), in which Mom-and-Pop rules of thumb, like revenue multiples, are used or at least referenced. However, in these cases the view is that it is clients being bought, not going businesses, even though some of the staff may transfer and you can be sure the multiples are adjusted for profitability. These exceptions are used only when profitability in that service practice is at fairly standard margin for that industry.

2. It is interesting, at least, to conjecture as to what extent M&A multiples become self-fulfilling prophesies, in the sense that they are derivative multiples at first, but then buyers and sellers come to expect them and thus they start driving deals as opposed to being derived from them. What in large part belies this premise, though, is that if the growth rates that drive rapid growth in an industry disappear, so will the higher multiples. But to some degree there certainly is a momentary sort of follow-the-leader phenomenon.

3. Public P/E multiples may be shown both ways (based on cash flows similar to EBITDA or based on net income) but in each case they are usually shown after entity income taxes.

CHAPTER 26

Qualitative Values Inherent in the Target Company
Next to the Auction, The Real Value in M&A

Coastal Delaware—November 1989

I, along with tens of thousands of other Washingtonians, have made coastal Delaware the nation's "summer capital" for years, especially in July and August when we march to the beach like penguins to their annual breeding grounds. And breeding grounds is not a bad analogy, considering the number of singles that accompany us old folks in our quest for sun and sand. But that November, I was at the coast on business, and it was cold and windy.

I had not even known that this small plastics manufacturing company existed, but I was growing impressed nevertheless with an industry with which I had been, up until then, unfamiliar. The plant, which was only a mile or two off of a highway that I had been using for years on our family beach treks, was about three acres in size, with all kinds of impressive machinery, and well kept up. It employed lots of people at the very low labor costs that were available in coastal Delaware at the time. It reminded me that over the years, most of the individual buyers and private equity groups (PEGs) I had represented on the buy side had expressed a high interest in manufacturing. The old American dream, I guess, of having a plant where the widgets just rolled off the manufacturing line into the hands of willing customers. What could have been bad about this one? It should have been an easy business to sell; it was doing about $30 million a year.

I was soon to find out. Its EBITDA margins were a paltry 2.5%.

Quantitative and Qualitative Valuation

I want to touch on an aspect of valuation that I have found in the course of my teaching to require a moment of reflection somewhere during the course. There is a tendency sometimes, particularly after I have covered the standard sections of M&A valuation for students and audiences, to become excessively focused on earnings growth rate as a measurable number, and multiples as a determining or derivable number, as a number abstracted from any real appreciation of the underlying business. Let's put that in English by saying the tendency is to get too bound up in the quantitative stuff (the math of valuation) at the expense of the qualitative stuff (which are the value drivers, for better or for worse, in the particular company being sold).

Two Law Firms

I can very simply express the idea of value drivers with an exaggerated and trite example that at least brings out several of the classic drivers while having a little fun. Let's imagine two law firms (B.I.G. Mouth & Associates, and the Boring City Law Practice Group). Let's say they both show exactly the same financial operating performance; that is, they each have $50 million in revenues and $15 million in net earnings before taxes.

Now I will give you for free that law firms and other professional practices tend to be valued or sold at around a multiple of three times their net earnings (EBITDA) or one times their revenues. So here is the quiz. How much is law firm B.I.G. Mouth & Associates worth, and how much is the Boring City Law Practice Group worth?

This is obviously some kind of a dumb trick, since obviously if the answer was really the same value for each firm, I would not bother posing the question. I know you know that, but it is a useful starting point in a simple discussion of simple value drivers.

Let's say that The Boring City Law Practice Group is a corporate practice with 1,000 attorneys that typically has 8,000 regular clients. B.I.G. Mouth & Associates, on the other hand, consists of a partnership between four famous and vocal litigation attorneys who typically, in the course of a year, represent three or four usually well-known (one might add well-chosen) and highly publicized cases each.

Of course the answer to their individual valuation would be very different now that we have taken a look beyond the numbers. The Boring City Practice would in fact likely to be worth maybe $45 million[1] but B.I.G. Mouth & Associates, as a law practice separate from its lawyers, would likely have little or no value, as it reflects two of the classic negative value drivers: a high concentration of customers (only 12 to 16 very unstable clients or major cases a year) and the lack of value in the practice itself (because all the real value is tied up in the personal, professional, goodwill of the four B.I.G. Mouth lawyers). Personal, professional, goodwill (very similar to over-reliance on key management) is not possible to pass on to a new owner and since it is not transferable, it is not salable . . . nor is an unstable client (customer) concentration. These are value drivers, however primitively stated.

Value Drivers Go Well Beyond the Numbers

The point here is that the value drivers of a business go well beyond the numbers. When I teach formal valuation to beginners and I describe value drivers in shorthand, I say they deal with the stability of, and the opportunity for, earnings in the future. Using that as a frame of reference, most value drivers are obvious: For example:

- The growth rate of earnings
- Protection of earnings from competitive or obsolescence threat
- Protection of earnings from undue customer concentration
- Protection from excessive dependence on key personnel
- Protection from product or service obsolescence, etc. (buggy-whip businesses)
- Quality of products and services
- Quality of management
- Diversification of customers and products
- Adequately protected proprietary products where applicable
- And more

Some of these will not necessarily be reflected in current performance, but may be latent in the company currently, both negative and positive. A business can be, on the surface and in the moment, performing well but headed for disaster. Similarly, a company's robust future may not immediately show up in its income statements.

To take another approach: Any value driver analysis of a business, at least in terms of the questions that can be asked, can be established with reference to these four points. For example:

- Profitable revenues:
    - Adequacy of gross margins (think of the effect of changing competitive cross-border product and service pricing with India, China, and Mexico; regulatory restraints on pricing; condition of plant and equipment; high margin proprietary products versus low margin contract manufacturing)

- Adequacy of net earnings margins (think of risk involved in lack of cushion from low net margins; inadequacy of return on capital invested)
- Ability to control expenses (think labor unions; local demographics; effect of capital intensive business in periods of high interest rates)
- Consistent and stable revenues:
  - Competitive threat (think barriers to entry; product obsolescence; and again of the effect of changing competitive cross-border product and service pricing with India, China, and Mexico)
  - Revenue stability (think customer or contract concentration; excessive reliance on key owner or employee goodwill or skills)
- Focus: A business with focus on a main revenue stream (business line) is a rule much easier to find buyers for than one that has become a mini-conglomerate. Usually if a Middle Market business has become a mini-conglomerate, it was by simply being reactive rather than being focused. This probably felt good while it is happening, but will prove a difficult sell later.
- Revenue growth rate:
  - Industry growth (a rising tide should float all boats, which probably means highly desired products or services)
  - Company growth (going against the tide may or may not be sustainable)
  - Overall growth (think about cycles and sustainability and the likely point the business is in a cycle)

Las Vegas, NV—October 1997
Buggy whips are not what they used to be
As usual, when I got to the part about industry obsolesce, I used the old hackneyed "buggy whip business" metaphor. When my presentation to the valuation conference was over, I retired to the bar for a beer and one of the attendees, actually a resident of Vegas, joined me. And pointed out to me that buggy whips were not at all obsolete in Vegas, but they had nothing to do with horses or buggies. Well, whatever.

Obsolescence, or . . . Go into Plastics, Young Man

Some of my readers may remember the movie *The Graduate* where the young hero is advised to go into plastics. It was probably good advice at the time, but not long after, it was bad advice. While there are some real exceptions, the plastics extrusion and injection molding industry, which was once thought to be the new frontier of American manufacturing, is in fact not a particularly good industry. Typically, it is job-order manufacturing, which means that the customer owns the molds and the products.

Picture products of a high commodity nature, like the plastic casing on the pen you might be holding right now, the cigarette lighter casing, or radio dials in your car. These are extremely low-profit items to the manufacturer, and furthermore, he is dependent in this case on the whims and vicissitudes of customers in the automotive industry and others giants often, who have often little mercy for these smaller Middle Market businesses. Job-order manufacturing is a very difficult business to be in, for sure, with low value drivers all around in terms of revenue stability, customer concentration, profit margins, you name it.

Again, intuition and appearances notwithstanding, to learn the value of a particular business in a particular industry, you simply have to peel back a few layers of the onion, especially when it comes to *industry analysis*. The industry a business finds itself in is no less important than the earth a plant finds itself in. The plant can either be a weed in an otherwise beautiful garden or a rose in a junk yard. It will make a difference to the gardener/harvester, because in either case he is not likely to want to stay around for long before moving off in search of roses in well-cultivated gardens.

How Quickly They Forget

And these comments are by no means limited to old-line industries like plastics or job order manufacturers. It is funny how quickly *cutting edge* can and does become old stuff. Only several years ago, cutting edge was computer box sellers, and then slightly later it was value-added systems integrators, who added some additional value to the technology products and boxes they integrated and assembled for their customers. Frankly, it is hard to give away many of these businesses, much less sell them, today. Hewlett-Packard and Microsoft are tough competitors.

When Race Horses Become Plow Horses: A Last Comment on Growth, When Growth Has Peaked

It is not always immediately apparent, but the owners of large Middle Market businesses that are otherwise successful and profitable but have captured either pretty much all of the market share in their sector (or, in other words, are not in a sector that has any growth left in it), obviously should not assume valuation multiples that anticipate growth in earnings or imagine themselves as attractive to financial investors (PEGs) and industry strategic buyers, who are keen on fast stand-alone growth unless there is some particular synergy there that does not involve stand-alone growth.

This is a serious negative value driver. I have seen it in some pretty big companies, and it is often an abrupt and sad awakening. Middle Market businesses, to be really attractive to either industry strategic or financial buyer/investors, need to be able to demonstrate the possibility of substantial growth (in earnings) or expect lower multiples and a difficult sales process due to a limited number of buyers, even if they are profitable. This does not mean these larger companies do not have value as merger and acquisition (M&A) sales-side candidates. They very much do, but often at the lower end of the multiple range, at least in terms of their stand-alone growth, unless there are particular synergies to a buyer beyond the stand-alone growth of the company.

The Use of a Value Driver Analysis Contained in a Preliminary Valuation Report

I discuss this elsewhere in this book (see Chapter 22), but a value driver analysis, particularly as part of a *preliminary valuation*, can provide an excellent midterm strategic and tactical planning tool to help Middle Market companies improve their businesses to eventually maximize value. Most clients should consider having such an analysis prepared by a competent investment banker with adequate training in valuation at least every two years or so. I believe most of them will find the value of this type of analysis far beyond what they might initially imagine it to be.

Chapter Highlights

- Middle Market business valuation is as much qualitative as quantitative.
- Revenue and earnings stability, followed closely by revenue and earnings growth, provide excellent starting points for a specific company's value driver analysis.
- Middle Market business owners need to be particularly alert to business peaks.
- A value driver analysis as part of a *preliminary valuation* analysis can provide an excellent strategic and tactical planning tool to help Middle Market companies improve their business to eventually maximize value.

Note

1. In fact there are very few purchasers for large law firms. These are almost always transferred by mergers, not purchases. Who would or could buy them?

CHAPTER 27

M&A Conventions and Establishing Balance Sheet Targets

Baltimore, MD—January 2000

The inner harbor in Baltimore is beautiful, one of the most visited places of all cities in the United States, but in January it is damned cold at 8 A.M. And I'd forgotten my overcoat. Karl and I were walking over to his offices in the historic financial district of Baltimore, just a couple of blocks off of the harbor, and my teeth were chattering.

"Vat do you mean they get my balance sheet for their offer? I verked all my life for those profits and I will keep them for myselv." (Karl had a slight German accent, as you may have noticed).

"Karl, I am afraid that is the convention," I said. "I am sorry you did not realize this sooner." (He actually did know and had been told this many times, but he liked to vent anyway, just for the pleasure of it, I suppose.) "Look, the best way I can describe it to you is that the balance sheet is kind of like an office building. If you buy the rents, you get the building. In a very rough sense, that is the way it works with a business acquisition. If you buy the business income, you get the balance sheet. Maybe a better analogy is that the buyer needs gasoline for the car, except in this case the car dealer has to supply the initial full tank. The gasoline is the balance sheet."

Karl's response was unprintable.

I added, "Well, you do get to keep some of it."

Conventions and Their Need and Basis

Conventions? Whose conventions?

Perhaps fortunately because my early training and expertise was as a CPA, after I began doing M&A, I fairly quickly got the relationship between what was in M&A terms the financial core of an operating business, as I will say again, its gas tank, its balance sheet. As I studied valuation sciences in the late 80's I also came to understand early on that certain assets on that balance sheet were a business's financial assets which were peculiar to each owner of a business but not to the business itself (cash and long-term debt if any). Finally I understood that a business is not an owner (an entity) and needed to be separated from ownership in order to make any sense of it as a business, per se.

Out of this knowledge came an understanding of the conventions that need to be applied to make clear what was being bought or sold. I also found that many M&A deals were done with little or no understanding of what conventions needed to be applied to be consistent from deal to deal and to truly understand what your client was selling and what they were getting as opposed to what they were giving up that was rightfully theirs to give up or not, to be paid for or not. It seemed to me this was like the blind leading the blind when it came to M&A deals represented by professionals who ether had only minimal accounting knowledge or at least did not have access to accounting knowledge. One of the other problems I suppose of dilettante representation of deals.

This is not to say that deals need to strictly follow conventions but where they are not followed it should be consciously and with an understanding of what the cost or benefit is of abandoning or using a convention. Many of the M&A deals I have observed were substantially misunderstood both by the advisors and their clients in terms of what the actual purchase price (deal value) was. For example, if a nominal stated value of $20 million involved giving up $2 million dollars worth of balance sheet items then the actual transaction value was only $18 million.

The Balance Sheet in General

It amazes me how many fairly large Middle Market sellers do not realize that they do not get to keep the accounts receivable, etc. (Karl's business did $16 million a year in revenues). I guess until the time comes to sell the business, they just have had no reason to think about it. They may also be confused by Mom-and-Pop business purchase transactions, where frequently the seller does get to keep his own receivables, etc. But in a real operating Middle Market business the balance sheet goes to the buyer, with a few important exceptions, and subject to some conditions.

I was eventually able to explain this to Karl (hammer it home through his thick skull would be more like it). He did not like it, though. He did not have to like it, but he did have to learn to live with it. Although I admit Karl had a certain Germanic tendency to shoot his messengers, I think he did it mainly for sport as opposed to meanness. He was actually a good guy at heart, and a very smart one to boot.

M&A Conventions in General

In Middle Market mergers and acquisitions (M&A), there are a number of explicit and implicit conventions. Conventions are reference points just like rules of spelling and grammar. In actually doing a deal any convention can be violated but by starting from the basic rule one can than determine the costs or gains from deviating form the norm (e.g., purchase price adjustments necessary to account for deviations). The important conventions are:

- A business is what is being sold or bought, not an entity (e.g., a corporation, etc.). Attributes of a transaction, to the extent they are solely a factor of entity activities (i.e., paying income taxes, financing the business long term) can and should be ignored while calculating the value of the business.
- Valuations that are based on M&A conventions (e.g., multiples of EBITDA, etc.) result in M&A Enterprise Value (which means the balance sheet is cash free/long-term debt free). Cash and long term debt are considered *financing* as opposed to *operating* assets.
- Since a business, not an entity, is being bought, the issue of a stock purchase versus an asset purchase is strictly mechanical, but tax considerations resulting from the mechanics ultimately may result in purchase price adjustments when the business is transferred from seller to buyer.
- The *ordinary and necessary* balance sheet (which assumes the correct balance sheet fully accrued and adequately reflected) goes to the buyer.[1]
- Balance sheets, are moving targets from day to day, so the establishment of balance sheet deliverable targets is necessary.
- There are three important balance sheet *dates* in an M&A transaction:
  - The balance sheet upon which the agreed targets are based.
  - The apparent balance sheet actually delivered at closing.
  - The *true up* (or corrected) delivery (closing) date balance sheet usually determined 30 to 60 days after settlement.
- There are three important balance sheet *targets* that are usually established:
  - Cash (if any)
  - Net working capital
  - Net assets
- Working capital by the preceding cash free convention is delivered, and therefore the target should be measured, without the inclusion of cash

but must never the less be adequate. To the extent that the removal of cash from the delivered balance sheet causes working capital to be inadequate either cash will need to be restored (to that extent) or a purchase price adjustment made.

Let's discuss each of these conventions and what they significance they have in the M&A world.

Entities and Businesses—Redux

If you and I each owned two identical businesses, but yours was owned through a corporation and mine was owned through a partnership, the *businesses* would have the same value, although the entity tax consequences might be quite different. Any difference in the value of the ownership interest as a result of being held in the *entity* will be solely attributable to the entity differences, and not to the underlying business. For example, comparable businesses with more or less aggressive tax avoidance strategies could not begin to be compared if entity income taxes solely attributable to the entity choice and/or degree of tax aggressiveness were considered. This goes as well for the owner's or entity's choice of financing itself. Businesses are not entities. Entities are not businesses.

M&A Balance Sheet Conventions, or, Who Gets the Balance Sheet?

In Middle Market M&A deals, the convention is that the buyer is purchasing not only the earnings stream of the seller but the sellers' balance sheet (at least most of it) as well. The buyer is buying the future earnings of the business, along with the assets that will produce them. Although valuations are initially derived mainly from earnings considerations, the resulting valuation includes the buyer's right to receive the *ordinary and necessary* balance sheet of the business. The balance sheet is a little analogous to the fuel in the gas tank. While car dealers may not sell cars with full tanks, it is expected in the Middle Market M&A arena that the basic fuel tank (the balance sheet) will be supplied and adequate for the job.

Put differently, the type of calculation that the parties perform, typically based on EBITDA or some close variation thereof (see Chapter 24), results in a value known as M&A Enterprise Value. Enterprise Value includes the key *operating* assets on the balance sheet, including the accounts receivable, inventory, equipment, accounts payable, accruals, etc., but not the cash and not the long-term debt, the latter two being *financing* assets.

M&A Enterprise Value and Debt

Enterprise value also assumes that the business is free of long-term debt. It does not have to be long-term debt free in reality, of course, but if there is any long-term debt, then either the seller will need to pay it off at closing or, if the buyer assumes it at closing. In other words, the assumed amount will come out of the seller's proceeds (e.g., by way of a reduced purchase price). You would not expect to buy a car that had a lien attached to it from the previous owner's unpaid car note. Whether the seller pays off the long-term debt out of his sales proceeds or the buyer assumes it will basically amount to the same thing. The important thing here is to understand that the long-term debt on a business has no more to do with its value then the mortgage on your house or the note on your car have to do with the actual values of those assets.

M&A Enterprise Value, Permanent Debt versus Operating Debt (Accounts Payable and Working Capital Lines)

Please notice that I said in the immediately preceding paragraph "long-term debt." That does not include operating debt, such as accounts payable, payroll accruals, etc., but rather debt that stands as a substitute for equity. In other words, debt that is only on the books because of the owner's long-term financing choices. Assuming he chooses debt financing, this is usually long-term interest-bearing debt (including the accountant's classification of some of it as due in the short term). However, it can also be debt that is called, and initially looks like, working capital debt (which would ordinarily be considered short-term operating debt), but upon careful examination is determined to be an equity substitute. A strong indication of whether it is an equity substitute or not is whether it is paid off annually, as a working capital line is designed to be. If a working capital line never quite seems to get paid off, then the portion of it that has not been paid off (the lowest balance the line gets down to every year) is probably long-term debt.

M&A Enterprise Value and Cash

In addition, M&A enterprise value assumes that the seller will to be able to take the cash, to the extent there is any, off the balance sheet, although this later presumption is often a function of negotiation between the parties. If the amount of cash that can be taken by the sellers or conversely needs to be left on the balance sheet is negotiated, it will usually involve two considerations:

1. Establishing a target amount of cash to be left on the balance sheet
2. Agreeing on a methodology for establishing the target cash (a typical methodology might be something like leaving 15 to 45 days' worth of needed operating cash in the business—but again, keep in mind that the starting point is the assumption that *no* cash will be left)

Other Limitations on What Is Included in M&A Enterprise Value

The convention that the buyer gets the seller's balance sheet needs one more clarification to be complete, and that is that the buyer gets the seller's *ordinary and necessary*[2] balance sheet to run the business. Another way to look at this is that the buyer gets the *operating assets*, and these basically consists of three classes:

- The working capital consisting of accounts receivable, inventory, and similar assets that change pretty much on an hour-by-hour basis as a result of the hour-by-hour operations of the business.
- The fixed assets, such as plant, equipment, and computers; office furniture; etc., that are necessary to operate the business (see also Chapter 28, *Special M&A and M&A Valuation Topics*, Valuing Real Estate on the Balance Sheet)
- The intangible assets, which usually reflect such assets as patents, copyrights, and other intangibles necessary for operations including overall goodwill (e.g., customers, reputation, ability to produce earnings)

    Purchase price of the business:

    $10 million EBIT times a 6 multiple = $60 million
    Identified tangible operating assets = $35 million
    Resulting implicit goodwill and other intangibles
    not specifically identified = $25 million

In general, then, all of the operational assets but not financial assets (cash and long-term debt) go to the buyer.

Other Nonoperational Assets beside Cash

Many Middle Market businesses' balance sheets also contain items that are not operating assets. Examples include real estate held for eventual expansion or investment, marketable securities, and assets that may be more related to the idiosyncrasies and practices of the owners, such as pleasure boats, planes, condominiums in Colorado, assets held for future expansion but not currently used (nonoperational in nature), etc. Either these assets need to be removed from the balance sheet or the business purchase price should be increased by their value if they are to remain. Obviously, if the buyer for some reason wants these nonoperating assets, then the business purchase price is increased by their value or of course they could be purchased separately.

Establishing Targets for Deliverables, Usually the Balance Sheet—A Moment in Time

As discussed above, a buyer is purchasing essentially three categories of economic assets:

- The income stream of the business
- The intangible assets necessary to run the business
- The balance sheet tangible *operating* assets necessary to run the business

The first and second categories are easy enough to pin down rather exactly with legal descriptions, language, and schedules and are embedded in the basic purchase price calculation. The problem is the third category, at least in terms of the individual accounts, such as inventories, payables, and receivables. It can be elusive and a moving target but it doesn't have to be.

Operating businesses will have a balance sheet by the end of the day that looks at least somewhat different in terms of its constituent parts than it did at the beginning of the same day. Since the buyer is entitled to the balance sheet, the problem is pinning down which balance sheet and at what point in time and of what is this balance sheet composed. The fact that balance sheet *totals and relationships but not individual accounts* will not look much different as a rule on a day-to-day and even week-to-week basis is where we derive our ability to pin down balance sheet targets. While accounts receivable may have gone down $2 million, cash gone up $500,000, and accounts payable gone down $1.49 million, the chances are that working capital and net assets (or net worth) will look pretty much the same at both ends of the day and, for the most part, will have only changed by profits and losses for that day.

EXHIBIT 27.1 Negotiated Targets and Actual Deliveries

Target Type	Negotiated Target	Actually Delivered at Time of Settlement	Difference
Cash	$ 150,000	$ 200,000	+$ 50,000
Working capital (ex-cash)	$ 600,000	$ 500,000	($100,000)
Net worth	$3,000,000	$2,950,000	($ 50,000)
Actual purchase price adjustment in buyer's favor (implies an operating loss of the same between negotiation and settlement or a withdrawal of profits)			($ 50,000)

The Balance Sheet: At the Time of Negotiation or at the Time of Settlement?

The Letter of Intent (LOI), which concludes the actual financial and business terms negotiation, is followed by a settlement within a reasonable period of time (approximately 60 days), and the usual convention is that the buyer will get the balance sheet (more accurately targets derived from that balance sheet) that existed *at the time or just before the time* of the LOI final negotiation. This is the balance sheet around which the negotiations usually took place. This is what the parties knew at the time and is one of the items the parties were negotiating for or about.

Another reason this particular balance sheet is used to create the basic targets is that during the 60-day period until settlement, the balance sheet (specifically, its net assets) will change by the amount of profits or losses the business incur during that period. Since the risk of loss remains with the seller until closing, the profits are also his. So if net assets go up or down they are therefore the sellers gain or loss. For an illustration of this, see Exhibit 27.1.

Working Capital Targets on the Balance Sheet

Establishing a working capital target will also require some negotiation between the buyers and the sellers. Although the assumption is that the targeted working capital for delivery at the time of settlement will be equal to the working capital at the time of negotiation (minus cash, since this is

M&A enterprise value), in fact working capital may not be deemed exactly adequate (ordinary and necessary) for the continued operation of the business. For example, this might come about, in cases in which the business has simply skimped along in the past with inadequate working capital and the buyer does not want to get stuck with that legacy.

In these cases, as well as establishing a working capital target in which working capital is in fact more or less adequate but for normal operating reasons tends to change over, say, the six to twelve months preceding the negotiation, several approaches are common in arriving at a negotiated target. Among these are:

- The average working capital (without cash) for X period preceding the balance sheet around which the negotiation took place
- The average working capital (without cash) for X period preceding the balance sheet, measured as a percentage of quarterly or monthly sales
- Comparison of other balance sheets' average working capital (without cash) maintained by companies in the industry, if close enough comparables can be found and proportionate size can be adjusted for

As a last remark on working capital, let me point out that when a rapidly growing business is being bought, there may be a need for additional working capital sufficient to fund that future growth. In M&A transactions, the assumption is that either that working capital will be furnished from the *future growth* or that it is the buyer's obligation to fund that. If he wants to grow the business further than working capital invested from the targets current rate of profit growth will provide then he should finance it. This is one of the reasons that for *buy side valuation calculations* (which are typically the DFE approach; see Chapter 24), the cash flow convention used will net operating cash flow (which is after taxes), adjusted for additional working capital needed for expansion. Having said this, however, this is rarely a concern from the seller's point of view. In other words, if the buyer wants to fund substantial additional growth, then the investment of additional sufficient working capital to finance that is his choice and obligation and will not concern the seller.

Net Worth Targets on the Balance Sheet

As I have said, the balance sheet just before the completion of LOI negotiation suggests the net worth target that has to be delivered at settlement (keeping in mind that this deliverable assumes net worth minus cash, since the buyer does not get the cash, as a rule), but no net worth target would seemingly need to be separately established. Rather the net worth deliverable would seem to be more or less an automatic result of having established targets for cash and working capital. It is the cash (if any) and working capital targets that need precision. The reason that does not entirely work and a net worth target needs separate establishment is due to changes in nonworking capital assets and liabilities that night happen occasionally between an LOI and a settlement.

Double-Counting Target Purchase Price Adjustments

It is important, however, in language drafting (I have seen this mistake made in practice, and it leaves everyone in confusion at settlement and the later true-up) to carefully avoid double-counting or unintended outcomes from purchase price adjustments that arise from the targets. Basically each actually delivered category as determined at settlement and then later verified at the subsequent true up date has to be separately calculated as against the negotiated target and then netted against each other in order to determine the overall purchase price adjustment.

- The excess or deficit of actual cash at the point of settlement from that negotiated
- The excess or deficit of working capital at the point of settlement from that negotiated
- The excess or deficit of net assets (net worth) at the point of settlement from that negotiated

Settlement of Differences—Truing Up

There is normally a period of 45 to 60 days after final closing and settlement (the true up) when balance sheet items *actually delivered* versus balance sheet *targets* are eventually compared and any resulting purchase price adjustments are made. Where the parties disagree about the actual amounts, disputes are typically settled by bringing in a third accountant or by arbitration. See the example shown in Exhibit 27.1.

Operating in the Normal Course of Business

Many, if not most, LOIs will include a clause that goes something like this: "between the date of this Letter of Intent and the closing, the sellers agree to operate in the ordinary course of business...." Obviously, if balance sheet targets have been established through negotiation, any deviation from those targets will show up as a deficit or surplus in one or more of the balance sheet actual deliverables. But actually, this clause is meant primarily to avoid having the seller do something really radical, like discontinue certain lines of business, change the nature of business, withdraw or refinance major assets, or otherwise do things that significantly change the underlying business or its financial structure.

The Balance Sheet and Normalization

As a rule, the balance sheet less frequently requires normalizing then does the income statement, as the primary transaction value is based on normalized earnings taken from the income statement.

Normalization of the balance sheet is important when balance sheet assets are significantly understated (or overstated, if they are operating assets like inventory) in terms of their value. The accounting convention, of course, is to reflect balance sheet assets at their historical cost, or in the case of liquid or working capital assets, at their lower cost or market; this is good enough most of the time, and no further restatement is required.

Occasionally, though, significant assets are reflected at a value that is significantly less than their actual value. Notice that I use the term *significant* twice here. The asset has to be significant in relation to the overall company assets, and the value understatement itself has to be material. I almost always see this in terms of large-ticket assets, whether operating or nonoperating (i.e., held for investment). In either case, these might include real estate, aircraft, vessels, etc.

Normalizing *Fixed Operating* Assets

If the asset is an operating asset (i.e., actually used in the operation of the business) and is being used at its highest and best use as an operating asset, then restating its value usually will not add nor subtract anything to the deal transaction value, since it is assumed that the value of the fixed assets (however they may be carried on the balance sheet) is reflected in the business's cash flows, which in turn have determined its purchase price. Again, an exception to this could be misstated inventories (a non-fixed operating asset), for example, which may in turn have an impact on the income statement (EBITDA) as the misstatement is applied to the differences between correctly stated inventories at the beginning and at the end of a year.

Other than inventories, other nonfixed operating assets, or as a result of just plain accounting errors, restating the value of other types of fixed operating assets does not affect the cash flow of the business, and therefore does not increase the business's value. Restating the value of the understated fixed operating assets does, however, emphasize additional values that are not obvious and might as well be shown to the buyer. Furthermore, showing these assets at their proper values may well highlight collateral for financing that might be used by a buyer.

Normalizing *Nonoperating* Assets

Of course, if the asset is a nonoperating asset, it will in fact either add value to the deal or be removed by the seller before the deal is completed. The question of whether these assets should increase the value of the deal or be simply withdrawn by the seller is more or less either a tax question and/or a buyer and sellers choice. If the purchase price is increased, then there is an additional (presumably capital gains) tax. If the asset is withdrawn, then there is (presumably an ordinary income) tax on the dividend. At this time, since dividend tax rates are and capital gains taxes rates are only slightly different, there is usually not that much tax difference between the two approaches.

Chapter Highlights

The primary M&A conventions are:

- A business is what is being sold or bought, not an entity (e.g., a corporation, etc.).
- Valuations that are based on M&A conventions (e.g., multiples of EBITDA, etc.) result in M&A enterprise value.
- Since a business is being bought, and not an entity, the issue of a stock purchase versus an asset purchase is strictly mechanical but may have a significant impact on final transaction value nevertheless, especially as a result of the tax consequences of the deal.
- The *ordinary and necessary* M&A enterprise value balance sheet (which assumes the correct balance sheet fully accrued and adequately reflected) goes to the buyer.
- Cash and long-term debt (financing balance sheet items) are not part of the value of a business (M&A enterprise value).
- Long-term debt can be:
  - Disguised as working capital lines of credit
  - Shown as short term on the accountants financial statements to the extent it is due within one year, but is nevertheless long-term debt
- Nonoperating assets should be either added to the purchase price or extracted by the seller before settlement.

- Conventionally established balance sheet targets may include:
  - Cash
  - Working capital
  - Net worth
- The balance sheet around which targets are negotiated is usually the one closest to the final pre-LOI negotiation date.
- The balance sheet against which actual delivered amounts are compared to negotiated targets is the balance sheet at settlement.
- There is normally a period of 45 to 60 days after settlement when balance sheet actual assets delivered versus balance sheet targets are compared and any resulting purchase price adjustments are made. The true up.
- Cash and working capital targets are determined by a variety of negotiated ways, including averages over a recent period and/or simply absolute amounts.
- Normalization of the balance sheet can take place with regard to both operating and nonoperating assets:
  - Nonoperating assets written up or separately valued are more likely to affect the final transaction value than operating assets.
  - Operating fixed assets written up may provide a better basis for senior debt financing by the buyer from third parties as well as provide better information to the buyer as to the total value of what he is getting form the balance sheet but a purchase price adjustment is usually not appropriate or called for.

Notes

1. In theory, anyway, a seller could keep the balance sheet, but this would result in a proportionate downward adjustment to final transaction value.
2. My accountant readers will recognize that *ordinary and necessary* is a term borrowed from the tax code where it is used in an entirely different context. However the term, as a succinct descriptive term, fits here quite well.

CHAPTER 28

Special M&A and M&A Valuation Topics

Overview

While this book addresses the issues of Middle Market deal valuation topics that arise in most transactions, assuming the sale of 100% of a profitable business, this chapter will be devoted to a few areas not yet covered, or at least not covered as thoroughly as they should be.

Specifically, this chapter will cover:

- The sale and valuation of real estate as part of an mergers and acquisitions (M&A) deal
- The sale and valuation of early-stage technology
- The sale and valuation of nonprofitable businesses
- The sale and valuation of product line and or contract(s)
- Valuation in later-stage private equity group (PEG) deals and venture capital deals
- The sale of minority interests to strategic buyers (stake-outs)
- True merger transactions
- Partial or mixed business acquisitions

Valuing Real Estate on the Balance Sheet

When real estate is involved in the sale of a Middle Market business, it gives rise to the perennial question: How should it be valued? Is it part of the operating business or can it, and should it, be separated and valued separately?

Is the Real Estate Separable from the Business?

Based on the discussions of the use of multiples to value a business's earnings stream in this book thus far, it should be clear that the multiples tend to be in the four, five, or possibly six range, and only much higher if there is justification of one or more of several types (see Chapter 23, *The Rules of Five*). In income-producing real estate, however the multiples are much higher as a rule, tending to be in the nine, ten, or eleven ranges. This increase is because real estate is considered a safer investment and therefore demands a lower return on investment (ROI) to its buyer.

So it should be apparent that if I separate the real estate from the operating business by treating it as if it is leased to the operating business (whether it actually is or not) and then separately calculate the value of the business and the real estate, I will usually get a higher total valuation for the combined value of the real estate and the business.

The actual process is relatively simple: Remove the real estate carrying costs (depreciation, taxes and interest, operating costs) from the business earnings statement and calculations, and substitute a fair market rental expense. The value of the real estate is then calculated as if a separate investment group owned it, operated it, and leased it to the business. In other words, a hypothetical rental profit and loss (P&L) statement is created, and the value is calculated based on capitalizing its net operating income at the higher multiples and then added to the value of the operating business. Exhibit 28.1 reflects the difference to the seller as a result.

Rental versus Sale

There are two choices when the real estate is separable but at least currently necessary to the business. (This is usually office rental space that, for one reason or other, the buyers wish to continue to use). It can either be sold to the business buyers at the higher value or rented to them at the appropriate market rates. There is no preferred method here, as either works, and the choice will be dependent on the desires of the parties.

Real Estate as Part of the Business

Things are not necessarily this easy, though. The real estate really does have to be separable from the business for the illustration in Exhibit 28.1 to make sense and be defensible to the buyer. For example, if the real estate is a very specialized manufacturing plant that could not possibly be used or rezoned for any other purpose, then it probably has no higher value then what it is being used for in the business and also is vitally necessary to continuing the business's operations. In that case, it is simply another balance sheet fixed operating asset that cannot be separated from the business.

EXHIBIT 28.1 Valuing Real Estate Separately

Real Estate Description: 20,000 SQ.FT.; Rental Rate $8/Foot; No Mortgage

	Real Estate Considered and Priced as Part of Business	Real Estate Treated Separately
	Impact on Earnings and Transaction Value	Impact on Transaction Value
Gross rents at market value for real estate (triple net)	($160,000)	$160,000
Real estate taxes	10,000	(10,000)
Interest expense	—	—
Operating costs	12,000	(12,000)
Net earnings (or effect on business's net earnings)	138,000	138,000
Typical earnings captilization rates for middle market business and for real estate	5×	9×
Transaction value effect	$690,000 (decrease)	$1,242,000 (increase)
Net impact on seller	**$552,000 (increase) in value**	

Operating Asset or Nonoperating Asset?

A good sanity check as to whether or not the real estate is an operating asset is to ascertain whether or not the real estate could be leased to a third party for investment and then leased to any number of possible alternative tenants and, if so, at what rental rate[1]? If the answer is that it could not be rented to a third party for any other purpose (or put to a higher and better use by rezoning into, say, a residential or better commercial usage), then separately pricing the real estate or establishing some arbitrary market rent that is not justifiable is not going to float in the negotiations with the buyer.[2]

If it could eventually be rezoned into a higher use (and therefore more value), then the solution, of course, is to either sell it to the buyer at a negotiated or appraised higher value or lease it to the buyer at a rate that is justified by its current best use (in the business), with the thought that if the sellers retain the real estate but lease it to the buyer, the sellers may well rezone it someday or provide a lease purchase option to a buyer.

If it is an operating asset, another way out of the dilemma of achieving total liquidity for the seller where the buyer does not want to purchase the property it could also be sold to a third party (investment group) and then leased to the new business owner/buyer. This an approach which often facilitates deal making.

Technology Valuation: Is It a Business Yet?

I want to devote some space to technology valuation, as there are some points that are peculiar to it. It is not unusual that an M&A banker is asked to represent a young technology company that may have invested tens of thousands of hours and no small amounts of money in developing some really nifty technology and, in the process, acquired a few clients. For example, in recent years I have been involved in a number of transactions where the cumulative investment (usually not counting sweat equity) in the development of the technology has been, say, $8 million, and yet the company when it came to us looking for a buyer had only $1 million in sales and a marginal net before taxes, if any. Let's call the EBIT(DA) $150,000. So what is the company worth? Is it six times $150,000?

You can see the problem. If we value it as business on trailing EBIT, it is not worth much, and yet the reflex reaction (often self-serving) of many buyers is to do just that. They may like to just glance at the P&L statement on the conventional notion that the value of economic assets are their ability to earn income for their owner and argue that the historical P&L is the best source of determining that.

Now it should be obvious that if the technology cost $8 million to create (or, more importantly, would cost that much to recreate), then the technology must, hopefully, be worth $8 million. Otherwise, a great deal of effort and money has probably been frittered away. If it is good technology—and it is critical that it be really good—it will be worth at least $8 million.

The value of technology is greater than its ability to produce a historical return to its owners if it has not yet been commercially exploited to the point where the capitalized income (EBITDA) is worth more than the cost of recreating the technology. The problem comes about when a technology enterprise is neither apparently fish nor fowl. It has some aspects of a business, some customers, some income, and some aspects of just being technology (not much business or income, at least yet).

I think sometimes, when confronted with these situations, that it would often be better if the young technology enterprise had no customers, no business. The problem, of course, is that the attention of buyers and investors tends to shift to the historical income statement, the current earnings situation, and does not place the emphasis where it should be, on the potential future income.

Part of this is a natural negotiating advantage that the buyer/investor at least *tries to establish* by adopting this perspective. In spite of this, as I have said, I have participated in the sale of several such business that produced only small revenues but were sold for substantial sums of money. For example, in two cases in recent years, the company revenues were under $1 million and net income was almost nonexistent—and both companies sold for well north of $20 million.

For example, while technology deals will involve ultimately their own unique transaction structures, which sometimes take the form of royalties. In summary there are three approaches to technology valuation in a transaction. Again, here, I am talking as much about preliminary valuation as about the dynamic valuation that results from the actual deal.

Approach 1: The Technology Reconstruction Cost Approach

This approach relies on the reconstruction cost of the technology. What it cost the enterprise to create the technology may be a good indicator of this amount, if it was accomplished efficiently.[3] This number can also establish a *baseline or minimum value* of the technology, assuming again that it is good technology that simply has not been, or had the chance to be, fully commercially exploited yet.

From a buyer's point of view, this approach might also include a time-to-market calculation—in other words, the time it would take a buyer to pursue creating the technology itself. There is an opportunity cost here of the lost profits to the buyer during the recreation process. There is also the issue of lost opportunity costs, associated with the fact that a competitor may achieve a market foothold that will be harder to dislodge later while the buyer is creating his own version of the technology. The old clichés of Beta versus VHS and Apple versus Microsoft come to mind. It is not always the best technology that survives or at least thrives. Sometimes, as in these classic cases, it is the one to get to market first.

Here is an example of the combined cost of reconstruction of software and time-to-market costs:

Cost of reconstruction of software two years	$8 million
Loss in software sales in two years while software is being developed	$10 million
Gross margin on software (or net income or contribution)	
20%: Loss in contribution margin	$2 million
Total cost of reconstructing software (value of existing software)	$10 million

Approach 2: The Trailing Earnings Approach

The second approach is, of course, to rely on the earnings the technology is producing for its current owners. As I said, in general, while a buyer may want to do this for the negotiating advantage it brings, a seller should resist this if there is greater earnings potential that can be demonstrated. But sellers do need to be realistic about discarding this approach. If they have gone down the wrong road with the technology, or their business model is flawed, or they are too late to market, then this approach might in fact be the most accurate reflection of the value of the technology. In fact, it might even overstate it. Few of us want to believe that our creations have little value, but it happens.

Approach 3: The Present Value of Future Earnings from Technology Approach

The third approach involves situations where there is some reasonable basis for projecting future earnings from the technology and the present value of those earnings (see Chapter 24 on DFE calculations). In the alternative or in combination, the present value of future earnings could be the present value of an exit strategy (like an initial public offering (IPO) or the future sale of the company/technology), which can also be estimated by applying present value financial calculations to the exit strategy.

Valuing the Nonprofitable Business

I am almost embarrassed to include this brief section, but I feel compelled to, since in my early days of Middle Market M&A deal making I read a book entitled something like *How to Price a Profitable Company*. Just from reading the title, I concluded that the author did not know how to price or do a deal with an unprofitable company. In fact, after I read the book, I concluded that he did not know how to value a profitable one, for that matter. Most of the ways of valuing (getting value for, would be more appropriate) a nonprofitable company are fairly obvious, but to be thorough, here they are:[4]

- Normalize earnings to profitability
- Forecast future earnings
- Separate the profitable divisions, product lines, or contracts from the unprofitable portions of the business
- Point out to buyers the synergistic benefits of acquiring the nonprofitable business, especially in an auction

■ A little more esoteric perhaps, but in bankruptcy situations nonprofitable business can, with, court approval, be simultaneously acquired and reorganized into profitability, as well as obtaining a better financing structure and balance sheet

Sales of Product Lines and Separate Contracts or Separate Divisions

Of course, normalizing and recasting the reported earnings (cash flows) of the selling company will sometimes turn a loss into a profit (see Chapter 7, on normalizing and recasting). But without really needing to discuss further the more obvious approaches in the above list, I would also examine whether or not there are profitable contracts, product lines, or divisions that could be unbundled and sold separately. These two also can be valued exactly the way that the future earnings from technology can be, which is with a DFE approach (see Chapter 24).

How Do I Know if It Is a Product Line, a Separate Contract, or a Business?

In determining whether a group of assets is a business versus a product line, a separate, or limited group of contracts (this is not always that clear in actual practice), there are three broad areas to examine:

1. A *business* has
   a. Varied products and services. The product-service mix establishes a critical mass to the business sufficient to allow the presumption of its continuity into the indefinite future even though the overall product or service mix tends to change over time.
   b. Is relatively well-established. Unlike a relative start-up, the history of the business tends to bolster the assumption of critical mass and sustainability.
2. A *product line* situation, or contract(s), may have:
   a. Only two or three products or contracts. As opposed to a mature business, there does not appear to be sufficient critical mass to allow confidence in the business's sustainability.
   b. The obsolesce or useful life of the current products (or contracts) can be known or estimated.
3. The owning entity may be a fairly new business without much history, but still suggestive of its ability to constantly renew itself with new product or service additions, and therefore be considered a business. It may also be an older business winding down operations to the extent that it has lost its identity as a business.

EXHIBIT 28.2   The Weighted DCF/DFE Approach for Venture Capital Investment Valuation

	Best Case Year 3 Exit Event	Worst Case Year 3 Exit Event	Projected Case Year 3 Exit Event
Earnings or cash flows	$ 10,000,000	$ 2,000,000	$ 6,000,000
Exit multiple in an M&A transaction (private sale)	7×	7×	7×
Exit value	70,000,000	14,000,000	42,000,000
Investor's (VC's) targeted ROI	35%	35%	35%
Present value of exit events	28,450,948	5,690,190	17,070,569
Average present value of exit events (premoney*)	$ 17,070,569		
Required funding	6,000,000		
Investor's % of ownership	**35%**	($6M divided by $17M)	

* In the alternative:
- Post-money is $23,070,569 (17,070,569+6,000,000).
- Investor's resulting ownership is 26% ($6M divided by $23M).

In valuing a product line or contract(s), a limited life must be assumed and estimated. The limited life will almost always have a ramp-up in revenues/earnings, followed by a ramp-down, often followed by no or very flat revenues/earnings.

And finally, a discount rate (not a capitalization rate or multiplier) will have to be identified in order to determine the present values of the associated cash flow streams, since the cash flows have a limited life, and no residual value (as in an ongoing business) is estimable or existent (see Exhibit 28.2).

Investment Value to Particular Buyers

The unprofitable company should also be analyzed, in whole or in part, by seeking possible synergies with certain identified buyers (Chapter 7) that might produce an investment or synergistic value that is irrelevant to the lack of profitability of the selling company on a stand-alone basis. Finding these synergies could be a combination of intelligence gathering and the negotiated auction (see Chapter 12). Starting from scratch, at least, this type of intelligence gathering is no small challenge, as a rule, and is where the investment bank that is capable or willing is really worth its fees.

Valuing Rapidly Growing Businesses for Venture Capital and Similar Investments—Is This Really Valuation?

You will recall that in Chapter 3, which deals with buyer types, I mentioned early-stage private equity investors, commonly known as venture capitalists (VCs). I include this type of investment in Middle Market M&A because it should be included. It is an equity investment in a Middle Market business, just like any Middle Market business purchase involving the whole business. It differs from the norm mainly in that it is often for a minority interest and is usually for a business undertaking that has to go a long way to prove itself.

I occasionally teach a seminar in valuing early-stage businesses for venture capital investments. In the late 1990s, when this type of investment was especially popular, so was the seminar. It was not unusual to fill up a sizable hall. One of the things I used to do was to hand out a spreadsheet that demonstrated a method of valuing venture capital investments that applied weights to different outcomes ranging from worst case to expected case to best case. In effect, it pretty much averaged the values from each case. The approach was and is known as the First Chicago method (see Exhibit 28.2). There is no rocket science involved here, and I have included an illustration of the approach. Anyway. I used to offer to have the spreadsheet emailed to whichever of my audience wanted it. I was always amazed that the group that requested it the most were, you guessed it, the venture capitalists in my audience. Maybe this had something to do with the sad results that soon followed most late-1990s VC investments. Many VCs, it seems, were just "winging it."

This approach, the venture capital method or sometimes the First Chicago method, is sometimes touted as a valuation approach. I suppose in a limited sense it is an approach to determining Investment Value (value to a particular investor), but it is not necessarily Fair Market Value. Put differently, it really is a way to have at least some pseudo scientific[5] basis for determining relative ownership interests in a VC investment; that is, as a practical matter, a partnership formed between the founders and the funders (VCs) to fund an early stage idea or business.

It may not be a valuation method other than as the term may apply to Investment Value, although it is sometimes called one by professionals, especially when they want to use an actual VC investment to argue the objective value of something, at least between two unique parties. Of course, the fact that a transaction actually took place is an accepted value indicator in some situations. This argument usually occurs in a negotiation or sometimes in an expert opinion in a courtroom. In fact, *early-stage* VC valuation is pretty much all based on pro forma projections as opposed to real value. It says that if I, the VC, put in *this* much money, and the project is *that* successful, then *this* is how we will split the profits. Maybe that is not really valuation. Maybe it is horse-trading with a lot of guesswork about the ultimate health of the horse.

Venture capital (and, at an even later stage, PEG) investing is about having an exit strategy or a "liquidity event" somewhere down the road. Usually, this exit strategy or liquidity event is either selling the business (an M&A transaction) or taking the business public (an IPO). The process is to try to estimate what the proceeds from either event will be and then use the DFE or DCF methods (Chapter 24) to determine what the present value of that future event will be.

You will recall from Chapter 3 that in general, the nature of the funding of these PEGs, whether early- or later-stage, is that they have investment horizons of five to seven years as they are, in one form or another, limited partnerships, and their own investors need to be able cash in or at least tally up within a time frame that more or less corresponds with something a little shorter than the life of the partnership (fund).

For example, let's say that I can resell (via M&A or IPO) the business for $100 million in three years, and that as a VC I want to achieve a minimum 35% per year return on my investment. The present value of that $100 million, then, is $40 million. If that $40 million assumes that the founders will need $10 million to get things going before the present value can ever reach $40 million, then the VC will receive 25% of the enterprise and future profits and the founders 75%.

Premoney versus Postmoney Valuation

Experienced readers will probably immediately note that in the example just given, I assumed the $40 million calculation to be a *postmoney* valuation. In other words, the value of the investment *after* the injection of the $10 million was $40 million, so therefore the *premoney* valuation is $30 million. The assumption here is that the company could not possibly get to a $40 million value without the $10 million in financing, a very logical assumption it seems to me in the case of early stage companies. However, I have observed, more often than not, PEG (VC) investors characterize the $40 million value as premoney, thus leaving the postmoney valuation as $50 million. This, of course, would have resulted in the investor only owning 20% ($10 of $50 million) of the project. I can understand this approach in much later-stage company investing, where the value of the company can be well-established and is already significant, independent of any new investment, but it amazes me when I see it in early-stage deals. Well, as they say, we do not make the rules, we just benefit by them.

The M&A Exit Event in Private Equity Group Investments

In Chapter 25, I compared the valuation of privately held companies with that of publicly held ones. The same approaches are used to estimate the eventual resale of the company (a private company transaction) or the IPO of the company (a public company valuation). As usual, the private sale if it is an interesting business will bring a multiple of something like six or seven times the before-tax earnings (cash flow). The public IPO will bring something like 15 to 25 times the after-tax earnings of the business. Exhibit 28.2 assumes a private sale (M&A exit) at a multiple of seven.

Valuation in Later-Stage Private Equity Group Deals . . . Valuation or Not?

In later-stage PEG deals, there is definitely valuation work going on that goes beyond attempting to establish the mere parameters of future "partnership" profit sharing. By definition, a later-stage or at least more advanced-stage company has real and measurable value as of now that goes beyond its future prospects, which should also be incorporated in determining value.

I refer you back to the discussion of premoney versus postmoney valuation. In these cases, one element of the so-called valuation will be in the nature of traditional M&A valuation of an existing business, and another element will be solely valuation on an "as if" basis, primarily associated with an investment by the PEG and a guess (educated perhaps, but a guess nevertheless) about what the future will bring as a result of the investment.

Private Equity Groups and Minority Interests

In the consideration section of this book (Chapter 18), I talk about the inadvisability of a seller taking or retaining a minority interest in a privately held business. Of course, this is frequently exactly what happens in these PEG deals, in both early- and later-stage capital investments by PEGs. Either the sellers retain a minority interest, or the private equity investors obtain one. So how does this reconcile with the advice given in that section of this book? It works, but the assumptions are two important ones that need to be carefully vetted by prospective investees, especially when considering the limited time and investment horizons of the PEGs:

- They (the PEGs) are risking (investing) a lot of money, sometimes making additional investments in future expansion, and believe they will have an exit or liquidity event in, say, five years.
- The selling owners (investees) will benefit from the investment and hopefully the sound judgment and assistance of the PEG investors.[6]

All of this suggests a second bite at the apple (later sale of the retained minority interest) for the original sellers if all goes well. That second bite may be well worth the risk of the minority interest retained too. I have represented clients whose second bite (say for a 35% interest) was substantially larger than the initial valuation when the PEG first came in.

Selling Minority Interests in a Business to Strategic Buyers—Stake Outs

One way for a developing company to raise capital for expansion and/or acquire new distribution channels and/or a big new customer is to take a minority interest investment from a strategic industry investor. For this purpose, a strategic investor would be defined as a larger operating business that wants to acquire some of the developing company's technology or intellectual property or processes concurrently with staking out a claim to acquire the entire company later. While this may not be a bad way to go, and in some instances is the only choice available for developing companies, it has a couple of landmines that owners should be especially alert to.

1. If the investor is also a competitor to the selling company's customers, its investment and consequent relationship may be the kiss of death to obtaining certain other customers. This becomes a self fulfilling prophesy then really making the developing company the captive of the investor at what will be eventually a value substantially less than if the developing company was able to do business on an unrestricted basis.
2. Strategic companies making this kind of investment will, as often as not, want to negotiate a first right of refusal for the later purchase of the majority interest in the investee company. This is not quite the kiss of death, but it can make selling the company's remaining majority interest on the open market very difficult. Competitive buyers will simply not, as a rule, want to waste the time or money in negotiating a deal when the rug can be pulled out from under them as a result of this right of refusal being in existence. In my view, these types of rights of first refusal should be avoided at all costs, unless there is no other way to raise the needed expansion capital. Another approach to this problem is to establish the first right of refusal in such a manner that it has to be exercised and accepted or declined at the investee's sole choice *before* taking the majority interest out to the M&A market.

True Merger Transactions

In a true merger transaction in the Middle Market, no or only modest cash typically changes hands. The buyers and sellers will tend to look at themselves as forming a new partnership, joining two or more businesses to be run together. The negotiation for determining who owns what in the new "partnership" is usually more a relative valuation exercise than an absolute one, and the basis of measurement is usually relative Fair Market Value or relative Investment Value).

Synergies are still an issue in this type of deal, as in all others. The question is who gets credit for them, if they are valued at all? There is a normal tendency for each party to want to say the synergies are coming from its side of the deal, but in fact, if there is no deal there will be no synergies, so many parties to this type of transaction will split the difference by either ignoring the synergies (this works) in their valuation or by splitting them in some fashion that has to do with the current operations of the constituent businesses.

Negotiations are key, for example:

• Value of Company A	= $20 million
• Value of Company B	= $30 million
• Value of combined companies	= $60 million
• Who gets the synergies?	($10 million)

But be careful of who speaks first about their perceived stand alone value. This issue (who speaks first) is as difficult in a true merger as in any other M&A transaction. I find generally that looking at and introducing a lot of relative factors up front without being highly specific about my own client's, stand-alone valuation is the best and perhaps safest way to get the dialogue going and avoid early entrenchment of positions. For example, I might start with something like this:

Item of Focus	Company A	Company B
Sales	$90 million	$60 million
Gross margins	22.5%	25.6%
EBITDA	$8.9 million	$7.2 million
Working capital	$4.5 million	$3.2 million
Net worth	$5 million	$5 million
Number of customers	4,310	10,200
Employees with government clearances	100	90
Compound annual growth rate last three years	15%	26%

Now, most of the above could be used to determine stand alone values for the companies, of course, but I find after participating in many of these deals that it is usually best to start with a lot of relative numbers, as in the above chart, and then let the parties ease their way into determining the relative value for the share exchange. The more comparison we can do, the more apparent the share exchange ratios may be.

This case is also one where stand alone valuations need to be approached very gently. I assure you, no independent valuator will understand as much about either of the two businesses or their prospects as the prospective merger partners will. The standard of value, to be technical here for a moment, is most akin to that of Fair Value, as used by the accounting profession. In that context, Fair Value is a sort of negotiated value that takes into consideration the facts and context in which a deal is done.

And of course, beyond the financial issues there are other difficult issues to be resolved. Keep in mind here that one or all parties may end up as minority shareholders, so resolving and documenting management issues up front is the key

- Is there to be a dominant company after all?
- Who bears layoffs/changes?
- Who handles management and decision making?

Partial or Mixed Business Acquisition Transactions

These can be tough to rationalize, but relying on normal M&A conventions helps you think through the issue, as usual. I recently was confronted with a problem that one of our bankers raised. The situation was that the client (buy side) was being asked to buy inventory (easy enough, just price it) and goodwill but no other tangible assets. Now remember that the convention is that the buyer gets the balance sheet (without cash). But what if there is no balance sheet? Or as in this case the buyer (our client) was being asked to pay for the inventory separately from the business but yet again with no other *tangible assets* being involved or acquired but also was being asked to pay for goodwill (based on the cash flows from the operating division that was being purchased). The obvious solution (it did take a little bit of thinking to get there) was the following:

The purchase price of the inventory (based on a physical count) was going to be:	$2.5 million
(Cannot be known until it is counted and priced)	
The value of the business, assuming that normal net tangible operating assets were coming with it was ($1 million EBITDA times 4.5) and was:	$4.5 million
The normal net operating assets (ex cash) for this industry were:[7]	$1.5 million
Therefore, the value of the purchase as a business (in addition to the inventory) was:	$3.0 million
(since the normal net assets of $1.5 million would not be delivered)	
Therefore, the correct reasonable offering price was ($2.5 million + $3 million), or:	$5.5 million

Chapter Highlights

- When real estate is in the deal, the first consideration is whether it is an operating asset (goes with the balance sheet) or a nonoperating asset (separately priced or leased to buyers).
- Nonoperating real estate can be valued by either capitalizing reconstructed net operating income as if rented, or by appraisal.
- In early-stage technology valuation, several questions arise:
  - Is it a business or just technology?
  - Should it be valued by:
    - Trailing earnings
    - Cost of reconstruction
    - Future earnings on a DFE methodology
    - Some combination of these methods
- Sales of product lines or contracts should be valued by a DFE method.
- One method of valuing a nonprofitable business is by valuing synergies for particular buyers although obtaining the information for this can be either easy or quite difficult.
- The formality of VC and PEG valuations is not necessarily as formal as one might expect, but the DFE and First Chicago methods are at least implicit in every such valuation and resulting negotiation.
- Premoney versus postmoney valuation characterizations can be inconsistent and provide dramatically different results to the partners.
- Exit events in PEG investments are either M&A transactions or IPOs.
- There is some justification for retaining a minority interest in the case of PEG deals, due to the fact that PEGs:
  - Often bring smart money to the business
  - Are desirous of maximizing value
  - Typically all but guarantee an exit event (for better or for worse) within four or five years
- Selling minority "stake out" interests to strategic buyers has two pitfalls:
  - Loss of potential customers
  - Granting rights of first refusal on later sales of the business
- True merger transactions are more relative value calculations for share exchange ratios then absolute stand-alone valuations, and the relative factors should be introduced to the parties carefully and gradually to avoid early entrenchment of positions.
- Pricing mixed-business sales can be most readily done by using standard M&A conventions.
- It is all ultimately in the negotiation, but relying on M&A convention goes a long way towards structuring a sensible deal.

Notes

1. I am of course excepting "sale and lease back" arrangements entered into as a capital raising device by an owner/user of special purpose property which also may be simply a way of financing that does not in and of itself change the character of the real estate as an operating as opposed to an investment asset.
2. Conceivably the characterization of a part of a purchase price as rents for an operating asset could be a tax or financing mechanical deal making device however.
3. "Efficiently" is key here, especially given the much cheaper outsourcing available from countries like India and Russia, which can create technology and software much more inexpensively than just a couple of years ago.
4. For this chapter, I have assumed a going concern concept, or at least partly a going concern concept, but it should be noted that some businesses are worth more dead than alive. In other words, their assets are worth more in liquidation.
5. "Pseudo" scientific because like in most valuation work the underlying principles are based on sound mathematical approaches (DFE, etc.) but the data that goes into the formulas are frankly guesses (art) and highly dependent on the judgment of the valuator which judgment may vary widely in quality.
6. And it usually will be sound judgment if it is a large PEG. The wild and woolly days of the late 1990s are mostly behind us, and in recent years, PEGs and VCs have become increasingly more sophisticated at analyzing deals. This is not to say that the recent influx of hundreds of billions of new dollars into this marketplace may not tend to eventually lead back to the past at least somewhat. When there are lots of dollars seeking a finite number of deals, danger could be just over the next horizon, for sure.
7. Normal net assets could have been determined by a number of approaches including typical normal net assets (ex cash...this is Enterprise Value after all) of businesses in the industry. In this case we took normal net assets related to sales as a percentage (15% in this case).

CHAPTER 29

Common M&A Taxation Issues
Brief Comments

Unquestionably there is progress. The average American now pays out twice as much in taxes as he formerly got in wages.

Henry Louis Mencken

I am proud to be paying taxes in the United States. The only thing is— I could be just as proud for half the money.

Arthur Godfrey

Prince Georges County, MD—2005

The stepchild, perhaps, of the Washington, DC, area, Prince Georges County (PG, as it is known to locals) is still an economic comer. The predominantly black middle-class population here is the wealthiest, best educated, and most affluent in the United States. Bordered by its richer cousin Montgomery County on the north, large parts of the Potomac River on the west, and its even earlier-stage cousins, Charles and St Mary's Counties on the south, PG, if not exactly a hotbed of Middle Market business, is certainly a maturing incubator of sorts.

Madeline's offices were in a mid-rise office building overlooking a strip mall. As I drove up, I thought, It's not a very pretty site, but at least it's functional for her particular type of business.

Madeline was a tough and talented business woman. She's had to be. And she was being tough with me. She said she already had an offer for $15 million for her business from a single buyer, and she wanted to scale my fee for representing her, based on only any incremental value I could achieve. I looked at this offer, and I did not think it really represented

$15 million. For one thing, it included a working capital target specified by this buyer of at least $1 million more than it should have been. For another, it included an unorthodox shifting of another $1 million dollars in taxes to her side of the deal. Finally, there was an earnout provision that was at least $750,000 unfair to her side of the deal.

Madeline thought she had $15 million on the table already. I thought, using conventional mergers and acquisitions (M&A) deal structures, that it was a $12.25 million offer. The first thing I would have to do in representing her would be to get back that $2.75 million. She did not understand that yet and I hoped I could explain it to her, as I could work like the dickens to increase her value by almost $3 million without getting paid for it or most of it. I would have to find out how reasonable she was under that hard crust. As for me, I knew I was not going to take this client on under those circumstances, for sure.[1]

A Brief Tax Overview

This chapter is intended only to be a brief overview of the most common tax issues that arise in Middle Market M&A transactions. It is certainly, as will be obvious, not intended to be a deep treatise on M&A taxation. It is focused mostly on the sales-side point of view and will not directly cover post-transaction concerns of buyers such as tax-based purchase price allocations and acquired asset amortization; the ability to achieve the benefits of net operating loss carry-forwards; or many of the myriad other M&A taxation issues that can arise. It is intended to cover only some very basic things, at a very basic level, for a client who wants an initial overview or an investment banker without tax training who needs familiarity with the concepts. The use of terms here is neither intended to be, nor is, precise, and most of the actual surrounding tax law regarding the areas this chapter speaks to is omitted from discussion.

In short, this is a chapter for laymen. I believe that 90% of the issues that arise over and over again in common Middle Market M&A transactions can be conveniently summarized as coming under one of the following groups:

- Entity type or selection
- Asset versus stock forms of transaction
- Other transaction structural issues
- Reorganization structures
- Presales event tax planning
- Postsales event reinvestment

Entity Selection: S Corporations versus C Corporations and Asset versus Stock Deals

Fundamental to any starting point for considering the tax consequences in an M&A transaction from the seller's point of view is the selection of corporation type. Under the Internal Revenue Code, a corporation (or its shareholders more accurately) can decide to be taxed as a subchapter C corporation, which is a taxable entity, or by way of a subchapter S election as a corporation that usually pays no taxes (an S corporation).

Virtually all taxes on the income of an S corporation are paid by, and by the consent of, the shareholders when they file their own tax returns. An S corporation is also commonly known as a *pass-through* entity, as its income and losses generally "pass through" to the share-holders.

The consequences of being a C or S corporation at their most basic level in an M&A transaction are that a C corporation, which sells its *assets* to a buyer as opposed to its *stock*, will generally pay a tax; whereas an S corporation generally will not. When the C corporation distributes the remaining proceeds of the sale (after the first round of taxes at the corporate level), the C corporation shareholders will be taxed all over again. In an S corporation, there is generally no corporate-level tax, so even though the gain on an M&A asset transaction is taxed to the share-holders, it is generally only taxed once, which usually provides a dis-tinct advantage to an S corporation over a C corporation in an *asset* type of sale.

An alternative structure for the sale of a business can be the sale of a corporation's stock. Here, the playing field is closer to neutral, as both C corporation shareholders and S corporation shareholders will generally pay tax once at capital gain rates.

The effect of all of this is to make an asset sale by a C corporation in most cases totally unpalatable, unless of course the buyer agrees to pay the taxes through a purchase price adjustment (i.e., reimburse the sellers) because of the double taxation situation that arises.

Prior to the Tax Reform Act of 1986, certain tax elections could allow a C corporation to avoid this double taxation, but that Reform Act canceled these elections. Gradually, as a practical matter over the years since 1986, buyers have come to realize that they cannot get a deal done with a C corporation on an asset purchase basis, at least without usually having to compensate the seller for the double taxation effect. I would say that at least 75% or more of the transactions done with C corporations as a consequence are for the sale of their stock and not their assets. So you would think that all is well whether the seller is an S corporation or a C corporation ... but that is not the case.

The problem is that the buyer, after doing a stock deal, does not really get the full benefit of his purchase price, as he cannot write off the assets he has indirectly acquired (keeping in mind that he merely acquired stock). So this typically gives rise to the buyer's choice of a Section 338(h) election, where he uses a Section 338(h)(10) election (by the buyers and sellers) to acquire the stock as an S corporation's stock and is then able to "step-up" the basis in the acquired assets (by hypothetically treating them as if it were an asset deal in the first place) and write them off. In these cases, the S corporation shareholders are taxable on some of the gain, which often results in ordinary income recapture. As a part of the negotiation, the buyer may or may not reimburse the S Corporation shareholders in effect for the taxes that result.

But the buyer will often want the seller to pay the taxes on the hypothetical 338(h) transaction as a purchase price adjustment or, in other instances, directly. So we are somewhat back to square one here, but this still gives the S corporation–asset seller a substantial advantage compared to the C corporation–asset seller when it comes to an M&A deal, as the former can more easily effect an asset sale without onerous tax consequences.

Of course, the sellers can refuse to pay the taxes attributable to the Section 338(h) election, but it is one more thing to negotiate, and if the seller wins this negotiation it may well be at the cost of having to give something else up along the line. All in all, the existence of an S corporation election is usually much better, as is provides more tools to lower the tax costs of an M&A transaction.

The Effect of Timing of S Corporation Elections and the Built-In Gains Tax

It might appear at first glance that the simple solution to this dilemma is to have a C corporation make an S election just before it is sold, but that does not work either. Basically, the rule is that whatever the business was worth at the date of election (built-in gain), that portion of the gain on the sale of the business will still be subject to C corporation double taxation.

Only ten years after the election is made does this rule (the built-in gains, or BIG, tax rule) expire. An election as an S corporation may still make sense if a business is rapidly growing, so that its value at the date of the election is only a small part of its value at the date of the sale, even if the sale is made within the ten-year period. I believe that most Middle Market business owners who still operate as C corporations should consult their tax counsel and a valuation expert/investment banker to decide whether to make an election now.

Other Transaction Structural Issues

It is not uncommon in an M&A deal for advisors to look at ways of characterizing some part of the deal price as compensation to the seller for services (subject to ordinary income taxes to the seller, but deductible by the buyer). This is often looked at as a compromise to enable the deal to get done. Its disadvantages are that if it is carried too far, the deductibility by the buyer will be at risk, and this is aside from the obvious disadvantage to the seller of converting what is usually taxed at a low capital gains rate into a much higher ordinary income rate. However, if it is carefully structured, there are circumstances where the risks and the reward of this approach will make sense to both sides.

Earnouts

For convenience's sake, I am going to repeat somewhat verbatim here the comments on taxation of earnouts from Chapter 19, which solely devoted to earnouts. The perpetual question in earnouts is whether or not they give rise to capital gains or ordinary income. The courts and rulings are mixed here, so one is left with the need to engage good tax counsel, particularly in *drafting* the earnout agreement to protect a client's position in this regard. In general though, the body of tax law and precedent would seem to support the notion that installment payments of uncertain amounts (earnouts) emanating from the sale of a business would be considered a part of the purchase price and reportable, for the most part, as capital gains income. Without trying to be tax counsel, let me offer some rough guidelines here:

- To the extent the earnout is tied to the continued services of the seller as an absolute condition, this can bode badly for capital gains treatment, as the payment may be treated as ordinary income to the seller as compensation or consulting services.
- If the earnout is consistently referred to as an element of the purchase price in the various agreements, this bodes better for capital gains treatment.
- If the earnout is constructed as a deferred payment note of some sort, reducible by failure to hit the earnout targets, this may help to support capital gains treatment.
- Deferred earnout payments that do not bear interest may be treated partially as interest income (taxed as ordinary income) and partially as sales proceeds (subject to lower capital gains rates).

But as I said, drafting here by tax counsel is everything.

The Effect of Tax Accounting Methods

Many Middle Market companies, especially in the lower end of the Middle Market, report their taxes on a cash basis. This results in timing differences between what is reported for normal financial accounting purposes on an accrual basis and what is reported for tax purposes on a cash basis. Assuming the client has saved money by reporting for tax purposes on the cash basis, someone will eventually have to pay the deferred and latent tax on the difference between accrual-basis income and the cash-basis income reported to the government.

Stock Deals and Cash-Basis Sellers

So, in an M&A transaction, who is liable for these latent but real taxes? If a buyer buys a corporation (a stock deal), this latent or deferred tax is an assumed liability of the acquired corporation and will go along with it from a tax law point of view. But in an M&A negotiation following the conventions, the liability is not an ordinary balance-sheet operating liability in the sense that I have used that term before (Chapter 27) on balance sheet conventions. So it is not one of those liabilities that by convention the buyer is automatically assumed to inherit—except, of course, by negotiation.

Assets Deals and Cash-Basis Sellers

The sale of the assets of a cash basis S corporation constitutes the sale or exchange of, among other things, its heretofore unrecognized accounts receivable, which would give rise to a tax to the selling corporation (or, more precisely, its shareholders) on those receivables, thus generating the taxes on the timing difference just discussed. So another form of built-in gains tax for cash-basis S corporation shareholders would be a day of reckoning in paying the taxes that were avoided previously by opting for cash-basis reporting.

Installment Notes and Cash Basis Tax Payers

Installment notes are less common in M&A transactions in the Middle Market (except for usually smaller deals under $5 to $7 million in transaction value) then one might expect, the principal forms of consideration being usually cash, earnouts, and then stock, in that order.

When they do occur, they have the interesting tax advantage that if these notes are qualified for installment reporting, no taxes are paid by the cash-basis seller until the payments are received. This is particularly attractive when the seller receives a market interest rate on the face amount of the note that is the equivalent of other investments he could make if he had the cash, because he is, in effect, investing the government's taxes on his own behalf until the time comes to report the payments. If the maker of the note is very credit worthy and the note is well secured, this can be a real boon to a seller.

Reorganization Deal Structures (Taking Stock)

Oddly enough, the reorganization sections of the Internal Revenue Code that deal with merger transactions (mainly Sec 368) do not appear all that commonly in Middle Market M&A deals, but an awareness of them at a very basic level is important. They do come up in at least some deals, and many clients are curious about them, being at least dimly aware that taking stock as part of their sales price *might be* tax free.

Let's start by clearing up that "tax free" remark. Even where taking stock actually results in the payment of no immediate taxes, this is simply a *tax-deferred transaction*, not a *tax-free one*. When the seller eventually sells the stock, he or she will be taxed, and his/her basis in the stock for determining gain will be the same as his/her proportionate basis in the business sold earlier, so the tax has merely been deferred. The only things certain in life are death and taxes.

Furthermore, any tax deferral in a reorganization type of transaction is solely on the stock, *not on cash* or other consideration taken in addition to stock.

Tax-free reorganizations are built around the concept of continuity of ownership interests in the surviving entity. Hence, these types of deals are more like mergers than outright sales of businesses, as the owners of the selling corporation will become in-part owners of the buying corporation. They may be accomplished by exchanging buyer stock for either the assets or the stock of the seller. As a rule, where there is cash or other nonstock consideration involved (boot), the *upper limits* of cash, if allowed at all (see B-type reorganizations below), will be around 50% of the overall deal price. However, there have been rulings that allowed a greater amount, and each transaction needs to be guided by expert tax counsel.

The Alphabet Code

There are seven types of reorganizations, A through G, and variations known as "triangular" (this is why code section 368(a)(1) is often called the Alphabet Section). However, only three of these are really germane to this light overview, as they are the ones that appear the most frequently in deals where an reorganization (stock exchange) is involved. They are A, B, and C reorganizations:

A REORGANIZATIONS   In an A reorganization, the structure must comply with the relevant state law for a statutory merger. These A reorganizations usually result in the acquiring corporation (in M&A terms, the buyer) acquiring the assets of the seller corporation in part for stock and in part for cash. The seller corporation ceases to exist, and the shareholders of the seller corporation end up with the stock of the buyer corporation, plus any other consideration received.

B REORGANIZATIONS   In a B reorganization, only stock and *absolutely no cash* can be used, and the acquired corporation usually continues its existence as a subsidiary of the acquiring corporation. Here again, in M&A terms, the buyer corporation exchanges stock for all of the stock of the seller corporation.

C REORGANIZATIONS   In a C reorganization, one corporation (the buyer) acquires the assets of another (the seller), which then distributes to its own shareholders the stock and other consideration received again, with the proviso that only the stock gets tax-deferred treatment.

While, as promised, I have barely touched on the topic of tax-free reorganizations, it is important to point out that these are very complicated, often suggest the need for advanced letter rulings from the IRS to see if they will work, and always require the assistance of expert tax counsel.

Disposing of Business Interests by Gifting Prior to a Sale and Charitable Remainder Trusts

Two popular devices for tax planning prior to the sale of a Middle Market business are the use of charitable remainder trusts (CRTs) and gifts (often of family limited partnership interests, or FLPs). Both, in effect, involve giving up some or all of an owner's interest in a Middle Market business before it is sold. In short, the recipient of the given-up share, whether it is a family member or a charitable trust created by the owner, become the sellers when the business is eventually sold.

Charitable Remainder Trusts

In this approach, the seller donates his interest to the charitable remainder trust, which is, in general, a tax-exempt entity that is then not taxable on the later sale of its interest in the donated business. In turn, the CRT (or one of its various forms) agrees to pay the donor (the original business owner) amounts of principal and income over a period of time. The business sales proceeds, of course, end up with a charitable organization. This type of presales event tax planning may be particularly good for:

- Owners who have sufficient other personal liquidity over and above the interest they that have just given to the charitable remainder trust
- Owners who are philanthropically inclined

The tax benefits should be obvious, as the entire value, if the business interest donated is later sold (since there was no tax on its sale), earns income for the donor and the charitable beneficiary on a larger portion of the sales price of the business (before taxes, since the entity is a tax-exempt entity) then would have been otherwise possible.

Gifts and Family Limited Partnerships (A Generation-Skipping Tool)

By shifting business ownership interests to other family members, either through family limited partnerships or a direct gift to the next family generation, the business ownership interest can be placed in the hands of heirs to appreciate prior to their sales, thus avoiding estate and capital gains taxes by shifting post-gift appreciation to the new owners. In addition, by receiving less than a controlling interest in the business, the value of such interest will usually be valued at less than a proportional percentage of the business. Minority interests are usually valued after taking discounts of as much as 20% to 40% because they would be difficult to resell to a third party, as they have by themselves no control over the operations of the business.

Divisive Reorganizations

Section 355 of the Internal Revenue Code (known as the Morris Trusts) allows the historical owners of a company to divide up the company's assets with no gain recognition, provided the owners transfer the assets to a separate business (controlled by the shareholders of the transferring company). This is in concept—and must be in practice—a mere shifting of the assets to a separate entity, but with the retention of at least 80% control by the shareholders of the distributing company. Tax-deferred distribution is basically the same intended outcome as contemplated by the Section 368 reorganizations section, referred to above.

Small Business Corporations

A shareholder in a qualified small business under IRC Section 1045 can exclude up to 50% of the gain on the sale of the stock, up to the greater of $10 million or 10 times his cost basis in the stock. A small business is any C corporation[2] with an active business not depending on the professional services, licensing, or reputation of its owners (among other exceptions), with aggregate gross assets of less than $50 million. Alternative minimum tax preferences apply to the exclusion, so the actual benefit is often less than what the tax savings would be otherwise. If the owner uses the proceeds from the sale of a small business corporation to acquire another small business corporation within six months after the sale of the first (a roll-over) there will be no tax until a later sale of the newly acquired stock.

How Much Do Taxes Matter During the Negotiation?

Keeping in mind that businesses do not pay income taxes, one would think that very little of the negotiation for the purchase and sale of a *business* would involve tax considerations, and in fact, that is *literally* true.

However, businesses are owned by entities, and that is where taxes come in. Depending on the form of the deal (assets versus stock); the nature of the selling entity (S versus C corporation); and the elements of consideration (cash, stock earnouts, balance sheet targets, etc.), the tax consequences can be significant. But I find it easier and more accurate to view the negotiation for the sale of a Middle Market business to consist of two separate negotiations, in effect.

The first is the sale of the business itself (e.g., negotiating a value based on multiples, auctions, and so forth that the parties can live with. The second and quite separate negotiation is about the tax aspects of the transaction. Thinking about the negotiation this way (just as thinking about earnouts as either incentive or comfort earnouts, as discussed in Chapter 19) can focus the mind on these two separate topics appropriately but as a rule, in practice, they are often just as jumbled together as the two different types of earnouts.

Chapter Highlights

The main tax elements or areas that appear over and over again in Middle Market deals are:

- Stock versus asset forms of deal structure
- C versus S corporations

- Section 338(h)(10) elections
- Timing of S corporation elections and the built-in gains (BIG) tax
- Purchase price versus compensation
- Tax treatment of earnouts
- Tax accounting methods and their effect
- Installment elections available to cash-basis tax payers
- Gifting of business interests prior to the sale of the whole business:
  - Charitable reminder trusts
  - Direct gifts and family limited partnerships
- Reinvestment of sales proceeds or their tax deferral (partial) in the sale of qualifying small business corporations
- Separating the tax from the business aspects of deal making

Notes

1. It is interesting to surmise that a C Corporation asset sale of $15 million may leave the owner who has a zero basis with only $8 million of after-tax proceeds, whereas a stock sale for $14 million may let her bank $10 million after taxes. Which deal is better? The $15 million sounds better at the cocktail party, but the $14 million deal puts an extra $2 million in the bank.
2. Organized after August 1993.

CHAPTER 30

The Business of Middle Market Investment Banking

For Consultants or Others Who Might Like to Do This Kind of Work

Mamas, don't let your babies grow up to be cowboys ...

Willie Nelson

Savannah, GA—October 1989
Peter was telling me one of the saddest professional stories I had heard in a long time.

At the quarterly meeting of our bank in Savannah, the one I had just recently begun to work with, Peter was telling me about Frank, who had been with the firm for three years and had just left. It seemed Frank spent the entire three years without a payday, and his wife and pocketbook had finally had it. Frank ran the firm's small office, which served Georgia and north and central Florida.

Peter told me that Frank had started out three years ago with incredible energy and enthusiasm. He had all the right background too: a graduate business degree, years of senior experience in financial services, and a personality capable of charming the leaves off trees. Peter said that by Frank's second year, he had churned up three very nice sales-side clients, and by his third year, two more. This is pretty good, actually, for a guy starting out fresh in the business. If even two-thirds of these deals closed, Frank stood to have a decent payday for all of his work. Somewhere well north of a million dollars would have been his cut.

The sad story was that none of them closed. The failures had nothing to do with Frank, either. Their causes were downright weird.

349

In one case, the sudden death of a client days before the closing raised estate problems that would not be resolved for years, and the business was taken off the market. In another case, a criminal action against a company he was representing, although later dismissed, eliminated any real possibility of a sales transaction at that time. In yet another case, the loss of a major distribution agreement by a sales-side client not long before closing was scheduled. You get the picture.

As I thought about this on the plane back to Washington, I reflected on why contingent-fee investment bankers got the big bucks. It was a question, obviously, of the chances of getting them at all. I made up my mind then and there that I would tell Frank's story to every prospective banker that came to me for advice. While it might be a little extreme, it really did happen. I have stuck to my word.

What Is Investment Banking?

Not everyone has had the experience of working for one of the larger Wall Street investment banks; therefore, I have found that students often are not even totally sure what the term "investment banking" covers. I know that most of the public has only a vague and mostly erroneous idea that it has to do with something like investment advice regarding stocks and bonds (wealth management). I always recommend that to start in this profession, after appropriate training, one must first self-declare that he is an investment banker, and then declare to the community that he or she is one. Of course, if one is to make that declaration, it is good to know what the term means. I also want to help overcome any reluctance to that imperative (declaration of one's profession) by briefly explaining what investment banking most commonly means in usage.[1] A good place to start is by some contrasts:

Investment banking is not commercial banking (these are the guys we make savings and checking accounts deposits with and borrow money from, with deposit insurance provided by agencies of the U.S. government). Although both groups are termed "bankers," they are not the same thing at all. Investment banks consult with corporations on M&A and capital formation and in at least a part of their operations manage other people's wealth and sell stocks and bonds and so forth. To some degree, the distinctions have been more obscure since 1999, when commercial banks were allowed to branch out into other financial services businesses (which had been prohibited for 66 years by the Glass-Steagall Act), but even now, strong firewalls have to be maintained between these two functions. For the most part, those commercial banks (almost always larger ones) that did branch out went into either wealth management (stock and bond advice) or investment banking as I am using the term here. For all intents and purposes, the investment banking business might as well be a separate company, in so far as operationally there seems to be little contact or synergy between that business and the traditional commercial banking business.

Investment banking is not merchant banking, either. Merchant banks (usually known in the United States as Private Equity Groups, or PEGs) invest their own money in acquiring companies. Investment banks do not invest their own money that way, as a rule and it is certainly not their main business although they may have organized a separate PEG to do so.

But, while large investment banks certainly provide wealth management services and stock-trading desks, these are also not usually what is meant by investment banking per se, especially as it is commonly used and as it is used in this book.

In short, investment banks either assist business (and sometime governments) to raise money and/or provide financial advice on transactions such as mergers and acquisitions. In the former case, they assist in raising capital by public offerings of stock or bonds and private placements of offerings with PEGs. A good way to think about investment banking, whether acting as agents and advisors in mergers and acquisitions (M&A) deals or in raising capital, is that this is a go-between function. The money involved is almost always someone else's and not that of an investment banking operation.

So get comfortable with the term. All you need is a broker dealer and securities licenses (discussed later in this chapter) and hopefully some experienced guidance (this is really important), and you are an investment banker specializing in M&A. If you come from another background, accounting or general financial consulting, or valuation for example, the term may initially seem unfamiliar and uncomfortable but this is what you are doing when you are advising clients on M&A and capital formation for a success fee.

Some Ironies of the M&A Profession

I hope my love for transaction work has somehow seeped into this book. I cannot imagine a better professional life, and there are few professions that are as well-rewarded, for those who can stand the stresses and the financial ups and downs. The deep satisfaction that comes from applying long experience and various skills to making "deals" is exquisite—at least until you have to think about where to find the next deal—but that is the nature of the beast. When we do really good work for our sales-side clients, we lose them.

While I know that many seasoned Middle Market bankers pride themselves on their earlier operations background and experience, I think most of them would admit, at least in their hearts that they are better deal people then operations people. You see, I believe you have to love what you do in order to perform at the top level of your profession.

Attention Deficit Disorder and the M&A Banker

I think that operations and deal professionals are different, just as managers and strategists are different within operations. Deal professionals have, I think, shorter attention spans. We often kid about deal people having some peculiar form of career adult attention deficit disorder, and maybe some of us actually do, but put in a more positive light I think that those attracted to the deal profession have wide and eclectic interests. We simply love learning. A former associate of mine used to say that we are a mile wide and an inch deep. There is lot to be said for that, although if that is the shape of our pond it is a highly unique pond in its own right. You need more than a wandering curiosity to succeed as a deal person; you also have to have the ability and tenacity to learn fast, very fast sometimes.

People Skills

People skills are critical. I personally think that it would be a heck of lot easier, at least in certain senses, to be a litigator as opposed to a deal attorney. A litigator can go for the throat of the opposition. Not that skill is not required, but the deal attorney's approach requires a great deal more finesse. It involves not going for the throat, maybe going just close enough to get the best possible deal for his client, but most of all *getting the deal done*. This requires people skills and a great deal of self-knowledge and self-management.

Maybe this is why young people do not usually succeed as full-fledged bankers in Middle Market banking and must wait, in most cases, until probably their late thirties or even late forties to begin to achieve success in the field. Of course, in defense of young would-be-bankers, there is also the issue that clients who are about to undertake a $50 million transaction simply usually feel better in the hands of perceived technical experience and maybe a little life experience as well.

If I were asked for the most important *nontechnical* attributes in someone considering entering this profession, I would say unequivocally that they are:

- Sufficient personal liquidity to survive the first two years
- If entry is first at the banker level, at least 35 years of age
- A real liking for people

- A real empathy for other people's views
- A love of diversity and change
- At least some financial background
- An analytic approach to problem solving

Entry Points to Investment Banking in General

So how does one get into this profession? It is not necessarily easy, but the classic routes each have advantages and disadvantages. If the Middle Market is divided into thirds in terms of transaction value, then the lower third would be transaction values[2] up to $150 million, the second third from $150 million to $500 million, and the upper third from $500 million up to $1 billion. I believe this framework is reasonably accurate and useful. I think they will give the reader a good idea of who does what in the Middle Market and serve as a good segue to the entry points into M&A investment banking. There are many variations of entry points into investment banking, but two with some subsets are classic. They are the small firm/big firm choice, which can also be expressed as the young person/older person choice and just as accurately as the financially secure person/nonfinancially secure person choice. Let me explain.

Boutique Banks, the Lower Third of the Middle Market

The lower third of Middle Market transactions are primarily executed by small but real boutique investment banks, typically with four to five bankers, with some competition from the regional banks (maybe 20 to 50 bankers). The boutiques are more likely to experience this competition when M&A activity is down and the regional firms reach down lower than their normally preferred deal sizes.

The upper third of Middle Market transactions are usually competed for by the large Wall Street investment banks and the larger regional banks. The same phenomena is true here in the upper third as in the lower third, as the Wall Street firms will tend to compete for smaller deals as the M&A market wanes.

The middle third is probably about equally done by all three groups of banks: the boutiques, the regionals, and the Wall Street banks. But most Middle Market deals are done by boutique investment banks, as most Middle Market deals are in the lower third of the market where these banks thrive and where most of Middle Market deals take place.

Direct Entry as a Banker through a Boutique Firm

Boutique investment banks, especially those in the lower third of the Middle Market, often operate on a financial structure that is known, not too pleasantly, as *Eat What You Kill* (EWYK). This financial structure handsomely rewards the banker (who is usually technically an independent contractor, although he looks and acts like a staff banker to the outside world and in all other respects and may even be a firm partner). When he succeeds by closing deals around 50% of the fee goes to the banker and the balance goes to the bank and then after overhead expenses the remainder is distributed to the firm partners.

In this model, the bank is owned by the partners who fund the firm through good and bad times, providing the support staff, expensive research capabilities, and credibility that a real investment bank brings to a prospective client. The house also provides the marketing and branding that are so necessary to successful Middle Market banking.

The problem, of course, is that while the EWYK banker is handsomely rewarded when he is successful (50% of say $600,000, three times a year, is not a bad living by any standard), there can be long dry spells between deal closures, sometimes a year or more. For a banker who has been at it for awhile and developed some financial reserves, these dry spells can be unpleasant but not fatal. In my experience, it takes from one to three years for a new banker to gain enough traction that he can count on *completing* at least a deal a year, depending on his contacts and experience at the outset. This means that the only likely entrants to Middle Market investment banking—at least into the boutique EWYK system—will be older, more experienced persons with enough financial reserves behind them to survive the initial one to three years and enough life experience to not lose heart too soon.

I have seen some accomplish this by combining outside consulting work with investment banking for their first couple of years, but even this is problematic, because it can make the bank uncomfortable about its potential liability for the consulting work or even where the consulting work is coming from. Will the consulting clients assume they are dealing with the bank? Is the consultant able to attract his consulting clients because of his affiliation with the bank? These are serious issues. Credible boutique banks are NASD (since 2007 FINRA) broker dealers, for reasons I will explain shortly, and are required to be aware of and supervise the activities of their licensed bankers. An investment banker doing outside financial consulting work can pose a problem for the bank in that regard, and many would not consider allowing this approach for that reason.

Entry through a Boutique Firm as an Analyst

An alternative entry point into boutique banking is as an analyst supporting the bankers with financial analysis, research, and memorandum preparation. This route at least provides a salary, an opportunity to learn, and the possibility of eventually graduating to becoming an EWYK banker with some kind of financial transitioning step. The problem here is that these jobs (unlike their counterparts on Wall Street, at least during the boom M&A cycles) are as scarce as hen's teeth.

Entry through a Larger Firm as an Analyst

The other classic entry point for the younger person without financial resources is to pursue the larger firm route. The route here is usually again through the analysis and support group. Of course, in this case, the analyst may be handsomely paid, at least again in the boom M&A and financial markets years, although job security can be a problem in the wane years. Something like 50,000 bankers and analysts were laid off with the financial and M&A markets collapses in early 2000 and a similar and certainly greater number in the fall of 2008.

One disadvantage of this route is that, just as in the smaller versus big-four accounting firm situation, the employee of the larger firm will definitely tend to get less client involvement and may be relegated into the deep dark closet of a relative specialist. A great number of these young people in both professions tend to become disillusioned within a couple of years (not to mention burned out from the much, much longer work hours (often 90 or more per week) combined with less autonomy) and drop out.

Entry through a Consulting or Other Professional Practice

A third approach I have observed, and even in fact counseled on, is the addition of an M&A practice (a true investment banking practice, not a support services practice) to a consulting firm that has fees coming in from other sources to weather the inevitable bad times. Often, this will be a smaller CPA firm, a valuation practice, or even a law practice. These types of professionals have a step up in entering the M&A investment banking field, because they already have a handle on a few of the important technical aspects of M&A banking and have a potential client source as well from the other part of their practices.

My observation has been that these approaches have been mixed in their success. When they do not work, there are typically several reasons why. The problem lies in the very different cultural (Exhibit 30.1) and economic structures (Exhibit 30.2) of the investment banking profession (large fees but long periods of no fees at all) as compared to other types of business services firms (moderate but steady fees).

For example, it is sometimes difficult to convince a partner in a CPA firm, that his partner the investment banker should be drawing a paycheck during the long fallow periods when he is producing no income. However,

EXHIBIT 30.1   Small Consulting or CPA Practice versus Sales-Side Investment Bank: Impressionistic Illustration of Cultural Issues

	Small CPA or Consulting Practice	Small Investment Bank
Personality of Practitioners		
	Agricultural: Gatherers	Hunter: Eat what you kill
Focus of Practitioners		
	High: Practitioners need and enjoy sustained focus	Low: Practitioners subject to attention deficit disorder
Partner and Practitioner Reactions		
	Cooperative Barometer: High	Cooperative Barometer: Low to Medium
	Competitive Barometer: Low to Medium	Competitive Barometer: High

when the banker produces a large fee after one of these periods, it seems it is just as tough for him to reconcile fee-splitting with his CPA partner when he is likely to feel that he has taken much of the big risk and should be rewarded with the biggest share of the upside.

This is part of the unfortunate side of receiving pay as large and infrequent sums of money, which is inherent in M&A investment banking but is nevertheless a fact of life. The differences that seem to emanate

EXHIBIT 30.2   Small Consulting or CPA Practice versus Sales-Side Investment Bank: Impressionistic Illustration of Key Financial Comparisons

	Small CPA or Consulting Practice (3 Practitioners)	Small Investment Bank (3 Bankers)
Number of clients	100	5
Average fees per client	$5,000	$400,000
Client retention	90%	0%
Marketing hours	5%, 300 hours	50%, 3,000 hours
Number of paydays	1,200	5
Administrative staff	1	1
Research staff	0	2
Gross Revenues	500,000	2,000,000

EXHIBIT 30.3　Small Consulting or CPA Practice versus Sales-Side Investment Bank: Impressionistic Illustration of Different Approaches to Marketing and Business Development

	Small CPA or Consulting Practice (3 Practitioners)	Small Investment Bank (3 Bankers)
Ratio of initial contacts to secured engagements	90%	0.06%
Therefore, initial contacts needed per year to secure 10 clients	11	15,700
Client understanding of services available	Low to Moderate	High and Focused
Therefore, what is marketed	Services and Firm	Primarily the Firm

(Exhibits 30.3 and 30.4) from these two different cultures can cause no small amount of conflict between the two groups. The more highly competitive investment banking culture can and does easily clash with the less competitive cultures of many business services firms. I have seen this bolt-on approach tried so far in law firms, consulting firms, and accounting firms. While I have seen a few real successes, the failures can tend to outnumber them unless they are handled properly—and properly usually means associating or partnering with a well-established M&A investment bank that can fund most of the costs during any fallow periods, without the need to divert the local practice from its main focus.

EXHIBIT 30.4　Additional Skill Sets Necessary for Small Consulting or CPA Practice to Create a Sales-Side Investment Bank

- Formal business valuation techniques
- M&A business valuation techniques
- Deal structuring techniques
- The M&A negotiated auction process
- Capital markets and banking knowledge
- M&A negotiation styles
- M&A conventions
- Basic securities law
- Basic contract and UCC law
- Accounting knowledge (consulting firms already have)
- Basic M&A taxation (consulting firms already have)

Lateral Entry from Firm to Firm

There is, of course, the not uncommon practice of moving from firm to firm. I believe this may be more typical in the larger boutiques, where a banker's own referral base (such as the CEOs of a few large but M&A-active companies) can make him an attractive candidate for a raid or at least to get a better deal from another investment bank.

This illustrates again the fact that perhaps half of the professional goodwill in larger boutique practice resides in the bank and about half in the banker. Fortunately, it is rare for all the top bankers to leave at once. Then there is the occasional newer firm, where there is really only one significant rainmaker. But in this case, the firm will not be particularly stable unless that rainmaker owns it, which he usually does.

Insufficient Knowledge to Be Successful

An all-too-common assumption is that knowledge of one aspect of M&A (e.g., accounting, valuation, law, etc.) is fully sufficient to build a practice and competently advise clients. Each of these is a very good start, but only a start. The wiser firms and more successful consulting firms that have decided to foray into M&A have brought in an experienced M&A professional or investment bank to establish the core expertise that they will need to enter this very different world form the one they are used to.

Cultural Issues in Investment Banking Practices— Some Further Thoughts

M&A investment banking is concerned with large sums of money, whether that is the proceeds to the client or the banker's fees. Large sums of money, as it has been sometimes been my sad and sometimes my pleasurable experience to observe, tend to bring out the real people behind what is all-too-often the facade they present to the world. The facade may or may not be in synch with the real person, but I can almost guarantee you that large sums of money will bring that real person out, in synch or not. It comes out in relationships between bankers in the same firm in the form of overcompetition to claim referred deals or quarrels about fee splits.

I suppose this is inevitable. I can already imagine some moralistic reader shaking his or her head knowingly while uttering something like "Those greedy money people." Actually, though, I think the competition here is no more or less intense than what is found in most, perhaps all, human pursuits, ranging from art to love, to science, to business, and so on. The difference is that the financial stakes, at least, can often be higher. In my opinion, it is very difficult (and unlikely anyway) for a *single* banker to close and manage more than three transactions a year. So when a dispute does arise between bankers, it may be over as much as a third or more of the banker's income for that year. This is enough to make anyone competitive. Add this inherently high-stakes competitiveness to the fact that bankers are people who are used to negotiating and more keenly aware than many others of the day-to-day tendency for people to prefer and rigorously defend their own self-interest, and voilà, you have a very competitive environment. It is critical to document any banker-to-banker fee split arrangements in detail and well in advance, and to at the same time remain flexible should circumstances warrant that the fee split be revisited. But any such changed circumstances need to be big ones.

As I said, I do not think bankers are unusual here, and much of this is due to the context in which they find themselves. To be successful in Middle Market investment banking also requires having social skills that cannot really be faked over time. The relationships in the Middle Market between bankers, their clients, and their colleagues is just too close to allow a banker with bad people skills to survive long. What I am trying to say is that usually these are nice guys and gals, in spite of the highly competitive environment.

Furthermore, in my experience the culture of an M&A firm can be tremendously influenced by its leadership. If the partners, or at least principal partners, appear to be meticulously fair and always above reproach in terms of honesty and integrity that culture will permeate down through the firm. This does though have to be combined with the partners willingness to quickly identify and remove any sour apples in the firm in this regard. It is easy enough to poison the entire apple barrel without decisive movement in terms of behaviors that are expected and others that will not be tolerated.

Teamwork and Mitigating Risk

The partners in Middle Market banks should go to every length possible to encourage, without mandating (some bankers, some very good ones, just will not be comfortable with this), teamwork on client engagements. This goes a long way towards neutralizing the natural competitiveness among bankers. In addition, the team approach not only builds relationships between bankers but also smoothes out the economic peaks and valleys inherent in Middle Market EWYK banking systems.

When two or more bankers split the 50% banker side of the fee, it engenders a sense of responsibility on the part of the banker who was invited into the deal (there is almost always a clear lead or initiating banker—typically a firm rainmaker—who was responsible for bringing the deal in house) to act in kind in the future to the banker who brought him in. In my own experience, when this type of system is introduced into a firm, it is met at first with a bit of reluctance but thereafter it is amazing how quickly most of the bankers begin to accept the team system and even come to rely on it as the best approach.

I mentioned before that in my view, it is very unlikely that a banker can manage more than three engagements in a year, especially all at one time. The team system greatly mitigates on behalf of bankers and their clients. The problem with the deal business is that it is lumpy. Engagements do not come off of conveyor belts neat and orderly, one deal at a time. They come in clumps and slumps. This is equally true about a deal's phases and stages. In the semifinal and final stages of a deal (the auction and the final LOI through closing), the time involvement on the part of the banker can be incredibly intense. In fact, when a banker is involved in two of these at the same time, he will have little time to do anything else, like develop more business (which I will talk about shortly) or even handle day-to-day human issues like vacations, illnesses, and family responsibilities. The team system obviously aids with this aspect of lumpiness during deal execution phases too.

The benefits of the team approach include the enhanced quality of service provided to the client. The client is happy because there is always coverage, and happy clients of course enhance the firm's and the bankers' reputations and referrals. But as I said, in the firms in which I have been involved in the management, I have never found it necessary to mandate the team approach. Most bankers, when they get a little experience, just simply prefer it. The occasional banker who insists on keeping all of his deals to himself had better be very good at both business development and deal management. I do not think many bankers can survive the Middle Market lumpiness as loners.

Financial Risks—Other

If I have not made it clear previously, Middle Market bankers can make a lot of money, or . . . not. If they do, it is only by taking on great risk. The risk is working very, very hard and ending up with no payday. The banker takes on myriad risks. But mostly, he takes on the risk that the deal will not get done.

Not many professionals will accept an assignment that may take up to a third to a half of the working year with no reasonable assurance of a significant payday of any type. How does one get that reasonable assurance? Bankers learn eventually to be very careful about the projects they take on. The opportunity costs of working very hard on a deal that cannot be closed for the sake of a small retainer are huge. It does the banker anygood in terms of his reputation, either, to take on deal he cannot complete for some reason.

A good rule of thumb, perhaps, is that a banker should have a confidence level of about 75% that he can get a deal through to the finish line. If 75% does not sound very high to you, well, it does to me. In fact, that is about as high a confidence level as is sane to have at the onset of an engagement. Even if the banker has thoroughly analyzed the client's business, the opportunity for deals in the clients industry, and so on, there are so many reasons that a deal might not be done that are out of the banker's control that in my opinion, 75% is a decent confidence level.

For example, the longer a transaction takes, the more things can go wrong, such as marketplace changes, and force majeure. I completed a transaction for a client in early June 2000 that resulted in a sale of his small telecommunications engineering support business for $38 million. He and I got in just under the wire. Had he not done the transaction then, within two months his business would have been virtually unsalable. The telecommunications crash was about to hit, hard and suddenly. The frenzy to lay thousands of miles of cable across the country, soon followed by overcapacity, came to a very quick end—and so did many of the business that served the telecommunications revolution and that had been incredibly attractive acquisition candidates just months before.

While I fortunately did not have the personal experience of losing a deal in the wake of September 11, 2001 (you do escape a few bullets, I guess, in spite of yourself), I can tell you that many, many financing and acquisition deals were put on hold or entirely cancelled as a result of the terrorist attacks. This phenomena is recurring even now as I make the final edits to this book in the Fall of 2008 in what will undoubtedly be recorded in history books as the "Great Crash of 2008" or something similar. Deals in excess of $75 to $100 million dollars are starting to get very shaky as financing debt dries up and public company buyers especially, are reluctant to make serious economic decisions. Whether this will be very short term is difficult to say but it too will pass.

There are endless other reasons for not closing that have nothing to do with the quality of either the business or the quality of the investment banking services. These reasons range from divorces to deaths to clients simply changing their minds. I believe that if these factors are taken out of the equation, one could realistically estimate the odds of success on most well-vetted sales-side engagements at 90%, but these extraneous factors are very real, and anyone considering Middle Market investment banking as a profession should be aware of them so as to allow some reasonable personal budgeting decisions as well as some emotional preparation for those occasions when these things not infrequently happen.

The first financial risk taken on by bankers is at the start of their careers. As I have said, a large number of Middle Market banks operate on an commission-only (EWYK) basis with their bankers. Combine this with the fact that it would be very unusual for a banker to actually *complete* a transaction during his first 18 months in practice, and you have some risk that he will run out of money and have to find other work just at the time when he is reaching the tipping point for the actual start of deal flow, which I believe is usually around 18 to 24 months. The gestation period for M&A deals and client relationships can be years, and of course, even after the banker is engaged, it can take six to twelve months or sometimes a lot longer to close a transaction.

Marketing: Half of Investment Banking Is Business Development

As I have said before, the irony of this business is that the more successfully you represent a client on the sales-side, the more quickly you lose him as client. While he is drinking umbrella drinks in South Florida, you are left with the satisfaction of having done a good job and the problem of where your next client is going to come from. I spent some years in the 1970s building a rather substantial public accounting practice. It was my experience that once you had a client on board, the stickiness of the relationship was powerful. You had to really do something bad to lose a client. As a result, the need for practice development, while it was there, at best needed to take up no more than, say, 10% of the accountant's working hours. It may be more now but really not that much except for a few senior business development partners.

That simply is not the case in investment banking. It is more realistic to assume that something like 50% of a banker's time at all levels of the firm will be spent developing new business if he is to be successful. Unlike public accounting or some consulting practices, there is little or no annuity feature to investment banking beyond the gradual building of a reputation for the bank or banker. The associated problem is that while a banker is executing deals, especially if he is working on more than one at a time, he is unlikely to have much time to develop more business. This is another way the banking business is lumpy and why it is critical to combine drip marketing (constantly staying in front of a lot potential deal flow through emails, snail mail marketing, and the like) with heavy continued personal networking. I recently heard one of our bankers describe this relationship as in a war metaphor the air force (the drip marketing) and the ground troops (local continued personal networking). Neither works very well without the other but when they are done together one plus one is greater than two by far. I guess "Force Multiplier" would be another apt war metaphor.

What a Banker Markets versus What He Sells

Assuming a banker is focused on the sales-side, another issue is concerned with what a banker is trying to market when he develops business. Middle Market decisions to sell are only occasionally motivated by an investment banker. There are some exceptions, of course, and occasionally the market situation in a client's industry will be either particularly conducive to selling or particularly threatening enough to warrant considering a sale at an investment banker's recommendation. However, an investment banker usually has little influence over when a client might decide to sell. The banker can supply information, but the client makes the decision—often for noneconomic reasons.

Most of the time, decisions to sell are made independently of the banker, whether they are for business or life situation reasons. So what a banker markets, when developing business, is ability to represent the client with excellence, in ways that are better than those of the competition. Since the banker has little influence on the timing of a prospective client's business sale, he or she will need to follow a business development approach that will put him/her in the right place over and over again, trusting that one day it will also be at the right time.

This approach suggests that a banker has to be in front of a lot of possible clients or referral sources in a year. Exhibits 30.1, 30.2, and 30.3 illustrate impressionistically at least the effort needed by a small investment bank to maintain, say, two to ten transactions a year. Obviously, when I use numbers like 17,500 contacts to net 10 clients (keep in mind that even all of these will not result necessarily in closed deals), I am being impressionistic, but I can tell you that it is an impression based on long experience and many conversations with other bankers over the years. In fact, I have seen similar numbers estimated by another quality investment bank.

Sellers, Not Buyers

If it is not obvious already, let me make one comment in the context of marketing and business development for sales-side bankers, to those who would enter these portals:

You are marketing for *sellers*!

Hopefully, that makes the point. Among the most frequent misperceptions I see in beginning investment bankers is the excitement they show when they find or have been approached by a buyer. It does not matter whether they have a sales-side client or not, just that they have found or been approached by a buyer. This is a lot like finding a pickaxe and thinking you have struck gold (assuming it is not a buyer willing to pay a retainer).[3]

I cannot imagine anything less exciting to an experienced Middle Market banker.

Buyers are simply not the problem when it comes to obtaining new business for an investment banker. Unless he emphasizes buy-side retained work, the Middle Market investment banker's focus is sellers, unlike business brokerage offices in the Mom-and-Pop world, in which buyers are almost as highly valued. Once a sales-side client representation is undertaken, the issue is certainly one of finding buyers, but in a sales-side engagement, well-vetted, the buyers will come readily and reasonably abundantly. In fact, the very nature of the negotiated auction process is such that, unless desperate, the last thing a banker wants is a single buyer. With a good sales-side representation, a banker wants and should be able to find multiple buyers.

Multiple Marketing Approaches

Among the possible approaches to the dilemma of the very large numbers of contacts necessary to achieve a very small number of engagements and then to get in front of these clients at exactly the right time though networking, drip and brand marketing. I believe the following are the best approaches, at least that I have found.

Becoming an Expert in an Industry

I believe that this is one of the most effective ways for an investment bank or a banker to achieve solid success, hands down. If he goes about it the right way, it suggests all kinds of opportunities to put himself in front of a large number of potential sales-side (and retained buy-side, for that matter) clients at exactly the right time. It is surprisingly easy to both actually become and be perceived as an expert in an industry. At a minimum, four things are necessary:

Initial Research to Understand and Choose the Industry   It is key to find the right industry and there are some things to look for in determining which industry (or industries) on which to focus.

First, it should be an industry where there is a lot of churning, things are changing, companies are consolidating. Frequently, this has been in the second wave[4] of technology industry acquisitions, with a few dominant players fighting each other but an otherwise fragmented industry with a lot of second-tier players who have enough good technology or business to be of interest to the dominants. An industry where the dominant players have already achieved enough dominance that the secondary players would be of little interest to them would not, of course, be a good choice.

Another consideration is the amount of banking coverage that an industry is already getting. Frankly, I have rarely found an industry where there is not room for one more investment banker expert. I suppose it is possible, but I think if that is the case, the churning cycle is probably toward the end anyway—which is the real reason to seek other opportunity industries in which to specialize.

Finally, it is important to pick a narrow enough niche. For example, specializing in "technology" would be far too broad now, although it might not have been 15 years ago. One would need to specialize in a subset of technology, like health care technology (and even a subset of that, probably), financial operations software, or a clear subset of telecom technology.

Publication in Industry Trade Journals and via the Internet   Investment bankers should demonstrate their knowledge of the specialty niche by drafting two to four articles or perhaps a white paper a year for publication either in industry trade journals or via broadcast email to a select database of industry players.

Interestingly enough, I have found this requirement to be somewhat intimidating to bankers. What will I write about, and where will I get the data? In the age of the Internet, data is more than abundant: The problem will not be finding it, the problem is more like being overwhelmed by it. A good concept to use in considering content for your articles is "News You Can Use." Think about what you would like to know in your own industry. All Middle Market businesses have great curiosity about what they might be worth; what other deals are being done; what the state of industry consolidation is; and so on.

This information is abundant and does not even require that much original research, to be perfectly honest. Having said that, however, there is nothing quite like original research, which usually means meeting, talking to, and getting to know the people in the industry. Everyone likes to talk to investment bankers about the subjects that interest them; namely, their money and their opportunities, their industry trends and their competitors. Remember that using others' independent research requires citation and attribution, but there is no shame in that. And avoid merely rearranging facts that are in the public domain (your readers can use Google, they have probably read it already). Your article should present information with a compelling new focus, drawing conclusions on or synthesizing the research you have done in a way that's interesting and unique.

Another thought to use in helping stimulate a banker's creativity is to think in terms of your opinions. I have known very few bankers who, no matter how shy they might be about writing, are unwilling to express their opinions orally, loud and clear. So do it. Just do it in writing. Do it conversationally. Do not at all worry about editing the first time through.

You or somebody else can do that later. Just talk. Anne Lamott, in her great book *Bird by Bird: Some Instructions on Writing and Life*, suggests that writers be tolerant of their "shitty first drafts." If professional writers can be tolerant of putting down essentially what they are thinking, and then get around to organizing and pruning it later, so can the rest of us. If all else fails, hire a ghost writer. Chances are, if you have been studying an industry for even a short while, you will have developed your own opinions even if you cannot immediately cite the data to support them. Write your opinions down first, and then either you or somebody else in the firm can supplement them with research where it is needed. Generally, if you have made a thorough study of your specific field, you will find that the research matches your views. Why? Because you have probably acquired those views from careful observations and your own reading. Even if the research proves you to be wrong, that itself is terrific, as it bring even more focus to your industry knowledge.

If a banker can publish two or three articles annually, in combination with the other approaches to developing industry expertise, he or she will soon be the "go-to" banker (or at least one of them) for people in the industry.

Development of an Industry Database of Players   Once again, this is a project that takes more time than skill—and probably not even that much time to create a basic list. There are abundant sources of lists of the companies involved in any given industry. These range from attendance lists at trade shows (see below) to purchasable lists from publications, trade associations, and services that sell lists. One thing is certain; If there is an industry, there is someone, somewhere, who has compiled a list of its players. On the other hand if no one has then be the first to do it.

This database will provide the source of addressees for self-published articles and also put some boundaries around the industry universe, which will come in handy in future research and just day-to-day contact information. If email is used, then good judgment would suggest that the emails contain graphics and articles of high quality, be reasonably spaced out (once a month would be the maximum), and provide the addressees with a clear way to opt out.

Attendance at Trade Shows or Industry Conventions   To develop and establish your industry expertise, it is critical to attend at least three or four trade shows or industry conventions a year where the players themselves gather. And that does not mean simply visiting exhibit booths to see what is going on. Two bankers with whom I have had the pleasure of working are quite skilled at this approach. They are "Energizer Bunnies™" when it comes to this technique. One of them sometimes rents a suite or small comfortable meeting room and, well in advance of the convention, invites carefully selected people, such as CEOs and officers of companies in his industry, to meet with him (usually sequentially, as these are often competitors). He has excellent success, usually having a dozen or so meetings in two days.

Another banker with whom I have attended industry conventions in his field of specialty is exhausting (and educational) to be with for two days or so when he is doing his thing there. He goes nonstop, maximizing every opportunity to get into a dialogue with the businesses officers. And it does not have to be the CEO. For example, he often establishes substantial leads, just by contacting the CIOs, who in the smaller technology firms are likely to be at the shows. He walks the aisles and they are flattered.

So what do these guys say? What kind of conversations do they have? Well for the most part, they just talk investment banking relative to the industry and the prospective clients' business. As I said, it is a rare CEO or owner who is not interested in the state of the industry, what his company might be worth, what his competitors are doing in the M&A arena.

If the banker has also established himself with published articles, he will most certainly have a high success rate in getting the ear of the right people. My observation has been that after a couple of years of this kind of sustained effort, a banker can just walk into the door of a trade show in his industry, stand there, and they (the industry players) will come to him.

SPECIALIZATION TAKES TIME   Achieving that stature in the chosen industry does take some time, though. Bankers I have observed and talked to, who have followed this approach, suggest that the real payoff begins around two to three years out. But when it comes, if the industry is chosen well and the follow-up is good, the payoff will be handsome. Keep in mind that the two principles of investment banking prospecting are to be there at the right time and to convince the prospective client that you have the skills sets to execute his investment banking transaction. There is no better way than industry specialization to do this.

SPECIALIZATION IS NOT WITHOUT ITS DANGERS   Specialization can be a risky strategy, though. The ebb and flow of M&A industry sectors are notorious. In Chapter 6, I talked about the problems of timing the sale of Middle Market businesses and the certainty that industries have their cycles. Add to this the macroeconomic cycles that also impact M&A activity, and you have a double whammy that suggests that putting all of your eggs in one exclusive basket may not be an entirely good idea.

It is the "live by the sword, die by the sword" approach. If your practice specialty is in an area that is experiencing either a valuation bubble or a great deal of activity (usually these two features co-exist), then all is well and good . . . until the bubble is over. Correspondingly, M&A activity closely tracks the macroeconomy, and when the latter is off, it is far better to have several practice areas to draw from in a period when there are overall fewer deals. A judicious approach, for an individual banker at least, is to blend perhaps one or two practice specialties with a general Middle Market approach.

From the perspective of an investment bank, the same thing is true. If for example, a bank has ten bankers, each of whom pursue one specialty as well as a general practice, then the bank is somewhat insulated from the slings and arrows of bubbles and cycles in industries, and at least somewhat better insulated from macroeconomic slumps as well.

Finally, the number of industry specializations a banker can take on is limited by resources of time, money, and focus. Committing to write three or four articles (an absolute minimum necessity) and attend three or four trade shows (again, probably an absolute minimum) is a significant commitment of time. Multiply this by several specialties, and the time and money commitments grow rapidly. Then there is the traditional conflict between quantity and quality, which must be taken into account.

All in all, it will depend on the circumstances of the bank and the banker, but I seriously doubt, in a small boutique (ten or fewer professionals), that more than one or two specialties per banker is reasonable. Too many specialties will overly stress your resources and focus, making the strategy counterproductive.

The New York Banker Style of Practice

There is another style (a somewhat cinematic one admittedly) of what I suppose you could call marketing, and that I call the New York Banker. This banker is the type who more or less creates deals out of whole cloth. For example, he keeps his ear to the ground in one or more industries, learns where the right M&A combinations might be, and between whom, and tries to instigate a deal between two parties who did not anticipate being in a deal of any kind at the moment, much less with each other. By patiently pointing put the advantages to the heretofore clueless parties, the banker gets something going.

I have seen more than one Middle Market banker succeed very well with this approach, but it really takes a lot knowledge of an industry or sector (without otherwise specializing in it) and reading a lot of general business media to boot. I also think it takes a certain type of very aggressive personality. I admire the style, but I am not particularly comfortable with it myself.

Being in the Investment Banking Business for a Long Time

This approach may seem rather obvious, and I would not mention it here but for the fact that it illustrates a little differently what I was saying about entry points into Middle Market investment banking. The difficulty in entering the business is largely associated with the length of time it takes to build a following and a reasonably reliable stream of engagements. This is true for individual investment bankers and for new banks. The pleasant outcome of long-term involvement in M&A is the fact that, having survived the early years, a bank or banker can be reasonably assured that transactions will come along. Maybe not as often as he would like, but often enough, especially when associated with the other active business development approaches that I am general discussing here, to be very rewarding.

A lot of this comes from building a reputation as a name in the business. Clients want to see that the firm is a player, and an experienced one that has been around for a while. When a firm has been around for a while, it is likely prospective clients will become aware of it from just sheer endurance. The marketing people call that "branding."

Covering Large Numbers of Middle Market Business Owners

Exhibits 30.4 and 30.5 illustrate, at least impressionistically, the problem faced by the Middle Market investment banking industry, and that is the need to be, and the effort required to be, in the right place at the right time. Hiring an M&A banker is not like weekly grocery shopping, where the vendor just puts up a store and waits. For many Middle Market businesses, their sale is a once- or twice-in-a-lifetime event. The banker must be there when the need arises. All of the tactics suggested here are different approaches to that idea, but at its simplest level, the law of just being visible in front of large numbers of prospective clients is an effective and critically necessary approach.

During its heyday, a once-well-known Middle Market bank—some would call it more of a business brokerage firm than an investment bank (and it was sometimes well known for the wrong reasons)—sent out vast quantities of direct snail-mail pieces to net thousands of potential clients a year.[5] Admittedly, this was viewed by many as an approach that was more focused on selling valuations for relatively large retainers than on quality investment banking, but it does suggest that the practice of contacting large numbers of potential clients can be effective. Unfortunately, it is also estimated to have only closed 10% of its clients' transactions, with almost 90% of its revenue coming from retainers (valuations) as opposed to success fees. But that was its style—it need not and *should not* be yours.

A number of legitimate investment banks, especially in the 1990s, took the same approach (mass mailers and seminars); some still do. Although it reached a saturation point in the late 1990s, and the activity level eventually dropped, particularly after the economic crash in early 2000, the approach

EXHIBIT 30.5   Impressionistic Illustration of Best Practices Annual Marketing and Business Development Strategies for an IB

Events	Discrete Contacts	Resulting Clients
I. Becoming an expert in a single industry		
1. Trade show and convention attendance (3 annually)	900	2
2. Research articles (3 annually)	600	
II. Being in the investment banking business for a long time		
1. Clients per year of business (2, beginning after four years)	2	2
III. Covering large numbers of Middle Market business owners		
1. Large snail mail or email (3 to 10 annually)	9,000	3
2. Seminars, panels (8 to 12 annually)	300	
IV. Networking with professionals who provide services to high net worth clients		
1. Lunches, networking events (50 annually)	2,450	1
V. Networking with other M&A support professionals		
1. Lunches, networking events (50 annually)	2,450	1
VI. Serving clients and executing engagements with excellence		
1. Corollary to II. Estimate that it increases yield in II by 50%	1	1
Total Contacts/Clients	**15,703**	**10**

can be effective if done tastefully and consistently over a long period, perhaps using the more modern approach of broadcast email (preferably with opt-in and opt-out alternatives for recipients who might consider this spam). These mail contacts do not have to be overt solicitations of clients, but can include invitations to seminars with other interesting news that will hopefully garner the attention of Middle Market business owners, who are always interested in keeping abreast of issues that concern their eventual exit strategies and/or their industries.

For example, in my own extended metropolitan area, there are approximately 5,000 Middle Market businesses. Staying tastefully in front of them ten times a year (50,000 points of contact) is simple enough and can be accomplished very inexpensively by using the broadcast email approach.

While not all of these emails will be opened (15% is a good estimate) it works better than direct snail mail where the estimated action rate is about 1%.

Combined with two educational seminars[5] a year (advertised with very tasteful graphics, and including real educational content), this approach can be very effective in terms of being in the right place at the right time and demonstrating that your bank is the one to represent the client when they are ready.

Networking in General

Let me just say this once: Networking, done properly is *the single best way to develop business*. Over many years of observing bankers, I have without any doubt observed a direct correlation between success and the amount of quality networking. By doing it properly, I mean:

1. *Make it a discipline* by scheduling a certain number of organizations and individuals to network with each month and each year. Anything less than once a week is less than wholehearted and less than effective. Keep a recurring list, and stick to it—sometimes over many years. This is another aspect of being in investment banking for a long time.
2. *Get involved in organizations*. Do not simply attend organization meetings. Get involved. Join committees. This is the way to develop close relationships with people, by getting to know them and working with them. Direct selling is unnecessary most of the time. When people know who you are and what you do, and they like you, they will refer business to you. Period.
3. *Maintain a list of contacts*. Drop them a note from time to time. The note does not have to be associated with direct selling of your services—and most of the time, it should not be. A simple "Happy Birthday" or "Hi, how is it going?" note is much better. Nobody wants to be plagued by self-promoting salesmen.
4. *Avoid the business card handout* kind of networking above all. Most people will throw these away and forget you if you restrict your networking to this style.
5. *Do not restrict your networking to business organizations*. Business people are often involved in charitable and arts organizations. Go where they go. Get involved.
6. *Be patient*. This approach takes time, but success here, while gradual is exponential as opposed to arithmetic.

Networking with Professionals who Provide Services to High Net Worth Clients

This can be an effective approach, although as usual there are potential pitfalls. Money managers and similar wealth management professionals often have a high net worth clientele, and, quite naturally, a number of that clientele are going to be Middle Market owners or executives. While this approach is very similar to networking with other M&A support professionals (see below), the thing to be aware of is that this class of professional sees M&A intermediaries through the opposite end of the lens. They see intermediaries as being a lucrative source of referrals back to them. After all, most Middle Market M&A business owners, having just completed a sales-side transaction, will likely be more liquid, more affluent, and more in need of wealth management services.

Networking with Other M&A Support Professionals

Accountants, attorneys, commercial bankers, business consultants, and valuation professionals can obviously constitute a good referral base (but see my caveats at the end of this section) for the same reason that wealth management professionals can. They also look at M&A bankers from the other side of the lens as potentially a good referral source back to them, as do wealth managers.

In truth, we are. I would say in perhaps one third of the transactions we encounter in my own practice, we are in a position to refer a client to at least one of these professional groups (with the exception of outside valuation experts, as they have little to do with M&A transactions once one has been initiated).

For example, the ability to refer to attorneys, usually arises from the fact that many sales-side clients would have had no reason to have a relationship with a transaction attorney and are seeking our advice in finding a good one. In the case of accountants, a similar situation arises. A surprising number of Middle Market businesses with well to the north of $10 million in revenues are able to get by with maintaining a fairly casual accounting system (at least some aspects of it) and are not necessarily audited either. About one in two transactions will see the client raising the level of pretransaction accounting services to avoid confirmatory due diligence problems and perhaps to increase the quality of their tax advice.

Accountants and commercial bankers are likely to be able to refer business, as they will sometimes know about a client's transaction before the client hires an investment banker. Attorneys, on the other hand, even more often learn of the transaction before the banker has been hired, and are a worthy referral source to cultivate. But an investment banker's ability to refer to a commercial banker is somewhat limited by the fact that the sales-side investment banker's objective often is to put his or her client out of business, but many commercial banks now have affiliated wealth management services of one type or another, and will be interested in the referred client's newfound liquidity.

My point here is that M&A bankers can be a very good referral source for these support professionals and, as such, can expect to receive referrals back. These guys are a major source of investment banking business over the years. There is another side of the coin, though: In my experience, many of these wealth management and other M&A support professionals can promise a lot and deliver little. In my own firm, we allow these professionals to address our bankers periodically, as a small part of our staff meetings. In many cases, we know that these professionals have addressed every other M&A bank in the last year as well, looking for referrals themselves. Who is likely to get the deal referral when it comes? Beats me!

And it is fair to say, too, that this is a problem for both sides. One thing that I believe is critical to understand in developing a referral base is that the old 80/20 cliché comes into play here quite handsomely. About 20% of the referral base you develop and cultivate over the years will produce about 80% of your referrals.[6] One learns quickly to recognize or at least sense the ones with whom, for one reason or another, you will develop a strong mutual referral relationship that will last through the years.

I am always very friendly (but internally skeptical) on meeting new referral sources. I am also very up front about discussing the 80/20 rule. There is no reason not to. It is true, and everybody knows it. The final rule I follow religiously is to treat those with whom I do develop a mutual referral relationship as very special. A sacrosanct rule is that if we receive a referral, we find a way to reciprocate. That is called "fertilizing the plant," and it is as effective in business as it is in agriculture. I am always amazed at the unfocused "everywhere, all the time" networkers I see; they seem to be trying to be all things to all people. They would be far better served to focus over time on the quality of their referral base, not the quantity.

A corollary to this is the fact that investment banking referrals are not going to come in large numbers as a rule from any one referrer. If I received one transaction referral every three or four years or so from my top ten referral relationships, I would have an incredible deal flow from just this one source. Again the idea here is consistency, not quantity.

Long-Term Exit Strategy Planning

Another approach to developing business stems from the combination of understanding that:

- Developing trust and confidence with a client can take a long time.

- Middle Market M&A engagements, unless caused by quick necessity of some sort on the part of the client (death, divorce, catastrophe), frequently can have a long gestation period or sale cycle.
- Almost all Middle Market businesses would do well to begin planning for a sale at least three years before executing it.

All of which leaves an opportunity to actually develop a sort of sub-practice of exit strategy consulting, which can not only be lucrative in its own right but also can provide a long-term pipeline of deal flow into the future.

One successful method I have observed (and have practiced in my own firm) is to obtain a consulting engagement with a Middle Market client that begins with a preliminary valuation, giving a detailed analysis of the client's business value drivers that the client, in turn, can use to reverse-engineer his company by knowing what will eventually bring about its maximized value when the time for a sales transaction actually arrives. We have found it helpful, in formulating these engagements, to include periodic pulse-check meetings and often, as well, to give a credit to the client for some of the fees paid to us against the eventual retainer when the sales-side engagement takes place. In this case, the credit that is, the client actually has an investment in the banker.

Serving Clients and Executing Engagements Well

Over the years, investment banks, like other professionals, develop whatever reputation they earn. A client I represented a number of years ago, a small international consulting practice, came up with the concept that an irritated client is far more damaging then a pleased client is helpful. This concept might be self-evident, but like most self-evident principles, nobody had quite expressed it the way my client did. The consultants, based on studies, learned that an angry client or customer will tell about eight people of his unpleasant experience, whereas a happy client or customer will tell only two people. This knowledge not only spawned a very lucrative consulting practice, but also had a profound impact on the way many, many large American, Japanese, and eventually other businesses came to approach the issue of quality of services and products.

Performance and Intensity in Their Clients' Interests by M&A Bankers

Investment banking results are a very big ticket item for clients. If you want to really irritate somebody, do something to his pocketbook. But if you want to create a friend and a referrer for life, perform for that client like there is nothing more important on this Earth at this moment. Live the transaction with him. Let him know you are fighting for him as if your own fortunes depended on it (of course, they actually do).

I have clients I have been using as references and referral sources for more than ten years. They will not hesitate to spend 30 minutes sometimes talking to a prospective client for whom I have used them as a reference. I am not going to suggest for a moment that you can be in practice for many years and have every client you deal with be exceedingly happy. There are always characters and problem clients out there, as well as clients who will tend to externalize their own self-created problems on you. However, a banker's goal should be to please 100% of his clients. If he is successful 90% of the time, he will eventually have a constant source of deal flow and a referral base to support his deal flow.

Richmond, VA—October 1991

"Give me an example of what you mean by intensity, Doug, since you talk about it so much."

Doug, a really successful Middle Market banker, and I were sharing a very bad and unhealthy fast food lunch in the front seat of my car. We were really in a hurry to get down to the Norfolk area in tidewater Virginia for a meeting with a food industry client, and it was the best we could do for lunch, I am sorry to say.

"All right, this is what I mean. Do you remember that food distribution deal that closed several months ago?"

"Sort of."

"For two days before closing, I tromped around that damned warehouse observing inventory counts, because my client's accountant was not available, everybody was shorthanded, and the inventories needed to be completed if we were going to be able to close. You have any idea what it is like to be in a 15-degree refrigerated warehouse counting frozen food packages?"

"No, never done that."

"Well, the deal got closed. I got a really bad head cold, and . . . the client sent me a referral a month later. Guess it was worth it."

"Guess it was. I see what you mean."

Like all of the other anecdotes in this book, this one is true, if slightly altered to protect the innocent.

Securities Law Issues

Under the Securities Exchange Act and the Uniform Securities Act (which is more or less a codification of or basis for many states' blue sky laws), it is clear that the solicitation for the sale of securities is subject to regulation. In the great stock market crash of 1929, approximately $25 billion dollars of securities became worthless, the Great Depression ensued, and the Securities Acts of 1933 and 1934 quickly followed. The primary thrust of both of these acts is fair treatment of investors, which requires full and adequate disclosure.

All sales of securities using interstate commerce must comply with the regulations. These regulations are generally administered by the National Association of Security Dealers (NASD); since 2007, the name of the regulatory body is the Financial Institutions Regulatory Authority (FINRA). This self regulating professional body is under the not-too-far-distant oversight of the SEC.

Part of the actual administration takes the form of requiring individuals involved in this type of work to have a securities license, thus becoming registered representatives. The most common licenses held by M&A professionals are Series 7, for federal purposes, and Series 63, for state purposes.

The investment bank itself is required to be a *broker dealer*, subject to a great deal of regulation designed to protect the public. The broker dealer is required to file quarterly financial reports and annual audits, and is held strictly accountable for maintaining minimum levels of capital.[7]

In addition, one or more of the partners of members of the firm will have to hold Securities Principal Licenses (Series 24) and, unless they hire it out to a consultant, a Series 28 license as a financial operations principal (Fin-Op). Although the Fin-Op license is by no means a piece of cake, especially for nonaccountants, none of the licenses is beyond the ken of the average financial professional. However, a week or two of serious study and testing can be anticipated for each of these licenses.

The sale of securities in an M&A transaction under both federal and state securities laws is clearly covered, but it is doubtful that Middle Market M&A activity was originally even thought of when the regulations were put into place.[8] The problem is that far more than 50% of Middle Market M&A transactions involve the acquisition of the owning entity's stock, particularly since the 1986 tax act, which made the sale of entity assets prohibitively expensive due the fact that they are taxed twice, once at the corporate level and then later, after distribution, at the shareholder level.[9]

Penalties for selling securities can be both civil and criminal and can also result in rescission of the transaction. Of course, transaction rescission could also lead to lawsuits, to which the unlicensed banker can be certain he will be a respondent when they are filed.

Another real problem is the sales-side client who deals with a fee dispute with his banker by threatening to point out to the authorities that the bank was inappropriately conducting regulated activity without being properly licensed. This has caused more than one nonlicensed M&A bank to walk away from or quickly settle a large fee that they had otherwise well earned.

For these reasons, many unlicensed investment banks took the leap in the late 1990s and became broker dealers. While it is not clear that this is a necessary step (ask ten law firms prior to the last five years or so and you would have gotten varying opinions[10]) many banks went forward anyway, in an abundance of caution. Now, for many of the better banks, it has become the norm.

I also believe that many of them found that getting properly licensed had the additional favorable consequence of adding a level of credibility that their unlicensed competitors might not have, giving them somewhat of a competitive advantage. What is clear is that the regulators really do not quite know what to do with these "strictly M&A" banks. They enforce the regulations as they must, but with seemingly little relevance to what the laws and regulations originally contemplated (again, the sale of securities to the public). It would not surprise me if a separate set of regulations eventually evolves to cover "strictly M&A" banks. Several drafts by the American Bar Association have been submitted to the SEC already. They are badly needed.

My last comments on the regulation issue:

- Consider establishing the broker dealer as a stand alone entity that only deposits fee checks and disburses fee splits, with no other expenses running through it. This will make the auditing and minimum capital complexities much easier to administer.
- Establish an expense-sharing agreement that allows the main consulting practice to guarantee the expenses of the broker dealer. These arrangements have been approved by FINRA, provided that the guarantor has the capacity to actually guarantee the expenses and that a careful record of the appropriate allocable or direct expenses is maintained.
- Do not mix any other activities (consulting, valuation service, and so forth) of the firm with the M&A activity of the broker dealer. Again, this will make record keeping, auditing, and minimum capital compliance much easier.
- Do not try to distinguish between asset and stock deals. Just run them all through the broker dealer. Even an asset deal may possibly take the form of a stock deal. And as such, it was probably offered in a manner that may have come under the provenance of the Uniform Securities Act at a state level.

Engagement Intake Management

I would like to finish up this section by sharing a couple of hard-won insights that hopefully may save the neophyte investment bank or banker from some of my own early mistakes.

Taking on Clients without Retainers or Commitment Fees   My advice? Never do this. Again, watch my lips: *Never do this*. I have already talked about the new banker's excitement in getting a deal, any kind of a deal. The deal (combined with the banker's inexperience) tends to blind him or her about the realities and vicissitudes of actually completing a transaction. One of these vicissitudes is client commitment, which I discuss elsewhere in this book. A client who has no skin in the game is not a client. He or she has not made a commitment to actually doing a deal. There are plenty of curious clients out there, willing to have you take on loads of work just to find out what their business might be worth.

One way to weed these out is require a retainer or commitment fee up front, in an amount significant enough to demonstrate the client's seriousness. When this advice was first given to me, I relegated it the old psychiatrists' mantra about how a patient who did not pay his fees on time was not committed to the process and therefore would not be susceptible to therapy. I initially thought that this was just so much malarkey to justify the psychiatrist getting his fees paid or the banker collecting some money. I soon learned that the advice reflects a real and deadly truth, which is ignored to the banker's detriment.

I would consider budgeting a retainer over several months (and have done so), occasionally reducing one a bit in cases where I really believed the issue was not one of lack of commitment, but I do not trust my own judgment enough to suspend the retainer altogether. In fact, I trust my judgment enough to be rigidly resistant to suspending retainers.

Vetting New Deals (Especially Capital Raising Deals)   All of us have our blind side when it comes to taking on transactions, even when the retainer is not an issue. The blind side can work either way, too. It can cause inappropriate deal rejection, as well as acceptance. Another way to sponsor the all-important issue of teamwork in boutique investment banks is to insist that all potential new engagements be vetted by a committee. The sense of teamwork, the minimization of acceptance and rejection error, and the discovery of hidden strengths or contacts within other bankers relevant to the vetted deal can be very productive for a firm.

The vetting process can be every educational, as well, from the point of view of less experienced bankers. The committee process tempers the zeal of less-experienced bankers, who are prone to making errors in the direction of accepting engagements that cannot be executed, especially in private equity and other capital raises. The process also tends to make the less experienced bankers more aware of the areas of experience possessed by their fellow bankers on the committee, who might actually help a deal get done.

There is more to a good capital-raising opportunity then simply the latest and greatest idea, even if it is the latest and greatest. Timing, management, capital markets appetites, and many other issues may have a great bearing on the likelihood of success. In my view, the tender balance between a great idea or company, and a company that capital can actually be raised for, is not learned easily or quickly.

> *First of all I choose the great roles, and if none of these come, I choose the mediocre ones, and they don't come, I choose the ones that pay the rent.*
> Michael Caine

Climbing the Deal Size Ladder   Yes, we all want bigger deals. We know they are easier to do, actually take less time, and frankly are more fun and prestigious. But I strongly disagree, and have thoughout my professional career, with the advice that says if you want bigger deals (clients) you should stay away from small ones. Do a good job with the small ones and your referrals will multiply. Both in investment banking and in public accounting, some of the largest clients I have ever represented were referred by some of the smallest clients I ever had. The only exception I make to this is to strongly recommend staying away from Mom-and-Pop business brokerage deals—not because they are small, but because they are a different business altogether, involving (as I have pointed out elsewhere) different techniques. Here, it is frankly easy to get pigeonholed as a business broker. Avoid that niche like the plague.

Success in Life and M&A

It may seem, from the sports (golf) analogies I have suggested in this book, that I may be some kind of fanatical sports fan. Actually, I am not. I rarely watch sports, with the exception of a few major golf tournaments. Fortunately I am married to a woman who more or less is a rabid sports fan, across the board. You name it, she watches it: football, the Kentucky Derby, golf, basketball. Her enthusiasm and total absorption when she is watching the latest sporting event on television make me grin, at least internally. She plays not a single sport, unless you consider gardening a sport.

While I feel that the cliché that sports including golf are a metaphor for life is often belied by the all too corny and trite comments made by athletes and coaches in their pre- and post-game interviews (they must give these guys all the same script), I also have had the pleasure to live during an era when one single athlete so dominates his sport that I do take notice of what he says... but mostly of what he does.

His name? Tiger Woods.

Of course I do not know this guy, and if I did, I might be disappointed in the actual person... or not. Who knows? But I have listened to his answers to the inane questions of sports commentators following his latest victory over men who themselves are elite athletes. The answers seem to be summarized in a few central ideas that all of us would do well to note.[11] And I can guarantee you these apply to the world of M&A investment banking. I want you to understand that when I talk about winning in this context, I am not talking about defeating someone. Winning is a very personal and private thing and has nothing to do with defeating the other side:

- *Forget about numerous goals.* Stay with the big picture. One goal is enough, and that is to just get better every day and success will result (i.e., do not spread yourself thin).
- *Losing comes with winning.* Get over it. Life continues, and there is always another challenge and another opportunity. Concentrate on that (i.e., do not get discouraged).
- *If you are going to play, play to win.* Learn to grind on every shot, every deal, every client relationship (i.e., pay attention to detail).
- *Never, ever, give a half-hearted effort.* Stay in the moment for yourself and your clients (i.e., if you are going to do this, do it all the way).

The $10 Trillion Opportunity

My enjoyment of this profession has been immense, and occasionally immensely financially rewarding (in between periods of wondering where the hell the next deal is going to come from, of course). It has had me on more airplanes than I care to mention, traveling to exotic places like West Africa and a lot of less exotic places like Omaha, Nebraska. I have been involved in more industries than I can remember, I have met more "characters" than in a Monty Python episode, and, at times, I have been called on to find creative juices that I did not know I had. I have had clients to whom I became so close they remained lifelong friends, as well as parties on the other side of a transaction who swore they would never talk to me again (or worse)—but many of them I worked with later, on other deals and we became real friends.

If you have to ask: Yes, I would do it all over again (I am still doing it, for that matter). If you have a wandering and wondering mind, a love of people, a relish for excitement and adrenalin rushes—in other words, if you are a "deal junkie," go for it.

Furthermore, in what has been termed the $10-trillion opportunity (somewhat of an exaggeration from our own research, but still in the trillions when it applies to Middle Market M&A), I see only good things and very hot markets (with some of the usual lulls, of course) in the future of the M&A intermediary profession. Without overly repeating an introductory chapter, a vast number (about 800,000) of Middle Market businesses will change hands over the next 20 years as a result of baby boomer retirements and technology advances, not to mention the cross-border movement to a one-world business economy. About 2/3rds of these will be sold with an estimated market value of $3.3 trillion. Almost 3.3 trillion anything is a staggering quantity to grasp. For instance, 3.3 trillion hours ago was 150 million years *before* the first dinosaur existed. A 3.3 trillion gallon wave would form a puddle 8 inches deep the size of Lake Michigan. How about 3.3 trillion equals the number of miles America drives each year (200 billion gallons of gas @ 17 mpg), the total barrels of extractable oil shale reserves, and the number of miles to the furthest star (Andromeda Galaxy) that can be seen by the naked eye?

Chapter Highlights

- Key characteristics of a successful investment banker are an enjoyment of people, a love of variety, and an ability to take huge risks.
- Most Middle Market investment banks are modeled on an "eat what you kill" (EWYK) basis and therefore difficult for younger people to enter, other than through an analyst position.
- Entry through a consulting or other professional practice can be done (see Exhibit 30.6), but barriers to this approach include insufficient expertise and experience, lack of licensing, cultural and economic clashes between partners, and lack of credibility.
- One half of a banker's or bank's time is spent on marketing tasks:
  - Mass marketing can be accomplished through seminars newsletters, databases, etc.
  - Narrow marketing through highly selective networking is very important to developing new business.
  - Impressionistically, it takes an estimated 17,000 to 20,000 points of contact to land an engagement.
  - A banker is looking for, and trying to be in front of, *selling* clients, not buyers, when he is marketing.
  - Being in the business for a long time, with a loyal referral base coming from quality management of previous deals, is the best way to sustain a practice.

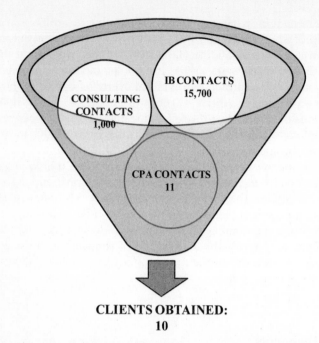

CLIENTS OBTAINED:
10

EXHIBIT 30.6 Small Consulting or CPA Practice versus Sales-Side Investment Bank: Impressionistic Illustration of the Funnel Effect

- Specialization is a great entry point to banking, but do not place all your eggs in one industry basket.
- The New York style of banking, while it can be effective, is not seen particularly frequently in the Middle Market.
- Consider establishing an exit strategy subpractice to develop good immediate income and long-term deal flow.
- FINRA, the SEC, and collateral legal concerns make it practically mandatory for a bank with any growth ambition to obtain the proper securities licenses and entities.
- There is a $10-trillion opportunity (more or less) out there.

Notes

1. This book is being final edited in September 2008 in the midst of the so called "deepest U.S. financial crises since the great depression." Over the last several weeks the distinctions between commercial banking and investment banking are undergoing enormous change at least in terms of how the industries are typically known to the public. With large

commercial banks acquiring large investment banks and vice versa there is a rapid blending of the two historically different industries. However as a matter of functional operations the two different professions will continue to operate separately even where under common ownership.

2. As I continually point out in this book, the important relationship contained in the rough rule of thumb is that transaction size can be estimated as around 50% of the revenues of the sold company. I continue to point this out, in appreciation of the fact that many readers will be reading only those parts of the book that interest them—and rightfully so.

3. While this book is sales-side focused, I want to make a distinction of course between the passive buyer, who simply announces he is available to purchase the right business, and the active buyer, who is willing to pay a retainer for an acquisition search.

4. The second wave of technology industry acquisition, seen from the perspective of my firm, has been with companies where the emphasis is not so much on technology per se, as it was in the mid- to late 1990s, but on business solutions applications. In many vertical industries, transportation and hospitality, for example, technology is no longer so much gee whiz stuff as it is real solutions to real problems such as optimizing hotel room bookings or airline seat sales. In each of these technologies while there are a few dominant players there are a number of secondary players too with great technologies and/or enough business to be attractive acquisition candidates to the dominants.

5. The national brokerage firm combined its huge national direct mail campaigns with what were reputedly very high-pressure scare-tactic seminars in very poor taste. This approach backfired as often as not, at least with the more intelligent attendees, but it also obviously landed a certain number of the gullible (and often greedy) types. The whole operation was more than a little distasteful and should hardly be dignified as investment banking. It was subsequently purchased by a large reputable national firm in the financial services industry, which has been cleaning up its act. Much of my information comes from conversations with former employees of the organization.

6. While it may have become a cliché, the 80/20 rule is actually yet another possibly observable instance of the Pareto Principle, sometime known as the Law of the Vital Few, developed by Italian economist Vilfredo Pareto. Whether this can be actually observed in this instance, I am not sure, but I can tell you that in a professional career of some length it feels very, very consistent with my experience.

7. Assuming that the broker dealer is set up strictly for executing M&A transactions, it can expect to satisfy the requirements of minimum capital by maintaining no less than $6,000 in equity capital at any time. This

can be more complex than it sounds, as this capital requirement can be affected easily by other balance sheet debt.

8. As of this writing, there is an ABA task force (June 2005) report recommending at least somewhat more sensible regulations regarding an M&A type of practice. Furthermore, certain M&A industry groups are taking a harder look at this. Hopefully the SEC and the FINRA will see the light eventually. The biggest problem is that there are 50 states that would have to buy in to and serious change ion the regulations and that why this process is likely to take a long time.

9. This assumes that an S corporation election is not in place, of course.

10. For example, some law firms, advised clients that obtaining the licensing would only call them to the attention of apparently otherwise unconcerned regulators. Others were reluctant to provide any kind of a clear opinion at all. And a few vigorously recommended full compliance. Everyone seemed to agree, though, that M&A transactions were not what the law was originally designed to protect the public from, insofar as the parties to these deals were not the "public," in the sense that buyers of businesses are either other business or super-sophisticated financial investors.

11. Most of these ideas, or their essence, are taken from an article or articles from a little-known golf writer, Wayne Defrancesco, who himself stands well above the golf writing crowd in terms of intelligent commentary on this elusive sport and, whether Wayne realizes it or not (I suspect he does), on life.

CHAPTER 31

A Postscript: The Capital Markets

Providence, RI—1989

I was on a small business White House advisory council in the late 1980s, and frankly, all of us were at a loss and scrambling to find sources of capital for very small Middle Market businesses, especially the early stage ones (that was the reason for the conference). Most of you will not remember those days and it is just as well, but my, how times have changed. Since then, the private equity and venture capital markets have been more or less born and changed the landscape of our Middle Market business economy exponentially.

Even as a novice financial professional (CPA), when I first heard the term "capital markets," I was not entirely sure what it meant. Did it imply the British sense of "capital" (the best) markets, or something else? If it meant that, I was sure my young wife would know about them and where they were, and had probably already shopped in them. I am kidding of course, more or less anyway. I came to learn that it meant just what it said . . . the place where you get the dough from the other guys.

OVERVIEW The capital markets. While they have not been an emphasis in this book (which largely focuses on Middle Market mergers and acquisitions, or M&A, transactions), the capital markets are a vital resource, and a source of capital with which investment bankers in the Middle Market need to be familiar. For one thing, investment bankers do not just represent buyers and sellers of businesses, but also businesses seeking capital. The reason for including this material is because of this nexus between M&A and the capital markets in general.

Except as a pedagogical device, it is pointless to separate these subjects, as it would be all but impossible to responsibly practice M&A without a relatively complete, if broad, knowledge of the individual funding sources within the overall capital markets. In fact, very few M&A transactions do not in some way involve the capital markets, either as a source of financing or as alternative of which a prospective client should be aware.

Many capital markets transactions are, in fact, M&A deals (the whole or partial acquisition of the assets or equity of a business enterprise). I want to address several of those capital markets[1] here in a more or less quick-visit fashion, as my readers will not need a long dissertation on each.

Furthermore, it would be impossible to address all of the capital markets; even if one were to do so, the list would be obsolete within a year, as these markets update themselves and change that fast. So this chapter will briefly discuss the relative cost of capital of each of the main sources, with a little bit about the process for each and the suitability (matching investors, objectives, and purpose) of each. I will use a couple of terms here several times that I want to define in advance:

- *Bucket shops* (sometime referred to as *widow-and-orphan shops* or *Boca Raton shops*): These are typically retail stock promoters (albeit usually licensed) who operate boiler rooms pushing less desirable stocks and investment schemes (pushing them frequently to the edges of the law, if not outside it). For years, many of these were located in south Florida.[2] Picture a large room filled with telephone banks and some group leader up in front exhorting the representatives to sell, sell, maybe even offering a gold watch to the one who performs the best this particular hour. Investees should avoid association with this type of operation at all costs due to their borderline unethical practices and a certain "taint" that comes with having dealt with them.
- *Best efforts offerings*: Public stock offerings that are not initially purchased (guaranteed in effect) by the investment banks that underwrite them.
- *Guaranteed underwritten offerings*: Public stock offerings that are first purchased by investment banks (or syndicates) underwriting them and then resold at a profit in the public markets.
- *Investee*: The party seeking the capital investment in itself or for itself.
- *Investor*: The party providing the capital.

COMMERCIAL BANKS   Nature of the investor: Heavily regulated. Risk-averse and highly conservative low specific loan profit expectations. Low margin for error. Heavily bureaucratic and in very small banks often political. Schizophrenic in terms of sales versus credit culture; will seem to be graciously selling a borrower at first, and often back off later, when actual deal terms and credit considerations are developing.

Suitability to investee needs and targets of the investor: Low risk. Profitable, nonearly stage businesses. Must have ample collateral available.

Good cash flow as well, but far less cash flow and character-oriented than prior to mid-1980s.

Typical terms and types: Revolving lines of credit against accounts receivable (A/R). Rates usually related to, but not as low as, big bank prime; think 7% to 9% usually. Term loans 5 to 7 years against equipment. Overall senior lender position, or specifically collateralized. Various performance and ratio covenants. At least annual renewal, except term loans. Will try for owner's guarantees. Usually strong covenants. Old School was 4 Cs of lending, in this order: character, cash, collateral, credit. New School order (post-late 1980s) is collateral, cash, credit, character. All four Cs are still important, in whatever order.

PIPEs: PRIVATE INVESTMENTS IN PUBLIC EQUITIES **Nature of the investor:**
Usually private equity groups (PEGs) specifically organized for this purpose.

Suitability to investee needs and targets of the investor: Medium-risk investor. Urgently needy investee, or sometimes, simply more convenient and transaction expense-wise, cheaper for investee.

Typical terms and types: Invest in ether common stock with warrants or convertible preferred stock.

Pros, cons, and details: Toxic death spirals are common in many PIPEs, where the market capitalization rapidly recedes, but the number of shares necessary to preserves the PIPE investors' position remains the same or similar formula protection. Downside investor protection of this sort is not always necessary for fundamentally strong public companies to offer investors, but if they are fundamentally strong, they would not usually be seeking a PIPE. PIPEs should only be a last resort for many investees.

IPOs: INITIAL PUBLIC OFFERINGS **Nature of the investor:** Primary (in a guaranteed underwritten offering) investor is actually an investment bank. Secondary investor (the purchaser of the stock in the public market) is the actual investor. Initially, the agent Investment Bank must be convinced. In a best efforts offering, the initial investor is the public market purchaser, who of course needs to be convinced.

Suitability to investee needs and targets of the investor: Only should be undertaken when large sums of money are needed ($50 million or more) and justified. Not for the weak-kneed. Stay away from bucket shop small offerings. Highly dependent on macroeconomic and market conditions. Tend to be trendy and cyclical (in and out of favor since early 2000). Not an exit; rather, an entrance into another kind of market (some people say an entrance to hell).

Typical terms and types: Cost of raise around 10% to 11%, including substantial ongoing professional fees, perhaps for a small public company as much as $2 million annually. Best efforts versus firm commitment. Minimum thresholds to break escrow or all or nothing.

Pros, cons, and details: Very difficult and restrictive to be a public company at the smaller end of the scale, since Enron and the ensuing Sarbanes Oxley legislation. Careful consideration is necessary before doing (if it can be done at all). Again, stay away from small offerings, bucket shops. Many small publics going private in this new environment. Huge expenditure of professional fees and management time. Once again, this is not an exit; it's more like an entrance.

PUBLIC SHELL REVERSE MERGERS **Suitability and pros and cons:** Although acquiring a currently publicly traded shell company is an easy way to become a public company overnight, shell reverse mergers are not an answer 99% of time. This neither produces capital, a real trading market, nor analyst coverage, and often comes with a "taint."

SWEAT EQUITY **Nature of the investor; suitability to investee needs and targets of the investor:** Poor, ambitious, not well connected investee. If successful, a good way to bootstrap and preserve equity, but usually is the only choice for those who do it.

Typical terms, pros, cons, and details: Results (or should) in a high discipline on processes, decisions. High failure rate, much naiveté; should obtain experienced advice before proceeding with the project; vet idea before wasting time.

FRIENDS, FOOLS, AND FAMILY (THE "THREE Fs") **Nature of the investor:** Naïve, friendly; potentially but not likely litigious. Not much money, but usually loyal to investees.

Suitability to investee needs and targets of the investor: Startups needing only small amounts of money.

Typical terms: Whatever the market will bear. Either fairly generous or frequently nonsensical terms, as not typically professionally advised. Probably should produce returns on investment (ROIs) similar to mezzanine debt: 18% to 25%.

Pros, cons and details: Not much of a source of capital usually, but at least something.

LEASING PROGRAMS **Suitability to investee needs and targets of the investor:** Usually offered by banks (more conservative and better terms) and leasing companies (less so on both counts). Good source of capital for equipment acquisitions for investees, as automatically secures investor's interest at least in relationship to other investors in the same enterprise. Also, an excellent source of capital for sale and leaseback deals, where investee already has the assets necessary to collateralize the lease.

Typical terms: 10% to 13%

REAL ANGELS AND WANNABE ANGELS Nature of the investor: Rarer than hen's teeth. True angels are very sophisticated and therefore not likely to offer easy terms. But best angel is probably the "wannabe" individual investor or angel clubs. If investor is a wannabe, then terms will be all over the place. Wannabes rarely actually invest, though.

Typical terms: A pricing point is mezzanine terms plus private equity terms, including warrants and ownership: 18% to 25%.

SBA PROGRAMS: SMALL BUSINESS ADMINISTRATION Nature of the investor: U.S. government–guaranteed loans. Somewhat bureaucratic, but probably no worse than straight bank borrowing. Program is a risk mitigation program for lenders, and may involve secondary market sales (resales) later by lending bank or institution. Many programs, but SBA 7(a) are the best known.

Suitability to investee needs and targets of the investor: Relatively small business loans. Can help persuade a bank, grease the skids. Wholesale <100 employees; retail or service avg. 3 year revenues <$6 million; manufacturing <500 employees; construction avg. 3 year revenues <$12 million; real estate loans for owner-occupied commercial property used in a business also available.

Typical terms: 7(a) (Maximum $2 million, 25 years, fixed or variable rates but pegged to lowest prime)

Pros, cons, and details: Standard commercial terms. A bit more bureaucratic. A bit more time consuming. The following are popular credit factors used by the SBA: *Equity*: Reasonable debt to worth ratio. *Earnings*: strong monthly cash flow projections. *Working capital*: Adequate level. *Collateral*: Personal guarantees required of every 20%+ owner.

SECONDARY PUBLIC OFFERINGS Nature of the investor: Just like IPOs, primary investor/screener is actually an agent in a guaranteed underwriting. Actual eventual buyer of the stock is secondary investor. Dependent to a great degree on macroeconomy.

Suitability to investee needs and targets of the investor: Suitable to post-IPOs willing to move more slowly (see PIPEs for contrast) or for founders' sales of stock.

Pros, cons, and details: Slower than PIPEs and other approaches. Should be compared to debt alternatives. A way for founders to get more liquidity. Needs a justifiable use for the money, or problems will arise shortly in overall cost of capital for the issuing company.

INDUSTRY STAKEOUTS   Nature of the investor: Industry player who wants to take a "wait and see" position to get "most favored nation" treatment on whatever fronts can be negotiated with a business it is interested in for some reason (technology?), at least if it becomes successful. Often a good way for investee to secure expansion funds.

Suitability to investee needs and targets of the investor: Minimizes capital of investor that is tied up. Provides an alternative and usually friendly source of capital to not-fully-matured investees.

Typical terms: There are no typical terms, each deal stands on its own. Will usually provide a chance, and terms, for a liquidity event for the investor, and possible additional collateral relationships, such as distribution agreements and rights of first refusal on sale of investee.

Pros, cons, and details: Terms, especially rights of first refusal on sale of investee, can be very problematic for investee (kiss of death). Can prevent investee, either technically or practically, from doing business with competitor of investor.

REGULATION D (REG. D) PRIVATE PLACEMENT OFFERINGS (RULES 501 THROUGH 506) OF THE 1933 SECURITIES ACT   Nature of the investor: Can be either an individual(s) known to investee or sold to previously unknown parties through a broker (again, be wary of bucket shops).

Exception to securities registration rules: Need some accredited investors: $200,000 to $1 million income and net worth rules,or any type of institution that participates in these markets. Rule 506 (the principal rule): up to 35 nonaccredited investors. Unlimited: both in terms of dollar offering and number of accredited investors.

Pros and cons: Investors' targets are either casual (if investor already known to investee) or passive/opportunistic, based on macro market and investment conditions. Investee needs to be careful here, as usually this capital has no other benefits associated with it, such as advice, contacts. etc. See *More pros, cons, and details* below.

Typical terms: All over the place: debt, equity type of terms, what the market will bear. Since usually not suitable for IPOs, institutional private equity or debt, can be expensive but, from investors' point of view, very risky. A reasonable frame of reference is the mezzanine market: 18% to 25%.

More pros, cons, and details: Early 1980s real estate booms sold as tax shelters to doctors, dentists, etc., until laws changed. Historically more litigious; probably more punitive civilly and/or criminally if investee violates rules. While an exempt offering, this is expensive, labor intensive and, unless prearranged, time consuming. Requires explaining what risks are very thoroughly, almost to the point of discouraging investors. Strict securities rules compliance necessary. Stay away from bucket shops.

REG. S OFFERINGS OFFSHORE SECURITIES SALES SAFE HARBOR RULE   Nature of investor: Buyers must be offshore and not prearranged, but fewer disclosure requirements than Reg. D. No United States solicitation (directed selling efforts).

Pros, cons, and details: Constitutes a speedy offshore way to sell securities and raise capital. But must come to rest outside of United States (cannot be resold within United States) for at least a one-year restricted period since 1996, which can constitute a major disadvantage.

EARLY-STAGE VENTURE CAPITAL (VC)   Nature of the investor: Sophisticated, institutionally backed limited partnerships. Exit horizons three to five years. Fund lives eight-plus years; Management lives on 1% to 2% fees, based on total invested capital plus 20% carried interests above a certain threshold return to primary investors.

Suitability to investee needs and targets of the investor: High-risk, high-reward investor. High-risk, high-reward investee. Early-stage company, therefore needs great management, great ideas.

Typical terms: Seeking usually at least a 35% ROI target. Governance agreement gives effective control, even though usually minority ownership.

Pros, cons, and details: Probably fewer than one in two thousand deals get done in early-stage VC. Hard to find capital. Out of favor since 2000. Very expensive financial and rigid nonfinancial terms. If things head south, investees will have ownership interest reduced (crammed down).

BUSINESS RECAPITALIZATION TRANSACTIONS   Nature of the investor: Usually institutional private equity players and sponsors. Equity often supplemented by mezzanine and other debt (leveraged buyout) in LBO recapitalizations.

Suitability to investee needs and targets of the investor: The investee who wants to take money off the table, but stay in the game. The investor who sees reasonable business maturity balanced with great opportunity.

Typical terms: Percentage of ownership determined at least implicitly using the VC present value approach (i.e., how much does each put in?). Strong corporate governance agreements and BOD seats to investors.

Pros, cons, and details: Good for partial liquidity; good if smart money (well-connected) partners; good for add-on investments. Often onerous redemption terms; can be very bad from debt leveraging to post-deal balance sheet. Can be very bad for investee if things go south; redemption and liquidation and first return priorities can be very painful to investee. Can be very good if things go well, as investee goes along to some degree for a second ride after first partially cashing out.

M&A TRANSACTIONS, EXTERNAL   Nature of the investor: Various, ranging from: opportunistic strategic buyers (worst case); strategic buyers (best case); strategic roll-up (private to public arbitrage, very best case); financial private equity (very, very good case).

Suitability to investee needs and targets of the investor: Investor targets vary with type of buyer/investor. Investee needs range from pure liquidity seekers (exit strategy sellers); financial resource seekers (merger or recapitalization sellers); intellectual or management resource seekers.

Typical terms: All deals: one-third cash, one-third stock, and one-third other. Most Middle Market deals over $10 million 85% to 90% cash, balance 5% to 10% other is usually earnouts. Auction process brings best terms by far.

Pros, cons, and details: A function of timing and the auction (you might say luck); highly dependent on skill of intermediary. Takes six to twelve months and more. Loss of control (usually 100%).

M&A TRANSACTIONS, INTERNAL, ESOPS, AND MANAGEMENT BUYOUTS   Suitability for investee: Where management has already been given too much control in cases of absentee ownership. Company not otherwise readily salable. Healthy company needed, because will need outside financing usually because of lack of management capital. Negotiation sensitivity is extreme, because of relationships with management, and may be subject to at least implications of management blackmail, especially in absentee-owner situations.

Pros, cons, and details: Tax rollover benefits to ESOP sellers. Valuation problems due to extensive regulation (IRS, U.S. Department of Labor). Company becomes semipublic in case of ESOP. Financing problems typical in MBOs. ESOPs of doubtful egalitarian usefulness in spite of the law's original intentions.

MEZZANINE FINANCERS   Nature of Investor: Institutional; medium-risk investors. Characteristics of both debt and equity investors.

Suitability to investee needs and targets of the investor/investee: Investor suitability: Relatively solid business with decent cash flow and prospects. Investee suitability: Where no room for more senior debt; often done in conjunction with other forms of financing at the same time from same or several investors.

Terms: Typically a coupon rate of 12% to 13% (but cyclically varies); plus an all-in rate (warrants, etc.) around 18% to 25% or 26%.

Pros, cons, and details: Provides good possible exits and returns on investment for investors through: liquidity event; interim cash flow payments; formularized valuation (e.g., five to seven times EBITDA). Cheaper than equity if no more debt can be taken on. Allows investee owner to reacquire the equity claim, unlike pure equity. Much more expensive than standard debt.

NONBANK BANKS   **Nature of the investor:** Large institutions (GE Capital, etc.). Provide big sources of project or term finance (usually no less than $5 to $10 million and up). Will mix cash flow and collateral based loans. More flexibility than a commercial bank, not governmentally regulated.

   Typical terms: Loan terms, depending on credit risk, and nature of loan; think in terms of big bank prime plus or minus.

   Pros, cons, and details: Only middle to upper end of Middle Market usually qualify (typically businesses with sales of at least $100 million and up).

FACTORS   **Nature of the investor:** Institutional investors, usually.

   Typical terms: Stated in terms of cost money (very, double-digit expensive). Stated in terms of fulfilling a need as a service provider may be rationalized as a useful, if discretely and occasionally used, device.

   Pros, cons, and details: Should only be used temporarily, as tends to be like an addiction that one cannot get out of. Can be offensive to certain of borrower's customers due to typical lock box process. Very, very, expensive (credit card rates and worse; 24% to 30% per annum is typical).

MERCHANT BANK SPONSORS (OR BACKERS OF FUNDLESS SPONSORS)   **Nature of the investor:** Groups of institutional or quasi-institutional (family office investors) partners, investing their own and other's money. Very sophisticated and smart money. Lots of money looking for a home. Tend to invest in *people* (with prior success) first, *ideas* a close second.

   Suitability to investee needs and targets of the investor: Can be entered into through two doors: Management with a head start on an acquisition, or highly experienced management looking for something to do.

   Terms will accordingly vary: Head start is stronger position (more like a financing or recap deal). "Looking for something to do" is likely (management gets 10% or so in options).

   Pros, cons, and details: Good way to get a new start. Smart money. Tough agreements, though, in terms of covenants, redemptions, overall corporate governance, etc. And why not? It is their money.

SBIR/SBRD PROGRAMS—SMALL BUSINESS INNOVATIVE RESEARCH PROGRAMS **Nature of the investor:** U.S. government, mandated to ten federal agencies a year that are required to award a portion of their R&D.

   Suitability to investee needs and targets of the investor: Good way to fund certain start-up technology plays. Consists of: Phase I Feasibility Study, 6 months, up to $100,000; Phase II Expansion, 2 years, up to $750,000;

and Phase III Commercialization, requires private sector financing, non-SBIR.

Other considerations: Must be "for profit," American-owned, and independently operated. Fewer than 500 employees.

PROJECT FINANCE   **Nature of investor and investment:** Actually, any number, and often many more than one investor, in any transaction. More of a way of structuring than a single source; debt and equity types match specific needs and collateral associated with those needs, (e.g., plant and equipment, working capital, accounts receivable financing, equipment leasing, etc.).

Suitability: Usually large and frequently offshore projects.

SPACS—SPECIAL PURPOSE ACQUISITION CORPORATIONS   **Nature of investor and type of investment:** Basically, a device to sell stock to the public before a company actually owns or conducts a business; a type of blind pool or blank check company. The company has 18 to 24 months to buy a business, then acquire the backing of 80% of the shareholders. It must not initially have a specific target in mind. If it fails to locate a target, it liquidates and pays back the money. Can range from very small to very large offerings.

Suitability to investor: High-risk investor with money to gamble as a blank check to promoters.

Suitability to investee: Usually high-profile investee with a following and a track record. Cuts through most of the problems and delays of going public in more typical way, since there are no operating businesses associated with it until it acquires one.

INDUSTRIAL REVENUE BONDS AND LOCAL ECONOMIC DEVELOPMENT PROGRAMS (TYPICALLY STATE AND LOCAL LEVEL)   **Overview:** Typically, these are arranged at a local municipal level. The basic technique is that a municipality, without truly assuming any liability of its own, and for local economic development purposes, will issue a bond of behalf of the investee. Also, many municipalities have local economic development programs that provide various resources to business that are not necessarily in the form of industrial revenue binds.

OTHER SOURCES   Other sources, just to be complete:

- *Credit unions:* Not normally associated with business but rather consumer markets, although could be a source of small business loans
- *Thrifts and mutual savings banks:* Usually real estate-oriented, primarily; can be a good source of real estate financing for businesses; a dying breed since the late 1990s

- *Federal government insurance programs* (e.g., OPIC)
- *Export/import bank financing*
- SBA export working capital lines

Notes

1. For another good reference text that lists some of these and some of these in more detail and yet others not reflected here, I recommend *Private Capital Markets*, by Robert Slee (John Wiley and Sons, Inc., 2004).
2. This should by no means suggest that all retail stock brokerage houses located in South Florida or in Boca Raton are bucket shops.

CHAPTER **32**

Another Postscript: The Unbundled Approach to Formal Valuation

Economics is extremely useful as a form of employment for economists.
John Kenneth Galbraith

Every man gets a narrower and narrower field of knowledge in which he must be an expert in order to compete with other people. The specialist knows more and more about less and less and finally knows everything about nothing.

Konrad Lorenz

For centuries, theologians have been explaining the unknowable in terms of the not-worth-knowing.

Henry Lewis Mencken

A Bird, a Plane?

I have commented throughout this book on the fact that most Middle Market "business valuators" do no such thing. Much more typically, they value entities that own businesses as opposed to valuing businesses alone. To the extent a formal valuator is doing a "business valuation," even though he or she is usually valuing an entity that owns a business, it would seem to make eminent sense that he/she start with the business underlying the entity which owns it. But business valuators usually do not start there.

Insofar as most business, as opposed to entity, valuations are based, or should be heavily biased toward, what businesses are *actually being bought and sold for*, I believe this factor should be more heavily relied on then it usually is by formal valuators. At the very least, it should be used as a sanity check when other methods, like cash flows to equity or debt and equity (inside an entity), are used to value entity securities or interests. Common sense would indicate this.

Certainly valuators commonly look at comparable merger and acquisition (M&A) transactions,[1] but in my view, they do so in an awkward or at least not fully exploited way. M&A comparable transaction methods are always based on before entity-tax cash flow equivalents (e.g., EBITDA), whereas the other methods usually (and in fact must) take into consideration entity income taxes.

So how does one employ this approach as a sanity check? Here is a hypothetical example:

The value of after entity-tax cash flows to equity securities
  holders when valuing an entity interest (assuming no debt)   = \$10.0 million
The income taxes applied to entity cash flows   = \$5.4 million
Implicit value of the underlying business in the M&A market[2]   = \$15.4 million
EBIT(DA) of underlying business   = \$3.0 million
Implied EBIT(DA) multiple   = 5.13 ×

Sanity check: Do M&A comparable transactions support this implied EBITDA multiple? If yes, then fine. If *not*, start over again.

While this may seem pretty simple and straightforward, as an M&A investment bank that also does formal valuations, we rarely see this simple check applied (or, alternatively, a bottom-up approach used by starting with the M&A business's market value). As a result, we sometimes see some pretty strange results when we apply the sanity check to other valuators' work.

Try it, it works. Arthur Schopenhauer, the 18th-century German philosopher, once not so famously said that a major problem with intellectual thought processes is that they are too often distanced from their practical roots by the development of arguments so abstracted that they lose sight of their beginnings.

At one time or another, it occurs to most of us with an exposure to the science of business valuation that much of this science is also highly abstracted, in that it involves concept built upon concept, resulting in decks of cards that can be shaky and unrelated to the handy referential point of what actually happens when businesses are actually sold in the M&A or securities markets. This is about the valuation of *businesses*—so why not take a look at where and how they are sold?

Finally, in conclusion, let me say just this.

Peter Sellers

Notes

1. Of course there are two problems, at least, when dealing with this data. The first is that it is inherently incomplete, in that it does not reflect exact deal terms or normalizations to EBITDA that might have been employed. The second problem is the perennial question in using this data, and that is whether or not we are using comparable Investment Value to a particular as opposed to general buyers. My answer to the first dilemma is that the other methods commonly employed have their own problems, and that is exactly why we use various methods when doing valuation work, as a sort of a test against each other. My answer to the Investment Value question is that all comparable transaction data inherently employs "Investment Value" of one type of another. It becomes useful in suggesting general-buyer Fair Market Value where enough buyers in a certain industry or market are paying similar prices.

2. Conversely, one might just as happily start by valuing the business separately using M&A comparables and then calculate income taxes at the entity level to result in entity securities valuations. This works equally well either way.

Index